HOTBEDS OF LICENTIOUSNESS

HOTBEDS OF LICENTIOUSNESS

THE BRITISH GLAMOUR FILM AND THE PERMISSIVE SOCIETY

Benjamin Halligan

berghahn
NEW YORK • OXFORD
www.berghahnbooks.com

First published in 2022 by
Berghahn Books
www.berghahnbooks.com

© 2022 Benjamin Halligan

Library of Congress Cataloging-in-Publication Data
Names: Halligan, Benjamin, author.
Title: Hotbeds of licentiousness : the British glamour film and the
    permissive society / Benjamin Halligan.
Description: New York : Berghahn Books, 2022. | Includes bibliographical
    references and index.
Identifiers: LCCN 2021052750 (print) | LCCN 2021052751 (ebook) |
    ISBN 9781800734869 (hardback) | ISBN 9781800734876 (ebook)
Subjects: LCSH: Pornographic films—Great Britain—History—20th
    century. | Pornography in popular culture—Great Britain—History—
    20th century.
Classification: LCC PN1995.9.S45 H345 2022 (print) | LCC PN1995.9.S45
    (ebook) | DDC 791.43/65380941—dc23/eng/20220207
LC record available at https://lccn.loc.gov/2021052750
LC ebook record available at https://lccn.loc.gov/2021052751

British Library Cataloguing in Publication Data
A catalogue record for this book is available from the British Library

ISBN 978-1-80073-486-9 hardback
ISBN 978-1-80073-487-6 ebook
https://doi.org/10.3167/9781800734869

Contents

Illustrations and Tables

Illustrations

Table

Acknowledgements

My thanks to: Abertoir (Aberystwyth), Michael Armstrong, Bettys (Harrogate), the Rt. Hon. the Baroness Blackstone, Oliver Carter, Rod Connelly and Bollox (Manchester), Rachel Hope Cleves, Douglas Crimp, Anthony Daly, Mark Duffett, Tony Earnshaw, Anne Etienne, Neil Gaiman, Keith Gildart, Judy Giles, Roland Glasser, Michael Goddard, Andrew Graystone, Peter Hardwick, Elin Hefin, the International Anthony Burgess Foundation (Manchester), Kevin Jackson, Aled Jones, Huw Jones, Mark Jones, David Limond, Stanley Long, Paula Meadows, Lucy McCaul, David McGillivray, I Mille Occhi (Trieste), Olaf Möller, Marc Morris, NYU Florence (Villa La Pietra), James O'Brien, Jade Munslow Ong, Alexei Penzin, Fran Pheasant-Kelly, John Roberts, Dame Elan Closs Stephens, Whitney Strub, Florence Sutcliffe-Braithwaite, Matthew Sweet, Talisman Fine Art, the Thatcher Network (and Rory Stewart), Ellie Tomsett, Christopher Weedman, Gavin Whitaker, Ioan Williams, Laura Wilson, and some who once worked in the areas explored in this book, and who have helped me in my research, but have asked not to be named or identified.

My thanks go to the library staff and archivists of: the universities of Salford and Wolverhampton, particularly (at both) James Anthony-Edwards; the Hugh Owen Library of Aberystwyth University; the London School of Economics; the British Library; and Llyfrgell Genedlaethol Cymru (the National Library of Wales). I am also grateful to Fahrenheit's Books in Denver. I must also acknowledge: the British Board of Film Classification; the archival work of the Adult Loop Database; the testimonies of the 'Magdalene Institutions: Recording an Oral and Archival History' project; the National Viewers' and Listeners' Association Collection (Special Collections, Albert Sloman Library, University of Essex); the work, and witnesses, of the Independent Inquiry into Child Sexual Abuse (IICSA), chaired by Alexis Jay.

This research was conducted at the School of Arts and Media at the University of Salford, and the Centre for Film, Media, Discourse and Culture at the University of Wolverhampton (with the approval of the Faculty of Arts, Business and Social

Sciences Ethics Committee). I wish to express my thanks to colleagues at the University of Wolverhampton's Doctoral College, and Research Policy Unit.

The cover image shows the Raymond Revuebar, Brewer Street, Soho, London, July 2016. Photo by John Hedges, and used with kind permission.

This book is dedicated, with friendship and gratitude, to Philip Waddilove (1929–2020), Stanley J. Long (1933–2012) and Leanne Bridgewater (1989–2019), who wrote: 'Push the sky over / and watch the stars fall out' (Bridgewater 2016: 75).

The Soul of Pornography

'It has been said', my late colleague, the great Welsh television director John Hefin used to claim (perhaps the source had been forgotten?), 'that every British film is, really, about class.' This was sometimes his first comment, in his first lecture, to first-year undergraduates on an Introduction to Film Studies course.[1]

This book is, in part, a stress testing of this arresting thesis. For John, British cinema was understood either to have been limited, even immobilised, by an inability to see beyond an ordering of reality via preconceived ideas of a hierarchical class stratification, or to have been energised by critical engagements with such an ordering and its concomitant prejudices. This book looks to the former tendency, but with one major proviso: that while I want to look at unconscious accommodations of preconceived ideas of class, I also want to find the junctures at which such ideas become manifest in a disordering way. To do this, I approach the material of this research – pornography on film, from the Summer of Love to Margaret Thatcher as prime minister, plus coda – as building blocks of imagination and fantasy. The intellectual's view of pornography as essentially utilitarian (that is, as a masturbatory aid or a stimulant to sex), typically then prompting a discussion of freedoms of speech versus censorship – as with Anthony Burgess's 1970 lecture 'Obscenity & The Arts' (Burgess, Greer and Biswell 2018: 49–79) – is not explored in this book. Rather, I read pornography as presenting ideals, aspirations, desires, possibilities, intelligence and rewards for its users, and utopian visions. And, in this presentation, in pornography, I find particular insights into the ways in which ideas of class order or fire imagination, and order or fire this fantastical take on reality. To do this, I take one step back from the material so as to consider how these fantasies can be interpreted as striving to anticipate, and then meet and match, the desires of their perceived audiences. Or, put simply, what did the pornographers think their audiences wanted to see? From this vantage point, each pornographic film can be seen to imagine its audience, as the fantasies it offers evidence a set of assumptions, conscious or otherwise, about the desires of that imagined audience. An example of a conscious element to this process is found in an interview with the hardcore Scottish pornographer John Lindsay, whose work is discussed at length below – who even, as with an election strategist, has identified his ideal constituent, as summarised in an interview for the pornographic magazine *Knave*:

> Who then is the ideal girl for a Lindsay film? 'She's about 17, big blue eyes, long blonde hair, slim body, medium titties. She's Lolita-like. Innocence ready to be seduced. That's what the average man wants.'
>
> It is to the average man, 'l'homme moyen sensual' [the man of average appetites] as the French so neatly put it, that Lindsay aims his films. Or rather at their fantasies. In an interview some three months ago on London's Capital Radio, John was asked by an aggressive American female why men liked seeing schoolgirls and suchlike getting up to naughty capers in his films. His reply was as candid as most of his conversation: 'Because of women like you'. (Duncan 1978: 71)

It seemed, then, as I began, that the research would order the analysis of the material thematically, around grouped sets of fantasies: from, at first glance...

- blunt proletarian opportunism in the blue-collar service industries...
- ... to sophisticated erotica around country houses;
- the 'lure' of the Soho gentlemen's clubs and some of the noted glamour models associated with them;
- ditto massage parlours;
- some kind of notion of pro-sex, 1970s feminism liberating the sexually frustrated housewife into infidelity;
- niche, ritualistic sadism and masochism;
- playacting schoolgirls;
- chambermaid(s) encountering guests who are late checking out of their hotel rooms;
- aristos 'swinging' with the younger set

... and so on. And the objectionable nature of such class prejudices (and frequent misogyny, homophobia and racism) could, at least initially, be set aside, because these were fantasies for unseen audiences, and not considered attempts to represent, even-handedly, various social groups. Thus, the more objectionable the films, the more relevant the idea of fantasy would be in terms of that fantasy underwriting and evidencing class prejudice. (And at first glance too, I wondered where the non-heterosexual material may be – if indeed it existed at all in this period, at least on a commercial circuit of sorts.)

But, surprisingly, the material, as it revealed itself, would not be ordered in this way. Rather, the pornography mostly presented itself along auteur lines: specific film-makers whose oeuvre was often characteristic with respect to both their concerns and overall interests, and their signature film styles. In a way, and in the context of the oft-noted timidity and frigidity of British erotica, each auteur figure was a pioneer and so was often quite individual – and some paid the price for this path-breaking (or just overstepping the mark), and for their roles in the, or a, sexual liberation of the British cinema. And, as individuals, they rarely shut up about their work. There was, in print and on screen, much reflection on what they did – and how and why, and where and when, and for whom and with whom – and on the embattled libertarian, and heroic, political import of all of this endeavour. This is true of Stanley Long (his 1971 documentary *Naughty!*), Lindsay (his 1973 documentary *The Pornbrokers*), Paul Raymond (the 1982 quasi-documentary *Paul Raymond's Erotica*), the figure of Mary Millington (in *Queen of the Blues*, Willy Roe, 1979 and, posthumously, with *Mary Millington's True Blue Confessions*, Nick Galtress, John M. East, 1980), arguably Peter de Rome (in the sense that his loops were often an add-on to sexual encounters: filming those he had spent the night with), and via the endless puff-piece profiles of such figures in pornographic magazines. Indeed, in addition to Harrison Marks's self-ghosted biography (discussed below; Wood [1967] 2017), de Rome (1984) and Long (Long and Sheridan, 2008) also wrote autobiographies, and arguably a number of female porn stars discussed here may have done so too (or lent their names to such books). Lindsay apparently also wrote an autobiography, *The Sexorcist*, which was published in some form, but I have been unable to trace a copy or bibliographic record, and Derek Ford wrote two self-serving studies of cinema and sexual exploitation (1988 and, co-written as Selwyn Ford, 1990). David Sullivan added a business guru twist to this subgenre, with *We Made £200,000: The Story of B.H. and D.S.* (co-written with Harry Marle and Bernard Hardingham, 1972, and in some additions 'with an interview with Lord Longford'), on his first three years in the pornography business. And the softcore film *The David Galaxy Affair* (Roe, 1979), made by Sullivan to advance Mary Millington's fame, reputedly contains autobiographical elements.

There seems to have been a similar tendency on the part of the film-makers to reveal the milieu too: so many of the films feature long sequences in Soho, or around the seedier areas of Piccadilly Circus – presumably the streets just outside the cinemas and clubs in which these films were being watched. *Snow White and the Seven Perverts* (David Hamilton Grant, Marcus Parker-Rhodes, 1973) even ventures inside the cinema club, to reveal a gaggle of masturbating men sprawled in front of a cinema screen – albeit in animation. The loop *Certificate 'X'* (possibly 1968, from Ultima Films) showcases the culture: a lone female hippy enters a Soho cinema club and undergoes paroxysms of autoeroticism as she watches loops, with a male filmgoer joining her.

The *Knave* interview with Lindsay is prime auteur-ism: Duncan presents Lindsay as a neorealist pornographer, and with discernibly characteristic creative tendencies:

> *The films reflect the personality of their maker: there's a mordant, anti-establishment, cynical humour about them. In* 100 Lines *the scene opens with a stunningly beautiful girl sitting at a desk in the full school outfit. She is doing her detention [etc] … Obligingly, she faces the camera so that it can record the repeated entry of [sic] the penis into vagina, and the girl's breasts heaving up and down in a lascivious rhythm of their own. (And they were pleasantly large breasts for a girl who was, I believe, only 16 at the time.)*
>
> *But it is typical of Lindsay that he should have shot such a film in a real school. Typical also that he should choose, as he does so often in his films, to clothe the models in uniforms [that] should make them taboo – as schoolgirls or girl guides or nuns … This is how John Lindsay sees himself: a social rebel, an outsider. He once told me that he looked upon himself as a mixer of love potions, someone who 300 years ago would have been called a wizard or a witch. (Duncan 1978: 27)[2]*

And, as to the libertarian impulse justifying or redeeming Lindsay's work:

> *'I pay a lot of tax,' he says, 'more than the average guy' … Recently the police came round to one of Lindsay's clubs, enquiring about the presence of any Soho protection rackets. They were told that yes, the heavy mob had been round with a 'pay up or else' demand. They were a bit put out when they eventually learned that was a description of a visit from the VAT [value added tax] men …*

Politicians, he says, would like to put a tax on pleasure. 'People who say they know better are forever censoring us people – the other people – or the peasants as they believe we are. Like cigarettes and alcohol which, admittedly, kill us. But they also censor sex, which doesn't kill us. Why is that? It's because they haven't actually sussed out a way of putting a meter on a basic human function.'
(Duncan 1978: 27)

And so, with apologies, I have perhaps inadvertently uncovered in a new cohort of British film directors, who may now need to be incorporated into histories of the British cinema. But their work is meagre (in quality if not quantity) and often miserable. Twenty years ago I began a similar process of, as it turned out, very slightly expanding the canon, around the life and work of British horror film-maker Michael Reeves (1943–1969; for the resulting critical biography, see Halligan 2003). And, while I have been gratified to see his name included and his reputation grow, I cannot say the same of the film-makers discussed, pretty much entirely for the first time, in the current book.

The operationalisation of my methodological approach to the material often raised the question of how little of it I could watch, before being in a reasonable position to offer comment. Nonetheless, researching and writing this book has resulted in too many hours of viewing joyless 'erotic' films of little or even no merit – frisson-less, and a paucity of entertainment, a paucity of aesthetics, seemingly some performers in distress, and often unpleasant encounters with reactionary and objectionable ideas. At times, even after only a couple of days, I found myself genuinely unable to recall whether I had already viewed yet another dire 1970s 'sex comedy' or washed-out hardcore loop that I may have forgotten to remove from my never-diminishing pile of 'to watch' films. They blurred into one underlit and dingy tale of sexual frustration and misfiring erotic gambits, across housing estates, rainy holiday resorts, and chintzy hotels. Note taking was difficult when there was so often little or nothing to actually note down. And even sourcing such films has been a pain, as so many are, understandably, out of circulation. In this, my methodological approach drew some comfort from my former colleague John Mundy's book *The British Musical Film* (2007), which, by the time it hits the 1970s, begins to evidence that Mundy's patience is so frayed that he seems to edge towards giving up trying to find something to say about the umpteenth Cliff Richard vehicle of diminishing returns. In that my experience mirrored Nick Roddick's excursions into the 'island of furtiveness [of] Soho cinemas' in 1982/83, for *Sight & Sound*, it seems that the material had not improved with age. On the 'films [that] run from the barely passable to the unspeakably tedious,' Roddick says, 'I don't quite know what I was expecting, but what I got was a two-week course in aversion therapy. In no real sense can the films be described as erotic; and, with one of two rare exceptions, they are not particularly distasteful. They are merely boring' (Roddick 1982/83: 18).

Some further notes around implementing my methodology seem appropriate here. Firstly, I place to one side summaries of specific definitions of 'pornography', 'softcore' and 'hardcore', and the related legal debates, and changing positions of censors, often around contested notions of obscenity. Related questions, as to whether naturalist documentaries and fetish films (for example, shots of feet) are, to use another ambiguous term, indecent, are not explored here. These discussions are well rehearsed elsewhere and, at any rate, wend to the inconclusive; Hawkins and Zimring are able to tabulate differing definitions of 'obscenity', 'pornography' and 'erotica' (1991: 26). Even the 1979 parliamentary Report of the Committee on Obscenity and Film Censorship struggles to attain a definitive position, and seems to conclude, at the outset and with respect to the same material discussed in this book, that such an attempt would be counterproductive (Williams 1979: 6). John Ellis, in part discussing this report in 1980, notes the 'combination of vagueness and moralism in existing definitions of pornography', and observes that, at any rate, 'definitions of pornography have an inhibiting moral force to them' – seemingly inhibiting critical engagement with pornography itself (Ellis 1992: 146).

My concern is around films that are unashamedly designed for, to a discernible and defining level, titillation and sexual arousal. This then covers films that have no other clear function (for example, films that just show sexual intercourse), or films that are erotic, but with very substantial elements of titillation (as with Derek Ford comedies, or Harrison Marks's relatively mainstream films, or, perhaps less certainly, the Joan Collins disco films). 'Pornography' is a catch-all term – for this study, as a general descriptor of the most forward element of all these films. This descriptor then excludes 1970s British 'sexy comedies' (the *Carry On*, *Confessions of...* and *Adventures of...* cycles, for example), as they may be understood to be erotic but contain, if thinking in general terms, less substantial or upfront levels of titillation. Roddick, therefore, would not have found such films playing in the depths of Soho – Barbara Windsor levels of fleeting nudity in *Carry on Camping* (Gerald Thomas, 1969) would have been insufficient. If a definition is to be demanded, I would defer to the Church of England's report on 'Obscene

Publications: Law and Practice' in relation to items to be 'entirely prohibited' (Board for Social Responsibility of the General Synod of the Church of England 1970: 15) – that is: 'publications [that] are patently obscene or pornographic and [that] are published as such' (10), and 'material [that] is plainly pornographic and [that] has no other objective or intention' (15). Within this paradigm, 'hardcore' can be taken, as it would have been at the time, to denote displays of sexual organs in a state of arousal – differentiating 'hardcore' then from 'softcore', which tended to titillating nudity. 'Glamour', as in the 'glamour film', is therefore my chief identifier – one signalling back to the earlier days of the evolution of the form, when erotic display was supposedly only a facet (rather than the facet) of the advertised female. This is an expedient euphemism, then as now, in terms of smuggling in material that would otherwise be a cause for concern or disapproval. And in respect to my assembly of materials, 'glamour' has been the password – to collections and informal archives, albeit mostly around curator-salesmen of 'retro-porn'. Glamour opens up the existential promise of moving into a certain world or accessing experiences, whereas 'pornography' suggests the demarcations of a tableaux vivant, to be surveyed and then put away.

Secondly, some material has been difficult to locate, and this has (mis-)shaped my survey scope. My limited engagements with Russell Gay, David Hamilton Grant and – although I place him beyond the timeline of this study – Mike Freeman, and the blind spot of the obscure Ivor Cooke, seemingly making hardcore loops in the early 1960s or even before, reflect this difficulty.[3] Gay's oeuvre seems to have mostly remained on 8-mm celluloid, Freeman's work stayed on limited circulation (i.e. mail order) video cassettes of some thirty to forty years ago, and Grant attempted to vanish but was rumoured to be subject to a contract killing (see Sweet 2006) – but beyond this, and into the video-release era of the 1980s, some pornography makers did not use names at all (either credit-less or pseudonymous releases). In addition to these gaps, I have sporadically declined to make good my being ill- or under-informed about some of the work discussed, flouting the minimum standard for academic researchers in the field of film history. In some cases, as with Lindsay's work, I wanted to watch a just-sufficient amount, but no more than that, and was happy to allow myself to be warded off by some of the more lurid film titles. Indeed, calculating how soon I could call time on reviewing his oeuvre, to allow me to curtail this element of the research, was a constant consideration; like many of the men who came his way, and about whom Lindsay complained, I wanted to exit the set hastily, leaving the action to continue unabated, after a premature termination. To tarry with the material was often to watch yet another stretch of sexual intercourse in close-up, prompting no further academic insights on my part, whatsoever.

I have adopted the same position of prudence too on the prospect of endless indistinguishable hours of silent, black-and-white loops from the early to mid-1960s, from small and long-forgotten production companies, featuring models shuttling between magazines and strip clubs. To compensate for this lack of very substantive exposure, mostly around hardcore films, I have tended to use, in my discussion of various auteurs' philosophical positions on sexuality, other elements of their writing – even with the danger of allowing the film-maker to interpret their own work. This has been mostly around hardcore film-makers (Marks, Lindsay, Triga Films, and Ford as an exception), as, in hardcore, one looks for a philosophy of sex, which can be extended to a wider reading of life. In softcore, in contrast, the philosophy of life may already be present, as the films embrace a wider world (their settings), and then situate sex in it (their pay-offs). So I have found myself thinking about meanings lent to Euston railway station and its people *through* one particular Lindsay hardcore loop (i.e. sex to place), and I have found myself thinking about the meanings of sex and eroticism *through* Derek Ford's filming of Essex (i.e. place to sex). In this respect, *Brief Encounter* (David Lean, 1945), in its engagement with ideas of place and eroticism, came to exert an even more extensive influence over this book than I initially anticipated.

One of the challenges of researching vintage pornography is navigating the way in which 'bootleg streaming … affords unprecedented access to previously elusive material, but often operates as a chaotic data dump, without even useful metadata', pushing researchers to juggle with multiple versions from multiple sources (official, levels of unofficial, fan archived), or finding that something once available has since been made unavailable (Strub 2019: 42). In all likelihood, there are other strains of filmed pornography production from this period of which I am completely unaware. But some of this may have been deliberately abandoned to obscurity, and I would respect the wishes of those involved, particularly performers, to be forgotten.

Thirdly, I took a principled position in relation to open access of academic resources, and so if secondary scholarly writing was not fairly immediately accessible, I have ignored it – abiding with some authors' choices of opting for marginality for their research. But I have tended towards the unearthing and integration of texts from the time, in terms of trying to tap into something of the mindsets of opponents of the Permissive Society, no matter how hysterical (in both senses) these texts were, or even when, in the case of some feminist writers, their later transphobic positions have been taken to render all their work déclassé. (Indeed, as I note below, this objectionable trait was already in operation in some feminist writing decades back.) I note too my debt to the blogger and reviewer Gavin Whitaker who, as GavCrimson, has spent nearly two decades rediscovering and reappraising, and mapping, British pornography and sexploitation film-making. This area has been all but ignored by academic researchers of post-war British film history across the last forty years. Indeed, this absence seems one to be of the few continuities across the entire field. This oversight is found in Armes 1979; Barr 1986; Murphy 1992, 2014; McFarlane 1997; Ashby and Higson 2000; Harper and Smith 2013; and Petrie, Williams and Mayne 2020. It is possible that an exclusionary quality bar was effectively in operation for these studies, or that the films themselves simply were not sufficiently or readily available. Their resultant absence is not an issue in these publications (which articulate their scopes), except in the lackadaisical, maximal case of Murphy. The volumes by Leon Hunt (1998), Matthew Sweet (2005) and I.Q. Hunter (2013) are the most prominent exceptions to this tendency, along with Robert Shail's edited collection (2008), by dint of the inclusion of Hunter. Pioneering work outside academia includes the writing (and film-making) of David McGillivray (1992) and Simon Sheridan (1999, 2011).

So, with this discovery of film-director-ness, this book was then to be divided along the lines of hardcore pornography and its auteurs, and softcore erotica and its auteurs, and with an interregnum concerning lifestyles and models. And this was to be in the strict context – I initially assumed – of a particular historical period: from the Summer of Love and the British counterculture (of 1967/68), as the 'free love' high-water mark, to the coming to power of Margaret Thatcher's Conservative Party (in 1979), with the outraged, moralistic and censorial in the ascent. This period was aligned to technological developments too. The popularity of the home video cassette in the early 1980s effectively ended the use of celluloid, so that pornographic cinema clubs were rapidly rendered obsolete, as was the equipment (and skills) needed for screening 8-mm porn loops (also known as rollers) at home. Even the set-ups needed to produce porn, with nominal professionals, could be dispensed with once the video camera became a means of production for niche do-it-yourself pornographers – from West German amateur 'Hausfrauenpornos' (housewife porn; see Hebditch and Anning 1988: 21), to videos shot after-hours in Manchester clothes shops of men dressing as women, with shop assistants giving a running commentary, to paedophilic material arising from, and distributed across, networks of abusers (see, for example, IICAS 2021: 27, 93–94).

To contextualise the magnitudes of the freedoms from the late 1960s to the dawn of the 1980s, in terms of British pornography, it was necessary to first address the post-war years and the ways in which eroticism was restricted or limited, as with food rationing. But these new freedoms and abundances were not suddenly constant or consistent across the 1970s: they remained in negotiation, contested at the margins of what was and what was not acceptable, subject to sudden removal, and generally vilified, and condemned from many quarters (right, left, feminist, ecclesiastical, establishment and anti-establishment). Those doughty pornographers who fought back, in the 1970s, sometimes talked of a time to come when all such internecine strife was banished: a libertarian utopia, in which sexuality is not a matter for shame, or restrictive legislation, or moral censure, but a gateway to good mental and physical health, and to a wholeness to the experience of adulthood. Such talk suggested that they knew that history was on their side. And this then prompted a desire in me to defy my strict time frame, and to close this book by travelling forward in time to that moment they had anticipated, in order to take the measure of that utopian aspiration, and explore what freedoms seemed to be in operation – that is, to find the moment at which the censor's scissors have been blunted (with the legal release of hardcore pornography) or simply kicked out of their hands altogether (digital distribution networks beyond the reach of the British Board of Film Classification). This coda would also allow me to belatedly offer a corrective to the exclusive heteronormativity, if not the predominant whiteness, of almost all the previous material under scrutiny. And two novels concerning the English gentleman under duress at the dawn of the twentieth century suggested the potential insight offered by such a move.

E.M. Forster's *Maurice* – a novel that explored the psychic damage of sexual repression, was restricted by Forster himself during his lifetime (and only published posthumously, in 1971) – does something akin to this jarring lurch forward in time. After a series of precisely situated scenes, which constitute the novel, Forster suddenly whisks Clive (who had abandoned the homosexuality of his Cambridge University years with Maurice, forsaking him for married respectability and a role in the judiciary) forward in time, up to the moment of his death:

[Clive's] last words were 'Next Wednesday, say at 7.45. Dinner-jacket's enough, as you know'.

They were his last words, because Maurice had disappeared thereabouts, leaving no trace of his presence except a little pile of the petals of the evening primrose, which mourned from the ground like an expiring fire. To the end of his life, Clive was not sure of the exact moment of departure, and with the approach of old age he grew uncertain whether the moment had yet occurred. The Blue Room would glimmer, ferns undulate. Out of some external Cambridge his friend began beckoning to him, clothed in the sun, and shaking out the scents and sounds of the May Term. (Forster 1971: 230–31)

Clive's inane, establishment life, after the sudden exit of Maurice some decades before, seems worthy of little further comment for Forster; the illicit experiences of homosexuality re-measure, jarringly, the life's chronology and intensity. Sexuality rereads life and offers, crucially, alternative, hidden histories.

I had thought that such a leaping forwards in time also occurred in the 1895 novella by H.G. Wells, *The Time Machine*. As I recalled, the protagonist travelled from the Victorian present to the future in his time machine, and then to a number of stops in the very distant future, finally returning to the present. Once back in the present he relates the story of his journey to his friends, including an unnamed witness, who presents the Time Traveller's narrative verbatim, and some bookending comments of his own. And, again, parallels suggested themselves: this time in the anticipated freedoms of a future of pure hedonism. The first time machine is sent 'gliding into the future', at which point '[t]here was a breath of wind, and the lamp flame jumped' (Wells [1895] 1969: 10). The flame could be read, as with church ornamentation, in terms of a symbolic presence of God; this time-travelling transition from a Christian to a secular era seems to visibly trouble God. The travel also overthrows the Christian structuring of the week, where six work days, followed by a day of rest, follows the timeline of God's creation of the world.

Once in the future, the protagonist encounters the 'graceful children of the Upper-world' (53), who exist selfishly, for play and pleasure alone – but in a 'colossal ruin' of civilisation (52) nevertheless, for 'this wretched aristocracy in decay' (71), where they are sporadically preyed upon by an underground of workers who seem to have mutated into cannibals. And the very distant future, towards 'more than thirty million years hence' (95) is post-Anthropocene, with only 'a monstrous crab-like creature' and a 'crowd of earthy crustacea creeping in and out among the green weed and red rocks' of an 'abominable desolation' (95). These stops in time, as I recalled them, could be mimicked for the structure of this book. The starting point would be those drab post-war years; the future would be the Permissive Age (as indeed it seemed to be for Wells: a workless leisure society); and the distant future would be post-millennium queer hardcore pornography of a type that would have been barely imaginable in the previous phases – barely, but just about. In one of her final books, Mary Whitehouse, the chief public opponent to the permissiveness, begins to touch on satellite television, 'decoders', 'Filmnet' and 'hard porn' on Thursday, and Sunday, mornings (Whitehouse 1994: 179).

But when I eventually reacquainted myself with the novella, I found elements that I had forgotten. The story ends with the Time Traveller departing once again, this time with a camera to gain proof of his access to other times. The unnamed narrator stumbles in on this moment of departure ('a ghostly, indistinct figure sitting in a whirling mass of black and brass'; Wells [1895] 1969: 103), and records:

> I stayed on, waiting for the Time Traveller [to return]; waiting for the second, perhaps still stranger story, and the specimens and photographs he would bring with him. But I am beginning now to fear that I must wait a lifetime. The Time Traveller vanished three years ago. And, as everybody knows now, he has never returned. (103)

Then, in an epilogue, the narrator reflects on the Time Traveller's fate or whereabouts:

> It may be that he swept back into the past, and fell among the blood-drinking, hairy savages of the Age of Unpolished Stone; into the abysses of the Cretaceous Sea; or among the grotesque saurian, the huge reptilian brutes of the Jurassic times. He may even now – if I may use the phrase – be wandering on some plesiosaurus-haunted Oolitic coral reef, or beside the lonely saline lakes of the Triassic Age. Or did he go forward, into one of the nearer ages, in which men are still men, but with the riddles of our own times answered and its wearisome problems solved? (105)

These speculations and uncertainties, in which the past seems as barbaric as the future (with its cannibal terrors), so that the future-to-come seems to be a return to the Dark Ages – a barer existence, entirely akin to, or even interchangeable with, the past, and with the Time Traveller perhaps stuck in an ambiguous either – better represent the disorientations of the encounter with pornography made before, during and after the Permissive Age. And the Time Traveller, anticipating Walter Benjamin's 'Angel of History' (see Arendt 1969: 257), questions the assumption that post-Enlightenment progress is forever forward to the better. Thus the Time Traveller 'thought but cheerlessly of the Advancement of Mankind, and saw in the growing pile of civilization only a foolish heaping that must inevitably fall back upon and destroy its makers in the end' (Wells [1895] 1969: 105). For Benjamin, reflecting on Paul Klee's 1920 monoprint 'Angelus Novus', history is not, as 'we perceive[,] a chain of events', but rather 'one single catastrophe which keeps piling wreckage upon wreckage' (Arendt 1969: 257), and a 'pile of debris' (258). *The Time Machine* anticipates and illustrates Benjamin's thesis – with a likeness between Wells's Time Traveller and Klee's Angel (in Benjamin's reading), for whom 'a storm irresistibly propels him into the future to which his back is turned' (258). And this heaping and piling finds an echo too in the multiplicity of bodies in pornography across this time frame: the single, posed female of glamour (of the 1940s and 1950s), through to the sequences of erotically posed females (of much of the 1960s), then couples making love along with – via a philosophical impulse, towards swinging, as will be discussed – copulating multiples (from the late 1960s onwards), and thereafter to pile-ons of scrums of bodies (towards and beyond the millennium). My chronology, then, mimics the narrative of *The Time Machine*; and my analysis, which also finds forgotten visions of futures in the past, shares the uncertainties voiced in that novella's epilogue. And any sociological bent in my analysis draws on the lesson of Forster – the other or hidden life story or stories, available via this history of sexuality, that can now, belatedly, be told, suggesting a more compelling narrative of society and codes of respectable living.

This is how the material under scrutiny shapes the organisation of this book. Particulars of the methodology will follow. Before this, however, and still in introductory mode, it is appropriate to turn to a blunt foundational example of class stratification, and codes of respectable living – the 1945 David Lean film of Noël Coward's *Brief Encounter*. This is in order to consider how John Hefin's thesis can prompt an analysis of the determination of the erotic imagination by class, even in the nominally, metaphorically 'buttoned-up' melodramas of propriety, which would seem to represent the polar opposite of the literal unbuttonings of pornography.

The Soul of *Brief Encounter*

Brief Encounter is remembered as a famously repressed film, even to the extent that it is sometimes read or reimagined as a closeted gay text (as with Medhurst 1991), in part prompted by Coward's discrete homosexuality, and perhaps even the film's title. Indeed, the philandering male protagonist of *Brief Encounter* could be taken as a certain 'bachelor' type, and would have been born roughly at the same time as Forster's Maurice. He is now middle-aged, still unattached, outwardly respectable, inwardly adrift, and looking for fulfilment in improper love affairs conducted surreptitiously, and liaisons in public places – before heading off to a posting in the colonies (and out of scandal's way, to mine the clichés). *Brief Encounter*, in the context of this study, which is in part grounded in film history studies, also marks the first and one of the few glimpses of familiar territory. So this choice perhaps lends some reassurance to the historian of British cinema that elements of the foundations of this study also rest on a film that is omnipresent in considerations of British film history; McFarlane observes that '[i]t seems that anyone who has ever written about British cinema has had to come to terms with *Brief Encounter*' (McFarlane 2015: 47).

Brief Encounter offers limited comic relief from its bourgeois romantic drama – a married mother, Laura Jesson (Celia Johnson), fails to begin an affair with an unmarried doctor, Alec Harvey (Trevor Howard) – by contrasting the pained and halting romantic entanglements of the middle-class protagonists with those of two lower-class workers. For the latter, a kindly if bluff railway station guard, Albert (Stanley Holloway), expresses amorous affection to the prim if shrill Myrtle (Joyce Carey), who presides, regally, over the station tearoom, and whose clumsily assumed airs and graces render her reticent to reciprocate. The middle-class romantic entanglement is so pained that Laura and Alec only kiss very belatedly in the film, after endless hesitation, soul searching, talk and reflection. Prior to that, erotic frissons are limited to looks and, almost unbearably, to the moment that Alec discretely places his hand on Laura's shoulder and squeezes it as he takes leave of her in the station tearoom without alerting an unwelcome interloper, a friend of Laura's, that infidelity is in the air. Laura first edges into 'emotional infidelity' (in the contemporary legalese associated with divorce and relationship counselling), then they kiss, and he leaves permanently for a new life in Johannesburg, South Africa. She momentarily contemplates suicide – an exit from an impossible situation, or self-inflicted capital punishment for her behaviour –

but returns to her husband and family life. The historical context of Laura's self-control is quite precise: stoicism under fire, the keeping up of appearances (including the mostly successful holding back of tears), and refusing to buckle under pressure, were qualities that were understood to have been necessary – essential even – to a London bombed and blitzed in the years immediately prior to the film's setting.[4] When urban societal collapse was understood to be a real possibility, this firm control of feelings, and the mandates of decorum and politeness, and maintenance of mores, all mostly via self-denial or repression, or hot tea pick-me-ups, can be read as a home front against the Nazi onslaught. Even the shoulder squeezing is a reassuring act. That import was painfully apparent with the juxtaposition of two Robert Capa images, placed next to each other in the 2011 exhibition Eyewitness: Hungarian Photography in the Twentieth Century (Royal Academy of Arts, London). The first was the 'Face in the Surf' image of the 1944 'Magnificent Eleven' shots for Life magazine – that celebrated split-second blur of an American soldier propelling himself from the sea onto the Omaha beach in Normandy, to meet his enemy and perhaps death. The second was 'London, England, evening tea in an air raid shelter' (1941), which foregrounds an elderly air raid warden, with a look of kindly concern, talking to an elderly woman, seemingly in a borrowed overcoat, perhaps fearful of the destruction of her home. They sit by tea-making items, on a barrel draped with a makeshift table cloth. 'Evening tea' offers a shaken dignity under pressure, to the determination, despite fear, on the face of 'Face in the Surf'. And both qualities, in the witnessing of this Hungarian photographer, are understood to have been equally essential.[5]

The particularity of the somewhat unglamourous (relative, that is, to the norms of female leads of this time) role of Celia Johnson in this is precise too: her 'station' in life, as Laura, is to be respectable and middle class. She cannot talk as freely of love or affection as the workers who momentarily and periodically share her space in the railway station tearoom (and who seem perhaps to have been sexually active, and so freer in that way too). Lean ensures that the shared space is nonetheless appropriately organised: segregation via an unforgivably long tracking shot in the first scene, which wrenches the viewer away from the tearoom counter and flirtatious banter, and finds Laura and Alec huddled over a table, nursing their drinks and their ethical and moral dilemmas. Such imbalance, and discarding of the 'lower orders' in this movement is, for McFarlane, 'one of the recurring problems of British cinema of the period' (McFarlane 2015: 57). But Laura nonetheless seems to set the example of propriety for the workers. If she cannot, who will? And her final reluctance to detach herself from her family maintains that cell of regeneration that will outlast the Second World War and come to repopulate, and shore up, the dull city suburbs of the film's setting. This is her class's role and destiny. Patterns of sexual behaviour in pre-1945 suburbia are seen to be either absent, or contained within marriage, or (for the working classes) somewhat ridiculous. Laura's crime, in this context, seems to be as much about an ambiguous measure of intimacy with Alec as seemingly missing sexual desire and dallying with thoughts of becoming reacquainted with it, outside the comfort and familiarity of her marriage.

Laura's wayward thoughts are manifest, or let rip, in a fantasy sequence, in which she dreams of escape to an exotic, intimate and safe space with the urbane Alec. The romance is clichéd – whether on the part of the makers of the film, or as indicative of Laura's limited mental creativity (she claims she feels 'like a romantic schoolgirl – like a romantic fool!' in this moment), or as playing to the assumed understanding of what the audience of *Brief Encounter* would read as fantasy. Prior to this, a shot in which Alec and Laura kiss in a rubbish-strewn underpass is suddenly revealed to be a revelry, when Laura's armchair, and Laura, fade into the foreground of the scene. This reconfigures Laura as a spectator or curator of her own memories, now briskly pulled back from her revelry into reality by the voice of her husband, from the family living room in which the armchair is actually located. Thus, the mundane everyday of the film, for a crucial stretch, is usurped by fantasy. But even in this, in the voice-over that represents her conscience, the incredible formality of Laura's language remains; the politeness and properness is seemingly neurological: 'I imagined being with him in all sorts of glamourous circumstances. It was one of those absurd fantasies, just like one has when one is a girl being wooed and married by the ideal of one's dreams'.

The societal example that we find in Laura is both actual and psychological: yes, the public example is how one behaves and appears, and indeed quietly lives one's life, and it exerts control over how one is seen in public (it is Alec who pushes for kisses, and Laura who worries about being seen). But the example is also how one ought to think, and the rhetoric one uses as one talks to (and scolds, and contains) oneself. This voice-over is followed by a complicated shot: Laura's face reflected in the window of her train carriage, but seemingly oblivious to the passing countryside and 'seeing', instead, chandeliers, and herself and Alec (in ball gown and dinner jacket) dancing. In this way, her reflection is effectively superimposed on her fantasy, allowing for material, present reality to be pushed back into the frame (the blur of the passing landscape, the sound of the train), which is otherwise full of fantasies of escape from suburban existence. So romantic fantasy is seen to contain the very conditions of its generation: both the dull suburbs and the plush escape, simultaneously within the frame, for a jostling between Laura's daydream revelry and her conscious awareness of her surroundings. She frames the vision of this imagined couple being 'perhaps a little younger than we are now, but just as much in love' – that is, imagining what might have been, had they met before she married and, by implication, before she had aged in or into that marriage. And then to Paris, in a box for an opera – Alec lifting Laura's fur coat from her shoulders, now erotically exposing the flesh that, before, he had reassuringly squeezed. And then to Venice, kissing in a gondola. And then to an open-top car, and then to the balcony of a ship, with a sunset reflecting in the sea, and then to a 'tropical beach in the moonlight, with the palm trees sighing above us', until the image returns to the dull British countryside, 'and all those silly dreams disappeared'. It is an incredibly chaste sequence, delivering only the exotic, and barely the erotic.

The cruel ripostes to such imaginings – the way in which the film ensures those 'silly dreams' really do disappear – come thick and fast, as with the sight of a railway station advertisement for Llandudno, which is included in the sequence of their first kiss. Llandudno would seem to be the limit of exoticism actually on offer to this couple: a windswept Welsh holiday spot (the weather of *Brief Encounter* is blustery and autumnal) rather than ball gowns and furs, tropics and ocean cruises. The romance, or the potential of the romance, is confined to wishful thinking and daydreaming. What, after all, actually happens? In terms of what Lean shows us: just a bit of one-off smooching.

Brief Encounter, like a number of British films from the early/mid-1940s, seemed to attempt to imagine the coming peacetime life – a validation of 'what we are fighting for' (or, less prosaically: why lives had been expended). And this *Brief Encounter* suburbia would need to fulfil the role of the peacetime utopia of wartime aspirations: quiet cul-de-sacs and semi-detached houses of modest size in which replacement lives could be generated. The nominal setting of the film is a fictional 'Ketchworth' – strongly signalling Letchworth, that pleasant garden city, given over to sympathetic town planning, a uniformity of appearance for its new residential areas, and fights in town pubs, that would come to find a place in the commuter belt for London workers, another locality, and a template for further regeneration.[6] Indeed, this would be just the kind of nest area for the 'marriage to post-war repopulation' noted above. And freedoms within that suburban utopia would need to be granted in order to create a second iteration of the home front for the Cold War – this time against the restrictions and dearth of fun understood to typify life on the other side of the Iron Curtain. For the fight against communism, there would necessarily be a lifting of repression and a loosening of mores in the West.

Even as the film pierces the respectable facade, and breaches privacy in rendering Laura's stream of consciousness (an inner monologue in voice-over, structured as a confession to her husband, in which she frets over her yearnings, chides herself for untoward feelings, or observes that those in sunnier climates are freer with their affections), the resulting revelations nonetheless reveal a sexual imagining that is entirely locked into Laura's own class. And class structures, here, determine sexuality in an entirely custodial way, imprisoning those who conform, punishing those who do not, as in *The Wicked Lady* (Leslie Arliss, 1945) and *Black Narcissus* (Michael Powell, Emeric Pressburger, 1947). The freedom to cross class boundaries, and the sexual possibilities that arise with that, will be bestowed on the next generation – that of Laura's children – and not on this one. (Tellingly, then, *Lady Chatterley's Lover*, the 1928 D.H. Lawrence novel that concerned just such cross-class desire, would not be published in an unexpurgated version in the UK until 1960 – perhaps, then, something Laura's children would have read.)

In his discussion of the evolution of the British strip club, Elsom notes the legal injunctions against moving nude models (self-moving, that is; rotating platforms with still models were deemed to be acceptable). So that, seemingly, in the mid-1960s, it was possible to see Paul Raymond's glamour models 'in lion's dens, on revolving stages, under waterfalls, even *in* ice' (Elsom 1973: 179; emphasis in the original). The Lord Chamberlain held the power to veto stage productions (and with Sir George Titman assigned to inspecting strip shows), and a common joke concerning this ran 'a nude was rude if it moved' (quoted in Capon 1972: 87). And this maxim even extended to shivering in the cold – making one model's task, of standing still while freezing (as her brother threw axes at her), impossible to the extent that a 1957 King's Lynn show had to end early (see Davenport-Hines 2013: 142–43). The idea of the immobile nude woman encased in ice surely goes to the heart of this discussion of British sexual repression of this period, from the close of the Second World War to the onset of the counterculture. In this respect, pornography can be anticipated as an essential melting of the ice in the British psyche – a defrosting of national frigidity. As *Brief Encounter* illustrates, this must be an operation of freeing imagination, and so loosing fantasy. British pornography, then, must be located between ideas of class and fantasy. The dialectical tension that arises from such a dynamic for Laura (erotic adventure versus class propriety) then defines her 'self', which can be read in those subjective sequences (revelry, voice-over) noted above – a modernist, cinematic stream of consciousness flourishes. But the ideological battles to come, as this stream of erotic revelry swells into pornography, prompts me to locate, more precisely, and in a post-secular way, that 'self' – not of the psyche, but in Laura's soul. After all, Lean disassociates: Laura seems to see herself. This then is not diving into the self, and being immersed in a subjective state. Rather, it is splitting the consciousness away from the body, as if the soul leaves the body, and so is able to judge the body and its action – and, if that stepped-away soul is still unsullied, to be able to right herself.

'Being Her Means Being Pornography'

Performers who flit through the films under examination in this book may have been in these films against their wills or desires. And a number of such performers seemingly met unfortunate ends. They have not always been, in the romantic Hollywood tradition, taken too young by a tragic caprice of fate or, as if unable to contain their talent, the victims of a terminal surfeit of hard living. Rather, I refer to those for whom their later lives seem to have been marked by a return to the grimier and grimmer ends of the sex industry, and who then disappeared altogether. This then is a variant of, as per Dale Spender's book, *Women of Ideas and What Men Have Done to Them*. While the 'done' remains the same (and Spender [1988: 14] notes how 'hundreds of women – often influential in their own time – have been made to disappear'), my concern here is with those at the bottom: the notional voiceless everywoman, down on her luck to the point of being exploitable, rather than the martyrdoms of notable women of ideas. But the way in which 'men have used punitive measures against' women remains, albeit not just for those who have 'challenged' men (ibid.: 8), but also for those who have merely been in their proximity. Even the reassuring cosiness of retro-porn nostalgia, which defaults to ideas of what was once 'naughty', and sports an inclusive wryness around the lack of political correctness in these earlier and freer times, has been very substantially tarnished by revelations or intimations of deep connections between some of the personnel encountered in these films and in seemingly vast and still mostly uncharted networks of organised sexual abuse.[7] It is striking that few voices from the period are heard about the actual conditions of the porn set for the female performer. As can be imagined, and as Paula Meadows recalls: the performer ogled by interlopers, groped, and in comfortless surroundings, 'no running water – just someone's back garage or something' (quoted in Hebditch and Anning 1988: 94). Such a power dynamic also goes some way to explain the exclusive whiteness of the film-makers considered in this book; a feudal system of exploitation would be weakened, in the context of the times, by the much greater vulnerability of non-white pornographers to the law.

Many of these films can be considered to be evidence for the prosecution, and 1970s feminist writing was quite clear on this matter. *No Turning Back: Writing from the Women's Liberation Movement 1975–1980*, edited by the Feminist Anthology Collective for The Women's Press, places the writing on pornography in the 'Male Violence' section, rather than the following section on culture (Feminist Anthology Collective 1981: 224–26). And yet the collective's first task is a critique of those who make the case for the benefits of pornography, with the collective examining the commonality of eroticism in consumer culture, and then assessing the psychological, physiological and physical/biological damage that such a commonality is causing and maintaining: 'Women are seen as the vehicles for the plastic myth of mechanical, perfect, inhuman, profitable sex. That reduces us to the level of objects to be raped or humiliated, and those situations are reflected in much pornography' (Women's Report Collective [1977] 1981: 226). This was more generally theorised by feminist writers as a wider patriarchal strategy of oppression, with pornography as the apex or zenith of a sub-strategy of objectification, and also a warning or threat or illustration of imminent sexual assault, requiring inculcation from cradle to middle age and beyond. Likewise, to feminist activists of this time, pornography was a heteronormative/patriarchal intervention – joining innumerable discourses aimed at making the vagina available to men, and in so doing reducing the status of women, further to the limited gains achieved through feminism. For the Leeds Revolutionary Feminist Group in 1979, these discourses are outgrowths of the Permissive Society (now filtered through to the liberal mainstream), and represent the basis for abandoning heterosexuality altogether in favour of lesbianism:

> Penetration
> Penetration (wherever we refer to penetration, we mean penetration by the penis) is not necessary [for] the sexual pleasure of women or even of men. Its

performance leads to reproduction or tedious/dangerous forms of contraception. Why then does it lie at the heart of the sexualised culture of this particular stage of male supremacy? Why are more and more women, at younger and younger ages, encouraged by psychiatrists, doctors, marriage guidance counsellors, the porn industry, the growth movement, lefties and Masters and Johnson to get fucked more and more often? Because the form of oppression of women under male supremacy is changing. As more women are able to earn a little more money, and the pressures of reproduction are relieved, so the hold of individual men and men as a class over women is being strengthened through sexual control. (Leeds Revolutionary Feminists 1981: 6)

Andrea Dworkin, in her 1981 book *Pornography: Men Possessing Women*, charted nothing less than the erasure of woman herself, across history, in favour of pornography – stages of (as per Dworkin's chapters) 'objects', 'force', 'pornography', 'whores', and feeding into the sole 'idea of woman as sexual provocateur or harlot, [as] so consistently postulated in pornography' (Dworkin 1984: 178). From here, Dworkin sees (as shared with the critical approach of this book) pornography as illuminating or activating a nexus of ideas and assumptions, determining cognition:

In the male system, women are sex; sex is the whore. The whore is pornē *[i.e. the shared etymological root of 'prostitute' and 'pornography'], the lowest whore, the whore who belongs to* all *male citizens: the slut, the cunt. Buying her is buying pornography. Having her is having pornography. Seeing her is seeing pornography. Seeing her sex, especially her genitals, is seeing pornography. Seeing her in sex is seeing the whore in sex. Using her is using pornography. Wanting her means wanting pornography. Being her means being pornography. (Ibid.: 202; Dworkin's emphasis)*

And, further therefore, that 'the genre [of pornography] insists that sex is conquest' (Dworkin [1978] 1988: 208; see also 209–10, 219–20). A testing of cognition in relation to pornography occurred in the 1983 public hearings documented in *Pornography and Sexual Violence: Evidence of the Links* (Every-woman 1988), which included Dworkin's contribution.

Less radical feminist positions than Dworkin's still tended to read female sexuality as the prized possession of the male – and (therefore) the matter over which, and through which, control was to be exerted by the male, or patriarchal society, and its functioning in general. This was a particularly generative set of ideas, channelling feminist writing of the 1970s into Women's Studies so as to address, often sociologically, contradictions of the moment, and to trace these contradictions back into historical periods, as with Dworkin's *Pornography*, and the work of Judy Giles (1995, 2004), as well as within the constellation of Michel Foucault's work. The theme of control was explored in relation to legal status, medical status and victim status (especially in respect to sexual assault) in the collection *Women, Sexuality and Social Control* (Smart and Smart 1979), and extended to encompass the entirety of sexual liberation, via the 'challenges' raised by contraception, in Hera Cook's *The Long Sexual Revolution* (2004).

In *Pornography*, for the chapter 'Men and Boys', Dworkin loops such perceptions back to childhood. For Lee Comer, this inculcation is the role of 'Toys, Books and Television', discussed in her chapter of the same name in *Wedlocked Women* (Comer 1974: 29–39); and for June Statham, these same things (and clothes) function as patterns of reinforcement, to be offset by 'non-sexist childraising' (Statham 1986: 97). In this was effectively a socialisation of sexual role models, as founded on rampant and institutionalised misogyny. And, with this line of argumentation, pornography seems the very logical outcome: women as objects of sexual desire, as their primary function, offsetting the problems and irritants of 'keeping' (to use 1970s parlance) the 'little lady' or 'her indoors'. Thus, the sexualised female nude becomes the chief interpretative frame, for the male, of the female in her entirety. Lacanian strains in psychoanalytical thought would be quite familiar with this trope in which man effectively 'creates' woman as a fantasy projection, even to the complete exclusion of the actual woman herself.

Another jokily pejorative term for the female partner, the 'trouble and strife' (Cockney rhyming slang: the 'wife'), was utilised by David Bailey for a collection of his photographs of his then wife, the model Marie Helvin-Bailey. The book is introduced, by Brian Clarke, with the unconsciously Lacanian comment that while Bailey 'has "invented" during his career several women whose images are now part of the corporate psyche', these pictures of Helvin are apart from his usual fashion photography and portraits, as they 'present another view of Marie, sometimes erotic, sometimes cadaverous, but always beautiful' (Bailey 1981: 10). From the intimacy of, the collection suggests, their shared home or hotel suites, and the sense of a consensual, sexually experimental life together, Bailey effectively seems to mount a provocation against feminist criticism across the 1970s. As can be expected, Helvin is seen modelling lingerie, a little black dress in PVC, elements of bondage gear, flirtatiously blowing bubble gum as if a (nude) schoolgirl, nude on the bed and the floor, in the bath and the attic, and in images reminiscent of the home studio of Bailey's fictional alter-ego in *Blow-Up* (Michelangelo Antonioni, 1966), played by David Hemmings. But Helvin is also contrasted with tailors' dummies in the frame – and as seemingly the nude object of private holiday snaps. And nude but for a missing face: firstly with a white towel wrapped around it (while bringing a tea tray into a bedroom, as if a latter-day harem); and secondly, obscured by a camera (as per Clarke's introduction: the woman is faceless/personality-less, until Bailey has utilised his camera to 'invent' as much). The final image of the collection is Helvin as if a corpse, on the bare floor of the attic, wrapped in string and (bar for her exposed genitalia), head-to-toe in newspaper. A wicker basket placed next to her could be for body parts, as if this was a scene-of-crime photo, a serial killer having been disrupted in his post-rape task of dismemberment. The newspaper headlines wrapped around her seem carefully selected: those words that can just about be discerned include 'father / her jea[lous] husband', 'blow-up', 'chump', 'dream', '...bate' next to her genitalia; and, across the head, 'have a go'. And the biographical note on the back cover that immediately follows the image shows Bailey and Helvin, young and serious: 'Mr and Mrs David Bailey'. Bailey's recreations of domestic eroticism at the dawn of the 1980s seem to bait critics of pornography by freely providing the evidence to substantiate all their accusations: seemingly demeaning practices of domination, degradation and humiliation, an air of violence, and women considered in solely sexual terms. And yet Bailey's rejoinder is the suggestion of a recasting of such power games and masochistic tendencies (on, of course, the part of the woman), in the context of sexual experimentation, and straight male-to-beloved obsessive adoration. Here, if the sexualised female nude becomes the chief interpretative frame, for the male, of the female, then this is seemingly the start of the relationship, not the end of it. And *Trouble and Strife* chronicles the way in which the relationship then develops into psychological maturity. One problem with such a position, here from the quarter of 'classy' erotica, is that it still denies the female autonomy, beyond an assumed choice to be submissive: she remains the object of attention of the unseen other (Bailey's shadow appears in one shot alone). So this liberation, for women, is reformist, and purely on the basis of the male retaining his dominant role. And it is a liberation that effectively shows, critically or otherwise, the validity and scope of the feminist critique of pornography across the 1970s.

No Sex Please, We're British

Yet to have acted, in the 1970s, on a sense of distaste or repugnance for the pornographic text would have been to have found oneself siding, by association, with the censorious moralists then in the ascendency, and with their own misogynies. And, indeed, the censorious moralists occasionally cited feminist positions as aligned with their own, despite ideological differences – as if porn, as an absolute evil, prompted a popular front, uniting groups at either end of the political spectrum. Ruth Wallsgrove expressed this disorientation in the feminist magazine *Spare Rib*: of finding herself, as a feminist, seemingly aligned with anti-feminists – as caught '[b]etween the Devil and the true blue Whitehouse' (Wallsgrove 1977: 44), whose 'reason for attacking pornography is precisely the opposite to mine' (46). She concludes:

> *I don't want to choose between Mary Whitehouse and the producers of [the pornographic magazine]* High Society, *between two equally unacceptable alternatives … I believe we should not agitate for more laws against pornography, but should rather stand up together and say what we feel about it, and what we feel about our own sexuality, and force men to re-examine their own attitudes to sex and women implicit in their consumption of porn. We should talk to our local newsagents – many of whom feel pressured into stocking porn – or picket porn movies, or walk down Oxford Street with our shirts off. We must make it clear that porn is a symptom of our sexist society … We must choose a third alternative – Women's Liberation. (Ibid.: 46)*

A middle way between the two was also possible, with prolific romantic novelist Barbara Cartland condemning both nude models and women's liberation when interviewed in, disconcertingly, the exploitation documentary *The Anatomy of a Pin-Up* (David Cohen, 1971).

Right-wing pressure groups around anti-pornography activist and spokesperson Mary Whitehouse also took the fight to gay rights (as Wallsgrove notes), to feminism (blamed in part for 'causing' infidelity and homosexuality, as discussed below), and to blasphemy. No quarter was permitted for any form of progressive justification, or intimation of the common freedoms of the 'Permissive Society', in this popular front. The Whitehouse position was effectively that of 'No Sex Please, We're British' (as per the name of the British farce, discussed below).

I will engage further with Whitehouse's ideas later, as I wish to layer these in, in relation to the evolution of the ideological positions of the Conservative Party in the 1970s, rather than try to assemble and summarise a coherent position on her part. However, it is now time to introduce Mary Whitehouse (1910–2001), founder of the Clean-Up TV Campaign in 1964, and of the National Viewers' and Listeners' Association (NVALA, sometimes abbreviated as VALA) in 1965, and a ubiquitous and rambunctious media presence from the early 1970s onwards.

Whitehouse's groups seem, in part, to have effectively enabled sexual abuse by allowing some of the figures that she associated with to assume a saintly persona via their roles in her networks. Ridicule for their upstanding and unmodish declared beliefs and standards, via the public derision that could come from a connection to Whitehouse, would only have further obscured their opportunism. Almost any 1970s political grouping would have had a concern for internal security and potential infiltration (and Whitehouse was well aware of the latter from the protests mounted from within the venues she spoke at), and yet in this instance, Whitehouse – even indicating a slight awareness that things were not as they seemed – seemingly did nothing.[8] More than just two examples would be possible, but the two most extreme examples follow nonetheless, concerning now-deceased figures whose crimes are well documented.

In her final autobiography, Whitehouse reproduces some comments on Jimmy Savile (1926–2011), an equally rambunctious public figure, further to watching, and seemingly being involved with, an episode of his BBC television show *Jim'll Fix It* (broadcast between 1975 and 1994):

> *Jimmy spoke very kindly about our work and he was very touched by the 'We've fixed it for Jim' medallion which we had specially made for him. The team responsible for the show is quite obviously committed to something way beyond just the production of a programme. Some of the stories they told about the way in which they get involved with the children were very moving, like the one about the little girl Jimmy said he was going to marry and they got engaged with a huge cuddly toy just a few days before she died. ... [Savile] added 'While Mrs Whitehouse possibly wouldn't agree with my personal lifestyle, it is through organizations like hers that there is some semblance of decency'. Well, I don't know anything about Jimmy's lifestyle and, in any case, it's no business of mine. (Whitehouse 1994: 88–89)[9]*

The lifestyle was one of serial sexual assault, of adults and children, across many decades, including terminally ill children – to the extent that it is difficult to think that the child mentioned in this passage was spared (see Davies 2015). Indeed, Savile seems to have engineered *Jim'll Fix It* to facilitate further abuse opportunities for himself (O'Mahony 2012). Davies also notes Whitehouse with respect to Savile's moves to establish a powerbase via notable acquaintances (Davies 2015: 276–77). The halo awarded then would hold good for intimate access to royals (the 'squidgy tape', noted below, included a discussion of Savile as a placating marriage go-between for an arguing royal couple; see Booth 2012), and cautious silence or rumour-dispelling endorsements from later generations of television entertainers (as with David Mitchell: 'Jimmy Savile and child molestation – it rings true without being true'; Mitchell 2012: 117).

A second example is apparent in Whitehouse's *Mightier than the Sword* (1986), which goes out of its way to expose the Paedophile Information Exchange (PIE). A Foreword by her then regular barrister John J. Smyth, QC, includes: 'I have no doubt that history will give her a place amongst that select band of men and woman who in the name of Christ have done so much ... behind every engagement [of Whitehouse's] there is a preparation of prayer and dependence upon her Lord' (Whitehouse 1986: 9, 10). Smyth was with Whitehouse at a Festival of Light rally in 1971, discussed below, was Whitehouse's go-to for legal prosecutions, and appeared on television with her – a partnership across more than a decade (Graystone 2021: 20, 85). Smyth had been accused of sexualised violent beatings of over one hundred boys and young men, accessed through his chairmanship of the Church of England Iwerne Trust, which specialised in running holiday camps (Graystone 2021: 185). This Foreword was written after Smyth had fled the UK for Zimbabwe (where he carried on as before, and was later charged in relation to the death of a boy; see Laville 2017), after an internal report commissioned by the trust, but not then made public, verified these allegations. He died before prosecution was possible (Williams 2018). Whitehouse notes that God was effectively informing her decision making in terms of allies and court appearances (see Tracey and Morrison 1979: 11, 15, 54); in this respect both Smyth and God badly let Whitehouse down, although God seems to have been more adept at ensuring a flow of cash into the group when needed (54). Whitehouse's sensibility and operations were very reminiscent of clericalism, which was the assumed authority base that enabled and accommodated child abuse in various church organisations, as abusers were afforded a respect that removed them from suspicion, and even questioning.

Despite the subsequent, and very substantial, blackening of the reputations of some public moralists of this time (more of whom are encountered below), as part of the revelations after Savile's death, it is disconcerting to find that some of broadsides emanating from Whitehouse, relating to the mechanisms of the corruption of the innocent, were quite correct – including in relation to strategies around paedophile rights. Likewise, a 2016 report into the derelict nature of the running of the BBC's weekly pop music chart show, *Top of the Pops* (broadcast from 1964 to 2006), with the event read as becoming an opportunity for serial sexual assaults across a number of decades, would have held few surprises for 1970s campaigners looking to 'clean up' television.[10] For Whitehouse, *Top of the Pops* was a showcase for violence and anarchy (Whitehouse 1978: 43), and resulted in, for example, group masturbation among 'small boys' (see letter reproduced in Thompson 2012: 101–2).

The issue for the moralists was not so much that of, as it were, public littering (the occasional deposit of unwelcome material, against which legislation already existed, so that pornographers could be arrested, tried and punished), but of a countrywide pollution. In this sense, with their seeming potential to cause such damage, otherwise unremarkable cultural artefacts and films are afforded a much-enhanced importance. As with all moral panics, this unwelcome material was perceived as changing the complexion of society itself and corrupting the very psyche of the nation, for Whitehouse and her associates – and particularly her academic attack dog, the prolific and apocalyptic writer David Holbrook. The idea of a spiritual battle over national and cultural identity, and the collective psyche, and with the British people themselves at stake, is a beguiling and energising notion in terms of considering British film-making and pornography. Perhaps pornography deserves such exaltation? This is not, after all, merely the violent, or the merely lascivious, or simply impious, forms of entertainment, as with so many other British Board of Film Censors (BBFC) certificated and commercially released films that attracted conservative ire.

My approach then is both historical and conceptual. That is, firstly, that the pornographic films are specific to their points of origin, and so can be considered as artefacts of a nation's culture – which is the historical frame of this study. Secondly, the pornographic films are generators and enablers of that sense of culture – which is the conceptual frame of this study. This approach, rather than re-engaging with an already articulate historical feminist or somewhat threadbare moralist critique, is the way in which this book will primarily consider British pornography. To do so, it will first be necessary to outline a conceptual approach to film and national identity, beyond the standard Film History paradigms that are typically deployed.

Methodology Note #1: From National Identity to Collective Imagination

What is the relationship between fictional film and a sense of national identity – specifically, for this book, a British national identity? Reading films in relation to a sense of national identity and culture, in the fields of Cultural Studies, Film Studies and Film History, has been a methodological challenge for film scholars. Any cultural artefact can be understood to express a sense of its belonging to (in the sense of originating from) a certain place and time, and critical methodologies often seek to tie its form and content to that certain place and time. But this is typically a linear, sequential progression: the cultural artefact is seen to reflect something extant, so that the film is in receipt of ideas from the outside world. The presentation of a station guard in *Brief Encounter*, for example, is understood to reflect how station guards were, or were perceived to be, during the period in which the film was made. So the film is not only in receipt of information, but it validates that information too, through the process of representing the typical. In this sense, the cultural artefact also effectively creates and so normalises, and then transmits back out, such notions. Therefore the cultural artefact is generating a sense of society too: a non-linear progression that reverses the sequence – now the reflection of society becomes the template for that society itself, against which, in my example, the normality of station guards can be measured. Arguably, *Brief Encounter* worked to show the audiences of its time how and how not to behave when beset by opportunities for infidelity. This process is typically understood by film scholars to be enacted with films that have at least a nominal engagement with social reality, and often deploy realism or naturalism. Indeed, McFarlane notes that *Brief Encounter* was received as high realism at the time of its release (McFarlane 2015: 58–59). The questions of fair and reasonable representations of minority or un- or under-represented or marginalised groups, particularly in forms of popular culture such as soap operas, flow from this thinking with regard to processes of normalisation. Indeed, as Comer (1974) and Statham (1986) understand about this process too, as noted above, a variety of cultural streams or discourses (toys, books, television, clothes) can come together, mutually reinforcing each other, to germinate and disseminate objectionable messages and ideas. Culture, in this transmitter sense, is read as being affective in developing feelings in the audience concerning right and wrong, appropriate or inappropriate, typical or unusual.

For Jeffrey Richards, in *Films and British National Identity*, the dissemination is a function of state – a way in which the state establishes and continues to talk about itself:

> *Once the national identity has been defined, it can be promoted and spread by a whole range of institutions, events, symbols and ceremonies ... The practitioners of both elite and popular culture, and later the mass media, therefore play a central role in defining and disseminating national identity, values and character. (Richards 1997: 2)*

This process is typically read as a soft propaganda model – akin to an Althusserian reading of media as an Ideological State Apparatus. Richards goes on to apply such a notion to a reading of film through, for example, a discussion of British character (equitable, selfless, virtue-endowed, morally superior, civil-minded) in terms of films that 'dealt with' (in the vaguest possible sense) the empire – the 'British Imperial Heroes' of *Sanders of the River, The Four Feathers* and *The Drum* (Zoltan Korda 1935, 1938, 1939 respectively). In these, 'the man is the message' (Richards 1997: 40). Or, for a later discussion of *Brief Encounter*, Richards is able to move to a more diffused form of reading: seeing beyond that which now feels like ripe melodrama (as the realism that McFarlane notes now seems terribly dated), Richards finds something that is 'both documentarily and emotionally true' – the former not literally but in relation to 'the precise evocation of a middle-class woman's existence in the Home Counties in the 1930s and 1940s' (ibid.: 124–25). Richards problematizes all aspects of received and recreated notions of national identity.

The transmitter model seems more appropriate to moments of state crisis than moments of social crisis. British film can be taken to have had a particular role during the times of state crisis – and the development and propagation of ideas of 'the typical' serve to shore up certainties endangered by a besieged or changing state (as associated with the ending of the British Empire, or times of war). During times of social crisis or upheaval, film can be read as being effectively in reception mode: mirroring, even trying to make sense of, a confusing reality. This results in the artefact that later seems to 'reflect the times'. For Sue Harper and Justin Smith, in confronting a body of films associated with one decade (the 1970s) in which a sense of national identity was understood to have been in a process of fragmentation (i.e. a social crisis), the receptive nature of the film medium is identified thus: 'Ever since its inception, the medium of film has had a unique function in negotiating the relations between social morality and the emotional hinterland of psycho-sexual life' (Harper and Smith 2013: 138).

The nature of this negotiation remains uncertain, despite the identified uniqueness of this function to film culture. However, the outcome of the negotiation is seemingly not a settlement across both parties (presumably 'the state' and its institutions, as the generators of 'social morality', and the people of the state), but that film culture 'was able to articulate an unusually wide range of responses to social change, albeit in a chaotic and often oblique way' (Harper and Smith 2013: 232). And this is said to be true with respect to a particular shift detectable across the second half of the 1970s and its 'ideological rupture in consciousness', and as related to (referencing Raymond Williams) 'new structures of feelings' (ibid.). Consequently, as with Richards's reading, film remains indexical – reflecting extant matters, dealing with found reality. In this sense, the films reflect or generate a sense of national identity, in the flow of typification or normalisation. But, for Harper and Smith, at a time of social upheaval, the circumference of the reflection is expanded. Areas of the reflection now include the non-extant, and psychology – that is, the felt or imagined or desired or feared, the 'mood of the times', as it were. And film seems to be trying to make sense of the confusion of social upheaval, consciously or otherwise – as if trying to locate what is typical, so as to normalise it for transmission, but being unable to find the typical, and so the transmission becomes garbled, but remains more enlightening in its garbled state than any questionable and selective shoring up of normality. This is an expansive critical approach, and one that moves to a consideration of auteur film-making (which identifies an interpretative singular intelligence behind the camera) over industry film-making (where the soft propaganda function can be read as the product of multiple intelligences at work). This means that, for their study, *British Film Culture in the 1970s: The Boundaries of Pleasure*, a full range of films from mainstream to avant-garde fall under examination (including some 'low' sexualised comedies too), as all the films can be read as striving to reflect/articulate more than found reality. Thus, *Confessions of a Window Cleaner* (Val Guest, 1974) is grouped with films that very actively sought to engage with, and deconstruct, 'difficult' social/sexual mores (from incest/child abuse to the 1970s persecuted queer underground) – Peter Whitehead's *Daddy* (1973), Laura Mulvey and Peter Wollen's *The Riddles of the Sphinx* (1977), Ron Peck's *Nighthawks* (1978) and Derek Jarman and Paul Humfress's *Sebastiane* (1976). *Confessions of a Window Cleaner* is 'nuanced' (presumably from such art house cinema) however, as this film (and the subsequent *Confessions* films) 'addressed a young, working-class audience' through 'pop soundtracks and denim fashions' (Harper and Smith 2013: 145). And the films, in this framing, merely 'display a new liberalism in their espousal of sexual freedom' and 'propose, without hint of irony, that sexual freedom can be available to all' (ibid.). My contention is that this end point of analysis, for Harper and Smith's catholic overview, can now be positioned as the starting point of an exploration of such 'new structures of feelings' and 'psycho-sexual life'. And, indeed, this might allow access to a deeper strata of national identity – to (pace Whitehouse et al.), some kind of national psyche that is particularly vulnerable and so, once assailed by pornography, may potentially damage a sense of national identity altogether. To move towards such an analysis, it is necessary to outline a more sophisticated model of reading film than along the lines of transmitter/receiver/reflector, and sense or no-sense maker. That is – to move away from discretions of film criticism to wider considerations (ideological, partisan, technocratic, rallying, 'spiritual') from those unversed in the discourses of film criticism, but espousing ideas of the role of film, and art in general, in life.

Within the standard paradigm of film history, via the idea of the theatrical play reflecting life (that is, in terms of deploying a straight naturalism or realism), the film can only really be read in terms of its relationship to found, material reality. So film is taken as a mirror to known life itself: indexical, familiar, representative, empathetic – a recreation of, a documentation of, life. But what if films are read as grounded within a sense of the familiars of that reality, but in the context of the immaterial: thought and psychology; that is, the immaterial as that which can be taken as the aspirational, fantastical, utopic, furtive, with film as reflecting or recreating ideas of fantasy rather than found reality? This is not a particularly unusual or abstract turn: whole swathes of media (lifestyle television, advertisements, the media discourse of politics) essentially operate along this line of departure. As per the cliché, the car advert is not so much selling a car as selling a lifestyle. And effective propaganda also conforms to this model to an extent: it needs to diagnose not only that which is wrong with found reality, but how the proposed remedy will (even if only via suggestion) right the situation. This is the conceptual turn I mention in terms of my critical approach to pornography – and my point of departure from standard Film History approaches.

But I need to identify a further stage of consideration in this. The makers of the car advert present a lifestyle, for which the car is presented as essential. For smaller and cheaper cars, aimed at younger buyers, this seems to include, as per the adverts, trips out with friends in the sun, informal sports and picnics in the countryside; the car allows transport of, and access to, a loved one, and the ability (in the car) to have some alone-time with that loved one. It is unlikely that this is the lifestyle to which the advert makers themselves aspire, so they are not speaking of their personal preferences, but of the preferences of the potential buyers of the car being advertised. But I now need to identify yet a further stage of consideration. The lifestyle presented is an aspiration (accessed via having the car), but also a *presumed* aspiration. That is, the lifestyle can be read as the makers' assumption or understanding or belief (bolstered, no doubt, by marketing data, focus groups and so on) of the kind of lifestyle that potential purchasers of the car would want to aspire to. The lifestyle to which they aspire will probably not be the lifestyle they may attain, and indeed the car will generally be more useful for mundane domestic duties and commuting than picnics or romantic intrigues. But this articulation of an aspired-to lifestyle, in the advert, then begins to reveal information about the nature of such aspirations, of such unknown and unseen people. That is, firstly, the advert reveals who the makers think their audiences are (and, typically, along gendered and biologically essentialist lines); and secondly, the advert reveals what the makers think their audiences themselves (a) think they are, and/or (b) would like to think they are. Put simply, the car advert makers are peddling an aspirational lifestyle to a group of unknown people, and that aspiration reveals the car advert makers' imagining of the imaginings or imaginations of the unknown people.

Much of this kind of thinking determines Roland Barthes-inspired approaches to the deconstruction of the semiotics of advertising, and the interplay of meanings beyond just, for example, the selling of packets of spaghetti. There even seems to be something in the visualisation of eroticism that organically prompts this critical framing, perhaps because of the violation of privacy through showing intimacy; John Ellis notes, in passing, the defacing of adverts on the London Underground in 1980, with graffiti and stickers – one such is 'KEEP MY BODY OFF YOUR ADS' (Ellis 1992: 152). He notes the way in which the slogan is redolent of the various problems with such critiques – melding representation and reality, finding a limited target for campaigning (over representation of the body), and how "'I" refers to the collectivity of women; "you" is either the collectivity of men who in an undifferentiated way "portray women", or (as is more probable given the address of most posters) the power elite of marketing personnel', so that 'the (male) viewer is left in the same relationship to the poster plus sticker as he was to the poster alone: he is the voyeur to women speaking to the advertisers as he was the voyeur to the women performing in the poster' (ibid.). As an aside, confined to an endnote, Ellis suggests a corrective: a 'sticker "Who does this poster think you are?" [which] would be a more effective way of confronting the attitude that advertising promotes' (ibid.: 169, note 6).

Another useful parallel to this complicated thought process can be found in the work of the French conceptual artist Annette Messager. Messager's series *Mes Dessins d'enfant* (My children's drawings, 1971–72) are childlike colour pencil sketches of, seemingly, Messager herself, as if made by an imaginary child of hers. The identification of the mother, in addition to the series title, is also apparent in the words scrawled next to the sketches (complete with spelling mistakes and letters the wrong way around): *Maman avec son chignon* [Mama with her hair in a bun], *Mama met du rouge à levre pour sortir* [Mama puts lipstick on to go out], etc. The sketches do not for a second suggest the kind of technique or artistic achievement one would expect for conventional art works in a gallery, so their existence in this context prompts a series of speculations. For these sketches, Messager adopts the imagination, and mimics the infant drawing, of her imagined child – in order to imagine how her imagined child would see her, with the drawings as the artefact of that imagination. The same is true of another series of 'better' drawings: *Comment mes amis feraient mon portrait* [How my friends would do my portrait] (1972–73). These friends may or may not exist, and at any rate it is Messager herself who has made these drawings, not the friends. Critical writing on Messager has then tended to the point of the identification of the self, in terms of reading the images as a way in which art interrogates a sense of self, or plays with ideas of performing oneself – as with, for example, Sophie Duplaix's essay on Messager, 'Playing with Forms of "I"', (Duplaix 2009: 10–21). This is quite typical in terms of evolving ideas of self-performance, and of identity politics in the 1970s, and then even in terms of ideas associated with business or lifestyle gurus ('how to make a good first impression'; 'how others see you, how you see yourself', and so on). And, finally, this became typical in terms of evolving ideas of how the pressures of social media demand the ability to deliver images that meet the idea of a certain look and lifestyle that one may feel one needs to project to others, and the potentially detrimental nature of such pressures (so that, in his analysis of social media, Ben Light is prompted to argue for the Internet as, counterintuitively, 'just another space of our everyday life rather than another world' [Light 2014: 19]). But the use of this concept in Messager's art, in terms of my moving towards a more useful or appropriate model of reading fantasy film, is that the images suggest a complicated series of assumed positions. In the childish sketch, one sees how:

(a) Messager imagines her imaginary child, or friends, to draw;

(b) therefore, in this, is something of what these people may be, or may have been, like (since they may or may not exist);

(c) from this comes the idea of how they see her: in the child's case, willowy and ghost-like, with towering full-body images; in the friends' cases, oval-faced, and with a natural look, for portrait-like images (these vantage points denote different heights on the parts of the drawers);

(d) and how, of course, Messager sketches herself.

My concern is with the idea of (b): the image that suggests an imagining of the thinking of unknown or non-existent others. For this, I cannot turn to a body of Freudian/Lacanian film theory, in attempting to chart psychology, or the idea of the projection of (rather than perception of) other people. This body of film theory primarily considers, particularly in its intersections with auteur theory, the film text to be the creative imagining of the film director, who is then cast as the patient, or the midwife of enlightenment about various psychological conditions – as with, for example, Kline's study of Bernardo Bertolucci's films as a 'dream loom' (Kline 1987). Although there is a substantial organisation of the films examined in this book by the film-makers themselves, in relation to the above-mentioned auteur approach, I do not read the films in the standard auteur way, which is the foundation for psychoanalytical approaches to film-making. Rather, the films summon up ideas about the aspirations of others, so there is a distance between the films themselves, and what seems to animate them – and this guides an analytical approach that, nevertheless, remains grounded in close textual reading.

Again, Messager's work offers a useful parallel: 'Back in 1971, with the series called *The Boarders*, I would put little stuffed sparrows on the clockwork mechanisms used in toys, and with keys I'd make them jump about. It was rather touching' (quoted in Pagé and Parent 2009: 154). In the resultant macabre objects, the preserved remains of the sparrow are brought back to motion (if not life) by a small motor. So while the effect might be a split-second recognition of a living, hopping sparrow, and a human reaction to this might be one of warmth and care, this recognition is very suddenly revised when one sees this taxidermy orthino-noid at work, to Frankenstein-like ends. Likewise, the films may seem to function 'naturally' at first glance, as one would expect, with narratives of love and lust. But one could think again and conclude that what animates these films can be considered as apart from the films themselves: not love and lust as the goal in itself, as with the advertised car, but love and lust as indicative of something else, which is akin to a lifestyle imagined as desirable for an unknown other, by the makers of the film. A clear pornographic tendency parallels this operation: the supposed 'readers' letters' to pornographic magazines – seemingly written by staff writers (despite Anne Hooper's protestations to the contrary, which open an edited collection of as much from *Forum* magazine; Hooper [1973] 1980: 7). In these, the staff writer imagines a reader's voice, and in this speculates on what this fictional reader may fantasise about, and then writes up the speculations that the writer imagines may appeal to the other imagined actual readers. It is no surprise then that, in this tangle, tangible scene-setting often occurs in line one of each letter:

> *'About 12 months ago I had my first orgasm after 20 years of marriage.'*
> *'I love going down on my boyfriend and giving him "a trip" as we call it.'*
> *'One morning I found a copy of your magazine on my front lawn.'*
> *'Shortly before our marriage 20 years ago, my wife, who was 19 at the time, lost all her teeth due to a severe illness.'*
> *'The recent fad of streaking now seems to be fading, but during a warm spell in May I did my best to keep it going.'*
> *'When I was 12, I was sent to an expensive boarding school in Surrey.'*
> *'My reason for writing to you is that I thought my long experience as a full-time homosexual may be of some use to others have who written to you on the subject.'*
> (Hooper [1973] 1980: 23, 64, 65, 67, 160, 222, 251)

And this opening gambit then becomes the recognisable basis for flights of fantasy. Indeed, the very set-up of pornography suggests this is, to an extent, an appropriate approach for the form: the inauthenticity of the biological reactions and emotions (the outer human skin and appearance, disconnected from the inner self, which may not be organically reacting at all), with the whole lot effectively prompted into motion by the presence of the clockwork mechanisms of the camera pointed at the love-making scene. And so Messager's reanimated sparrows seem like apt metaphors for pornography.

This approach then maintains some distance from other methodological approaches that have evolved to pornography – most ably articulated in Jeffrey Escoffier's work on gay hardcore of yesteryear. Escoffier, in 'Sex in the Seventies: Gay Porn Cinema as an Archive for the History of American Sexuality', cites Laura Kipnis: pornography is 'acutely historical. It's an archive of data about our history as a culture and our individual histories – our formation as selves … Pornography is a space in the social imagination as well as a media form' (cited in Escoffier 2017: 88). While my approach recognises and builds on these attributes, the proportions are quite different. Escoffier notes the 1970s as the zenith of gay pornography in the United States – and central to an age and culture of libertinism. For Escoffier, the documentation of gay or queer cultures transfigures the films with an inescapable and valuable documentary impulse, as 'even pornographic movies preserve some historical evidence of the quotidian sex lives of gay men in the seventies' (ibid.: 104). And the antecedents or parallels are via acclaimed film-makers such as Richard Leacock, D.A. Pennebaker and John Cassavetes (105), allowing for an anthropological or sociological impulse in the recovery of yesteryear's pornography. Even Peter de Rome's gay porn (often fantastical, ritualistic, musical) is taken as 'homorealist' (107) – a category that 'walks a fine line between documentary and fantasy' (109), and delivers 'memory images' (110, Escoffier's italics). And so, in conclusion, 'it is possible to contribute to an ethnography of sexual encounters among gay men in the seventies using homorealist porn movies' (113). The vibrancy of the films, and the out-ness of the culture they drew on or reflected, is such that 'reality superabounds', to use André Bazin's term (Bazin 1967: 27), with documentary realism unavoidably manifest on the screen.

But the case was quite different for pornography – gay or straight – in the UK. This culture was furtive and with limited access, and private wherever possible. It seemed unsure of its right to exist, beyond the boundaries of 'red light' districts – which is why, for the casual visitor finding him or herself in Soho, the experience could be so shocking. And that equivocation has, to an extent, remained intact. So British pornography seems a minor concern: slight happenings, filmed in private, that only really begin to make sense, or justify their existence, when considered as accesses to other imaginings, rather than as skimmed off from an extant culture. The direction of travel then is quite different: British porn, in my conception, points to historical fantasy images rather than 'memory images'. This then responds to the feminist critique: the analysis seeks to deconstruct the very content of patriarchal inculcation, via an access to its purest and so most debased discourse: filmed sexual exploitation.

If the pornographic films contain within them intimations of their imagined viewers' desires, which will then be the way in which I will, in part, read these films, then a further question arises: how do these pornographic films effectively function in respect to imagined viewers' desires? And external pressures on this question are apparent, for this is not a case study scenario (pervert A enjoys film B because it combines violence with sex, to refer to a typical concern of the BBFC of the 1960s and 1970s) but a universalising of this idea of imagined viewers' desires. One almost has to think of some kind of collective imagination that exists outside the viewers: a free-floating smog of ideas that seeps into domestic spaces and pollutes those within them. In the Church of England report *Obscene Publications*, it is an 'unwarranted pollution of the social atmosphere' (Board for Social Responsibility 1970: 12). This is why the battle is on the spiritual plane, for Whitehouse and associates. And even in terms of feminist thought, Wallsgrove notes the lack of a '*causal* link' between pornography and rape, but that 'they are linked in spirit' (1977: 44, Wallsgrove's italics). Here, in a classic (albeit unversed) Judeo-Christian theological turn, 'evil' resides without, engulfing those vulnerable unfortunates in its proximity. To fight evil becomes a physical matter: the destruction of, or locking away of, items that contain intensities of evil – putting the genie safely back into the magic lamp. So those who have the means of production (cameras, models, lights, rooms, editing facilities, outlets for distribution) have the ability to intervene into, and damage, this collective imagination. This then delivers a very specific potential for those film-makers: not just something as trivial as makers of entertainment, or makers of art, but something more akin to agents shaping the way a nation desires. So, rather than any expected psychoanalytical approach, as centred on an individual figure (the lone viewer and their desires, and speculative reasons for them, and so on), I wish to take as a starting point an approach that draws on Joseph Stalin's reading of writers as the 'the engineers of the soul'. But desire, and the soul, are now familiar: that potential endangerment of the soul for those ranged against the

Permissive Society, and (therefore) the soul read as the terrain of battle between desires and propriety of *Brief Encounter,* and that battle as determining life and personality itself.

Methodology Note #2: Erotic Engineers of the Soul

Stalin borrowed a phrase coined by the novelist Yury Olesha, 'the engineers of the human soul', for a general conversation with authors in the home of Maxim Gorky, on 26 October 1932.[11] This was only months before the ending of the first Five Year Plan – given over to the radical reorganisation of agriculture in order to increase the pace of industrialisation – which would be announced as a success, and engender further medium-term revolutionary strategies to consolidate the USSR's position as an industrial world power. The second Five Year Plan would run from 1933 to 1937, and would include improvements in transport – one area in which the first Five Year Plan had exceeded targets (albeit accidentally; see Hunter 1973). Stalin's thinking about the role of writers can understandably be placed, then, at this juncture, with new priorities now spreading to classes not covered in the first plan. The position, and so role, of the artist is understood to be in the realms of an idea of a collective psychology.

The second Five Year Plan included work on the railway network, and the prospect of shuttling rural citizens into new and alien stretches of the country; how they would react would have been a reasonable concern. These were citizens who, only some years before, may have been entirely rustic; Lieberstein notes that '[o]f the 12,600,000 workers and employees drawn into industry during the first Five Year Plan, 8,600,00 were former peasants' (Lieberstein 1975: 53). So some finessing of such social upheavals, in terms of developing a modern, urban sensibility, or a more advanced or sophisticated mindset for the populace, perhaps fast-tracked across a couple of generations (peasantry to proletariat) would have been welcome. In addition, this identification of the role and use of the artist in society then allowed for rearguard action against artists whose work sought to undermine societal cohesion and purpose – as it once had. A.A. Zhdanov, who would codify and operationalise Stalin's position ('Zhdanovism' or the 'Zhdanov Doctrine', as then popularly associated with socialist realism) had identified the intelligentsia as actively, damagingly reactive:

Gorky once said that the ten years from 1907 to 1917 might well be called the most shameful, the most barren decade in the history of Russian intellectuals; in this decade, after the 1905 Revolution, a great many of the intellectuals spurned the revolution and slid down into a morass of pornography and reactionary mysticism ... deserters from the camp of revolution to that of reaction, hastening to dethrone the lofty ideals that the best and most progressive representatives of Russian society were fighting for. (Zhdanov [1947] 1975: 518–19)

In the most straightforward way, Zhdanov's conception of the role of the artist was in respect to the battle for ideals. And, in the most concrete way, this battle was literal: those who had lost their lives fighting for the same things that the writers deign to satirise and attack.

So at the point of considering the achievements of the first Five Year Plan, Stalin's concern in 1936 turned to the matter of the developing intellectual life and its wider functions. From 'Changes in the Life of the USSR in the Period from 1924 to 1936', on 'the question of the intelligentsia [including] workers on the cultural front', Stalin hailed 'an entirely new intelligentsia', which – unlike the previous iteration, who had been entirely within the orbit of the ruling classes – was now 'bound up by its very roots to the working class and peasantry'. This was true not least as now '80 to 90 per cent of the Soviet intelligentsia are people who have come from the working class, from the peasantry, or from other strata of the working population'. Consequently,

the very nature of the activities of the intelligentsia has changed. Formerly it [the intelligentsia] had to serve the wealthy classes, for it had no alternative. Today it must serve the people, for there are no longer any exploiting classes. And that is why it is now an equal member of Soviet society, in which, side by side with the workers and peasants, pulling together with them, it is engaged in building the new, classless, socialist society. (Stalin 1953: 685–86)

As Clark notes, this positions the worker-writers 'as intermediaries between the educated and the masses, and as such provide "levers" of the cultural revolution' (Clark 1978: 197). Zhdanov expanded on Stalin's position in a speech for the Soviet Writers' Congress of 1934:

The weaknesses in our literature reflect the fact that consciousness is lagging behind economic life, a state of affairs from which, obviously, our writers are not exempt. That is why unceasing work on educating themselves and improving their ideological weapons in the spirit of socialism are the indispensable conditions without which Soviet writers cannot change the consciousness of their readers and thus be engineers of the human soul. (Zhandov [1934] 1950: 17)

And the remit of 'changing' was reiterated as 'remoulding' in his closing directives to the Congress:

Create works of great craftsmanship, of profound ideological and artistic content,
Be the most active organisers of the remoulding of people's consciousness in the spirit of socialism,
Stand in the front ranks of the fighters for a classless socialist society!
(Ibid.)

To engineer a soul or a psyche, which might then be termed, in a classic propaganda fashion, as working to manipulate the psychology of the Soviet citizen, can reasonably be taken as needing the ingredient of projection or fantasy. The artistic works look a few steps ahead – to the world to come. And from this perspective, a series of ethical framings of the present can occur: read what is right or wrong as what works for the collective good, or does not, and so speeds up or hinders the progression to the world to come, respectively. And such an ethical sensibility also encompasses the need to be resilient during times of social upheaval, for the times to come, which will be those of social peace. Thus the projection or fantasy becomes the justification of the upheavals and hardships of the present too. In the use of Stalin's position on art and society, aligned to communism, and for the doctrines of socialist realism, reality was understood to be rendered in two registers: critique of the present, and intimation of the near future – diagnosis and cure, suffering and then reward; in Eagleton's terms 'the development of the productive forces, free from the stymieing and blockages of pre-history or class society, to the point where they can give birth to a surplus sufficient for the abolition of labour and the fulfilment of the needs of everyone' (Eagleton 2010: 101–2). So the heroes of socialist realism do not flounder around lost in the world, but seem inexorably pointed in the direction of their (or their children's) salvation. And this is an affective endeavour: seeking to inculcate change through art. Clark offers a commentary on the results, in Soviet literature: that '[s]ome writers were so carried away by the Five Year Plan cult of technology that they depicted industrial machines as actually impressing their own rhythms and harmonies on the psyche of the workers who operated them' (Clark 1978: 190), aligned with a universal effort whereby 'social institutions were seen as a sort of assembly line for retooling a human product and turning out the new Soviet man' (ibid.: 192), '[t]he most dramatic illustrations' of which 'can be found in the books about "alien elements". One such source, and a particularly rich one, is the book commissioned to celebrate the White Sea–Baltic Canal project [*Belomorsko-Baltiiskii kanal imeni Stalina* of 1934], an undertaking that used thousands of convict laborers. On almost every page the authors describe how the "human raw materials" were "reworked"' (ibid.).[12] And the reworking itself had both psychological and biological benefits: one character here, an engineer and a former member of the bourgeoisie, developed a quicker pulse and reactions, as well as a faster mind, once he began working for the greater Soviet good, and this new tempo also changed and regulated his breathing patterns. During this process, he experienced a complete disassociation from his former self. This is the kind of position that, in 1932, would be relayed into thinking about mutually enforced and enforcing capitalism, and sexual oppression, by Wilhelm Reich – so that socialism strikes a virtuous and non-censorious relationship with the sexuality that it liberates: 'Only through socialism can you achieve sexual *joie de vivre* ... Socialism will put an end to the power of those who gaze up towards heaven as they speak of love while they crush and destroy the sexuality of youth' (Reich and Baxandall 1972: 274).

One final note is that the White Sea–Baltic Canal book, in its material sense, is then considered an essential tool in the toolbox of the worker:

> It was even argued [by proponents of the Five Year Plan] that books should have a direct effect on production itself. Occasional slogans in the literary press reminded writers that 'The Book Is an Instrument of Production', and 'In Order to Conduct a Successful Spring Sowing Campaign We Must Arm Each Kolkhoz Member with a Book, and Likewise Every Sovkhoz Worker and Each Poor- and Middle-Peasant Household'. At a rather higher level of sophistication, a joint appeal of the Education Commissariat and the Federation of Soviet Writers

described the writer's function as 'raising the morale high, inspiring the masses for the struggle, ruthlessly exposing indifference, stagnation and desertion, all of which undermine the plan'. (Clark 1978: 196)

(The Western counterpart is simply that the material item is essential for the worker's leisure, rather than labour.)

From this vantage point, a clear demarcation becomes visible between films that effectively work on expanding the 'soul' (that is, via the work of the artist-engineers: films that dare to show the projection or fantasy, and so educate and galvanise), and films that may stand on the brink of showing this, but cannot or will not. That bar may be entirely due to the regulations of the day. And that bar is apparent in the example of *Brief Encounter* too. This is not just a matter of maintaining propriety, and what can be seen to happen, or should not happen (and so may not happen) to the couple – to be straightforward: sexual intercourse, and a new life together – but also the way in which the imagery itself is limited or curtailed or ambiguous. What is it that is not seen? *The Servant* (Joseph Losey, 1963) ends with an orgy, at the point at which the aristocratic protagonist, seemingly having suffered a nervous breakdown, has been reduced to a bedroom-confined, drink-induced stupor. He falls to the floor and crawls on his hands and knees, and with his former sense of sexual propriety (which was aligned to an appropriate fiancée) now abandoned. Weedman reads the orgy as the moment of the final reversal of power, between upstairs and downstairs (the aristocratic and servant classes), in the context of a crisis-inducing 'crossroads' moment (social, political, artistic) of 1963 (Weedman 2019: 116–17).

But the orgy cannot be seen for the flux of visual metaphors and stylistic flourishes that obscure it. In fact, read literally, this is not an orgy at all: Losey provides images of people walking with some difficulty around a bedroom, some with cognac in hand, or sitting listlessly and staring into the middle distance, and some kissing. The latter group includes the servant kissing the aristocrat's fiancée. For McFarlane this is a 'party sequence, in which the house is invaded by 60s swingers', but he also notes the implicit: 'a pervasive acrid aura of sexuality' (McFarlane 2015: 142, 143). De Rham, also writing on the film, hedges her bets, with 'the final "orgy" scene (as it came to be known)' (De Rahm 1991: 154), whereas Palmer and Riley find not only an orgy (and note Losey's agreement on this term), but also see drugs in the hedonistic mix (Palmer and Riley 1993: 60, 61, 45). Losey recalls deliberately wanting to shoot an orgy at which nothing happened – which begs the question: how, then, is it an orgy? (quoted in Ciment 1985: 230–31). Palmer and Riley also note the jarring shift to visual stylisation for the final third of the film – which effectively then offers a further way of not showing the orgy – as arguably upsetting the aesthetic unity of the whole film (Palmer and Riley 1993: 51–55). For example, the camera seems to join the guest in its lurching about. And all these writers orientate their readings to a homosexual subtext in the film that, arguably, completely fails to break surface.

Losey seems as bold as can be, within the strictures of the time – even almost twenty years beyond the epitome of British buttoned-up emotions, *Brief Encounter*. And, indeed, *The Servant* was passed uncut by the BBFC on 30 September 1963, albeit awarded the 'X' certificate. The unintended consequence of working in the area of implied rather than shown is that censorship, or self-censorship, can result in that unexpected problem of making matters look substantially worse than they actually are: the more that is cut away, the worse the (surmised or implied) offences that must not be shown. Ken Russell was fond of telling a story about the removal of the naked wrestling scene between two male protagonists in his 1969 adaptation of D.H. Lawrence's *Women in Love* in some South American countries. This resulted in the scene of hyper-heterosexuality – now a cut from a door being locked from the inside to two sweaty, unclothed and panting men lying in front of a roaring log fire – being referred to as 'The Great Buggery Scene' (cited in Baxter 1973: 180). (But even the film uncut, despite its heterosexuality, was warmly received by the British 'barely covert' gay film magazine *Films and Filming* in December 1969, with a cover photo of the naked clinch, at a moment of exertion, and the enticement of 'more pictures inside'.) And it is this juncture – where the muted suggestions seem even worse – that makes for the tipping point: the time at which it seems better to allow a modicum of the forbidden than, in banning it, suggesting more extreme possibilities. And, indeed, this juncture could be taken as the very foundation for the 'Swinging Sixties' in London: to begin to allow rather than to continue to disallow.

As an example of the disruptive consequences of disallowing, one thinks of the famous Lewis Morley photograph of Christine Keeler, taken in the Establishment Club in 1963, at the height of the scandal ('The Profumo Affair') over her relationships with a Soviet military attaché and a British politician, and the perceived state security liabilities. This was a scandal that was understood to have helped promote *The Servant*, as the scandal broke at the time of the film's first release – and one could note the similarities of appearance between Keeler and

Sarah Miles, who plays Vera in the film (two working-class figures who find themselves in the locale of misbehaving aristocracy). And, in relation to this magnitude, for British intelligence officer Peter Wright, the prospect of yet another scandal and, with this, the Conservative Party driven further from office, was one that scared MI5 and MI6 to the extent that they covered up any homosexual variant, in the figure of the confessing 'Cambridge spy' Anthony Blunt (see Wright, Greengrass 1988: 213–14, 230, 340–41).[13] Profumo was, in this reading and in relation to permissiveness, not so much an aberration for the party of decency and the family (and so on) but, as Wayland Young (1963) put it, something already within 'aspects of Conservatism'. In Davenport-Hines's later reading, the Permissive Society seems to have been materialised by a number of electrifying 'good time' girls (Pamela Green, Stockport's Norma Ann Sykes aka Sabrina, seen in an early St Trinian's film, Keeler and her friend Mandy Rice-Davies, and Diana Dors), gaining exposure via newly emboldened newspapers (now wielding an osmotic sexual frankness gained through coverage of legal proceedings) and nightclub shows – all of which suggest swinging and leisure and sexual freedom in a secular, post-marriage capitalist mode, freeing the 'insulated lust' of the 'English sex parties [which] fell short of orgies' of the 1950s (Davenport-Hines 2013: 126). Comedian and writer Bob Monkhouse's recollections of partying with Dors in 1952 is quite different: a 'continuous showing of blue movies on a big screen' (Monkhouse 1994: 97–98), at first manipulated into having sex for others to watch (through a hidden two-way ceiling mirror), followed by an actress of the day engaging in bestiality for the same crowd (ibid.: 100–101). Dors blamed her manipulative husband Dennis Hamilton for some of this, in her autobiography *Swingin' Dors* (with cover copy of 'I've been a naughty girl! A frank and full account of the wild life I have lived – and the men I have loved'), (Dors 1960: 101, 122).

Morley's contact sheets show a variety of standard glamour poses, mostly with a cross-legged Keeler seen from the side, sat in the chair to obscure her breasts but showcase her legs, and glancing, flirtatiously, over her shoulder.[14] But when sat with the chair backwards, so that Keeler's legs are on either side of the chair's pinched 'waist', and breasts blocked from view by her arms, which are positioned so that the elbows rest on the top of the chair's back, the resultant image suggest something quite different. The V-like back of the chair (in fact, a knock-off of the more famous Arne Jacobsen chair) suggests the black pubic triangle of this (then) most notoriously sexually active of glamour models – as if the exalted epicentre of this sexual activity, into which the Conservative government has fatally fallen, which is her vagina, has appropriately grown to cover a third of her body, or even dissect her body altogether. It could be a latter-day variant of Gustave Courbet's scandalous painting *L'Origine du monde,* but now the vaginal 'V' explodes outwards (rather than inwards) and upwards, contained only by the knowing, come-hither look on Keeler's face. In this way, Morley's rendering of Keeler comes to suggest an overgrown, even superhuman, vagina, thrusting forwards at the viewer, and that, with Keeler at the centre of her times, this vagina now hovers disruptively over once polite British society.

And the counter to this tendency, then, is the 'begin to allow' – which could then logically extend to the bluntness of pornography. Here, especially in hardcore, nothing is implied, and all is shown.

Pornography, in these contexts of Whitehouse on permissiveness, of ideas of film and national identity, of Stalin on the role and agency of the artist, is therefore read as showing the possible – the near future that will right the unacceptable present (in the most immediate way: sexual frustration replaced by sexual abundance). And that 'possible' is presented as a battleground: between the censorious who feel that the independent existence of this promise is detrimental to the individual, and so to society at large, and the pornographers, who may speak of libertarianism, but effectively seem to work to supply a series of promises for an assumed audience. The promises themselves then engender, in the manner of socialist realism, rituals and understandings and codes of behaviour: the very clichés of pornographic narratives. And all this lifts the pornographic texts out of the standard modes of reception, especially as regards the transmitter/receiver models of film and national identity, and into a spiritual realm. The soul is endangered, for the censorious, by pornography. The soul is being engineered, for the libertarians, by pornography. And Stalinist terminology around such an idea is consistent with Whitehouse's writing too. And even Max Caulfield, in a mid-1970s hagiography of Whitehouse, noted Stalin's position on the artist as a pole in direct contrast to NVALA's prescriptions for the BBC (whereby less inherent leftist establishment bias would allow for artistic voices from the political right; Caulfield 1975: 88).

My critical and analytical approach to pornography is therefore located between two sets of ideas, both of which are removed from any materialist impulse – even as the pornography itself seems entirely materialist in orientation, illustrating objects of desire that can be possessed or owned. In terms of its historical reception across the timeline of this book, pornography is like a spiritual battle for the soul of man. In terms of its essence, in the period under examination, pornography evidences sets of working assumptions about the fantasies of man. The next chapter seeks to identify or explain the terrains of the historical reception. And, beyond this, the remainder of this book seeks to identify and explore the assumed fantasies, as created by my canon of British pornographers.

Notes

1. Further discussion, as related to such an idea, can be found in Hefin's (2007) thoughts on casting predominantly Welsh actors for his film *Grand Slam* (1978). The dynamism of the result, for 1970s television films, needs to be considered in respect to Raymond Williams's identification of the pre-emptive self-deprecation of Welsh figures in popular culture at that time (D. Williams 2021: 57). The Introduction to Film Studies course ran from 1994 to 2001 in the Department of Theatre, Film and Television Studies at the University of Wales, Aberystwyth, and was mostly delivered by the two of us. On Hefin's teaching and position in Welsh media culture, see M. Williams 2021a and 2021b.

2. While the film itself seems to exist, styled as *One 100 Lines* on its title card, I have been unable to find the date of its making or release. Lindsay's preferences for presenting performers as schoolgirls in his films resulted in numerous legal problems, discussed below. It is instructive that while the *Knave* article goes into Lindsay's work in detail, and discusses his legal problems (including from the 1974 loop *Jolly Hockey Sticks*), a 1982 profile of Soho sex cinemas for the respectable auteur-centric magazine *Sight & Sound* notes *Jolly Hockey Sticks* as ambitious, but remains unsure of its national origins, let alone its director or the trouble it occasioned (Roddick 1982/83: 21).

3. Cook or Cooke has remained mysterious – see Hebditch and Anning (1988: 213) and Carter (2018). The former reproduce the rumour of his hardcore film *100% Lust*, featuring Christine Keeler. Since this film has remained as hearsay (and then also in relation to other figures encountered in this book), it is possible that it does not exist, but it has the persistence of a story originating in slanderous state propaganda arising from the Profumo scandal, some years later. A comparable incident of attempted character assassination concerned Marianne Faithfull 'caught' receiving oral sex from Mick Jagger, and incorporating a Mars bar, during the Redlands bust, discussed below; see Faithfull and Dalton (1994: 113), Todd (2016). This rumour was referenced in *Performance* (Nicholas Roeg and Donald Cammell, 1970), with a Mars bar glimpsed outside the Powis Square pad of Jagger's character.

4. The actual year of the film's setting is not entirely clear, but it could reasonably have been read as contemporary to its year of release – if the lack of discussion, or evidence, of the experience of wartime life, is discounted.

5. I say 'painfully apparent' because, as I approached the images, I saw that for a fellow visitor, whom I estimated as old enough to have had direct experience of this time, they were too much: he had retired to a bench and was weeping silently.

6. My thanks to Jill Patterson, and her father – my guides to Letchworth. See also Stephenson (2002) on the influence of Letchworth on subsequent urban planning. Edgar Wright's use of Letchworth for *The World's End* (2013) suggests a form of arrested development for those

unable to leave, tending their pints in the same pubs and succumbing to entropy while their school friends, long since departed, live fuller lives.

7. Retro-porn readings permeate the pre-#MeToo majority of recent studies of British exploitation cinema. On #MeToo and film culture, see Boyle 2019.

8. For activist infiltration of a Festival of Light rally in Westminster Hall, which involved members of the Gay Liberation Front dressing as nuns (and so dodging the way hippies were being screened and barred from entry), see Green (1988: 380–82) and Grimley (2014: 183). The resultant protest involved heckling, cushion throwing and dancing. The bill for the habits was footed by Graham Chapman, of Monty Python, who would play the figure mistaken for Christ in *The Life of Brian* (Terry Jones, 1979) – a film discussed below.

9. The Savile quote is from the coverage of the award ceremony, in the NVALA newsletter, *The Viewer and Listener*, of January 1978. The newsletter is much given over to pre-emptive attacks on the 1979 Williams 'Report of the Committee on Obscenity and Film Censorship', then in preparation (and discussed below), and paedophilia. Prior to the quote, Savile is disconcertingly clear: 'It goes to show that happiness is not necessarily connected with the sordid side of life' (Anon 1978: 1). The accompanying photograph shows Whitehouse in the background behind Savile, and a child perched on Savile's thigh.

10. See Chapter 9 of Volume 2 ('The Jimmy Savile Investigation Report') of Smith's report into sexual abuse at the BBC: *The Dame Janet Smith Review* (Smith 2016).

11. Other variants are 'of the human soul' and 'engineer of souls'; for the source reference, see (Gorky et al. 1977: 25–69).

12. The project itself featured in dissident writing as a particularly fatal one for the prisoners involved.

13. Blunt confessed in 1964, the year after the Profumo scandal broke. Wright (1988) notes that the Profumo affair was understood to be a Soviet intelligence operation in some quarters of UK and US intelligence (270), and that the example of Profumo was still unnerving Conservative prime ministers in the 1970s (372–73). Indeed, the 1973 scandal surrounding Lord Lambton (Antony Claud, photographed 'in bed with two prostitutes, smoking a joint'; Holden 2004: 196) initiated by the husband of the call girl Norma Levy, 'who later told press that she voted Tory because they had always been her best clients' (196), suggested that Conservative sexual double standards merrily continued. Sir Henry d'Avigdor-Goldsmid mentioned the scandal in the House of Commons directly in relation to the Profumo affair, but even then seemed unwilling to name the matter directly – 'the events of ten years ago' (197) – as if a collective Conservative traumatisation remained.

14. The contact sheets, along with the chair itself (its varnish now somewhat blistered, but the chair clearly never had much in the way of finish) were included at the outset of the Victoria and Albert Museum exhibition 'You Say You Want a Revolution? Records and Rebels 1966–1970', of 2016–17. The photoshoot was intended to promote a film about Keeler, which ran into censorship difficulties; see Farmer 2018.

PART I

The Permissive Society and Its Discontents

CHAPTER 1

Two Notional Regimes of Permissiveness

... not only of Soho but of other hotbeds of licentiousness ...
—Quite Contrary: An Autobiography, *Mary Whitehouse*

Mary Whitehouse to Margaret Thatcher

The fear of toxicity, of pornography, contributed to the founding of the Festival of Light. Capon's 'official' history of this evangelical Christian pressure group talks of 'the rather euphemistic term "moral pollution"' (Capon 1972: 13) and 'the dangers of moral pollution' countered by 'Christian moral standards' (20) against a 'systematic corruption of the young' (24).[1] Car stickers were produced – 'Moral pollution needs a solution' (29) – and a Statement of Intent was drawn up, which noted '[t]here is clear evidence that a determined assault is being made on family life, moral standards and decency in public entertainment and the mass media ... We, like many others, are concerned about the environmental pollution of all kinds that is damaging the world today' (20). The statement confusingly conflates two things: a perceived actual assault (against family life, etc.), and a perceived representational assault (in 'public entertainment and the mass media') – that which John H. Court, in his Christian reading of pornography, refers to as 'visual pollution' (Court 1980: 84). But the general campaigning terminology does not tend to dally with such nuances, as, for Whitehouse, 'the power of television' is 'to create and change patterns of thought and behaviour' (Whitehouse 1972: 40), mobilising those who are horrified to see in this an abrogation of responsibility from broadcasters wielding such power, not least because this abrogation recalls the 'decadence of the Weimar Republic which had paved the way for Hitler's Germany' (93). 'There's nothing left is there, but for the parents of the country to rise up and say that we haven't borne our children and built our homes to have them undermined like this', Whitehouse claimed (44), and, furthermore, that 'broadcasting is used [ideally] for the building up, and not the breaking down, of our country and its people' (58). It is in this way that the stakes around the Permissive Society are, from this anti-permissive quarter, nothing less than saving society itself. The Permissive Society is the creation of secularism, Whitehouse argued in a paper on 'mental pollution' for the Royal Society of Health in 1974, and with that world historical event comes a second Fall of Man (see Tracey and Morrison 1979: 155).

But the campaigning response to this doom-mongering, on the part of Whitehouse, is jarringly different in tone. This can best be gauged in the ITV *World in Action* documentary 'The State of Denmark', which was broadcast 23 May 1970. Here Whitehouse avoids visiting the locations of the depravity in favour of Elsinore Castle and some brief shots of her outside sex shops: '[i]magine the headlines – "Mrs W. at Sex Fair!"' she later commented, and '[a]nyway, it was the last place I wanted to go' (Whitehouse 1972: 95).[2] But these 'hotbeds of licentiousness' nonetheless seemed to have whetted her appetite for a besieged and anarchic tour of university debating societies the following year. Of the University of Manchester experience, it was

> [o]nce again the same deadly revolutionary techniques I had met at Oxford. Terribly difficult to deal effectively with in the few minutes given for summing up, they leave one mentally and physically exhausted. I went to bed in the early hours of the morning, with not a trace of colour in my cheeks, but no regrets – only experience can teach the tactics of the New Left and how to counteract them. One of these days I will, I hope, learn how to explode with an amusing turn of phrase, the poverty of it's [sic] case and the weakness of its strategy. (Whitehouse 1972: 121)

In this tour, Whitehouse seems to have cemented her persona as an idiosyncratic iconoclast: the respectable-looking (lower-middle class) housewife with an undeniable gift for public debate and a masochistic taste for going head-to-head with the purveyors of smut and permissiveness (albeit dialogues in which she rarely paid attention to their responses).

But whether she realised it or not, this intervention was more than pantomime: Whitehouse was playing a role in a post-1968 attempt to shift the mainstream of political discourse (the so-called 'Overton Window') very substantially to the right. Future Member of Parliament Neil Hamilton, vice chairman of the Federation of Conservative Students, invited Whitehouse to speak at the University College of Wales, Aberystwyth, in 1971 (and Whitehouse returned the favour, inviting him to address NVALA; for both, see Whitehouse 1972: 117). Hamilton had a taste for intimidating provocation – in the same year he appeared at an Aberystwyth student hustings dressed as Mussolini, surrounded by a posse of henchmen dressed like fascists. A photograph of the group descending the Arts Centre steps appears in the 15 March 1971 issue of university magazine *The Courier*, and coverage notes 'Herr. Hamilton's entrance', with lights off, music playing, and a 'slide of a swastika on the screen' (Anon 1972: 3). Red-baiting followed with an article in *The Courier*'s 'Hard Rain' series: '[f]reedom will only be restored to our people when the apparatus of the socialist state is destroyed once and for all' (Hamilton 1971: unnumbered [4]). *The Courier* soon had material to run an exposé titled 'Neil Hamilton – Informer', reproducing a letter in which Hamilton 'sought to solicit information on student unions' misuse of funds ... [as with] contributions to dubious organisations, e.g. Dambusters, Anti-Springbok, Anti-Apartheid, etc.' (Smith 1971: 3). Hamilton, in response, and again mimicking a fascist coup, publishing his own, one-off (Hamilton 1972) spoof usurpation of the magazine, called *Feudal Reactionary* ('Incorporating *The Courier*'). This 'Special Silver Wedding Edition' proclaimed 'Homage to the Royal Couple' with an article conveying the good wishes of the Aberystwyth students to the royals, and citing 'our national prophet Mr Enoch Powell' (ibid.: unnumbered). Powell, then the Conservative Member of Parliament for Wolverhampton South West, would speak to the university's Conservative Association in February 1974.[3]

Here, in puerile but embryonic form, is the hard-done-by sensibility targeting a supposedly socialist state of the politically correct middle classes, busy stifling the market, and biased against any conservative reasoning – but immediately sidelining such voices through the control of the media. These oppositions, as enacted in Aberystwyth student politics, would be writ large by the end of the decade (as impossible as it would have been to imagine in 1971/72), with the Overton window – reflected, in part, in a parliamentary continuum from Powell to Hamilton – well and truly shifted.[4]

In relation to such debates, Whitehouse's rhetorical strategy did not seem so much to counteract these 'tactics of the New Left' but to sidestep them. In 'The State of Denmark' she talks to a cleric, a politician, and a member of the Color Climax Corporation. Her approach to dialogue seems to occur in four stages. Firstly, and briefly, a statement of fundamental theological certainty – so, for the cleric's equivocation around not enforcing Christian positions on non-Christians, Whitehouse responds that pornography is, on the basis of its engendering thought of adultery, 'plain, straightforward sin'. Secondly, this is often enforced by a personal verification of such an idea – she places herself, or the people whom she says she represents, into this discourse: they are clearly all personally offended. In this, an 'us and them' divide is posited. Thirdly, there is a blast of unsubstantiated conspiracy. In 'The State of Denmark' this takes the form of liberal politicians being beholden to shady lobby groups, artists seeking to profit financially from pornography, and elements of the public being manipulated (by the left, by the liberals, and by proto-fascists). And, finally, disconcertingly, substantial conversation can follow around policy and politics. In this way, a theological position is strengthened through personal validation, and that becomes the foundation of tedious political critique, and thus Whitehouse effectively theologises politics. But the results are often hopeless. 'The State of Denmark' includes footage at a Color Climax hardcore pornography shoot, to preface Whitehouse's encounter with the company. While their identified representative ('I understand that you're the manager of the largest distributor of pornography in Denmark') talks of the healthy and healing aspects of sexual fantasy, and notes the damage that a Christian upbringing can do, Whitehouse asks whether the sellers of pornography feel no shame (the answer, for her audience at least, is self-evident), notes the damage to Denmark's reputation (although, as if contradicting this, the documentary also references the brisk tourist trade throughout), and declines an offer to visit one of their shops, stating that she has a flight to catch. And this was a company distributing, albeit legally, child pornography during these years – as with the thirty-six loops in the 'Lolita' series with girls of 7–11 (see Taylor and Quayle 2003: 44; also Sheldon 2011), and a male variant (the 'Lover Boy' series), and even *Barbarian Sex Rituals* (1972), showing male circumcision and female genital mutilation. (At this point, discussion in relation to the Danish abolition of censorship was seemingly exclusively around the ethics of bestiality and depictions of rape, rather than paedophilia, on film; see Kronhausen and Kronhausen 1976: 50–51, and Larsson 2017a, respectively.) Nordstrom, in the one sour note in a celebration of Danish hardcore pornography, records that the company distanced themselves from the production of paedophilic material, possibly in the early 1980s 'when public opinion started to rage – [in that] that they had only purchased such filth from abroad' (Nordstrom 2012: 316). The Williams report, further to a trip to Denmark in the late 1970s, also notes the differing legal positions around production and distribution, but that, in terms of the majority of sex shops containing 'a wide range of the most extreme forms of pornography', 'a significant proportion of the publications we saw featured children ... [however], the authorities appeared to assume, in the absence of evidence to the contrary, that the children were photographed elsewhere than in Denmark' (Williams 1979: 212). Joop Wilhelmus was a major producer of child pornography magazines across the 1970s in the Netherlands and Scandinavia, as with the magazine *Lolita* (which also requested readers to submit amateur child pornography for publication, for payment) – a practice that seemingly sprang from his radical libertarian-leftist positions of the late 1960s.[5]

Paedophilic pornography was something about which Whitehouse was later to take a particular stand, and agitate for legislation (see Sutherland 1982: 154–57). And British 'stranger danger' campaigns occurred a few years beyond this, in the 1980s, fronted by figures such as Jimmy Savile and Rolf Harris – as with 'Jimmy Savile Introduces...' the book *Stranger Danger,* on 'what a child needs to know about strangers' (Keller 1985), and Harris's fronting of the information film *Kids Can Say No!* (Jessica Skippon, 1985).[6] For Whitehouse, morals and ethics seem to be a dogmatic matter rather than anything to do with actual behaviour. Caulfield claims that, despite Whitehouse's feelings that she had been taken advantage of by the documentary-makers, 'The State of Denmark' made her a national celebrity (Caulfield 1975: 97). And Enid Wistrich, whose time as chairman of the Film Viewing Board of the Greater London Council (GLC) from 1973 to 1975 resulted in her targeting by Whitehouse and the NVALA, noted that Whitehouse actively courted the media limelight (Wistrich 1978: 53, 66, 70). Indeed, in her appearance, and further to my own approach later in this book, as aligned with decentring Thatcherism, Whitehouse seems to anticipate the late 1970s figure of Thatcher herself. This was not the modernising, urbane and flirtatious Thatcher figure remembered, probably very atypically, by Christopher Hitchens, and who once playfully mock-spanked him at a party ('she smote me on the rear with the parliamentary order-paper that she had been rolling into a cylinder behind her back ... As she walked away, she looked back over her shoulder and gave an almost imperceptibly slight roll of the hip while mouthing the words: "Naughty boy!"'; cited in Kulze 2013). This was, rather, the Saatchi & Saatchi makeover reinvention of Thatcher as a prudent and proper, albeit outspoken and moralistic, suburban housewife, and 'the rediscovery of her origins as the "grocer's daughter", [which] aimed to revise Thatcher's upper-middle-class image' (Sutcliffe-Braithwaite 2018:

148; see too Kleinman 1987). The latter quality was the very 'ordinariness' that 'was so central to Thatcher's construction of an alternative imagined political constituency ... a large central mass of British society, self-reliant workers, not privileged or hugely wealthy, not part of her imagined "underclass"' (Hilton, Moores and Sutcliffe-Braithwaite 2017: 156), and identified by Thatcher as her '"quiet majority", echoing Nixon's image of the "silent majority" in the US' (Sutcliffe-Braithwaite 2018: 158–59). That template persona, complete with domestic but dressy outfits, is visible in 'The State of Denmark' – and so, once the figure of Thatcher (of 'Thatcherism') materialises, it is with elements of Whitehouse.

Picturing Permissiveness

What supposedly was Whitehouse's nemesis – the pollutant of permissiveness? Essentially, with respect to this study and the beginnings of allowing over disallowing, the base answer can be: activities that would seem to evidence sexual freedom. And freedom is considered with respect to a freedom to act – 'permission' (to which 'permissive' signals) having been granted, or taken, or assumed – in sexual ways without fear of meaningful judgement or punishment. This is not to say that permissive agents, or consumers of permissive media, in these terms, maintained a total indifference or blankness in the face of possible censure. Permissiveness must be occasioned by a sense of misbehaviour or transgression. And this is the essence of pornography: if it were a matter of guiltless biological event and nothing more, as is often noted, there would not be a sense of permission being taken or exercised; and nor would this permission taking be presented as a thrilling matter. So it is a 'Permissive Society' that allows for, or declines to move against, permissiveness.

Historically, this permissiveness was read as mythical matter. John Selwyn Gummer's 1971 book, *The Permissive Society*, is subtitled *Fact or Fantasy?*, as if even the conception is ontologically suspect. To this should be added that 'permissive' itself is invariably taken to be a pejorative term. After all, as Jeffrey Weeks notes, 'those who were supposedly chief advocates of the "permissive society" would rarely have used the term' (Weeks 1992: 249). And the vagueness of the idea provided infinite grounds for criticism, from those who would consider freedom of expression in relation to avant-garde art, to those who encountered and endured the 'torrent of erotica' leading to 'sex pollution' (from Edward J. Mishan's survey of the state of sexual mores; Mishan 1972: 14, 15).

A brief sociological overview of permissiveness can be found in Christie Davies's *Permissive Britain* of 1975. Davies starts his study by noting that '[t]he term "permissive" is not a very useful one except as a general description of the social changes of the last twenty years', and that James Pope-Hennessy was identifying a new generation, with a 'driving wish for freedom from tradition and convention, whatever the cost', as apparent in the 1920s (Davies 1975: 8 and 11 respectively, the latter quoting Pope-Hennessy). This 'cliché' he finds to be contemporary, at his time of writing, in the positions of Whitehouse. Mishan likewise begins his lengthy address of the Permissive Society, which was the central contribution to an edition of *Encounter* magazine on 'Sex & Culture', with such a proviso too (Mishan 1972: 9, footnote 1). Weeks also starts his consideration of 'the permissive moment', in his wider study of sexuality and society, by noting that 1960s permissiveness 'had become a political metaphor ... a charged and emotive term, obscuring, in its ambivalence, more than it illustrated' (Weeks 1992: 249). Likewise, Cliff Dallas quotes W.I. Thomas's dictum in respect to the counterculture and the 'Swinging Sixties': 'If enough men define a thing as real, it is real in its consequences' (Dallas 1979: 127). Thompson and Collins (2007: 219, fn 2) note 1950s and early 1960s uses of the term 'permissive society'. Stuart Hall problematizes the origins of this 'real', in relation to the legal basis of the policing of behaviour:

> *Permissiveness ... is difficult to define. Descriptively, we may agree that the tendency of legislation [across 1957–68] was to shift things in the general direction of a less rigid, looser, more 'permissive' moral code. But the term has a stronger connotative value. Did the legislation also express a society where moral standards and values were being eroded? Did it, perhaps, even promote such a trend? Here we are no longer in the realm of pure description, but have entered that terrain where the term 'permissiveness' performs the role of a powerful ideological counter. (Hall 1980: 2)*

The actual legislation that is typically noted in terms of a new 1960s age of permissiveness is the Abortion Act of 1967 (legalising pregnancy termination), the Sexual Offences Act of 1967 (decriminalising sexual acts occurring in private between consenting males over the age of 21, in England and Wales), the Family Law Reform Act of 1969 (lowered minimum age for marriage without parental consent from 21 to 18), the Divorce Law of 1969 (allowing for mutually agreed divorce, rather than the need for 'matrimonial offence'), and the Family Planning Association's 1970 decision to make the contraception pill available to single women. Thus, for Cliff Dallas, 'a number of much-publicised legislative innovations ... could be regarded as shifting the legal definitions of morality in a permissive direction' (Dallas 1979: 127). To this, one could add that, around 1970/71, wardens in British universities seemed to cease rusticating undergraduates caught 'after hours' visiting Halls of Residence of members of the opposite sex – a U-turn that was presented as a concession, but nevertheless one that seemed to have the effect of deflating or tempering student radicalism, and one of its campaigning causes, of the years immediately prior.

Considerations of pop culture artefacts seem to offer as much insight as collated statistics around the numbers of children born out of wedlock across the 1960s, or the ease of uptake of oral contraception and divorce, or the increasing age of marriage in this decade, or the growing distrust in the forces of law and order. Bridget Pym, in her study of political pressure groups and the Permissive Society, makes this move almost straightaway: the 'Permissive Society' is a cultural phenomenon, and so is best considered, very briefly in her case, via cultural artefacts, along with the various evolving matters of governance: the publication of *Lady Chatterley's Lover* in 1960, the satire boom of *That Was the Week That Was*, the publication of *Honest to God* (discussed below), the Profumo scandal, Swinging London, the miniskirt, the Beatles and the Rolling Stones, and Whitehouse and the Festival of Light (Pym 1974: 9–11). Cultural artefacts can be taken as embodying permissiveness or the myth of permissiveness – picturing it and promoting it: both an illustration of, and an engendering of, that which is now available, and what greater freedoms might look like and mean. To this end, a closer scrutiny of some indicative cultural artefacts of this moment yields some answers, and allows for a sense of the mythical (in the sense of a shared set of beliefs) nature of the Permissive Society. And vinyl LPs, along with 8-mm film loops, might be said to be a comparably portable, collectable, lendable bit of analogue media, and something that also points to, or offers a transport to, ever-new stops-offs for the modern bachelor's idea of glamour.

The gatefold record sleeve of *Beggars Banquet* by the Rolling Stones (released December 1968) seemingly shows the band (and dog, cat, goat and sheep) in the final satiated phase of a lavish banquet, perhaps in a castle or stately home (stone steps, large fireplace, bookshelf-lined walls). Tony Palmer, in his overview of popular music, sees in the image 'the remnants of an orgy that might have been, [with] grins of seedy self-congratulation across their lips' (Palmer and Medlicott 1977: 248) And John Roberts notes 'the image of the "band" as commune ... as a site for musical and social experimentation' in relation to countercultural albums of this period (Roberts 2020: 22). The Stones photo (by Michael Joseph) is black and white, with clumsy colour touch-ups of faces, and the setting and clothes are of an ambiguous time frame. These dandies could be taken as the scandal-courting Stones of Swinging London or the debauched court minstrels of an earlier age (a role not so removed from beggars). The image is within the gatefold, with an 'RSVP' on the front of the album, itself styled as a cream-coloured party invitation to such a banquet for the listener – or, at least, signals to a kind of aspiration for as much – one that the listener might arrange with the help of this 'debauched' LP for an ambient and suggestive soundtrack. This, after all, was the era of taking records along to parties, and the potential cultural cache that could be accrued accordingly.

The gatefold for the Jimi Hendrix Experience's *Electric Ladyland* (released October 1968), featuring a photo of nineteen naked women by David Montgomery, is much more straightforward in presenting, as it were, the sensational world of permissiveness. The naked women look at the camera – or meet the eye of the person who has stumbled upon this scene, seemingly in a black room, and from whose perspective the photo seems to have been taken – as if waiting for the next step to occur. The back cover of Syd Barrett's *The Madcap Laughs* (released January 1970) features of photo by Mick Rock of Barrett, with a mystery naked woman in the background – reputedly when the photographer arrived, the woman was already present, and so photos were taken of Barrett 'at home', irrespective of what or who was found there. The woman strikes a pose in the background, while Barrett would seem to stare at the photographer – but his eyes are obscured under a tangle of hair. The flat is bare, and distinctive with its orange and blue striped floorboards (apparently a paintjob spontaneously undertaken by Barrett himself), which seem to lock a crouching Barrett into a position on something like an amended chess board. The suggestion is of a bohemian and surreal world, recreated in this living space, through which unclothed women casually wander. The moment is mirrored in porn itself: the Mayfair loop *Groovy Girl* (director unknown, possibly 1972) ends with a nude Caroline Dell sat by a record player at home, the Rolling Stones' *Out of Our Heads* LP (1965) prominently displayed. *Soul Rebels*, by Bob Marley and the Wailers (with a December 1970 UK release), seems to refashion Che Guevara, with (to the surprise and annoyance of the group) 'a female guerrilla fighter brandishing a machine gun and sporting a khaki shirt, tantalisingly parted to the tips of her nipples' (Grant 2012: 179).[7]

Beggars Banquet, Electric Ladyland, The Madcap Laughs and *Soul Rebels*, in a 1970 LP collection, clearly indicate what would have been considered to have been happening in fashionable circles – and this is before any of the records themselves have even hit the turntable, with Hendrix's '… And the Gods Made Love' or, from the Stones, 'Stray Cat Blues' adding explicit mood and information. Even in looking to those who shirk a 'wild men of rock' category – as with Genesis, only recently out of Charterhouse School – Paul Whitehead's mock medieval pastoral of courtly love for the cover of *Trespass* (October 1970) has been slashed by a jewelled, serrated knife (seen as a *trompe l'oeil* on the back cover). In this gesture to cultural vandalism, older modes of courtship are over, or even scorned by the generation of 1970. And even the coordinates of then-current paradigms of courtship seem thrown up in the air, with a gender-fluid, Pre-Raphaelite-like David Bowie on the cover of the British version of *The Man Who Sold the World* (US release: November 1970; UK release: April 1971). Bowie, with long blond hair and a quizzical expression, reclines on a chaise longue in a flowery Michael Fish dress and seemingly knee-high leather boots, playing cards strewn on the floor before him.

Philip Larkin's mock elegiac 1967 poem 'Annus Mirabilis' is an obligatory reference for all studies of the British Permissive Society. Larkin is precise about the intrusion of such erotic possibilities for the young (and which is also charted via cultural artefacts): 'Sexual intercourse began / In nineteen sixty-three / … / Between the end of the *Chatterley* ban / And the Beatles' first LP' (Larkin 1974: 34). My ellipsis covers '(Which was rather late for me) –', then reprised as '(Though just too late for me) –'. So Larkin was already looking on at something happening, or beginning to happen, for others, and which could have been for him had he only been born a few years later – resigned and mostly regretfully, he removes himself from this contemporary narrative.

An alternative to Larkin's defeatism comes in *Carry On Camping* (Gerald Thomas, 1969). After seeing a naturalist film in a dreary suburban cinema (seemingly frequented by businessmen), and finding in the film the notion of sexually liberating his sexually disinclined girlfriend, Sid James (as Sid Boggle), 56 at the time of filming – then nearly a decade older than Larkin – makes deceptive (and backfiring) arrangements for nude camping with Joan Sims (as Joan Fussey), then

39. Some payment is exacted from Boggle for this: the trip obliges him to dress as a hippy for a psychedelic concert in a field. When the potential of the sexually liberated boarding school girls, who are also camping, proves too dangerous for the relationship, Joan reverses her position, seemingly as a matter of damage control. The film ends with a zipped-up tent. *Carry On Camping* includes an anti-permissive figure in this set-up: Kenneth Williams as an asexual Puritan, Dr Kenneth Soaper, overseeing the schoolgirls. Conceivably this is an in-joke: a Rev Dr Donald Soper had seen great danger in 'pornographic reading matter', now freely available at 'the average [railway] station bookstall', and the reader of such 'sexual literature', capitalising on the increased amount of post-war leisure time afforded the worker, 'becomes progressively enfeebled and unable to concentrate' (Soper 1961: 45). Perhaps, thus piqued at the station, and as per *Brief Encounter*, the reader of this 'matter', in transit and so safely away from the family home, may be tempted to aspire to infidelity? And, indeed, the naturalist film equivalent, in *Carry On Camping*, does trigger the attempt to refashion innocent camping into a sexual stratagem; the work of the makers of naturalist films, like Arnold L. Miller and Michael Winner, can be read in this context. Soper, in his contribution to the 1961 collection *Does Pornography Matter?*, is also able to link pornography directly with alcoholism as twin detrimental evils to which society exposes the common man – and so his concern is patrician as well as restrictive (ibid.).

But this is not just yearning, or envy, on Larkin's part. Larkin's own fictional dealings with sexuality, prior, had centred on comic tales of figures driven nearly insane by being unable to deal with sexual encounters on their own (admitted uncertain) terms. The frustrated student protagonist of the novel *Jill* (of 1946), who stalks a young woman with whom he has become obsessed across Oxford, eventually self-induces something of a mental breakdown. The tangible possibility of eroticism, particularly in terms of offsetting the chilliness and austerity of a wartime winter university term, upends his previously ordered world. And the once shy and hardworking northern grammar school boy is pushed to a level of calculated or casual misbehaviour that outstrips his louche southern public school counterparts. For the sexualised public school girls of Larkin's posthumous novellas *Trouble at Willow Gables* and *Michaelmas Term at St Bride's*, the matter is reversed: avoiding lesbian clinches with predatory older girls at school (mounted via the offer of late night Latin tuition in the dormitory) until a bewildered innocent, undergoing a comparable breakdown, belatedly 'succumbs' to a lesbian encounter while at university, initiated by one of her former tormentors, and with whom, to her initial horror, she is allocated a shared room.[8] Even the title of a later novel, *A Girl in Winter* (1947), suggests the promise of eroticism suspended in a state of deep freeze. So the aged Larkin, when observing the U-turn so painfully apparent in the new order, can be forgiven for his amazement at the suddenness, and miraculous lack of consequence, of the freeing of the young to act as they will in these matters: 'And every life became / A brilliant breaking of the bank, / A quite unlosable game' (Larkin 1974: 34). The brilliance would, by 1967, become a casual norm for 'High Windows': 'When I see a couple of kids / And guess he's fucking her and she's / Taking pills or wearing a diaphragm' (ibid.: 17). This seems like the casualness or ease of sexual relations, as now positioned away from wedlock by mutual consent: a resuscitating of sexuality beyond legal/social restraints and confines around a nexus of marriage/procreation/family, as policed by social mores, and suddenly released, mostly unfettered, into the everyday.

Jeffrey Weeks, in his study *Sex, Politics and Society*, notes, of this post-war period (and, as per Larkin's witness, culminating in the late 1960s), 'a redefinition of female sexuality', and that consumerism 'was partially constructing a female sexuality' (Weeks (1981) 1992: 258). But to finesse this construction, a heightened sexual imagination is needed, with an extension of the scope of erotic possibilities. This is not so much a matter of feeling assured that the contraceptive pill will mitigate the danger of unwanted pregnancies, further to spontaneous sexual encounters. It is more a matter of, having first acknowledged this assurance to be the case, speculating as to what then might occur during a night out, with women (as per the inequity of male heterosexual dominance in such matters) as yet unmet. And so this understanding or perception is one that engenders changes at micro levels: what to wear out, how to wear it, who to talk to, what to say. Permissiveness for Larkin, and across the LP gatefolds, seems an idea or point of aspiration, or new horizon, or realistic example or prize, as exerting unavoidable psychic force on those who see it, or have heard of it – even if now self-declared as too old to participate in it. In this sense, it is enough that, in the years around the 1967 Summer of Love (with San Francisco and, to a lesser extent, London as its epicentres) the new idea of permissiveness exists.

The sexual world in which Larkin and *Carry On Camping*'s schoolgirls find themselves would also, at this time, concern mainstream, popular film-making. In *The Pure Hell of St Trinian's* (Frank Launder, 1960), the boarding school girls seem to exist as two types. Firstly, as an amorphous mass of rowdy urchins in gymslips, with unkempt hair bursting out from battered boaters (rude and undisciplined but recalling, as presented in this uncivilised or 'natural' state, something of Lewis Carroll's photographs of young girls, as discussed below). And, secondly, particularly in the case of Rosalie Dawn (Julie Alexander), the fully mature and sexually confident young woman, albeit affecting a coy poise. Rosalie is very much the same kind of physical 'type' favoured by Harrison Marks as his models in the 1960s, as also discussed below; she eventually winds up performing a variant of Salome's Dance of the Seven Veils in a harem. Launder arranges a number of the latter shamelessly for his leering camera – as with a sequence in a gym in which the girls adopt glamour 'health and exercise' poses or a catwalk with a variety of club hostess-type glamour outfits, followed by Rosalie stripping while delivering Hamlet's 'To be, or not to be' soliloquy, as the highpoint of St Trinian's 'Festival of Culture'.

As the film opens, after an arson attack on the girls' school, both types disrupt the resultant court case: the former through contempt of court, the latter by trying to seduce the presiding judge. But these schoolgirls are sexualised seemingly by their being in proxy to older males. Society had not started swinging at the point of *The Pure Hell of St Trinian's* in a way that it would be for the subsequent film, on the other side of Larkin's 1963, *The Great St Trinian's Train Robbery* (Sidney Gilliat and Launder, 1966). For the latter, the girls and female teachers are encountered as already integrated into cultures of sex: the girls are mostly blonde and insouciant, and with miniskirts and stockings that seem more a stripper variant of schoolgirl uniforms. One teacher (Margaret Nolan) is seen moonlighting as a stripper, and the headmistress is first encountered as, the film tentatively suggests, a 'kept woman' or prostitute in a garish boudoir.[9] By the time of Launder's 1980 *Wildcats of St Trinian's*, the film quite logically included topless models of the day and nudity, as with a nude swimming race. The film opens with a montage of pre-pubescent girls dancing, and the legs of dancing girls, in stockings, suspenders and high heels, with a disco soundtrack, and ends with the girls, at a grass-skirt boat party, being spanked with cricket bats and saucepans. The schoolgirl sexuality of *The Pure Hell of St Trinian's* is more akin to the Yardbirds' 1964 cover of the blues standard 'Good Morning Little Schoolgirl': suggestive lyrics that nonetheless do not fully eclipse a sense of young innocence ('Can I go home with – / won't you let me go home with you? / so I can hug, hug / squeeze, squeeze, / if you let me, / I can tease you, baby'), but with more directly sexualised suggestions communicated sonically (through the urgency of the undulations of Eric Clapton's guitar solo, across a guttural refrain of 'oh-ah-oh-oh-ah'). So in *The Pure Hell of St Trinian's*, eroticism seems to exist a priori, and before the swinging society: the schoolgirls are 'naturally' sexy, and the film, as if unfairly prompted by this, tends to 'naughty'. One seems invited to imagine them stepping from the hockey fields of 1960 (or even from Launder's proto-*St Trinian's* film, *The Happiest Days of Your Life* from 1950) straight into the nudist camps of *For Members Only* (aka *The Nudist Story*, Ramsey Herrington, 1960), *Nudes of the World* (aka *Nudes of All Nations*, Arnold Louis Miller, 1961) or (and as schoolgirls being spanked too) the Kent nudist camp of *Pussy Galore* (also known as *Nudists Galore*, Ivor Cooke, 1965). And the same societal tension exists in this nudist context too, for *Nudes of the World*: between the free-thinkers ('we girls decided to spread the gospel of naturalism') and conservatives (the local villagers who condemn these 'depraved creatures', undoubtedly heading for a 'wicked end', camping on the land of a Lord's estate). Lest Miller's film be understood to have reflected a substantial cultural battle of the moment, Szreter and Fisher note the 'almost invisibly small group' of British nudists, across this period and indeed after, in their survey of 'intimate life' before 1963 (Szreter and Fisher 2011: 270).

In *The Pure Hell of St Trinian's*, the school and pupils have been sold as a job lot to an association of rich businessmen. The local spiv, Flash Harry (George Cole), warns the older set not to come across like 'a bunch of scrubbers who have been nugging it [i.e. acting like a prostitute] around some female borstal institution': their education seems to consist of ensuring that a nascent sexuality does not sully their respectability, and so the promise of a rich husband – as also accessed or captured via their nascent sexuality. The girls are 'all my assets', for Flash Harry – 'well, until the fifth form grows up'. The threat, by the time of *Wildcats of St Trinian's*, is from the hard left; Harry is now a union official, with the schoolgirls' burgeoning sexuality now diverted into feminism – even manifest in a union office / anarcho-punk squat. The left represents a desexualisation, in 1980; 'wildcat' strikes and individual autonomy, rather than the 'wildcats' of the previous films, to be tamed and domesticated.

The template that had been set here, of the sexy schoolgirl, was then to come into common use – from *Baby Love* (Alastair Reid, 1969; tagline: 'Would you give a home to a girl like Luci?') to *Twinky* (aka *Lola*, Richard Donner, 1969; tagline 'She's almost 16, he's almost 40'), to *Please Sir!* (Mark Stuart, 1971, in which the miniskirt seems to be school uniform), relocated to Australia for the British-style girls boarding school of *Picnic at Hanging Rock* (Peter Weir, 1975), to *Killer's Moon*

(Alan Birkenshaw, 1978, in which LSD-dosed asylum-escaped madmen besiege a schoolgirl trip to the Lake District). Pornography's appropriation of this template was inevitable, as with John Lindsay's casting preferences: 'Lolita-like, innocence ready to be seduced. That's what the average man wants' (Duncan 1978: 71). Softcore model Fiona Richmond's 1973 LP, *Paul Raymond Presents Frankly Fiona* – featuring Richmond narrating stories of lust over Anthony Newley's easy-listening score – explores this dynamic directly. For the track 'My First Time', Richmond supposedly recalls the thrill of being watched by a Physical Education teacher while at school, leading to her first orgasm, and then a second time with the teacher himself – 'and soon after, he left the school. But now I was well in on the game, and my last year was blissful'.[10]

The problematic elements of these schoolgirl-centred fantasies are discussed in relation to David Hamilton's films, below. But their totemic use nonetheless suggests a new and unencumbered generation, born into enlightenment rather than innocence. The Permissive Society, in this light, seems like a rearguard action: a move to simply try to accommodate this phenomenon – particularly, as for Weeks (1992), with respect to new consumerist practices. Or, for critics of these changes, the Permissive Society is the hothouse in which guileless innocence prematurely rots into jaded experience.

Night Falls on Soho

What then were these consumer practices – in actuality? I suggest a consumer split between the more downmarket, as against the less downmarket. For more downmarket, I am referring to Soho cinema clubs, under-the-counter purchases, 8-mm films ordered from the back pages of pornographic magazines, and other unknown distribution/screening arrangements – including, seemingly, working men's clubs, and orgies/swinging events run on a scale from amateur to professional, meaning from front rooms to brothels. I am considering less downmarket in a relative sense: films screened quite legally, this time BBFC certificated, but that very directly signalled their pornographic or erotic content. Many of these films were also made in 'continental' versions, which meant the inclusion of hardcore material (whether from the actual performers, or via hardcore 'inserts' from anonymous performers), for X- and R-rated and pre- sumably unrated releases outside the UK (although I have found it difficult to

Illustration 1.1 The bright lights, the glamour and the mythology: *Soho Striptease* from 1960, directed by Pete Walker as 'Reginald Drewe', 8-mm box. Photograph by the author.

verify this persistent myth – extended cuts have rarely since surfaced). And this tendency also seems to have been in operation for 'offcuts' too, which seemingly did not (and still do not) circulate, and presumably must have been made for private use. One such was *Performance Trims* (actually screened at the 1970 Wet Dream film festival, with a prize awarded, and later at a Frankfurt porn festival): a ten-minute compilation of 'the outtakes, devoid of soundtrack, of the sex scenes between [Mick] Jagger, [Michèle] Breton and [Anita] Pallenberg' (Glennie 2018: 180), and, apparently, mostly of close-ups of Jagger's genitalia, from the film *Performance* (Nicholas Roeg and Donald Cammell, 1970). But more typical were simply alternative takes with more nudity and boisterousness – as was probably the case with Tony Tenser directing tavern scenes for an anticipated Continental cut of *Witchfinder General*, once the actual director was away (see Halligan 2003: 132–33).

Two distinct ambiences are associated with each side of this split. This is the difference of a sense of possible nights out (for the heterosexual male) in the

1970s. On the one hand, this might consist of surreptitiously scoring overpriced hardcore porn from a Soho sex shop, and then being able to view this on an 8-mm projector at home, or sitting in a small room in the dark (the Soho cinema club, or temporarily repurposed flat), having just bought membership, surrounded by heavy-breathing strangers, all watching hardcore porn loops, and hoping that the police do not arrive (or were not already present, in an undercover capacity), or viewing the same material in a booth in the curtained-off back of a sex shop.[11] Membership technically meant that the cinema club was private, so the films could simply sidestep the need for BBFC certification, and even the reach of the Obscene Publications Act – unless the police infiltrated the club, at which point audience masturbation would translate into 'running a disorderly house' and temporary closure (see Hebditch and Anning 1988: 217; Kerekes 2000: 196). But this did not necessarily mean that your night out resulted in being turfed out of the club that you have just joined. Raids could seemingly occur a few times in the single day, and John Lindsay commented (to the *Daily Telegraph* in 1978): 'Our customers simply stay where they are and wait for the raid to finish. We guarantee to re-open again in thirty minutes anyway. We have an unlimited stock of films' (Quoted in McGillivray 1992: 84). Thompson numbers fifty-four sex shops and thirty-nine cinema clubs operating in Soho between 1976–82; (Thompson 1994: 44).

On the other hand, the night out might consist of a visit to, say, Raymond's Revuebar – conceivably in the company of an open-minded romantic partner, or with work or business associates, to sample 'glamour' and 'choreography', albeit with overpriced drinks foisted on unsuspecting punters, and perhaps encounter and socialise with the models, some of whom could also be seen in the pornographic magazines of the time. In these matters, money would allow further levels of access, and of privacy.

My first night out is a matter of supply and demand interaction – but what is supplied (illicit documentary-style footage of nudity and actual intercourse) remains a matter of fantasy and desire, and something that, while mostly unavailable in decades prior, was now available from sex shops (open late or all-night). My second night out, on the other hand, is a matter of aspiration to a certain kind of lifestyle, and one seemingly free of the squalor of Soho. But it is also a matter of supply and demand, not least because being in the 'wrong' class would not bar entry to wealthier strata and locales. Consumer power in the secular and permissive age enables both. And many of the films discussed in this book also show or advertise these two worlds: the films talk of possibilities, and the locales of these possibilities – as with clubland in *Paul Raymond's Erotica* (Brian Smedley-Aston, 1982).

This is some remove from the locale of those achievements – the 'growing squalor and exploitativeness of pornography in major cities' (Weeks 1992: 251), the '[r]ow upon row of shuttered shops [in Soho], all containing wares of matching uniform ugliness' (Sutherland 1982: 9), the 'moral and physical grubbiness' of Soho of 1974, as a district that 'had become not only disreputable but also squalid: a malodorous enclave of run-down buildings, rancid hallways, peeling fly-posters, urine-soaked alleys, refuse-spewing dustbins and recumbent, grubbily shrouded figures on park benches, stale perspiration and cheap booze scenting their slipstream' (Willetts 2010: 348, 310). The existence of this enclave prompted Reclaim the Night activism, against the 'grotesque market of commercial sexism', where the protestors were met with physical violence from staff at the New Swedish Cinema Club in Brewer Street, and then from the police who arrived to 'protect pornography and attack women' (Soho Sixteen Support Sisterhood 1981: 222–23). In Leeds, feminist activists simply torched sex shops and then issued a press release (Angry Women, Leeds [1981] 1984: 49). What was clear was that Soho in the 1970s was not like Denmark's Christiania commune, in the sense of an autonomous zone of shared sexual freedom, but was a locale of sexual opportunity, in which permissiveness could be bought.

But what of the experience particular to each night out? Roddick's survey of Soho in the early 1980s provides details of Soho cinema club-going:

The cinemas advertise no times of showing, merely opening hours. In some cases they advertise the duration of the programme, though this is not always reliable: a 'full 2-hour programme' in one case lasted 55 minutes … [but] it makes little difference where one comes in or goes out. And anyway, films frequently have reels missing … [t]he films often promise scenes of anal intercourse, but since this is still illegal in Britain, even heterosexually, the scenes are usually cut … [t]he most startling thing about Soho's sex cinemas is that they are, virtually any time during the afternoon or evening, around three-quarters full. Not counting video peep-show booths and view-before-you-buy sex film shops, there are – or were when I did this survey – 36 sex cinemas in Soho, comprising 39 auditoria. (Roddick 1982/83: 18–19)

In genuinely hardcore houses, conditions vary. Some are relatively plush if slightly run-down cinemas, others are stuffy basements with the walls painted black and electric flex hanging loose ... [s]ome have cashiers' desks and proper tickets; others simply have a table littered with styrofoam cups of congealing coffee, from behind which a man takes pound notes. Prices vary from £2 at the Continental Blue Film Club ... to £4 at the Spartacus Gay Cinema Club ... [t]he clientele is almost, but not quite, exclusively male. A number of cinemas advertise 'Couples welcome', and couples do occasionally take up the offer. Single women are unknown ... it is hard to generalise about audiences. They range from adolescents to OAPs [old age pensioners], with many of the cinemas advertising concessionary rates for the latter. The one consistent impression I gained was that sex flicks were very popular with businessmen on their way home. (Roddick 1982/83: 20)[12]

For his 1970 survey, *The Danish Sex Fairs*, Jean-Claude Lauret begins with visits to Soho and Piccadilly Circus to sample British pornography, seeking to illustrate the way in which 'London is not Copenhagen' (Lauret 1970: 7):

There is always something sordid about these places. One has to look for them, search around those 'hot streets' where everything suggestions the exploitation of sex. Half-concealed club entrances, young touts offering the best striptease show, the most daring, the sexiest, the most beautiful girls, and a lot more...

Although not clandestine, such places seem accessible solely to the initiate. Tolerated, but with the threat of a possible police raid ... [d]uring one of my visits to London, I watched such a shop for a long time ... [a] door would open, the customer would disappear into some back room while the salesman, chewing on a soggy cigar, would, for some strange reason, make a show of busying himself, for the benefit of some unseen observer.

Curious about that back room, I walked into the shop one day. For once, my indifferent English was of use to me, since I could not possibly be a plain-clothes policeman. (Lauret 1970: 6–7)

In the smoke-filled back room, Lauret notes cellophane-wrapped packs of five pictures, being perused by 'a few stiff, respectable-looking gentlemen' (ibid.: 7), but when he goes to leave without buying any pictures he 'unwillingly caused a small incident': 'It was customary to pay the "entrance fee" by some purchase. The salesman was on the point of insulting me, the thug appearing behind the pseudo-tradesman. Let us dip in our wallet, then, and buy one or two packs of pictures' (ibid.). A persistent rumour is that those seeking paedophilic material would be invited to return to the shop after hours for the exchange, only to then be given a beating by both tradesman and thug in a back alley – but such a rumour would have had its uses, as a cover for those actually trading in such material.

In this light, Continental cultures of pornography, for Lauret, seem entirely wholesome and integrated into mainstream society in an unremarkable way. Once back in Denmark, for the SEX 69 fair, and standing in a crowd watching hardcore loops, he notes a man standing behind him and unselfconsciously masturbating (Lauret 1970: 23), and then recalls his own porn-induced revelry:

> In order to caress you furtively with our eyes, young ladies, we have forgotten all those explicit positions, those bodies displayed in their total intimacy. You are offering us your legs and your thighs bit by bit. And bit by bit, we are remodelling you to the image of our desires. You are the proof that in the Kingdom of Denmark there is room for dreams, for sanity. (Ibid.: 24)

And, further to these shades of pornographic milieu, one could note the burgeoning trade in underage male prostitutes just minutes away in Piccadilly Circus (subject to only occasional police dragnets during the 1970s), where the windows of the Wimpy burger bar and the notorious Playland Amusement Arcade were used to flaunt the 'Dilly Boys' on offer, so that the 'Piccadilly rent boys were an integrated and colourful aspect of the capital's fugitive demi-monde' (Reed 2014: 111).[13] Lauret seems not to have strayed beyond straight pornography and prostitution during his time in London; had he also looked into the Dilly Boy culture around Piccadilly Circus, he would have been even more dismayed. The rent, here and in Soho, were subject to society figures, such as art dealer and Rolling Stones associate 'Groovy Bob' (Robert Fraser), at least one royal family staff member, 'Backstairs Billy' (William Tallon), for gay foursomes in Clarence House on the Queen Mother's favourite sofa, middle-class professionals (as depicted in John Schlesinger's *Sunday, Bloody Sunday* of 1971), and predators of the most dangerous kind.[14] The latter gained eventual exposure via the Yorkshire TV two-part documentary *Johnny Go Home* (John Willis, 1975), on the twilight world of Piccadilly Circus and the meat rack, which followed the activities of Roger

Gleaves, sex offender and self-appointed Bishop of Medway of the Old Catholic Church, of the Guild of St Dismas, then running a series of hostels for runaway boys, and a related murder trial.[15] Uniformed figures who appear to be social workers, working with Gleaves, are seen in Euston railway station, picking up runaway boys and shifting them into slum-like dwellings, a life of prostitution, and imminent danger. (It is difficult to think that Whitehouse had not watched this, not least as the title provocatively suggests a kind of sequel to *Cathy Come Home*: the documentary details the misuses of a charity facade, exactly as per Whitehouse's own associates.) But even in this documentary, the rent was subject to blame: rough young boys, feminised in their glam get-up, opportunistically leading on hapless businessmen. And even this Soho social interzone seems to have delivered material of high pornographic worth.

Daly records, of his time as a rent boy, some elements of films and media use: from photographs for blackmail purposes (Daly 2018: 52), or for personal use if too specialist (for example, pederastic; 309), or photographs and 8-mm filming as part of sexual encounters, perhaps with the participants only dimly aware (124, 344), or even filming requested as part of themed role playing, with the 'punter' taking a starring role. The resultant films could be shown to add a 'risqué dimension' to dinner parties and swinging events (130), or to whet the appetite for those arriving at upmarket gay orgies. It was not clear to those caught up in the film-making what then happened to the films themselves – which seemed to remain underground, or surfaced many years later (sometimes as part of compilations of 'vintage' porn or as evidence in various prosecutions).[16] Daly notes links between Soho 'porn barons' and Playland, which must then have supplied rent boys to film-makers (314), and even the use of rent boys to mind Soho shops for a couple of hours, with the owner claiming he was preoccupied with a family matter – timed to coincide with pre-arranged police raids, and for which the rent boy would be arrested and charged (241). This technique was also used for any young man at a loose end in the area who looked like he would welcome some cash in hand, and it seems to have still been in operation in the mid-1990s (see O'Toole 1999: 130–32).

Even today, the remnants of 1970s British pornography, along with Color Climax films, still speak of this anarchic culture. Both are presented with makeshift DVD covers and suggest either retro-porn of historical interest, and/or films made during freer times of expression. Thus one Soho shop (at least during a visit in Summer 2017), in their basement, offer 'Original 60s 70s 80s Movies ... We have all your favourite classic XXX videos available on DVD', and collections include, from Malmo Films, the black-and-white *Home from School* and *Teach Me!* Malmo was noted in the 1970s as a centre for porn production (see Larsson 2017b). The (homemade) back cover to these promises: '6 rare amateur Super 8-mm Erotic Movies from the early 1970s, recently discovered in a deceased collector's attic. This recently discovered footage is a must for any collector of vintage erotic movies'. Thus the makeshift presentation frames the films as possessing a certain select cultural capital – seemingly verified by the way in which these films have been serendipitously saved and now bequeathed from beyond the grave, or as akin to finding the frozen possessions of an arctic explorer from an earlier age. And the proprietor assured me (although without deploying this terminology) that the customers for John Lindsay films tended to be those curious for the illicit material of yesteryear, with its unfamiliar codes and tropes – especially as the majority would have been too young to have seen his films the first time around.

Police raids were also a part of the operation and culture of Soho in the 1970s – seemingly related in part to police corruption, which existed at unprecedented levels around Soho, and eventually led to a dozen officers being jailed in 1977, and many more suddenly opting for early retirement (see Cox, Shirley and Short 1977: 140–211; Williams 1979: 40; Sutherland 1982: 164–71). Stanford connects successful prosecutions of sex shops to Lord Longford's investigations into police corruption, as part of his report into pornography (Stanford 2003: 331). And, conceivably, the sporadically substantial increases in the seizures of 'obscene items' by the Metropolitan Police across the years of concerted anti-permissive campaigning and Longford's investigations might have reflected the need to be seen to be reacting to such pressures (or, alternatively, warding off suspicions of corruption or police inaction, as argued by Bleakley 2019); see Table 1.1.

Corruption arrangements seemed not just a matter of paying off the police, with money and/or prostitutes, to avoid raids, or stage managing raids further to tip-offs, allowing for the Obscene Publication Squad to evidence actual arrests (Cox, Shirley and Short 1977: 173).[17] Rather, the relationship between the police and Soho pornography seemed so entwined, particularly in the early 1970s, that Soho could be viewed as a police protectorate – even enterprise. Police and pornographers holidayed together, and attended the same Masonic lodges (Cox, Shirley and Short 1977: 174). For example, Detective Chief Inspector George Fenwick, who had been the operational chief of the Obscene Publications Squad at one point, was sub-editing the porn magazine *Janus* for one of his supposed targets (to whom he would 'recycle' confiscated material by overseeing its delivery

Table 1.1 Total number of obscene items seized by the Metropolitan Police, by year.

1963	397,274
1964	63,585
1965	39,065
1966	50,409
1967	57,849
1968	26,000
1969	35,390
1970	71,053
1971	139,395
1972	1,038,206
1973	273,366
1974	184,702
1975	202,242
1976	173,993
1977	375,484
1978	1,229,111

Note: These figures presumably include all items from busts of individual sex shops. But it is unlikely that much stock was kept in these poky shops – perhaps only a couple of hundred items at any one time. So the increase in the early and late 1970s conceivably reflects police action against warehouses and supply chains. In terms of police corruption in the early 1970s, it is very possible that the same individual items were counted a number of times: confiscated by arrangement and surreptitiously returned, only to be confiscated by arrangement again, and so on. Data in this table is drawn from two reports: Board for Social Responsibility of the General Synod of the Church of England (1970: 8) and Williams (1979: 264). For context, Hyam notes the seizure of a quarter of a million photographs deemed 'indecent or obscene' by the Vice Society between 1868 and 1880 (Hyam 1991: 69); during the quieter stretches of the above table, this figure was only doubled, then, some one hundred years later.

straight back to him), and advising on content for other magazines (Cox, Shirley and Short 1977: 172).[18] Such a concern was unavoidable to Lord Longford, who commissioned a sub-report on the 'police tariff' system (no copies of which survived (Willetts 2010: 256–57).

Gangland enforcer 'Mad Frankie' Fraser recalled, seemingly speaking of the mid-1960s, the careful accommodation of territorial claims in terms of generating money from pornography. This was, in his case, to avoid upsetting rival gangs (the Richardsons, in an uneasy truce with the Krays), to be able to move against any interloper competition from smaller gangs (whose operations would be attacked), and with the police paid off to allow operations to flourish for a limited period (which might also include paying for tips-offs, should a police raid be deemed necessary). In this case, it was a matter of 'something to do with blue films': a mobile sex cinema – an improvised arrangement, but one that ensured a flow of cash:

> What used to happen, people would rent flats, preferably on the fringes of the West End, Holborn, Tottenham Court Road, where they have quite big rooms, and they'd have [sic] 'Brussels Sprouts' – touts – who would go around looking for men on their own and invite them to see blue films which were then all the rage and very daring. It was all done with a projector and a screen; there were none of them videos in those days, and the films were pretty mild by today's standards. The punters used to have to pay about a tenner – it wasn't cheap, but there was nothing of the corner game [confidence trickery]. Once the punter said yes, it was a genuine show he saw. They got value for their money. (Fraser and Morton [1994] 2000: 209–10)

The final comment, with Mad Frankie as the honest criminal, may reference the 'con-men who take your money, usher you into an empty room and let you wait – for nothing' (Petronius 1969: 247). Mad Frankie gives a takings figure of £2,000 a week, which would suggest in the region of thirty entries a day, at a tenner (£10) per person.

Soho's association with pornography predates the historical scope of this book by some decades. Joseph Conrad, writing in 1907 about 1886, opens *The Secret Agent* with a description of one of the many London shops that effectively were outlets of pornography:

[A] square box of a place, with the front glazed in small planes. In the daytime the door remained closed; in the evening it stood discreetly but suspiciously ajar.

The window contained photographs of more or less undressed dancing girls ... a few books, hinting at impropriety ... customers were either very young men, who hung about the window for a time before slipping in suddenly; or men of a more mature age, but looking generally as if they were not in funds. (Conrad and Mallios [1907] 2004: 3–4)

By 1960, the milieu was one that may have seemed mysterious and dangerous, but with opportunities for the venturesome (or foolish) – as per the subgenre of now forgotten Soho-set erotic potboilers with sociological pretentions: Roland Vane's 1951 *Sinful Sisters* (blurb: 'sinister side-streets of Soho and the garish glamour of London night clubs') and 1953 *Vice Rackets of Soho* (cover: 'This story exposes the white slave rackets [that] flourish unchecked in London's square mile of vice'), John Brandon's 1953 *A Scream in Soho* ('Intrigue, violence and murder in London's underworld') and John Bateman's 1957 *The Soho Jungle* (cover: 'A powerful story of a city's centre of desire'), for example. Richard Wortley's *Skin Deep in Soho* can be considered a late addition to this pool, with added middle-class credentials. The book opens by grandly invoking John Galsworthy, the new figure of the 'pop sociologist' in Marshall McLuhan, and unresolved issues arising from Puritan traditions (and with Wortley thanking his wife for her 'patient support' in his investigations) – all in extensively dealing with 'a stripper called Tina' (whose photos are on the dust jacket, and the book's spine, and inside, and to whom the book is dedicated), and the dives and characters of Soho in general (Wortley 1969: unnumbered ['Author's note']). The dust jacket note on the author mentions a middle-class upbringing, modern history at Oxford, and working for the BBC as a producer; 'I am married with two small children, and even more predictably live in Hampstead'. In the context of the moral crusades against permissiveness (discussed below), this does not seem so ridiculous: a humanist impulse and moral nonchalance about the subcultures of Soho. Elsewhere, Tina herself introduces the culture – as with various (presumably ghosted) books by glamour stars of the day, such as Mary Millington, Maureen Flanagan (1974) and Fiona Richmond, as well as Mariella Novotny, associated with the Profumo scandal. From the dust jacket of her 1971 novel, *King's Road*: 'Does her name ring a familiar bell? She is, indeed, the sophisticated beauty who gave those incredible, larger-than-life parties which shocked Britain a few years ago – parties [that] included the highly controversial "Man-in-the-Mask" soiree (the menu complete with a full-plumed peacock and dressed badger)'.

Beat Girl (Edmond T. Gréville, 1960) presented Soho as exerting a gravity field towards imminent depravity, pulling in waifs from St Martins School of Art (just around the corner) and nearby coffee bars. For the young teen Jennifer (Gillian Hills), a perfect storm occurs: both aversion to her new French stepmother (whom she investigates and outs – first as a stripper, and then as a prostitute), and Soho opportunities to exert her autonomy by rebelling, culminating in the low/high point of her performing a striptease at a party. For the farce *No Sex Please, We're British* (Clive Owen, 1973), in which the proprietor of the Aphrodesia shop is played by gangster and occasional actor John Bindon, the opposition to this culture is seen to be equally problematic. A milquetoast bank clerk, played by Ronnie Corbett, is mistakenly sent large consignments of pornography – first magazines and then 8-mm loops, including the fictional titles *Winnie the Pouf, Jack and Jill Forgot the Pill*, and *Teasy Rider*).[19] He scrambles to hide the material from the imperious bank manager (Arthur Lowe), who, shocked and distracted by the open displays of the sex shops he sees on his morning commute, launches a Whitehouse-style 'clean up Britain' campaign. The pornographers behind the shops merely seem to be local wide boys, prone to sleeping in, in bedsitters, and who have rebranded themselves as the Scandinavian Import Company.

A 'Soho cinema' had effectively adapted the subgenre of Soho-set erotic potboilers with sociological pretentions – with the violent crime and strip clubs of *The Small World of Sammy Lee* (Ken Hughes, 1963) as something of a forerunner in this. *Confessions of a Sex Maniac* (aka *The Man Who Couldn't Get Enough*, Alan Birkinshaw, 1974) has its dissipated young protagonist (an architect who draws inspiration from breasts, an innovation that occurs to him as he switches from architectural books to pornographic magazines) wandering around Soho. Adverts are seen for *Diary of a Half Virgin* (possibly *Eva - den utstötta*, Torgny Wickman, 1969), *Wife Swapping French Style* (aka *Hot Game of Sex*, Jean-François Davy, 1971), *Sex of their Bodies* (possibly *La ragazza dalla pelle di luna*, Luigi Scattini, 1974), *Love-Hungry Girls* (aka *Dangerous When Aroused*, Jack Angel aka Eddy Matalon, 1973), *Love Makers* (*The Lovemakers*, Sidney Knight, 1972) and *The Reluctant Virgin* (Cesare Mancini, 1971). And *Emmanuelle in Soho* (David Hughes, 1981) attempts to reimagine Soho as classy and fashionable – furs and cars, choreographed strip shows, the plush interior of a mews flat, Teacher's whisky and Cinzano vermouth, women having sex in a sunken Jacuzzi in the midst of a party, nymphomaniac call girls, and with girls essentially using the men they encounter for their own ends. This is the context in which the film attempts to materialise a British 'Emmanuelle' – and in Soho, despite the crime, also shown, and in the company of irredeemably seedy compère John M. East – so as to achieve a worthy parallel to the worldwide brand of the original, and French, *Emmanuelle* (Just Jaeckin, 1974).[20]

This attempt indicates the second ambience – the less downmarket – which sought to purge this squalor from the prospect of erotic adventures. Indeed, Willetts (2010: 310) offers his description of Soho in relation to the regeneration that Paul Raymond envisaged – and later notes Raymond's celebration of Thatcher's coming to power in 1979 (ibid.: 346) as good for business, and with a concomitant bonus as enabling his 'self-portrait as the Soho sex industry's Mr Respectable' (ibid.: 367). From this perspective, the Soho of the early 1970s could be taken as an enclave of Victorian destitution, and with some of the homeless presumably born in the Victorian era. This was the subject of the tour of the down-and-out and flophouse environs conducted by James Mason in *The London Nobody Knows* (Norman Cohen, 1967), with Mason sometimes only a few steps ahead of the wrecking ball. Such areas had survived wars and the blitz, but would not survive inner city regeneration. According to Elsom:

> *Paul Raymond, when he altered the design of the Revuebar, challenged the assumption that the middle classes were expected to slum when they went to see strip ... He changed the atmosphere of strip clubs and, by so doing, altered the style of the product – and also perhaps the sexual fantasies for which they catered. He also improved the standards of management, paying the girls good salaries, protecting them from harassment by over-eager clients, and thus raising the level of self-esteem among strippers (Elsom 1973: 183)*

> *Paul Raymond had a clear idea of how to civilize strip clubs – he installed chandeliers, thick carpets, glass windows and a décor reminiscent of the expensive section in Lyons Corner House. (Ibid.: 185)*

And this sensibility also extended to the editorial position on pornographic magazines; the *Club International* editor Steve Bleach recalled that Raymond

> *wasn't particularly fond of the more downmarket magazines like* Razzle *and* Escort. Club International *was more his sort of thing. The photography was*

quite classy. Escort, *which I helped to revamp, was based on reader response, on people sending in letters as well as photos. He loved the sales figures it generated, but he could never warm to Shelley from a council estate in Doncaster in a lime-green basque posed on a brown Dralon sofa and pictured against flock wallpaper. I admit, it could be quite shocking wading through stacks of photos like that, not because of the nudity but because of the home furnishings. (Quoted in Willetts 2010: 391)*

Elsom advances the theory that Raymond's problems with the police arose from the way in which he sought to make the strip club respectable to 'respectable' classes. Thus Raymond's 'Revuebar was the first club not to confess its guilt in advance by showing a proper sense of shame', and so acted as a provocation to the police (Elsom 1973: 182).

'Our Moral Climate': The Permissive Society as Decline

What did the existence of Soho – this intersection of permissiveness and squalor at the heart of London – mean for others? Permissiveness, in the Conservative discourse around British society, is typically historicised (it has a period: the late 1960s) and is seen as both symptom and illness. What is permissive, here, is way beyond sordid bedroom-matters: it is crime on the streets, poor behaviour in the classroom, gambling, drug use, and irresponsible parents undermining family units. In short, the permission that has been taken is a permission to ignore considerate modes of living. This was a powerful narrative that, despite a level of internal equivocation on the Permissive Society on the right, came to represent a – if not the – major gloss on a political strategy of neoliberal reforms for the 1980s.

Margaret Thatcher, in a major speech in Harrogate to the Conservative Central Council (1982), declared her intention of a 'counter-attack' on a Permissive Society that had 'steadily and deliberately vilified, ridiculed and scorned' values, as associated with 'morality' (Thatcher 1982). Such a counter-attack had been planned for some time; Matthew Grimley locates Thatcher promising 'a reversal of the permissive society' as far back as 1970 (Grimley 2012: 80). But Grimley also recognises the grandstanding nature of such bluster; Thatcher would mostly fail to promote or support actual legislation that would achieve such reversals (see ibid.: 79–80, 88–89; and Greenwood and Young 1980). And Durham notes that a number of those sympathetic to the Conservative position may have accordingly, and quite correctly, felt disappointed and/or duped and used, especially in matters around restricting reproductive rights (Durham 1991: 22, 168–69). And this is in the context of, as King notes, Whitehouse herself and related pressure groups having 'received greatly improved access to Conservative leaders and a more sympathetic hearing' since the Conservative election victory of 1979 (King 1979: 169).[21] Whitehouse, reacting to insufficient legislation (in relation to the Indecent Display Bill of 1981) commented: 'I never thought I would live to the see the day when a *Tory* government would "licence" pornography… for the Conservatives to even contemplate going down in history as the party [that] effectively legitimised pornography – that is incredible to me' (cited in Sutherland 1982: 169–70; Whitehouse's emphasis).

Archival documents provide a taste of this courting and then betrayal. Thatcher, writing to Whitehouse on 19 April 1979 (that is, less than a month before being elected to power), suggests the idea of a BBFC-style ratings system of television, that 'education about sex should be based on Christian principles', floats concerns about the availability of artificial contraception for 'minors through doctor's prescriptions', talks of legislation on 'indecent displays in public places', notes the concern of child pornography, acknowledges the right to religious education, and signs off with 'if there are any points you would like to pursue with me please let me know'. It almost sounds like NVALA in power. The tone was soon to change. Writing back to Whitehouse on 9 September 1979, and on the other side of her election victory, Thatcher notes that no immediate or extraordinary action will be taken around concerns about grants to various organisations working in sexual health and advice (including the Albany Trust) and producing booklets on family planning. And she calls into question, more generally, the veracity of Whitehouse's information about the official nature or otherwise of such publications.[22] Then, in a letter to Whitehouse dated 2 October 1979, Thatcher declines to rethink the age of consent for females: 'I remain entirely unconvinced by the argument of the Joint Working Party on Pregnant Schoolgirls and Schoolgirl Mothers that the current law … is inappropriate in modern times'. Writing to Whitehouse on 15 February 1982, Thatcher declines to go any further around legislation restricting sex shop licensing – that the controls available are a satisfactory limit: 'In our view, and contrary to what you suggest in your letter of 2 February, these proposals will avert the potentially serious social consequences that might have stemmed from the unrestricted spread of sex shops'. Thatcher reiterates that there is nothing more to be done in terms of fresh legislation, as

Whitehouse has been told before, and notes that the home secretary is aware of the situation, and is engaging in various bureaucratic matters around it too. The letter ends without the direct solicitation of Whitehouse's help (as per the April 1979 letter): 'I am grateful that you should have written to let me know of your concern. Please continue to write in that way. It is most helpful'. And in a letter dated 14 December 1982, Thatcher simply refers concerns regarding Channel 4's programmes to the watchdog, the Independent Broadcasting Authority, as if Whitehouse is essentially no different from any other complaining letter writer.

The same brush-off is apparent in a letter of 23 February 1983, with respect to video cassettes – but here Whitehouse seems to have had enough. This reply is heavily annotated, seemingly by a much-vexed Whitehouse: 'cannot agree' sits next to Thatcher's comments on the efficacy of restrictive legislation already introduced and, written next to Thatcher's signature:

> MORAL
> FALKLANDS
> IF SHE WOULD ONLY GIVE THE SAME LEAD.
> [illegible; 'right'?] to expect supp.[ort] and backing from Government

The break was clear: the 'moral lead' that Thatcher took in launching aggressive military action to protect the sovereignty of a Crown colony was not to be afforded to those endangered back home. Reforms, for Whitehouse, have been left to wither in the hands of the bureaucrats; she writes, across the top:

> My message [illegible] we believe that [the] sex/violence industry is out of control and that she [Thatcher] is the only one who can work through the fossilised 60's mentality of [illegible] which characterises the permanent civil servants at H.O. [the Home Office]. 'No [illegible]' has been their watchword. I don't think even they would dare say 'No P.M.'

To Thatcher's sign-off that reforms need public support to succeed, Whitehouse writes 'what a burden to place! but cannot with one's hands tied'. And, scrawled at the bottom: 'I come back to it – children most at risk. Parents cannot alone protect their children'.[23]

In the place of such dangerous and damaging permissiveness was to come, in Jeffrey Weeks's term, a 'new moralism' (Weeks 1992: 277); or, for Grimley, paraphrasing Keith Joseph, a 'remoralisation of society' to meet a 'crisis of values' (Grimley 2012: 78).[24] Thatcher outlined this position in a broadcast television interview with journalist Brian Walden for 'Weekend World' (London Weekend Television, tx. 6 January 1983; see Thatcher 1983), even as she failed to respond positively to Whitehouse's calls for the same. On the origins of this idea, see Samuel (1992), who also traces the recovery of the positive sense of Victorian values (from a socialist demolition across the 1970s) into fashion and tourism in the 1980s (ibid.: 11, 14), and through a return to classroom strictness and punishment, promoted by the champion of corporal punishment, and pedagogue, Sir Rhodes Boyson (ibid.: 12–13). Foucault provided a historical overview and dismantling of myths of Victorian propriety in the first volume of his *History of Sexuality* (1976/1978, French and English editions respectively). But Thatcher's target may have been those old enough to have had Victorian parents or grandparents (perhaps as fondly recalled after the Harrogate speech in Bettys Café Tea Rooms, over tea and the cake trolley) – and so with a direct memory of lives lived with those values.

In 1974, Joseph had been clear about a position on the Permissive Society that was less inclined to liberal accommodation:

> *There is moreover a commercial exploitation of brutality in print and in film which further debases our moral climate. And how is it that a generation that rejects the exploitation of man by man and promises the liberation of women can accept the exploitation of women by pornography? The left, usually so opposed to profitable commerce in trades beneficial to the public, systematically defends the blatant commercialism of the pornographic industry. (Quoted in Denham and Garnett 2001: 262)*

In this, permissiveness is an ideological enemy, and not just a matter of an excess, perhaps of finite duration, to be tolerated. As Grimley notes, Joseph's position on good behaviour was found at the intersection of economics and society: a healthy economy would be undermined by poor social values, and poor social values in turn held the potential to derail economic prosperity by seemingly misshaping the economy and its development (Grimley 2012: 82), as per Kenneth Soaper's position. For this, Grimley draws on Joseph's 1974 speech at Edgbaston – remembered for the notorious phrase 'our human stock is threatened'. Denham and Garnett situate Joseph's speech with the rise of the far right, seemingly Joseph's semi-sympathies for the 'frustrated decent people' in the ranks of the National Front, and an edging towards opening up a discussion about the reintroduction of capital punishment (Denham and Garnett 2001: 254). But Grimley is too easy on Joseph. The speech has a eugenic impulse to it, and as noted at the time too, both in terms of this threatened 'stock' and expressing frustration at the high birth rates among 'unmarried ... deserted or divorced' women, some of whom are of 'low intelligence, most of low educational attainment ... [and] unlikely to be able to give children [a] stable emotional background', and whose offspring then may be 'the future unmarried mothers, delinquents, denizens of our borstals, sub-normal educational establishments, prisons, [and] hostels for drifters'. For this scenario, Joseph calls for proactive birth control policies (Joseph 1974). Pragmatically, Caulfield also notes that illegitimacy results in the need for more financial support from the state, to care for the children – and while men are 'robbed of unsullied partners' (Caulfield 1975: 20). Consequently, the satirical magazine *Private Eye* referred to Joseph as 'Sir Sheath' – and indeed Whitehouse differed from Joseph on the matter of birth control use per se.[25] The controversy surrounding the speech was such that the phrase 'human stock' was, it was later suggested (including by Thatcher herself, at Joseph's memorial service), not Joseph's but Sherman's – but Joseph himself was careful to ensure attribution remained to himself alone (see Denham and Garnett 2001: 265, fn 88).[26]

Denham and Garnett note Joseph's linking of 'broken, fatherless or strained homes' with 'juvenile delinquents' (2002: 195), for which he found evidence in his 1971 visits to approved schools and remand centres (ibid.: 196). But Anthony Daly, who must have seemed very much of that difficult background (a young Northern Irish exile in London, brutalised and coerced into working as a rent boy), describes Joseph's alleged attempts to seduce him, and then his sexual assault at the hands of associates of Joseph, during a drug-fuelled gay orgy with various other Conservative Members of Parliament, and some other males then under the age of consent (Daly 2018: 78, 81), and Joseph's later attempts to apologise to him for as much (ibid.: 143–49). In this light, Joseph's interests may have been straightforwardly predatory and criminal, rather than academic and legalistic, or a bizarre mixture of the two – and taking his positions seriously, even for those inclined, is a much harder task. At best, it would seem that Joseph's position on permissiveness is selective, and at worse straightforwardly hypocritical (indeed, Denham and Garnett [2001: 272] note Joseph's erratic behaviour at this point). However, in Daly's recollections, Joseph articulated a series of connections about his own life that were reflected in his ideological thinking: early childhood homosexual encounters, this distraction giving rise to a poor academic record, possibly illness, finding security and refuge in marriage and family, but then guilt in relation to his sexual infidelity – and with a rent boy the age of his own son (Daly 146–49). In this way, crucially, permissiveness mitigates against the foundation of the restorative family, potentially robbing the individual of his ability to reach his potential.

This interlinking of behaviour, economics and society was not so much towards the idea of a political economy, but to propose a moral economy. Such an idea was bluntly articulated in 1977, in a televised discussion between Thatcher and William Buckley. Their main concern was the level of union power, to the extent that (with an imperialist's logic) those British industry managers naturally antipathetic to the Labour Party would nonetheless support the Labour Party for fear of finally losing control of their workers, should a Tory government come into power. The managers' reluctance to move to confrontation, to finally enable industrial modernisation, may undermine the operation of capitalism and so (in a series of logical fallacies from Thatcher) deny humanity to the human:

> Capitalism has a moral basis. The reason being: unless you have economic freedom, you will have no other freedom, at all. So the whole of the capitalist society is on a moral basis. The basis is that the individual is here to develop his or her talents. He cannot do that without both political freedom and economic freedom. The only kind of society under which you can do that is a capitalist society: to be free, you have to be capitalist ... The precondition of freedom is capitalism, so it has a moral basis. Now, certainly, if you have freedom, you have freedom to do good or freedom to do evil. So, obviously, it's the essence of choice.

Buckley, some minutes after, relates the problem of such industrial trends of the time to sexual misbehaviour of the time, in citing interviews with just such managers in the *Daily Telegraph* on

> the problems of dealing with shop stewards, none of whose concerns were with productivity – all of whose concerns were with the cantankerous complaints of individual workers about this, that or the other. There was, according to one of them [an interviewee], a total absence of an effective sanction. There isn't

anything that you can do to somebody who refuses to cooperate at the margin. As he put it, it was the industrial equivalent of the pill: all kinds of licentiousness can go forward without any dark consequences.[27]

Keith Joseph asked: 'Are we to move towards moral decline, reflected and intensified by economic decline, by the corrosive effects of inflation? Or can we remoralise our national life, of which the economy is an integral part?' Unsurprisingly, then, Joseph's orientation seems to have been to Whitehouse as much as economists: 'Let us take inspiration from that admirable woman, Mary Whitehouse ... [who, despite the odds] set out to protect adolescents against the permissiveness of our time' (Joseph 1974). And Whitehouse reciprocated the praise (see Denham and Garnett 2001: 267). Caulfield's strange biography of Whitehouse opens with this synchronicity: the 'unknown, middle-aged woman, a schoolteacher in the Midlands, [who has] set out to protect adolescents against the permissiveness of our time', who then finds Sir Keith Joseph 'squarely within [her] camp' (Caulfield 1975: 1).[28] Denham and Garnett note the orientation to Whitehouse was in the context of Joseph's feelings about creeping post-war permissiveness, apparent in the anti-establishment sneers of left-wing theorists, the oppositional or even anarchic cultures now found at universities (and against which Neil Hamilton had attempted to intervene and provoke), and '[d]rugs, drunkenness, teenage pregnancies, vandalism, an increase in drifting – now called by new names, but basically vagrant' (quoted in Denham and Garnett 2001: 266).

Digging deeper into the 1970s thinking of the Centre for Policy Studies – surprisingly, considering all the rhetoric – offers little to no further nuance or considered thinking through of this position. Sherman's internal document of May 1977, 'Self-Interest and Public Interest', is difficult to take seriously: obscurantist, crudely platitudinal and pseudo-philosophical as it moves towards assembling a mystical foundation for neoliberalism, which would be little more than, as per Hugo Young (2013), the 'materialistic individualism' of Thatcher's children: 'People who claim to care for the masses' interests and not their own, are humbugs or power-hungry – or both. A man who is not a patriot cannot truly love humanity in general ... all experience goes to show that excessive power to the state inhibits service and generosity, and intensifies selfishness'.[29] 'Nation, Government, Society, People', of September 1977, is clear about the current blocks on freeing service and generosity: '[F]undamentally, the new socialism, Fabian, Marxist, St Simonien, etc., invariably reflected the certainty of members of the educated and authority-wielding classes that the men of enterprise, the self-made businessmen, merchants, were unfit to wield economic power, [even] though it was the creation of their own work, vision and thrift'.[30] In the terms of this study, this dispute anticipates the coming battle for the levers of power between Oxbridge or Fabian man, and Essex Man. A structural change in society was clearly understood to be necessary to wrest power from the 'educated and authority-wielding classes' and their buffer zones, and so free the economy: 'If our values are to survive and reassert themselves, the hand of the State must be prised away and pushed back'.[31] In this identification of the enemies, or enemy sensibilities, of economic progress, Sherman comes to articulate his reading of the moral economy:

> I have referred to the atrophying of economic muscles; but what about moral impulses; moral responsibilities; can they remain immune? I fear not. It is not just that people abnegate responsibility for their own livelihood and their children's physical well-being. Step by step, moral responsibility goes with it. Parents are no longer held by the opinion of their neighbours to be responsible for their behaviour.[32]

That is: state provision, in robbing the individual of responsibility, also robs the individual of the need to provide for others, and so that natural instinct withers and dies, to the detriment of both the individual and society at large. It is in this way that morality and the economy are, in theory, connected – albeit, in practice, with a tension between neoliberalism and neoconservativism (as anticipated some years prior, in the Tory equivocations around the Permissive Society, as argued below). And this Tory/Thatcherite sensibility could, at times, be said to be accommodated by some schools of neoliberalism while, at other times, remain at odds with neoliberalism in general (Sutcliffe-Braithwaite 2018: 148–49). Translated into pornographic terms, and as explored later in this book: one could read the aspirational lifestyle pornography associated with Mary Millington as neoliberal (materialist: individualism and success, and due rewards – unencumbered by senses of propriety or morality), and our council estate gay porn as a neocon-servative fantasy of the logical consequences of political liberalism or the welfare state.

Whitehouse also articulated a speculative causal belief in the connection between what was understood to be morally proper and the health of the economy. Here, the once noble male is now beset: the Permissive Society allows too much access to, or the promise of, extramarital affairs at the very crisis point at which feminism has vengefully undermined man's self-worth and dissipated his role:

> *It could be that the assault on the masculinity of man, the rejection by women of their own femininity, drains sexuality of its deepest personal and social meanings, and drives men to see women in terms of their sexual parts rather than as whole personalities. If women deny men their instinctive role as father, husband and provider, while they may find sexual partners more easily than ever before, man's own deep sense of rejection and inadequacy may drive him to fantasies of sex and violence and even crime. It could well be that the very liberation that women claim as their right will deprive our civilisation of the intense male motivation and vitality that first creates the family, and then the economic and cultural drive that secure its safety and growth. (Whitehouse 1978: 89)[33]*

In Sutcliffe-Braithwaite's discussion of such positions of the time, the idea of self-interest is mitigated by the family – which breaks or dilutes self- into family-interest: the concern for immediate others, then, as the motivation for bread-winning; and, in reverse, that the weakening of the family then becomes detrimental to the familial connections, and so to the social fabric, underpinning wealth. So, for this mindset, '[s]ocialism had thus caused economic, but also *moral* decline' (Sutcliffe-Braithwaite 2012: 512; author's italics). In this respect, for Thatcher herself, the return of the family unit was both the prize of the vanquishing of socialism, and the motor of the new economy (ibid.: 517). It is therefore little wonder that permissiveness, understood as the very antithesis of family unit discipline, was to come to be, for Thatcherites, a fundamental, and deserving, shibboleth.

So the regrettable 'Sexual Revolution' of the times may, for Whitehouse, have been seen to result in a catastrophic trashing of the basic functioning unit of the economy: the heterosexual family. This is the 'long-term effect on the male sex if it is denied its natural fulfilment' (Whitehouse 1978: 88), and the first step on this slope of denial is for women to be less feminine – repelling the husband, and driving him to other women, as above, or pornography, or homosexuality (ibid.). My point is not to highlight such an obnoxious and ridiculous position from Whitehouse (and indeed this is only the half of it: the plot behind pornography in the UK is, for her, via Soviet Communism, as discussed below), but to note the essential similarities between Whitehouse's thinking and that of Joseph, Sherman and Thatcher. Indeed, Joseph's fascism is more repellent than Whitehouse's theocratic delusions. But all three were to define their positions in relation to the Permissive Society, and all three note a state of sexual anarchy as endangering financial stability.

These positions, in effect, belatedly actioned the expectation articulated some years before, in 1967, by Jonathan Aitken. Aitken opens his report on 'Sex and the London Scene' with a prematurely world-weary question: 'The only remaining interest in London's sexual revolution is the speculation about the date when we can expect to see the counter-revolution ... The pendulum of tolerance has swung so far towards permissiveness that soon the inexorable pattern of history will produce cries of "Bring back puritanism – all is forgiven", even from the lips of London's most prominent libertines' (Aitken 1967: 94).[34] The cause of the counter-revolution, for Thatcher, was to exorcise the toxic legacy of the generation that Aitken identifies, and who came of age in the immediate post-war years: 'We are reaping what was sown in the sixties. The fashionable theories and permissive claptrap set the scene for a society in which the old virtues of discipline and self-restraint were denigrated' (Thatcher 1982).

The qualified use of the term 'permissive', even if unintentional, is nonetheless telling (unintentional, as this was a tub-thumping speech for public consumption, and she goes on to justify her calls for order with unsourced and presumably common wisdom about children longing for rules, and the like). Is there a strain of permissiveness that is not 'claptrap'? Permissive reason? This is the heart of the contradiction: deregulation, the shrinking of the state, neoliberalism and the hollowing out of institutions, is philosophically aligned to permissiveness. The permissiveness is the freedom that, for Conservatives of this bent, is the very allowance of freedom that restores choice and dignity to the individual, and unshackles potential to allow for a renewal of society. Thus, for Aitken – after noting that Christine Keeler was 'young, attractive, amusing' and 'obviously enjoyed [her] occupation', and so the Keeler affair 'severely damaged the myth that prostitutes are the hag-ridden deadbeats of civilisation' – observes that 'the prostitute can make a real financial killing, and it is not for nothing that the modern call girls like to be known as "business ladies"' (Aitken 1967: 97) Thereafter, concluding his observations of the times, Aitken bemoans the ending of National Service (a compulsory period in the army for all young men), complains that

'Britain's influence, both moral and economic, is plummeting in the world' (297), complains about traffic congestion in central London (297), complains that young people work idly in 'fashionable occupations [when] they could be making some real contribution to British business' (301), complains about the tax rates (302), complains again about the penchant for 'the latest vogues' among the young (305), complains again about the tax rates (305–6), and closes with a call for a renewed interest in 'the fulfilment of honourable materialistic ambitions' (307) as, seemingly, the only chance to salvage the country. The energising appetite to take advantage of new freedoms by those in the know – and Aitken's study is about the figures he groups together as the 'Young Meteors' – is one that has been effectively waylaid by permissiveness:

> *In reality there is a desperate shortage of young people prepared to train and work for the really big responsibilities in tomorrow's Britain, and this is potentially the greatest danger facing our country. Young Londoners may be amusing in conversation, enterprising on the dance floor and adventurous in the double bed, but when it comes to big commercial enterprises they are naïve innocents. (Aitken 1967: 300)*

This suggests that a delineation of types of permissiveness is now necessary (rather than just declaring that the moralists were confused, or wrong), after some further historical definition.

Thatcher's other bugbear was socialism, identified as the incubator of 'fashionable theories', and as the mindset of the vilifiers, ridiculers and scorners of the Conservatives in the 1970s, as particularly firmly embedded in the newer universities. This was the socialism with which she associated the Labour Party of the 1970s.[35] Joseph also took up this theme of the damaging mindset of socialism in his Edgbaston speech. And for baffled and paranoid social commentators such as Christopher Booker, the chaos of the 1970s had arisen in an unwelcome continuum of the 'overblown fantasies of the 1960s' – an inexorable tide: the disorder and immobilisation of strike-afflicted Britain – 'the universal sea of "Delayed", "Cancelled", "Non-Operational"' (compared to which, Czechoslovakia, of Christmas 1978, is 'light, warmth and jollity' [Booker 1980: 172–73]). Added to this is the refusal of workers to accommodate themselves to the technocratic society (Booker reaches for parallels to the future class warfare of *The Time Machine* [ibid.: 165]), with the wrecking of the near future in full swing, exemplified in the 'horrible mistake' of the new town of Milton Keynes (ibid.: 148). So Peter Jenkins's study, *Mrs Thatcher's Revolution*, can be identified and understood to occur through *The Ending of the Socialist Era* (the book's subtitle). What was ending was a period in which too many permissions were granted, or those who used to grant permissions (be that in the family or a state body) were effectively stripped of their powers to do so. In psychogeographical terms, one could imagine walking through the small hills of vermin-infested rubbish and debris accumulating in central London during the 'Winter of Discontent' (a period of widespread strikes in the public sector, across 1978/79), and on to Soho, with its seemingly unchecked culture of sex shops, sex shows and prostitution, and find that these two scenarios were actually of one piece. Indeed, the obscenity trial in the UK around one of the novels that made such a connection (with the time for sexual exploration on the part of one of its characters made possible by strikes), albeit in a North American context – Hubert Selby Jr's *Last Exit to Brooklyn* of 1964 – is typically mentioned in relation to the onset of the Permissive Society of the 1960s. These ideological ideas translated directly into anti-permissive activism by the political right – with pornography as the chief target.

Notes

1. On the constituency of the Festival of Light itself, see Whipple 2010.
2. For Whitehouse's commentary on the making of the documentary, see Whitehouse 1972 (95–102), and also Caulfield 1975 (94–97).
3. Powell and Whitehouse were neighbours in The Wold, in the Claverley area, on the Wolverhampton outskirts. Whitehouse made much of the fact that she was not from a metropolitan elite, but retained an outsider status, and so was able to speak the common (Midlands) people's truth to degenerate liberal power. Paul Foot argues that in promoting concerns around matters of immigration, Wolverhampton became Powell's way of presenting himself as the voice of the disgruntled (white) people – despite the fictional nature of these concerns (Foot 1969: 61).
4. Smith concedes that Hamilton was a likeable and amusing student, despite his views. Neil Hamilton became a Member of Parliament for Thatcher's government in 1983, which must have suggested at the time that the joke was ultimately on his Aberystwyth opponents. He is now remembered for the decades of damage and scandal he brought to the Conservative Party, including in relation to, ironically, financial bribes (the 'cash-for-questions' scandal of 1994–97); see Wells, Wilson and Pallister 1999. Issues of *The Courier* are archived in the Hugh Owen Library, University of Wales, Aberystwyth.
5. Rumours persist that some or even much of this material was sourced from the UK. These rumours may have arisen from the way in which John Lindsay's tendency to cast adult performers as 'English schoolgirls in uniforms' for a number of hardcore loops was at the

invitation of Wilhelmus (who also features in Lindsay's *The Pornbrokers* documentary) – at least in relation to Kerekes's speculations about various court hearings involving Lindsay (Kerekes 2000: 194). Wilhelmus was jailed for incest in 1992 (a charge that was contested by a number of those involved), and he died shortly after being released, in possibly suspicious circumstances (according to Vermaat 1994, at least).

On the Scandinavian porn culture of these years, see Stevenson 2010, Nordstrom 2012 and Larsson 2017b. The Danish position was in part predicated on the idea, articulated by the Danish Forensic Medicine Council, that access to pornography aligned to 'different sexual tendencies' meant that 'deviating sexual tendencies are thereby neutralized' (Olympia Press 1971: 255).

6.   Harris was jailed in 2014 in relation to sexual assault, including of minors (see Walker 2014).

7.   On these seemingly contradictory positions on the liberated 'new woman' of the 1960s, in the eyes of the Rolling Stones, see August 2009.

8.   The novellas were published in 2002 as *Trouble at Willow Gables and Other Fictions, 1943–1953*. For these, Larkin wrote under the pseudonym Brunette Coleman – and so wrote from a position of a vernacular imagining of a female author chronicling schoolgirl antics. Jill herself is identified as a pupil at Willow Gables in *Jill* (Larkin 2005: 112), and in which the protagonist also adopts the trait of writing as if a female, for stretches of the novel. For a wider discussion of Larkin's schoolgirl fiction, see Rowe 2001. 'Annus Mirabilis' was published in *High Windows* in 1974.

9.   Margaret Nolan (aka Vicky or Victoria Kennedy) appeared in *Goldfinger* (Guy Hamilton, 1964) as a masseuse, and as the gold-painted silhouette in the opening sequence of that film, as well as naturist films (*It's a Bare, Bare World!*, William Lang, 1963), and 8-mm films for Harrison Marks, as discussed below. Her final appearance was as a barmaid in *Last Night in Soho* (Edgar Wright, 2021).

10.   It is not impossible that this was an attempt to tap the market of visually impaired pornography consumers.

11.   For the culture of booths, see Derek Ford's *The Sexplorer* (1975), and for the 1970s sex shop experience, see *Rude Boy* (Jack Hazan and David Mingay, 1980), in which the protagonist eventually abandons his job of minding the cash register, in a desultory way, of an unheated late-night Soho sex shop, and tending to requests for 'harder' material, in favour of working as a roadie for The Clash.

12.   Critical engagement with pornography from film historians and theorists at that time in the UK also included a weekend seminar on pornography in cinema and the visual arts, convened by the Society for Education in Film and Television, and running at the Institute for Contemporary Arts (ICA) on 17/18 May 1980. Critical framings were feminist, and in relation to gaze (pace Mulvey 1975) and psychoanalytical theories; some of the papers were collected in (Screen 1992). Four years earlier, the ICA occasioned substantial controversy with the 'Prostitution' exhibition/performances by the COUM Transmissions collective (see Ford 1999; Dwyer 2000: 10–52; and Tutti 2017).

13.   See too *Dilly Boys: The Game of Male Prostitution in Piccadilly* by Mervyn Harris (1973) for the operations of this subculture at the time, including the notorious pick-up area of the 'meat rack' (although scandals continued to surface well into the mid-1980s; see Lancaster 1986: 25). Hyam notes the beginnings of the underage rent culture in the Piccadilly area as relating to the closure of boy brothels in 1837 in Mile End and Spitalfields (1991: 63). Actor Peter Wyngarde's self-titled 1970 concept album survey of modern sexuality (rapidly withdrawn at the time)

mentions a character who 'one night went to troll the Dilly', in the song 'Hippie and the Skinhead'. On Kenneth Leech's work with rent boys in this area, see (1973: 58–61).

14. Fraser would use a telescope in his flat opposite to select his prey, and arrange for him to be sent over (see Vyner 1999: 262). On Tallon, and with news of a rent boy in Clarence House eventually turning up in the *News of the World*, see Quinn 2015 (113–16). Backstairs Billy's gay bar chat up line was 'Why don't you come back to the house for tea, and you can see?' – the walk between locations, Soho and the royal residency, was only twenty minutes (169).

    Sunday, Bloody Sunday makes substantial space to communicate the strangeness and delinquency of autumnal London nights of 1970, including an encounter between the protagonist, a gay middle-aged doctor, and a rent boy, on the meat rack – with the intimation that something complicated and emotive has happened between them previously. The doctor is robbed for his troubles.

15. On the reportage, see the documentary-maker's tie-in publication (Deakin and Willis 1976). On Gleaves, and the cooperation and charitable funding his organisation received, and the murder of a young resident of one of the hostels, Billy McPhee, by men in the employ of Gleaves, see HC Deb 1975. *After Cease to Exist* (COUM Transmissions, 1978), which intercuts a Throbbing Gristle concert/happening with a BDSM scene of (seemingly) a castration, by Cosey Fanni Tutti, included a recording of 'a pathologist discussing a murdered teenager's body found at a roadside. Thee [*sic*] victim had been killed by a homosexual ring by Bishop Gleaves', according to Genesis P-Orridge, as quoted in Ford 1999: [*sic*] 12.27 (such a pathologist discussion occurs in *Johnny Go Home* but was not audible on the soundtrack of the print of *After Cease To Exist* that I saw). Throbbing Gristle would later, certainly by happenstance, rework Elizabeth Manners's sentiments ('D-I-S-C-I-P-L-I-N-E – discipline' 1971: 205) for their 1981 single 'Discipline' – a song frequently performed live, and at very extensive length, featuring innumerable chants of 'discipline'. For some audience members, during a performance at Heaven nightclub in London (21 June 2009), this proved simply too much, and exits were made; the group's constant alienation of the audience continued, then, into their last handful of concerts.

16. Correspondence with Daly, September 2019. The orgies in question were in Mayfair. As discussed later in this book, more contemporary gay pornography on film seems to be utilised by male prostitutes as part of their own self-promotion. And, in another continuum, heterosexual play-acting, then as now, seemed to occur even during the most absolute of homosexual activities. Harris notes this 'code' whereby 'the boys should deny any sexual gratification as this would simultaneously undermine their masculinity as well as their self-conception of themselves as not being homosexual' among rent boys of the time (Harris 1973: 71, and see also 104–5, 118).

17. Peter Wright notes in *Spycatcher* that British Intelligence also utilised prostitutes – but for honeytrap operations against Soviet targets – whereas left-wing group members, 'since many of them lived promiscuous lives', were not susceptible to erotic espionage (Wright and Greengrass 1988: 310, 360).

18. Fenwick was one of those officers eventually gaoled (Travis 1999).

19. This is an exaggerated scenario, but far from fanciful: unsolicited letters offering pornography by subscription, through discrete mail order, and sometimes containing samples too, were not unusual. The letters would sometimes suggest that they were intended for another recipient, or note that the recipient's address has been obtained from a like-minded, unnamed friend.

20. On East, who both appeared in and curated historical British glamour, see Sweet 2005: 310–17.

21. For an overview of Whitehouse's campaigning and the Conservative Party in the late 1970s, see Durham 1991: 76–98. For a brief summary of Thatcher's favourable view of Whitehouse in the early 1970s, see Moore 2013: 184–85.

22. Presumably Whitehouse's concern was with respect to the Paedophile Information Exchange's work with the trust, as noted below, and on which Whitehouse had publicly spoken prior to this letter. If so, Whitehouse was quite correct – a joint pamphlet was planned (see IICSA 2020: 88–94).

23. These letters ('Letter Thatcher to Whitehouse': Box 4, for 19 April 1979, 9 September 1979, 2 October 1979, 14 February 1982, 14 December 1982, 23 February 1983) are held in the National Viewers' and Listeners' Association Collection, in the Special Collections of the Albert Sloman Library, University of Essex.

24. Sir Keith Joseph was Thatcher's close confidant, and co-founder of the Centre for Policy Studies with Alfred Sherman – and, in this, one of the co-architects of Thatcherism. He was viewed as a guru to the Conservative Party of the 1980s. In this discussion, then, through tracing the evolution of various ideas that would then be understood as Thatcherite or Thatcherism, I am keen to decentre Thatcher from Thatcherism – following the lead of writers such as Brooke (2014) and Hilton, Moores and Sutcliffe-Braithwaite (2017). From this perspective, Thatcher is often read as capitalising on, rather than being the genesis of, defining trends – such as ideas of individualism and equality (Robinson et al. 2017: 272); and, indeed, that Thatcher (and the Thatcherism of the 1980s) is not always a consistent or logical outgrowth of Thatcher and her positions of the 1970s – as per Whitehouse's chagrin.

25. '[E]specially as I am on record as being against the issue of free contraceptives for all, and known to be much exercised about the activities of some of the contraceptive lobby.' See letter: Mary Whitehouse to Keith Joseph, 23 October 1974 (Courtesy of the National Viewers' and Listeners' Association Collection, Special Collections, Albert Sloman Library, University of Essex).

26. For Sherman on the speech – claiming the real problem, beyond a few oversights in terminology, was a media backlash, and that this cost Joseph his leadership ambitions, and then his well-being – see Sherman and Garnett 2007: 55–61. For a mildly apologetic commentary on Joseph's position at this time, see Denham and Garnett 2001: 265–76. For opposition Members of Parliament attacking Joseph's misrepresentation of the data on which his argument was founded, see Holden 2004: 192–93.

27. 'Firing Line' with William Buckley (tx 19 August 1977, PBS).

28. A photograph of the two of them is included in the book. The book's strangeness comes from the way in which the author, despite full subscription to Whitehouse's ideals, is seemingly sexually aroused by the thought of her, across a number of passages, in a way that is positively *Trouble at Willow Gables*: 'Were it not for the slightly tell-tale signs of ageing around the throat, her high colouring, trim, unflabby figure and zestful movements would lead you to believe that she was still in her early fifties, an outdoors woman who energetically refereed lacrosse matches or stalked sheep trails in Welsh hills ... I found her in a bright red trouser suit, at once functional and attractive'; 'this tall long-legged, chubby-faced blonde'; 'a rare pleasure [for her, as a youth] was to cycle home with the sting of cool rain on her face; nor did she ever lose the sense of pleasure at walking through wet grass in her bare feet' (Caulfield 1975: 3, 31, 32 respectively). Such passages are included here as a rare access to nonconformist Christian eroticism (although Caulfield himself confesses to Catholicism), and a counterbalance to so much else in this book – beholding the sensuality of the athletic woman in nature, who

is undiminished by domestic settings or late middle age (rather than supposedly rendered desperate). Caulfield's is the furtive fantasy, as arising from glancing across at the woman in an opposite church pew. But he is right in recognising something: the idea of sexless anti-permissive campaigners, as envisaged in *House of Whipcord* (Pete Walker, 1974), seems quite wrong in some respects: the Christian position of these years was sometimes one of first admitting to sexual feelings as a way of talking about self-policing them.

29. Alfred Sherman document of May 1977, 'Self-Interest and Public Interest', held in the Centre for Policy Studies document archive, London School of Economics.
30. Alfred Sherman document of 2 September 1977 (Houston), 'Nation, Government, Society, People', held in the Centre for Policy Studies document archive, London School of Economics, p. 7.
31. Ibid., p. 34.
32. Ibid., p. 29.
33. Whitehouse's prose here reads as if it has been ghosted.
34. Aitken would become a Conservative Member of Parliament before, during and after Thatcher's government.
35. For a cynical, satirical take on this reading of universities at this point – or, at least, a take that chimed with Thatcher's position – see Malcolm Bradbury's 1975 novel *The History Man* (adapted for television, and broadcast in 1981). A young, seemingly Marxist, sociologist lives in a semi-squat, undermines the governance of the university for his own gain, maintains a troubled open marriage and, when caught having sex with students and staff alike, ensures that the accuser (a public school boy, whom he victimises) is bullied out of the university. The novel is set in 1972, and so could be said to reflect the 'march through the institutions' of the protesters of 1968, some four years on, and once a foothold has been gained.

CHAPTER 2

An Anti-Permissive Front

For the respectable and nominally progressive *Encounter* magazine – which typically concerned itself with literature, politics and sociology – a notable economist and social commentator offered some punditry on the disconcerting sexual openness of everyday society of 1972:

> Never have styles among women during the summer months been so openly flaunting. Knee-high black boots focus the spectator's eye on the full length of a thigh that, through a vestigial skirt, can be seen to merge, on seating, into the opulent rotundities of the buttocks. Picking one's way through a railway station, the bouncing jaunt of girls in over-tight silk slacks offers tantalising visions of pneumatic bliss ... One cannot but sympathise with those members of Women's Lib who watch aghast a trend that so blatantly submerges the individual character of women in a flesh pond of sexuality. For men can hardly be expected to avert their eyes from the manifest eroticism of fashions that have made of otherwise ordinary females an essential part of the furnishings of the sex-permissive society ... To put it mildly, it is a nuisance for an ordinary healthy man to be exposed to sexually inviting attire on the way to work. (Mishan 1972: 9–10, and fn 2)[1]

What, then, did this Soho-isation of day-to-day society mean? Mishan's vision of being involuntarily dunked into this murky 'flesh pond of sexuality' (although he seems as aroused as horrified) now warrants further exploration. Lord Longford (Frank Pakenham) attempted to do just this – akin to missionary work in a heathen nation.

To what extent was the United Kingdom understood to be teetering on the edge of a moral precipice by Longford and his co-thinkers? And it is this 'understood' that remains my primary concern: the myth of permissiveness that exerted itself, its particularities (especially with regard to the example of Denmark), and varying attempts to grapple with, and capitalise on, permissiveness. This first occurs with Longford, moving from a debate in British parliament to forming a ragtag anti-permissive front of commentators, personalities, campaigners, activists and criminals.

Lord Longford Intervenes

In the April 1971 House of Lords debate, 'Pornography in Britain' (HL Deb 1971), everything was present: acknowledging the counterculture's preference for love over war, the 'grave aesthetic menace if pornography is allowed to go forward unchecked', deference to soapbox thunderers David Holbrook and Elizabeth Manners (discussed below), recovery of the idea of Puritanism, concerns about underwear adverts seen on the London Underground and on buses, suspicion that cinema has 'decayed more rapidly' that other art forms, intimations of a silent majority of moralists in the country ready to fight the pornographers, the 'Old Boys Club' in operation ('I certainly make no criticism of the film censor himself [Trevelyan], whom I have highly regarded since he was kind to me at our preparatory school'), *Growing Up* (and a request to the minister of education, and 'mother of lovely children', Thatcher, to stop it being shown in schools), *Midnight Cowboy*, Ken Russell's *Women in Love*, *Flesh*, suspicions of the anti-Christ at work, unreferenced (bar a generic quote from Lenin) claims of a Communist plot behind the spread of pornography in the West, concerns with 'marital infidelity and the neglect of pre-marital chastity', and sex education. And, from Viscount Norwich, praise for Longford's mission: 'This morning I read in *The Times* about Lord Longford's own personal Calvary through Soho; through the world of Scandinavian sex magazines and striptease. I, too, have stood breast high – if your Lordships will forgive the expression – "amid the alien porn"'). Longford concluded by praising a debate that 'I feel, even by the standards of this House, is a debate that will long be remembered'.

The eventual paperback publication of his informal committee's resultant report, by Coronet Books in September 1972, emblazoned the word 'pornography' across the cover (red on white, for maximum impact, and broken in the middle – so 'porno' is the first word registered), with minor notes above and below about the investigation, and this being the 'full text of the report'. By this point, Longford had been nicknamed 'Lord Porn'. He had visited Danish sex clubs as part of his investigations (in one of three groups of his associates detailed to do this, each with £10 to spend), but had stormed out of two different ones once the performance began – the latter at the point at which a transgender performer had handed him a whip; the *Guardian*'s headline the next day was 'Peer defies the Whip'. Whitehouse herself was unavailable for this trip – she was in Rome to meet the Pope to show him a copy of *Oz* and *The Little Red Schoolbook* (see Sutherland 1982: 116; Stanford 2003: 323–24).

Longford's report now reads like a conspiratorial, hysterical, unscientific and anecdote-heavy telling-off. The report rarely distinguishes between material under discussion that would have clearly fallen foul of the Obscene Publications Act of 1959 (amended 1964), such as paedophilic films and bestiality, and that which would not have troubled the police at all, despite clarity in some parts of the report as to what would constitute illegal pornography; and it terms homosexuality as 'deviation' (Longford Committee 1972: 35 and elsewhere; such a position would have been somewhat idiosyncratic as late as 1972). Problematic names surface as involved in the preparation – problematic in respect to later revelations about their own activities across these years (and indeed, Longford's contributing authors note attendance at screenings of films that showed the sexual abuse of minors). One is pushed to conclude that their involvement in the report's preparation furnished a further layer of subterfuge to their activities. Longford was clear to note that the idea of the inclusion of 'practising pornographers' among the contributing authors was not one to be taken seriously (ibid.: 12) – they engaged in an 'exploitative and contemptuous manipulation of a vast public' (56) – and yet an avuncular and earthy figure such as Stanley Long would have grounded the flights of fantasy.[2] In this way, the Christian perspective that Longford mentioned (ibid.: 14, and see also 18), in terms of the 'social evil' (15) of pornography, could be achieved unsullied. And John Ellis directly relates the report to 'an exposition of the Nationwide Festival of Light's position' (Ellis 1992: 149). But this Christian perspective is essentially 'High Church' – or, put another way, ridiculously, and ignorantly (in relation to progressive Christian thought of the time), Old Testament – and this despite Longford's Christian socialism. The issues with the report illustrate Eagleton's position, of 1966, of a lacuna in theological thought as detrimental to the entire enterprise of 'a renewal in Christian thinking' – which is that 'we have no single, adequate, interpretative account of the relationship between the church and the social developments of the industrial revolution over the last one and a half centuries in Britain … [and so] much of our present theorising about Christian responses to industrial capitalism has necessarily to be done in a void' (Eagleton 1966: 57). The Longford Report essentially entrenches old oppositional certainties as guidance in terms of cultures of sexuality in the early 1970s, as if reacting against the rapprochement between Christianity and the modern world.

In the report chapter 'Broadcasting', an ideological position breaks surface in respect to a number of acclaimed television dramas (such as Ken Loach's 1966 *Cathy Come Home*):

> *The essential formula is the same ... that human miseries and misfortunes are due to our circumstances rather than to our nature, and that therefore blame attaches only to society, collectively, rather than individually to men and women who compose it. Thus, marriages break up and love is lost for lack of proper housing, drug-addicts go to their deaths because they have been deprived of comfortable homes and loving care, and drunks huddle helplessly under bridges, the injured innocents of a cruel and callous social system. (Longford Committee 1972: 233)*

The position on the blame for the misfortunes of others could not be clearer – and is also, in its theological vintage, Old Testament too. It perhaps also channels a general beleaguered right-wing anger about that way in which the BBC was effectively an organisation of and for, as Muggeridge was claiming, 'liberal human-ists' (quoted in Bakewell and Garnham 1970: 164, 165), who seemed to have been reduced to pamphleteering. The writer of *Cathy Come Home*, Jeremy Sandford, is roundly condemned by Richard Sturgeon, for example, in 'the progressive organ of the reactionary right', for his sympathy for the 'self-inflicted plight of the more feckless members of society', and so on (Sturgeon 1967: 19), in a way that recalls Kenneth Allsop's condemnatory survey of the infiltration of middle-class socialists into the arts, skewering the culture of the 1950s into the 'Angry Decade' (Allsop 1958).

But who was articulating as much, in Longford's report? The authors of this section include Malcolm Muggeridge, Dennis Delderfield, Cliff Richard, Jimmy Savile (albeit seemingly failing to contribute; Davies 2015: 280) and Peregrine Worsthorne. Muggeridge, close to Whitehouse, had coined the term 'Festival of Light' (Capon 1972: 15), and Cliff Richard appears on the front of Capon's history of the festival, which was initially read in the media as 'virtually a Whitehouse/Muggeridge anti-porn crusade' (35), and then as a 'Muggeridge/Whitehouse/

Longford anti-porn crusade' (103). The allegiances then are clear. Savile has been discussed above, but some who baulked at Muggeridge's new found Puritanism of these years did so in the knowledge of his reputation as a serial sex assaulter (see Levy 2015; and Seaton 2015: 220). Muggeridge and Whitehouse are pictured on the back cover of Caulfield's biography of Whitehouse (1975), at the Festival of Light rally in Trafalgar Square. So beneath the thundering, harmonic Christian voice of these two figures is straight criminality. And Muggeridge's charismatic, parsonic vocal qualities were clearly exceptional – as was in evidence in the television debate regarding the release of *Monty Python's Life of Brian* (Terry Jones, 1979), for *Friday Night, Saturday Morning* on 9 November 1979. Here, Muggeridge and Melvyn Stockwood (then Bishop of Southwark) caught John Cleese and Michael Palin in a pincer movement. Stockwood, in full ecclesiastic regalia, expressed fluster, frustration, annoyance and then (doubly empurpled) sharp condemnation, while Muggeridge delivered melodious, sing-song sentences and seemed to drift into a trance-like state, as if channelling God's own position on Monty Python back to the television studio (which was a tropical sunset-themed set, with Tim Rice as the host).[3]

The Longford Report provided plenty of partisan condemnation, well beyond the matter of pornography (as per the reading of *Cathy Come Home*) but little insight, even as a 'field report' from those lost in the field as they attempt to survey and address the new landscape of promiscuous Britain. This work was, specifically, intended to help with the drafting of parliamentary legislation; the Terms of Reference set out the need to 'tackl[e] the problem of pornography' in a way that 'would command general support' (Longford Committee 1972: 12) The report arose from the debate that Longford had initiated in the House of Lords on pornography on 21 April 1971 – the success of the first UK run of *Oh! Calcutta!* seems to have triggered these discussions, not least in respect to a fear that a filmed production would be made and distributed in the UK (ibid.: 22). For Longford, the production is noted as having 'contributed to the general public's idea of what was acceptable', so that some denounced it because 'it shifted the limits of publicly permissible sexual display in a direction they saw as harmful to society's well-being' – and hence 'Archbishop Lord Fisher joined the debate to argue that the public display of human genitals was an invasion of everybody's privacy' (ibid.: 22) The report collates a number of differing ideas and opinions (from groups, expert witnesses, letters, recollections of discussions, etc.), with an eventual majority position (rather than a unanimous one) that was pro-censorship.

But what was actually at stake, as implied in Longford's Christian rhetoric, was the erosion of the mental and spiritual health of citizens, through the ways in which pornography has resulted in an attack on the moral and ethical workings of society. The term 'sex pollution' (Mishan 1972: 15) is apt: things 'in the air', that are harmful to one's well-being.

The battle, for Whitehouse, was for the spiritual good of the nation-state. And Whitehouse was precise: much of her correspondence seems to have been gathering evidence (particularly from the BBC), further to the application of pressure on weak links in political culture. Thus, politicians with slim electoral majorities were particularly susceptible to such campaigns from the Christian conservatives. And the Christian churches, seemingly bar the mobilised evangelical elements around the Festival of Light, had not led the crusade to 'clean up' Britain, or even been particularly interested in being part of that strain of activism. Path-breaking theological thought at this point – South Bank theology, the re-emergence of social teaching in the Catholic Church (this was the period between the close of Vatican II and the beginnings of Liberation Theology) – would have had little time for parochial concerns around, say, the shelf positioning of *Knave* magazine in a newsagent on Crewe railway station. Rather, public clerical figures such as Bishop Trevor Huddleston and Father Daniel Berrigan SJ argued, and lived, and with danger to themselves, lives that revolved around activism against the obscenities of state violence in apartheid South Africa and imperial slaughter in South East Asia, respectively.[4] And the same could be said of Reverend Kenneth Leech's work with the dispossessed of Soho (noted below), or Father Michael Cleary's seeming complete immersion in the impoverished lives of his Dublin parishioners (as documented in Peter Lennon's 1967 *Rocky Road to Dublin*). Indeed, this work was formally aligned to the actual 1970 position of the Church of England (as per the 'Obscene Publications' report): that while outright porno-graphy was to be banned, 'it is also important not to be so obsessed' with nominally 'legitimate' sexual expressions in 'potentially sublime relationships', 'as to neglect those obscenities such as war, famine, poverty, slums, race hatred, which threaten the very existence of the human race' (Board for Social Respons-ibility 1970: 14).

In *The Pseudo-Revolution: A Critical Study of Extremist 'Liberation' in Sex*, David Holbrook seems to suggest that the Permissive Society, which he aligns with the 'sexual revolution', has arisen from a new phenomenon of being able to watch other people having sexual intercourse. It is now 'almost impossible not to see this frequently' (Holbrook 1972c: 5). And so live sex shows on the Continent and, in the British context, pornography, are, mutatis mutandis, the very generators of the Permissive Society. And these generators, in turn, are arising from an influx of perverts, or newly converted perverts, and the liberal institutions who counter criticisms against this degeneracy. This observation is included at the very outset of Holbrook's *The Case Against Pornography*, which seeks to intervene in the discourse:

> *Until recently, pornography was suppressed in our society and was the pre-occupation of a few disturbed individuals. Yet today not only is there permissiveness, but sick and sadistic fantasies are being thrust into people's lives on a massive scale. Because of the so-called 'sexual revolution', extremists who wield power over television, press and screen can censor and prevent open discussion of the problems of sexual explicitness and obscenity. Those who control the media have rigged the debate, so that many now feel it is all 'harmless'. (Holbrook 1972a: unnumbered [i])*

And John Trevelyan, Secretary of the Board of the British Board of Film Censors (BBFC), in his introduction to John Elsom's *Erotic Theatre*, advanced the arresting (Freud-grounded) theory that our own sexual uncertainties are to blame for the confusions from which permissiveness arises (Elsom 1973: xiv). In *A History of the Modern World* (1983), commentator Paul Johnson went so far as to claim that Lytton Strachey and the Bloomsbury Group's effective 'intellectual takeover of the modern world' (via, for example, Strachey's gossipy critique of *Eminent Victorians*, of 1918) had near-fatally weakened patriotic British society, thus 'leaving behind' (as summarised by Strachey's biographer, Michael Holroyd, on Johnson) 'a national emptiness which became the homosexual recruiting-ground at [the University of] Cambridge for Soviet espionage' (Holroyd 1995: xxxiv).[5]

All these voices can be placed in a subgenre of media commentary across the 1970s, but with a particular intensity during the early 1970s, bewailing the downward moral spiral of society, as enabled by the ending of deference, the undermining of patriotism and non-'standard' sexual practices. Scapegoats were needed. Kenneth Tynan's erotic stage revue *Oh! Calcutta!*, which premiered in New York in 1969, and then in London in 1970, was a substantial target in this (for the sketches themselves, see Tynan 1969; for an overview: Sutherland 1982: 96–

103, and Saunders 2017). And an anti-permissive hit list filmography came to be assembled too, around films that, as essentially commercial releases and with artistic pretensions, may have strayed into respectable cinemas in the suburbs. Three had seemingly been mostly overlooked by the censorious the first time around: *Flesh* (Paul Morrissey, 1968), *Witchfinder General* (Michael Reeves, 1968) and *Midnight Cowboy* (John Schlesinger, 1969). So this was made good for a 1971 batch: *The Devils* (Ken Russell), *Straw Dogs* (Sam Peckinpah), and *A Clockwork Orange* (Stanley Kubrick). And belated additions included *Language of Love* (Torgny Wickman, 1969; on the British release history, see Smith 2018), *Last Tango in Paris* (Bernardo Bertolucci, 1972), *La Grande Bouffe* (Marco Ferreri, 1973) and *The Exorcist* (William Friedkin, 1973). NVALA members would sometimes have to endure these films, as part of waging a media campaign against them – which was no small hardship; even John Fraser, for his study *Violence in the Arts*, confesses that *The Devils* would have been too much for him, and so he 'could not bring' himself to view it (Fraser 1974: 179). A further strategy was seeking divine intervention directly. Longford, and Festival of Light and Salvation Army members, prayed synchronously about the Greater London Council considering offering certification to Jess Franco's *How to Seduce a Virgin* (1974), once the BBFC had declined to do so. The film was passed, on a vote of 44 to 36; see Thrower with Grainger 2015: 27.

It seems conceivable that the 1971 films were targeted because they marked the ending of the relatively liberal period of the BBFC under Trevelyan, and the start of his successor Stephen Murphy as Secretary of the Board, on 1 July 1971. Trevelyan, profiled in the *Daily Mirror* in 1970, had clearly felt his time with the BBFC was over, and the task completed – and that a bureaucratic process alone remained, around determining boundaries of certificates: 'Already he knows there's little you can keep from adults in the sexy, swinging Seventies. His principal role is defending children against [the] drugs, violence and sexual brutality that cash-happy producers are longing to put their way' (Malone 1970: 12). And a two-tier certification system was put into operation, relieving the BBFC of absolute judgement: some films blocked by the BBFC, such as nominal sex education films ('white coaters'), were released anyhow on the approval of local councils – which nonetheless, with the right pressure applied, might result in police raids on the cinemas.[6] In the event, Trevelyan's belief in a diminished censor's brief turned out to be ill-founded. Of Murphy's first months in office, Trevelyan later recalled, post-Festival of Light:

I left him with a problem by having, with Lord Harlech's approval, issued an 'X' certificate for a somewhat modified version of Ken Russell's film The Devils ... My successor soon had another serious problem. The film Straw Dogs, *which the Board passed, was violently attacked ... It was bad luck for Stephen Murphy that very soon after this film the Board had to make a decision on* A Clockwork Orange. *(Trevelyan 1977: 217).*[7]

By 11 March 1972, calls were made in the press for Murphy to resign (ibid.: 219–20). Meanwhile, Kubrick himself had withdrawn *A Clockwork Orange* from circulation in the UK, for reasons that remain obscure but are generally understood to have been around threats made to himself and his family, further to the continued tabloid coverage of supposed copycat violence (see Krämer 2011: 117–19).

Other common targets included hippies, trendy clerics in the Church of England, youth gang violence against pensioners, recreational drug use, and sex education. The documentary *Growing Up* (Arnold L. Miller, 1969/1971), conceived and narrated by the sexologist Martin Cole, and which discussed and showed male and female masturbation, was a particular rallying-point as it brought together education and sex on film. It was 'a rotten film' for Whitehouse, 'which makes children no more than animals' (quoted in Caulfield 1975: 118), and that was still a concern a decade later, as identified early on in the Report of the Committee on Obscenity and Film Censorship (Williams 1979: 3).[8]

NVALA archival material contains some illuminating documents with respect to their operations, centred on Cole, and around at least one screening of *Growing Up*, which was at Milham Ford School, in Oxford, in the summer of 1976. The screening was at the behest of a young science teacher (with the film borrowed from their spouse), in a lab classroom with the blinds lowered, to the amazement of the girls present (including the school's head girl), who were perched on high stools throughout. In part this was arranged for the specific benefit of some of the girls, who were perceived to be naive and vulnerable. The screening is noted in a letter from the then secretary of state for education, Fred Mulley, to Mary Whitehouse, who was soon agitating for the removal of the headmistress – via an orchestrated letter-writing campaign, and direct interference in the school governance, via an 'insider'.[9] But the actual first alert was raised via a complaint, originally from Plymouth Brethren parents of pupils, and relayed via others, first to the headmistress (who took a dim view of the complainants), and then as discussed between the headmistress and school governors, to whom she conveyed her dim view. The insider was a NVALA member or sympathiser who, rather than going through standard procedures, simply sought to bring about change via external NVALA pressure. This was a campaign of alarmist letters to local newspapers, which included elements of public naming-and-shaming. The resultant NVALA campaign failed, and has long since been forgotten.

An eleven-page letter from NVALA, dated 11 May, but without a year – and seemingly not by Whitehouse, as she has edited the text – may well be in connection with this Milham Ford screening, as *Growing Up* was seemingly very rarely screened at schools (and NVALA have archived the letter with correspondence around the screening). The letter responds to a teenage girl, who has seemingly written to say that she has read an article of Cole's. Cole, the letter replies, 'has no qualifications for writing on the subject of sex education for the young, other than a relentless enthusiasm. And judging by what he has written, it is a thoroughly unhealthy enthusiasm at that'. Other, and very explicit and bullying, advice follows: her feelings for one female teacher do not make her a lesbian, and 'this is something you must note carefully – you could, by constantly masturbating, ruin your chances of a happy sex life in the years to come'; 'oral sex is officially classed as a perversion. It is unnatural, unclean and unhealthy'.[10]

Cole appears again and again in the context of information compiled for NVALA: an internal document, 'Dr Martin Cole film', marked 'private and confidential', drawing information from the *Daily Telegraph* and *Men Only*. Cole had recently founded the Birmingham-based Institute for Sex Education and Research (and possibly *Growing Up* was then back in circulation for the Milham screening via the institute). The report picks up on a *News of the World* article that Cole was working with Mariella Novotny (whose novel *King's Road* is noted above), to create a bank of pornographic films, either self-produced, or a library: 'The combination of Cole and Novotny may mean that the communist movement in this country will be actively working to break down the present legal framework [*sic*] even that of common law ... The communists would see Cole as a vehicle for cracking the law. If this is so, what might be the means of achieving this?'[11] The document speculates the pornography will masquerade as sex education, and around matters of mental health, and be presented as helping in 'the repression of certain types of crime', and any voices raised in dissent will be challenged publicly through a 'campaign by left-wing agencies in the media'. So any legal challenges to Cole's initiative will fail on the back of befuddled public opinion – 'so opening the way to a flood of blue movies and sex parlours across the country'. Additional

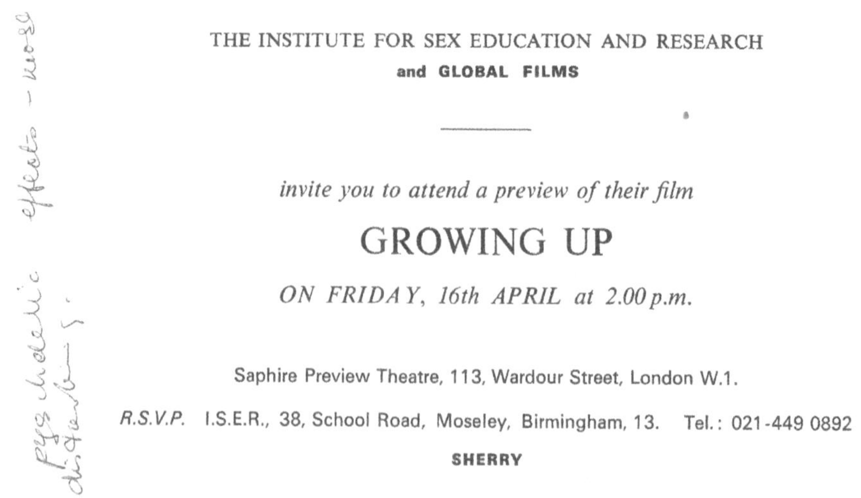

THE INSTITUTE FOR SEX EDUCATION AND RESEARCH

and **GLOBAL FILMS**

————————

invite you to attend a preview of their film

GROWING UP

ON FRIDAY, *16th APRIL at 2.00 p.m.*

Saphire Preview Theatre, 113, Wardour Street, London W.1.

R.S.V.P.   I.S.E.R., 38, School Road, Moseley, Birmingham, 13.   Tel.: 021-449 0892

SHERRY

Illustration 2.1 RSVP to an invitation to a screening of *Growing Up* (Arnold L. Miller (1969/1971): onscreen masturbation, followed by sherry. Notation by the National Viewers' and Listeners' Association (unknown hand): 'Psychedelic effects – most disturbing'. Invite from 1971. Courtesy of the National Viewers' and Listeners' Association Collection. Special Collections, Albert Sloman Library, University of Essex.

films were in fact made, such as *Sexual Intercourse* (1973) and *Impotence and Premature Ejaculation* (1975), both directed by Cole, in collaboration with the artist Trevor Denning.

It was in the field of education (or, more generally, the gatekeeping of culture to which children may be exposed) that permissiveness, as related directly to the theme of sex, was best configured as damaging.[12] Elizabeth Manners, headmistress of Felixstowe College, and content with her description as the 'educational Mary Whitehouse' (Manners 1971: 5) assembled these concerns for *The Vulnerable Generation*. The argument advanced in this book is that an increasingly debased popular culture for the young was a bridge to student militancy, so that Marxism itself was being operationalised as a pick-up technique – something to which Manners had also been subjected, albeit with the seducer rebuffed: 'I can still see the utter astonishment on the face of my would-be lover when I answered him with the rest of the [Engels] quotation, conveniently ignored by those who would cite Communist scripture to their purpose' (ibid.: 111). Manners relates the maintenance of innocence to a slower music tempo, discussed in relation to Rolf Harris's 1969 cover of 'Two Little Boys' and Simon and Garfunkel's 'Bridge Over Troubled Waters' (1970), along with Ken Dodd and Val Doonican. This is preferable to (and would ultimately be more profitable than) 'the frenzied jungle beat of *Top of the Pops*': 'Let us for goodness' sake – and I use the word advisedly – rescue sex both from the gutter of commercial exploitation through which it has been dragged and from the plane of exhibitionism, even status-symbol, where it now sometimes rests' (111). *Top of the Pops* is later referred to as 'sedulous anti-culture' (179). The solution to our 'now reaping the bitter harvest of the permissive society' is given in her address to the Felixstowe Rotary Club (5 March 1970): 'It has ten letters: D-I-S-C-I-P-L-I-N-E – discipline' (205). For Rhodes Boyson, that bitter harvest included eroding an absolutist sense of right and wrong, so confounding the master/pupil relationship. He recalled a meeting with respect to a boy he had suspended as headmaster at Highbury Grove school (therefore, between 1967 and 1974):

> I was then put under pressure to bring him back in the school, which I refused. I was then persuaded that there would have to be a full conference in the school about him, and I went over with the boy's housemaster to one of the house rooms, where there were numerous officials, school attendance officers, psychologists, social workers... all sitting round with the boy and his parents in attendance. The Chairman started the meeting by saying we were all guilty. He got no further, since I stood up and said to my housemaster, 'Since you and I are not guilty at all, we are in the wrong meeting', and we left the meeting. It was never reconvened, nor did the boy come back to my school. (Boyson 1996: 68)

Condemnations such as those by Manners sought to prompt or prime organs of the state to begin to exert control over the sexual anarchy. And, tellingly, the two most notable show trials that resulted were around the idea of children exposed to permissiveness: the first concerning the May 1970 'Schoolkids' issue of the underground magazine *Oz*; and the second, the 1971 attempted publication of a translation of the 1969 Danish guide for schoolchildren, *The Little Red Schoolbook*, which also involved Elizabeth Manners as an expert witness in the trial that followed (see Sutherland 1982: 111–26; Travis 1999; Travis 2001: 248–54, Carlin 2007: 132–44; Limond 2012). The intervention of Lord Longford can be seen in this context: a substantive investigation into pornography, even to the extent of propelling the Lord into Danish sex clubs – which can be read either as an attempt to co-opt and so keep a lid on the opponents of the Permissive Society, and/or to channel their concerns into a parliamentary programme of action (Longford, as a socialist Labour peer, would have had a certain function in these respects). This investigation and report would, presumably, seek to correct the liberalism of the Church of England's own turn-of-the-decade report, Obscene Publications: Law and Practice (Board for Social Responsibility 1970). Both these reports would discuss the Danish culture of pornography, but Longford's would draw on first-hand encounters of pornographic culture, at home and abroad – with contributing authors venturing 'behind enemy lines'. Eventual financial backing was secured for Longford from the tobacco industry (see Stanford 2003: 317). These reports can be taken as formal porn reports #2 (General Synod) and #3 (Longford). In this timeline, report #1, *The Obscenity Laws*, was drawn up by the Arts Council of Great Britain and published in 1969, considering the usual touchstones (Lawrence, *Last Exit to Brooklyn*), taking 'the so-called permissive society' as read, considering the example of Denmark, and including, in an appendix, a draft bill to repeal the Obscene Publications Acts of 1959 and 1964 (Arts Council 1969: 33, 57, and 38–41 respectively).[13] This report had a North American counterpart which, in its perceived liberalism, was a call to arms for Christian conservatives too: the 1970 Presidential Commission Report on Obscenity and Pornography. Report #4 seems to have attempted to right Longford's with a view to coming legislation – this was the government's own Report of the Committee on Obscenity and Film Censorship (Williams 1979).[14] Whitehouse and Holbrook, as well as Court (1980), undoubtedly felt their writing also constituted reports, although there was a formal NVALA publication directly attacking Williams too, *Pornography: A Matter of Taste?* (Anon circa 1979/80): that the Williams Committee report 'will turn Britain into a dumping ground for continental pornography', including approving bestiality material (2), and demanding, presumably pre-emptively, that necrophiliac material is immediately outlawed (11). Various marginal groupings, such as the Society of Conservative Lawyers, also issued publications, which are indexed in Williams (1979: 245–49), and to this list, I will add *Gay Left*'s own overview (Blachford 1978: 16–20). This canon of writing might also include the debate on pornography in the House of Lords (HL Deb 1971), published in Hansard, Trevelyan's autobiography (1977), which was first published in 1973, and Simpson's later reflections on the experience of the Williams committee report (1983).

Longford's report was unusual in that it was the less vexed by the potential dangers of catching works of literary merit in the crossfire; the Church of England fretted about John Cleland's *Fanny Hill*, James Joyce's *Ulysses*, and *Lady Chatterley's Lover* and *Last Exit to Brooklyn* at relative length. But it was quite clear, as noted above, that 'material that is plainly pornography' is to be 'entirely prohibited' (Board for Social Responsibility 1970: 15).

One of the first steps in advancing the counter-attack on the Permissive Society seems to have been around identifying, in *The Little Red Schoolbook* and then beyond, the external moral threat posed by Scandinavia. *The Little Red Schoolbook* would have been an obvious target for the anti-permissives; on pornography: 'Porn is a harmless pleasure if it isn't taken seriously ... you may get some good ideas from it and you may find something that looks interesting and you haven't tried before' (Hansen and Jensen 2014: 114), and with the suggestion of alleviating boredom in school lessons with pornographic magazines (see Moorhead 2014). But around the matter of paedophilia, evidence for the prosecution was present too: for Hansen and Jensen, '[i]n the old days people used to talk about "dirty old men". Children were told they were dangerous. This is very rarely true. They're just men who have nobody to sleep with' (111).[15] And the Petronius guide to 'underground' London outlines the suggestion of starting a pop star fan club in order to access young fans: that 'happy hunting ground' where, '[w]ho knows, you may even deflect [fan club members'] passion from their idol to yourself, and at least give them more than an autograph ... there are the schools – comprehensive or not. Here you are on your own. And watch out – or you may end up doing a stretch' (Petronius 1969: 3, 98–99). The perception of youth and youth culture had gone from merely hanging around and synchronised dancing (as with Michael Winner's Billy Fury musical of 1962, *Play It Cool*), to hanging around in anticipation of sexual adventure. Even Big Ben is seemingly converted into a phallus in the opening pages of Frank Habicht's 1969 collection of photographs, *Young London: Permissive Paradise*.

The Continental Threat

Swedish and Danish liberalisation, and the far-reaching moves against censorship in these countries at this time, and Amsterdam's red light district and related sex culture, were posited as a fate that awaited suburban Britain – and presumably with Soho as the beachhead.[16] Whitehouse openly voiced this fear: 'Do you think the Danish situation might develop here?' (1972: 100). The authors of the Longford and then Williams reports both visited, and wrote about, the Danish experience. And, indeed, pornography was being smuggled in from Denmark, via refrigerated trucks full of Danish bacon (Cox, Shirley and Short 1977: 166), and Amsterdam-based Italian Lasse Braun shot hardcore loops in the UK, and in UK settings. A number of these were compiled into *Sex-Maniacs* by Gerd Wasmund, with a 1977 director credit given to Mike Hunter, which opens with shots of a Rolls Royce, on an erotic assignment, skimming past Buckingham Palace, the Houses of Parliament and Trafalgar Square.[17] The intercutting between London scenes and hardcore sex sequences (seemingly with British performers, such as John English) could be said in this context to illustrate exactly the fear that Danish liberalism would be exerted through European integration. One of the films compiled, first released as *English School Girl* (1977), even films pupils exiting their school, from a predatory over-the-road position, before shifting to sex, including urophilia, seemingly (but quite clearly not) with such subjects. Such UK-shot but Continent-released pornography illustrated that a scalable intensity existed in UK hardcore film production; something like *No Morals* (director unknown; released by Tabu Films in 1979 in West Germany), also with John English, is a relentless orgy – albeit with the classic trope of the husband returning from work and horrified as he surveys the scene (which seems to include both his wife and two daughters). Or, presumably even worse, Braun's *Gurken Club* (possibly late 1970s) shows continental businessmen visiting London – taking a taxi from Trafalgar Square to the titular brothel, which includes cucumber use as part of the orgies that ensue – as Britain offers even more depravity than the mainland.

Erotic and pornographic film-makers, and Paul Raymond in particular, played up to this sense too, of Continental Europe as enabler of sexual freedoms – and hence the racy magazine *Continental Film Review*, and the ubiquity of the 'Swedish model' or 'French au pair' or 'Danish student' as a type; in softcore: the Italian model of *Her Private Hell* (Norman J. Warren, 1968), the West Germany au pair in *Secrets of a Door-to-Door Salesman* (Wolf Rilla, 1973), the Swiss au pair in *Layout for 5 Models* (John Gaudioz, 1972), and the Chinese au pair in *Au Pair Girls* (Val Guest, 1972). But the continental myth is present way before: the prostitution ring of *The Flesh is Weak* (Don Chaffey, 1957) seems to consist of Soho-based Italians, and Lawrence's young Lady Chatterley 'had been sent to Dresden at the age of fifteen, for music among other things', where, with friends at 18, '[t]he young men with whom they talked to passionately and sang so lustily and camped under the trees in such freedom wanted, of course, the love connection' (Lawrence 1960: 6, 7). Thus she gained a pre-marriage taste for the sexual encounter that would not then confine itself exclusively to her husband, once he was war-wounded and impotent. In terms of British exploitation film, even as far back as *Nudes of the World* (Miller, 1961), the progressive naturalists are seen to pit their internationalism (in that naturalism is shared by different nationalities, and the film's theme song is 'Ooh la la'), against a Little Englander mentality, in the figure of the postmistress, who wishes to close down the nudist colony. *That Kind of Girl* (Gerry O'Hara, 1963) effectively dramatizes the myth that any continental European girl represents an imminent sexual threat to young British men. This time a sexually transmitted disease-carrying promiscuous blonde au pair endangers the pending marriage of a lower-middle class British couple; he is tempted away, and she, in turn, is pushed into further premarital sexual activity with him in order to counter the au pair's offer (the relationship is only fully restored once the au pair has been repatriated). Some years on, with the young man now freer to take advantage, for *Grand Slam* (Hefin, 1978), a comedy of difference then comes to the fore with the jarring juxtaposition of sex with an *Emmanuelle*-like Parisian stripper 'interrupted' (via a leaking sound bridge) by the young man's father snapping him out of his continental recollections because of changing traffic lights on the rainy streets of a Welsh village through which they are driving a hearse.

When Wayland Young notes, for his 1965 'state of the nation' survey of love and sex, that '[i]n England, almost everything to do with sex has always had a foreign name' (271), one is prompted, in the light of the positions of both White-house and Raymond, to ask whether sexual intercourse itself is considered a foreign tendency – or, at least, and perhaps even worse, un-British. But ever further fears seem to arise from a distrust of the project of European integration on the part of Whitehouse – which was to become a reality in 1973 with British membership of the European Community and the Common Market. Even continental cuisine may have been an issue. Elizabeth David's *Italian Food* threatened to eradicate the carbohydrate stodginess of the British post-war diet (23), isolating, for David, the 'English housewives' who, 'a school of writers claim',

are weak in the head and must not be exposed to the truth about the cooking of other countries: must not be shocked by the idea of making a yeast dough, cleaning an ink-fish, adding nutritive value to a soup with olive oil, cutting the breast off a raw chicken in order to fry it in butter rather than buying a packet of something called 'chicken parts' from the deep-freeze and cooking them in a cheap fat or tasteless oil substitute.

If I believed that English women really needed this kind of protection – censorship it almost amounts to – I would have packed in cookery writing long ago. (David 1966: 25)

For David, in this Introduction to the 1963 Penguin edition of her book, it seems almost sensuousness itself, and finger-encounters with soft flesh, that are wrongly held to be an anathema to the British housewife – waiting to be liberated by the experiences and flavours of the Continent. And where are so many of the Italian ingredients to be found? In the groceries and delis of Soho.

Whitehouse, as a lower-middle-class nonconformist, who would have come of age in the years between the wars, may have harboured a fear of both European communism or (and as refracted particularly in the UK) socialism of the 1930s, and continental (or even British or Irish) Catholicism. The latter might even have harked back to the ostracization of Catholic converts in the 1800s – for Mercer, an occurrence to

appal relatives, friends, colleagues and former teachers ... [c]onversion seemed to fly in the face of loyalties to school, university, and even to country. Catholics were linked in the popular mind with disloyalty to England, with foreigners, particularly in Latin countries, with popular superstitions, or with Irish immigration ... with notions that Catholicism was associated with priestly domination, financial corruptions and sexual deviance. (Mercer 2016: 199–200)

Christopher Hollis's 1935 *The Church & the Modern Age*, from a quite different social vantage point to Whitehouse's – Hollis was at Eton, Oxford with Evelyn Waugh, and then teaching history at Stonyhurst College – had grappled with just these dynamics too. Hollis spends time distancing socialism from Catholicism, on theological grounds, in order to anticipate modern Catholicism's non-partisan embrace of the modern world (the legacy of Pope Leo XIII, particularly the 1891 encyclical *Rerum Novarum*), seemingly promising the conversion of the United Kingdom, in turn, as part of a European project – ushered in by trade.

Whitehouse devotes entire chapters to Denmark in *Whatever Happened to Sex?* ('The Danish Myth'; 1978: 158–78) and *Who Does She Think She Is?* ('Something

Rotten...?'; 1972: 95–102) – a culture that Holbrook sees (and, for context, as way worse than the 'perversion' of lesbianism; 1972d: 94) in terms of group sex and bestiality, in his *Sex and Dehumanization*. This may be 'psychopathological and perverted' but it is nonetheless the logical outcome of liberal society (ibid.: 20, 21), and an outcome that then first stuns and then immunises attendees to its depravities (ibid.: 183).

It is striking that North America was rarely a target – not least because much of its permissive cinema in this period seemed to be more organised around an ideological programme for a freer society, and integrated into new lifestyles, and this included a renaissance in gay pornography too (see Schaefer 2014; Conkelton and Newland 2014; Halligan and Wilson 2015; Bronstein and Strub 2018). It seems very possible then that Atlanticism rather than any European impulse steered the thrust of the British anti-permissives. Whitehouse, writing to then Prime Minister Edward Heath in August 1971, and selecting the grounds of her argument along the lines of Heath's preparations for economic union with Continental Europe, was quite concise. The threat was an influx of West German pornography, a 'moral pollution' potentially destabilising the axis of the European Union:

> *We stand on the threshold of entry into the Common Market. The first essential for its success is the establishment and maintenance of respect and trust between member countries. If Britain is flooded by the effluent of a highly organised German porn industry, then the whole basis of cooperation between our two countries could become soured and bitter. (Quoted in Thompson 2013: 277)*

Elsewhere, Whitehouse had speculated that the ever-present vitality-sapping pornography was reducing Denmark's males to a state of defenceless sexual exhaustion. In the context of the Cold War, it was clear who was to benefit from such a collectively dissolute nation: the Soviet Union. She finds scraps of evidence to support this supposed political strategy on the part of the enemy: the May 1919 'Communist Rules for Revolution' – without citation here, but now held to be a faked document (Whitehouse 1978: 106; see also Durham 1991: 170–71); the dramatic increase in Soviet naval activity around Denmark since 1960 (Whitehouse 1978: 107); the inability of liberals to take the idea of far-left infiltration seriously (ibid.: 241); a document from the Italian Communist Party (PCI) on the need for more sexually explicit films (ibid.: 240–41); and similar observations from former

FBI agent W. Cleon Skousen in his 1958 book *The Naked Communist* – that pornography, and sexual liberalism in general (pro-abortion, pro-divorce, pro-homosexuality, etc.) weakens the West. The latter idea resulted in the 1979 NVALA leaflets on 'Current Communist Goals' (see Durham 1991: 169), *Pornography: A Matter of Taste?* which reiterates the same argument (Anon circa 1979/80: 9), and a transcription of a speech by Count Nikolai Tolstoy, *Politics and Pornography*, exposing Stalin's secret bedside stash of porn (Tolstoy 1981: 4). Whitehouse also seems to have accused the Front for the Liberation of Mozambique of flooding South Africa with pornography – presumably to weaken the Apartheid regime – in her testimony to the 1979 parliamentary committee on Obscenity and Film Censorship (Williams 1979: 94).[18]

Following up just one of these sources sheds further light. The PCI document referenced by Whitehouse (1978: 240–41) is given as quoted in a letter to the *Sunday Times* of 9 August 1970. The letter itself is from the Dowager Lady Jane Birdwood, and reproduces comment from a (supposedly) PCI journal called *Cinema Documents* (with no further citation information), which welcomes the 'downright scandalous', and claims that pornography is 'entirely free of the restrictions of ordinary moral rules', so that the makers of such films 'eat away at the very roots of bourgeois society' (Birdwood 1970: 7). This is not quite a directly causal matter, with pornography as strategically weaponised in the overthrow of the West, as NVALA would have it, but standard countercultural exaltations of perceived anti-bourgeois cultural discourse of this time. Birdwood herself was a Whitehouse acolyte: she established the London branch of NVALA, was involved in initiating legal action against *Oh! Calcutta!* (walking straight from a performance in the Roundhouse to Kentish Town police station), and was described in one obituary as '[o]ne of Britain's most prolific racist and anti-semitic propagandists ... [who] bridged the respectable right of the Conservative Party and the street Nazis of the NF and BNP [National Front and British National Party, and her] racism and anti-semitism attracted a layer of wealthy right-wingers who would not have dared associate themselves with openly Nazi groups' (Lowles 2000: 17, 21). Her work for NVALA included speaking at a 1971 rally further to a screening, claimed to be for children, of *Growing Up* – a rally advertised, with appalling taste, as showing opposition to what would be a 'veritable moral gas chamber for six hundred of London's children'. Her co-speaker, Louise Eickhoff, was also an NVALA associate – a consultant child psychiatrist and long-term campaigner against sex education from a clinical anti-permissive quarter, cited approvingly for

COME
TO THE
CAXTON HALL

(WESTMINSTER)

7.30 p.m. Wednesday
6th October 1971

A MEETING TO PROTEST AGAINST THE
SHOWING TO 600 CHILDREN IN LONDON
ON SUNDAY 10TH OCTOBER
OF DR. COLE'S FILM "GROWING UP"

SPEAKERS INCLUDE

LOUISE F.W. EICKHOFF. M.D. D.P.H.

Consultant Child Psychiatrist, Selly Oak Hospital, Birmingham.

THE DOWAGER LADY BIRDWOOD

If this showing is allowed to take place, the Conway Hall, on this Sabbath Day, is likely to become a veritable moral gas chamber for six hundred of London's children. All parents, whether apprehensive about their own children or not, should treat this as a matter of grave concern and take the opportunity afforded by the meeting of registering their protest, remembering the words of Christ. "Whosoever shall offend one of these little ones that believe in me, it is better for him that a millstone were hanged about his neck, and he were cast into the sea". They will also have the opportunity of reviewing the whole subject of sex education.

Illustration 2.2 Poster: Anti-permissive rally against a screening of *Growing Up*. Courtesy of the National Viewers' and Listeners' Association Collection. Special Collections, Albert Sloman Library, University of Essex.

this as one of the witnesses of the Longford Report (Longford Committee 1972: 229–30). For example: Eickhoff blamed sex education for an 'anxiety state' giving rise to accusations of sexual assault from a 10-year-old boy at boarding school, which she claims (after examining the boy) to have been unfounded. And, later, that sex education (which is little better than pornographic film-watching) itself leads to pregnancy in girls as young as 12 on a 'sex-seeking path', with contraception then offered post-abortion, giving rise to 'an ever-greater avidity on their promiscuous paths', with 'suitable training' the only solution (Eickhoff 1967: 864–65; and 1975: 99–100 respectively).

Whitehouse fretted over and/or rehashed this Communist plot angle in her various books across decades (see, for example, Whitehouse 1972: 112; 1986: 104–5; 1994: 191–92). A general position seems to have been that British intellectual culture itself was a 'Marxist revolutionary industry', as reported or surmised by Caulfield (1975: 2; see also 140). Tracey and Morrison also note an additional position, which seems not to have been given much public exposure by NVALA in the 1970s, but can also be understood in relation to the threat of communism: that the depiction of violence potentially turns viewers into pacifists, and so less likely to support military action abroad (Tracey and Morrison 1979: 84–86). So pornography joins pacifism in this respect: 'The answer to pacifism lies, as it always has, in whether you believe in peace at any price, even the price of freedom from godless dictatorship within our own country' (quoted in ibid.: 86).

What is not considered by Whitehouse (but is touched on by Birdwood), and could have been drawn from a closer analysis of the pornography culture of Scandinavia and the Netherlands, is the revolutionary/anarchic political aspirations of the 'sexual underground' (Gert Hekma's term; Hekma 2013), itself as allied to Freud, Marx, Reich and Marcuse, and the experience of free love. Braun's *Prostitution Call Girl* (1971), for example, with a vaguely bisexual threesome (two males and 'Tiffany'), offers both a narrative and aesthetic shift beyond the standard couple interaction – illustrating multi-climactic sexual possibilities beyond the one individual termination point more typical of British porn. Braun's loops, from a pedagogical, 'happening' position, may have actually lived up to the anti-permissive fears.

This position, from which the free Permissive Society was understood to critique and exorcise, eventually, all bourgeois precepts, rules and practices, was exactly what – in their hysteria – figures like Whitehouse and Holbrook feared and warned against: permissiveness as a gateway to non-capitalist, if not fully communist, arrangements. This foray into radical politics might have offered some comfort to Whitehouse, both in terms of more correctly identifying anti-bourgeois sentiments as the root rather than Communism, as the permissive project was understood to have stalled and then degenerated. The sexual revolution was 'partial, and being more about money than pleasure', so that the 'sex industry now sought profits while disregarding the real desires of people' as '[s]exuality was used for exploitation' (Hekma 2013: 59). And, indeed, the UK was particular in its

Illustration 2.3 Proposed radical import of Continental pornography: Lasse Braun's harem in 8-mm: 'I like sex. Pornography is beautiful'. Photograph by the author.

capitalisation on an entirely depoliticised heterosexual pornographic imagining on the other side of this moment – as apparent in the films of John Lindsay, in which sexual access and exploitation are considered as one (as discussed below). Pornography in this respect was calibrated as pure entertainment, exactly akin to Whitehouse's general position on most broadcast media – that it should delight and move, as per her comments on *Jim'll Fix It*. An engagement with this 'sexual underground', and indeed with some sociological and academic framing, was only belatedly mounted by Whitehouse's associate John H. Court, for *Pornography: A Christian Critique* in 1980. Court cannily reads into Longford's critique a principled position against objectification (Court 1980: 10), as understood by feminists too (11), and engages with the co-opted theorists of sexual liberation (such as Reich and Marcuse) – as if the experience of the university debates of the 1970s has begun to impinge on the Whitehouse mindset, only to then collapse into conspiracy theory. Thus homosexual pornography is a vanguard to societal acceptance of such biblically prohibited practices (55); and with homosexuality and paedophilia closely associated in Court's discussion, and with children who are victims of the latter unable to turn to the police for fear of murder (55–56; it is not clear from whom: either homosexuals, paedophiles or the authorities themselves); pornography is, again, seen as communist entryism (58–59). But even Court, let alone Whitehouse et al., is far from the mark. Some radical groupings around homosexual then-subcultures had no designs on societal acceptance in this way, but on remaking society per se – as in the experience of the gay/queer Brixton squatting scene of the 1970s, or radical Italian thought around gay liberation from Mario Mieli, which was partly forged in London gay activist circles too, and sought to rethink and energise the relationship between homosexuality and radical feminism (see Cook 2011, and Mieli [1977] 2018: 208–53, respectively). The anti-permissives, in their unwavering fixations on the poles of moralism and assumed Victorian values, remained blind to such emergent groupings. This left any Whitehouse mindset ill-prepared to comprehend the coming AIDs crisis with, for many looking on, anything approaching Christian values (as Daniel Berrigan SJ would attest from a quite different Christian position; 1989) and, thereafter, ushering in decades of crises for the various Christian denominations unwilling to countenance practising homosexuals in their flock or, openly at least, in their leadership. The long legacy of wider influence on Anglican thought was one of exclusion; for Robinson-Brown, an institution of 'sexless Christianity', so that '[t]he Church becomes a safe haven, then, for those who are fundamentally anti-body, anti-desire and anti-sex', as arraigned against communities of non-white, non-heterosexual 'bodies [who] are regularly shunned and eluded' (Robinson-Brown 2021: 6).[19]

Thus, in this NVALA scenario, Denmark and Sweden are presented as wild, communalist pornographic frontiers beyond the reach of British law – exactly as figuring, ironically, in the imagination of the supposed readers writing letters to *Forum* magazine:

- *I am likely to visit Denmark this year and while there I might be tempted to purchase porno films, magazines etc. to bring back home. Would I be committing an offence by bringing back this sort of thing?*
- *I was brought up in Sweden in a family that even by Swedish standards was liberal for its time.*
- *I went to Denmark last summer for an archaeological dig, and entered a different world which made me dissatisfied with my own.*
- *In the bar of my hotel last evening I got talking to a Dane of about my age (I'm in my late 20s), and after chatting for a while he asked me outright if I'd be interested in being photographed for the porn market.*
  (Hooper [1973] 1980: 22, 220, 242, 273)

And Denmark was mythologised into the imaginings of the aroused male – as with Harrison Marks's *The Danish Maid* (year unknown; Maximus Films), with its dream of sex with the titular character thrown into humorous relief when a teddy boy is awakened by a knock on the front door of his flat, to discover that the maid he has requested is so British (rather than Danish) and unsexy (in the context of the times) that she is, in fact, a camp man in drag.

Thus Lauret, for his book *The Danish Sex Fairs* (which was translated and published in English in 1970), conducted an experiment of sorts: to track items of mail he sent from Denmark to France, some containing Danish pornography, and some with only the padding that would tantalisingly suggest 'documents' from Denmark.[20] The high percentage of mail then 'lost in the post' prompts him to observe, slanderously: 'Has the association Denmark = pornography taken root in [the postman's] repressed psyche? The envelope could be surreptitiously slipped in a pocket, its contents gloated over during the next strike' (Lauret 1970: 64).

The central concerns in anti-permissive commentaries are couched in terms of an assault on something understood along the lines of '[t]he psychic health of the community' (Holbrook 1972c: 197), leading to 'psychic impotence and loss of creative power in our dealings with reality [so that] the prevalent cult of dissociated sex is thus a threat to the *imagination*' (Holbrook 1972d: 8; Holbrook's italics). Such concerns are not dissimilar to Victorian warnings to youth regarding the consequences of the sin of self-pleasure. And the commentaries seem to dare literally to go to the places that Whitehouse (and her various books) would not venture: as with the fieldwork of Longford's witnesses, or in David Holbrook's *The

Pseudo-Revolution: A Critical Study of Extremist 'Liberation' in Sex ('[a]t one point in the preparation of this book I went to see a film called *The Sin Seekers* at a Cine Club in London'; Holbrook 1972c: 14).[21] Holbrook also provides sketchy sex advice to counter the prevalence of debased permissive tendencies – sex with Holbrook would incorporate a foundation of an 'imaginative experience [achieved] by reading, say, Jane Austen or Donne' (Holbrook 1972a: 9). Thus the psychological and biological is reconnected, overcoming or dodging the '[d]ehumanisation' which 'must inevitably follow if we attempt to divide whatever we mean by "sex"' from a *'meaningful relationship'* (1972d: 7; Holbrook's italics) – as is the case with hedonistic freedom, and as is the entire basis of the production and consumption of pornography. But his advice would be potentially undone by the fake orgasm, as his validation of his unfashionable preference to 'make love joyfully' arises to an extent, he claims, from a reading of the female's reactions (1972a: 9). All this attempted straitening or curtailing of sexual experience or preferences could be read, pace Reich's concern with 'the imposition of antisexual morality' (Reich and Baxandall 1972: 162), entirely in relation to the 'sexually crippled and therefore decent petty-bourgeois housewives capable of following the dictates of morality and with the sexually disturbed men who, with relative ease, are able to suffer monogamy' where *'the impairment of genital sexuality creates the conditions for the acceptance of marriage'* (ibid.: 164; Reich's italics); that is, that the propagation of sexual moralism is the condition of denial of sexual dysfunctionality.

Fieldwork excursions into darkest Soho are undertaken by Holbrook, and Whitehouse's and Longford's proxies and witnesses, and by Longford himself, and the cultural artefacts then pored over and discussed at length.[22] In Holbrook's case, the details are such that his *Case Against Pornography* begins to read as a compendium of erotic writing in its first few chapters. But pornography is seen to have spread to all walks of life, rather than be contained in Soho, and so has become potentially accessible to all – '[o]n my local railway bookstall can be seen the cover of a book showing a number of naked people performing some witchcraft ritual, and this all seems, today, socially acceptable. Books on necrophilia etc. are to be found even in small town bookshops' (Holbrook 1972c: 143). This perspective is one in which the counterculture has become the official culture, and those who, like himself, would warn against the opportunists promoting a libertarian free-for-all have lost their traction with government, church and schools – where teachers are enthralled by the idea of allowing children autonomy (an autonomy promoted by *The Little Red Schoolbook*). Holbrook seems to have spoken from experience in this respect, as his obituary in the *Daily Telegraph* records:

> His [anti-pornography] views caused problems when, in 1971, he was appointed writer in residence for two years at the progressive Dartington Hall School. The staff, he recalled, resented his presence, 'not least when I found that libertarianism had progressed to outright decadence: the children were taking drugs and their sexual lives [had] fallen to the level of a thoroughly decadent sensualism. There was much drunkenness and the headmaster, a homosexual, was often absent, keeping an antique shop in Plymouth'. (Anon 2011)[23]

The four Holbrook books used here originated in this period (they were all published in 1972), one of which seems, cattily, to make a point of quoting the Dartington headmaster previous to the antique-dealing homosexual, so as to praise his cautious position on sex education (Holbrook 1972d: 203–4).

As the Danish exemplar figures so strongly, and as the hubris of the anti-permissives is so vague and ill-informed, it is perhaps reasonable to consider the full impact of extremes of sexual revolution at this point, as manifest in the films of Color Climax. Their paedophilic material can be considered as intended for a niche market. But this general paedophilic ambience is something I consider below in the films of David Hamilton, all of which were distributed quite legally in the UK, and therefore represent the most mainstream quarter of film-making discussed in this book. But the bestiality material may not necessarily also be squarely aligned to another niche market. And this material circulated illegally in the UK, seemingly from the early 1980s, with an underground of bootleg videotapes (apparently also sold in Soho), given a generic title of *Animal Farm*.

The tapes were probably different in content, but consisted of footage culled from Color Climax's bestiality films, such as *Horse Fuckers*, *Lady Dog*, *Dog Loving Lady*, *Dog Orgy*, *Horse Power*, *Horse Lovers*, *Animal Bizarre* and so on (no dates known), all of which featured Bodil Joensen. The dog in question was Joensen's beloved companion, Spot, whom she had nursed back to health, having collected him as a puppy from an animal hospital; she wore a locket with Spot's photo around her neck throughout her life. The *Animal Farm* tapes also included footage, presumably of a higher quality, from one the most notorious films of the early 1970s, *Bodil Joensen – en sommerdag juli 1970* [Bodil Joensen – 'A Summerday' July 1970], Shinkichi Tajiri and Ole Ege, 1970). This documentary captures the way, or suggests or presents a way, in which Joensen initiates her sexual relationships with her animals, and would seem to exist (as presented in the documentary) contentedly in this world – at least at the time of the film's making.[24] The proximity of the film-makers to the sexual action suggests an abandonment of any distanced, 'objective', framing – so that viewers find themselves in the midst of the events, and so are forced to find a position on them. At the same time, there is no revised Lawrencian sentiment of a stirring oneness with nature: the filth, the flies and the dirt on the barn floor, and on Bodil (in spite of what seems to be her natural film-star appearance), suggest a descent into the 'lower' order of nature, or a reversal of evolution. The film evidences a kind of total freedom: a revolutionary erotic-ecological occurrence of returning to live and love with the animals, even a proto-feminist separatism (as no men are needed). And this was presented then as one such far-flung erotic option at the time, along with paedophilia – both tendencies feature in the 1981 'Polysexuality' issue of *Semiotext(e)*, (Peraldi [1981] 1995: 'Animal Sex', 90–106; 'Child Sex', 108–34), amongst more relatively standard concerns, such as extreme BDSM practices. *Bodil Joensen 'A Summerday'* explains the traumatic biographical context for Joensen's retreat into the world of animal sexuality which, in part, also related to her profession of animal breeding. In this sense, while explicit, the film is not directly provocative in suggesting bestiality as an avant-garde sexual practice – but presumably, for Color Climax, it could be sold in this way, and for the derivative *Animal Farm* tapes, it would be taken as an endurance test experience, sometimes at parties (at the point at which domestic VCRs were becoming commonplace). But even at the time, *Bodil Joensen 'A Summerday'* seems to have refused to allow itself to be confined to a genre of erotica – as with the Commune films and orgiastic actions of Otto Muehl and associates. Both Joensen and Muehl wrong-footed the Wet Dreams organisation, with Tajiri writing in *Suck* that he regretted, in accepting a prize from their festival, that he had associated his film with the limitations of pornography (Tajiri 1973: 166), and the festival-goers actively intervened to stop a live Muehl happening, which was then retrospectively theorised in a number of ways by those involved (including Germaine Greer and Heathcote Williams), and categorised as 'the Limits of Obscenity'; see Levy 1973: 219–32.[25] Color Climax's bestiality, as well as female genital mutilation films, seem to have been more an attempt to indicate the no-limits potential of the genre – and that fascination will always find new ideas to fix upon or behold. Certainly, in truth, the genre in itself is one that rapidly expends its potential for fascination: there is only so much that can be seen in terms of close-ups of coupling, which all soon blur into one.

Two Obscure 'Danish' 8-mm Loops

As an addendum to this consideration of Denmark, it seems appropriate to now encounter, ahead of the central engagements with their makers, two films that resonate with this sense of the moral Danish danger, and evidence a kind of mythologisation of it, within the British pornographic mindset.

Both films are obscure in origin, with virtually all production information missing. But my European Common Market-type model, in selecting them, is straight import/ export. The first loop concerns a Danish intrusion into the UK: *The Danish Maid*, directed by Harrison Marks, perhaps at some point around 1964–66 (the film seems mid-point from late teddy boys to early hippies). The film, black and white and silent, is semi-hardcore, in the sense that the male arousal is quite clear and the sex seems unsimulated. My second loop concerns, I think, exporting a couple to Denmark: *Danish Surprise*, of unknown director (but it certainly seems like a John Lindsay loop, in terms of the choreography of the foursome, and the various complementary love-making positions adopted). The film is entirely hardcore, in colour, and with sound. This was released by Color Climax, with two dates associated with it: the 1970s, and 1980. An English-language title card suggests it had a UK release.

The Danish Maid concerns a man who hires a maid from an agency to clean his flat. She arrives, begins to clean the flat, revealing 'provocative' underwear beneath her coat to do so, then massages the man, who is now in his underpants, before they move to the bedroom for sex. But a knock at the door awakens the sleeping man – still, in fact, in his armchair – so that this sexual encounter is revealed to be a dream: the actual maid has arrived and who, like the agency receptionist who fielded his initial call, is a camp man in drag. The flat-dweller looks directly at the camera, sharing a look of amused exasperation with the viewer (this Marks-style twist is far from unique to this film). The Danish-ness of the maid here is translated directly into her being immediately sexually available – in stark contrast to the Britishness of the actual maid who is (within the context of the film) so undesirable that she is a 'he'. The agency is identified, via a title card, as Puff & Poof Domestic Services – We Aim to Please. This then is a pornographic version of *That Kind of Girl*: the appearance of an Eve-like Continental European in the UK, who then tempts the Adam-like British character into sin. Marks and the anti-permissives thus share a sense that 'they (the Danish) are not like us (the British)' – although for Marks this is entirely a benefit, whereas for the anti-permissives it is a detriment. The only other analytical reading that this loop can reasonably hold is that the

Danish manifestation is in an erotic dream: the Danish-ness is within the psyche of the male – his imagination is already eroticising (or infected by) a sense of difference and Continental promise. Had any of Longford's team seen this in a cinema club, they may have concluded that the film-makers joke and rejoice in the idea of temptation, with the soul only too ready to be corrupted.

Danish Surprise seems to concern one couple who meet another couple in a restaurant. Their wives soon approach each other's husbands, which then gives way to an extended foursome. (As typical for Lindsay, this is a simultaneous but mostly detached double-coupling – so avoiding a sense of male bisexuality.) There is little more to say of the film itself: the action is in one room, which itself seems unconvincing as a restaurant. But the dynamic is telling: a naive tourist couple (British?) presumably enticed into this spontaneous sexual experimentation with a 'local' (i.e. Danish) couple. And the restaurant itself, and the dress of all involved, suggests some sophistication. The 'surprise' then is the ease of this transition: the naive couple surprising themselves in (a) their rapid adaptation to this 'Continental' form of sexual freedom, once abroad, and (b) that the Danish couple engage in sex much as the tourist couple. This establishes a sense of a European middle class, with things to learn from each other, and similarities as the basis of this learning, and an enthusiasm for the entire exchange – the very integration of the European project that is met with distaste by the anti-permissives. Again, had a Longford investigator seen this, Matthew 5:30 may have come to mind (cutting off the hand that commits the sin is better than allowing the sin) – the soul as imperilled by its proximity to sinfulness, although there are no second thoughts evidenced around any such conundrum in the film itself. The issue is that both films are pure sin: they simply reproduce the offending acts in a moreish manner – or record this instance of sin, and the damned souls partaking. There is, in this, as per the creeping secularisation of the society of the 1970s, no mitigating frame of reference of moral transgression occurring; the films just are moral transgressions, although few films offer such a dramatization in itself. (Peter de Rome's US-shot *The Destroying Angel* of 1976 is an exception – with a Catholic priest surrendering to homosexual temptations, against the counsel of a guardian angel, who, at one point, joins in a tryst anyhow, making it a threesome.)

Illustrations 2.4 to 2.12 *The Danish Maid* (Harrison Marks, 1964–66 [?]): the idea of Denmark as intruding into the very dreams of the bachelor – assailing the British psyche with the erotic promise of greater European integration, 8-mm images. Screenshots by the author.

Illustration 2.13 Color Climax's *Danish Surprise* (John Lindsay [?], year uncertain): in Denmark – when casual restaurant conversation gives way to partner-swapping, as indicative of the moral contamination available on the Continent. Screenshots by the author.

'Christian Morality Is Already Undermined'

One part of the issue for the anti-permissives was that their natural ally and amplifier in these matters – the Church of England – had, at least from its intellectual core, failed to offer much in the way of wholehearted condemnation of the state of the 1970s. And the reason, the anti-permissives understood, was that the Church had itself been waylaid by a liberalising spirit, at the start of the 1960s, in the form of South Bank theology (also known as South Bank religion) and its variants, and with this had come an abrogation of a duty to criticise sinfulness. Indeed, articulating such criticism was understood to potentially damage this South Bank tendency, which was towards a non-judgemental scoping of what people actually thought as the basis for a renewal of Christianity, rather than the task of imposing doctrinal thinking on the masses, for ever-diminishing returns. So even on the thorny question of 'Lust or Love', Douglas Rhymes, the Canon of Southwark Cathedral, can dismiss the received paradigm of debate, as built on given moral positions, and justify this dismissal against those who would accuse him of 'trying to undermine Christian morality' on the grounds that 'Christian morality is already undermined in that it is unheeded and rejected by many' (Rhymes 1964: 29). Thereafter Rhymes turns to the film *Room at the Top* (Jack Clayton, 1959) – shocking, at the time, for its seeming amorality on sexual matters – to explore wider contemporary questions of attitudes to life, including for the figure of the homosexual, in his 1964 book *No New Morality: Christian Personal Values and Sexual Morality* (55, 91–93).

John A.T. Robinson (then Bishop of Woolwich), in his foundational South Bank text of 1963, *Honest to God*, was quite clear as to the collateral damage necessary for Christian renewal: 'The last thing the Church exists to be is an organization for the religious. Its charter is to be the servant of the world' (Robinson 1963: 134).[26] And that world is to be found in 'the "depth" of the common', and as accessible in 'open[ing] oneself to the meeting of the Christ in the common, to that which has the power to penetrate [the found world's] superficiality, and redeem it from its alienation' (ibid.: 87). The Anglican Church was therefore to find a new 'function of worship' – 'to make us more sensitive to these depths; to focus, sharpen and deepen our response to the world and to other people beyond the point of proximate concern (of liking, self-interest, limited commitments, etc.)' (ibid.).

Edwards, in his edited collection on *Honest to God*, took Robinson's book and Alec Vidler's edited collections *Soundings: Essays Concerning Christian Understanding* (1962) and *Objections to Christian Belief* (1963) as evidence of 'A New Stirring in English Christianity', which he likens, in terms of a new pole of orientation, to the Oxford Movement (Edwards 1963: 22). Paul Johnson, addressing nothing less than the way in which 'our familiar culture, in its political, social, economic and creative aspects, is [as understood by some] soon to perish, from a combination of external assault and internal decay' (Johnson 1977: 1), would later place *Honest to God* in a post-war trajectory of a Christian counter-Christianity theology, as wishing to dissolve Christianity altogether – that is, those who 'openly accept, welcome and indeed wish to hasten the secularizing process ['towards, with apologies to Rudolf Bonhoeffer'] religionless Christianity ... [or a] Christianity without Christ' (ibid.: 120). And, from here, with 'the readiness with which this type of moral theology accepts sexual promiscuity (and aberration)' (ibid.) the scene is set for unchecked, unchallenged promiscuity. Manners was much of the same opinion; *Honest to God* left the faithful '[d]eprived of the old religious certainties of right and wrong', which is particularly irresponsible, she indicates, for children (Manners 1971: 55; her later chapter, called 'Honest to God?' mounts a general attack on Church of England liberalism; 117–29). Edwards and Johnson seem united in recognising a sea change (for the better, and for the worse, respectively), but are short on the implications, in terms of sexual morality, that could arise from this new sensibility. And this seems also to have been the limit of Robinson's liberalism too, for his 1970 book *Christian Freedom in a Permissive Society*. Here, the Permissive Society is reassuringly only a stage in the progression away from patriarchal structures and towards a 'mature society' (Robinson 1970: 72, 242). And, in terms of challenges thrown up in this progression, Robinson now differentiates between the erotic ('which is good') and the pornographic ('evil and undesirable'; 79). He bemoans the damage done to ecumenicalism by the 1968 papal encyclical *Humanae Vitae*, which reaffirmed opposition to artificial contraception (114–22), which would have been seen (as it was at the time by many Catholics) as a step back to the 'seizing-up church' rather than onwards to 'the exploding church', in Robinson's terminology (243). Indeed, the effect of *Humanae Vitae*, McLeod notes, was to now quarantine contraception-using Catholics, who had anticipated a relaxation on this position in the years immediately prior to the encyclical, outside the church – exactly the concern of the damage that would arise from imposing dogma on congregations (McLeod 2010: 166–69). This status of being 'outside' then made such a Catholic subset permissive by default, in the effective 'revolt among the laity' that followed (as Saunders and Stanford term it, in *Catholics and Sex: From Purity to Purgatory*, 1992: 72). And this being outside meant that the couples, and indeed the priests who advised, 'off the record' (155), that they would not condemn the use of contraception, were exerting autonomy in defiance of instruction and official thinking around personal sexual matters. David Lodge's 1980 novel regarding Catholic sexuality across these years, *How Far Can You Go?*, nuances the lived experience of this matter. In the constant negotiation between purity and sinful living, for his characters, the Rubicon-crossing choice to use contraception then shifts that lived Catholic experience (and Catholic allegiance more generally) away from doctrinal guidance, leading to a slow erosion of church or clerical authority.

Moreover, figures such as the Reverend Kenneth Leech would perform the work of reconceptualising sexual morality in permissive times, through a praxis process of, as it was then termed, 'contextual theology' (roughly: putting these ideas into practice, and so testing and modifying them). Leech concludes, in reflecting on his work as a 'mission' to the Soho downtrodden, that

> there is a desperate need for more beat priests, more hippy priests, more gay priests, more revolutionary priests, and one of our major problems in the Church is that so often we draw our ordinands from a fairly monochrome section of the population. (Leech 1973: 89)

And, to achieve this, it must be a matter of doing away with the 'parsonic voice':

> With [such] voice and mannerisms goes the image of the nice, refined clergyman, very fragile and easily shocked, insulated from the real world of conflict and suffering, protected by his collar and dark suit from real human contact. So many youngsters feel that the priest is not really human, and that to talk about sex, for instance, would shock and shake him. Too often I am afraid they are right. (Ibid.: 89–90)

The paperback cover of Leech's *Keep the Faith Baby* – illustrative of what this mission meant – pictured a young man in Piccadilly Circus, with a rent boy appearance, taking drugs intravenously. It may, of course, have been staged – this was the era of the New English Library's paperbacks, the garish covers of which sought to shock, and these may well have been what Holbrook was complaining about, in 'small town bookshops' (Holbrook 1972c: 143) – but the intention, in terms of situating the ideas of the book, remains the same. Leech may well have been aware, as per Daly's experiences, of the connections between broken homes, drug use, male prostitution, violence, blackmail and even murder, reluctant performers in pornography, and the brutal opportunists lurking on the edge of this vortex, such as the so-called Bishop of Medway of the Old Catholic Church.

That unwelcome, counterproductive 'parsonic voice' had then reappeared, ventriloquised through figures such as Whitehouse, Manners, Birdwood, Holbrook, Longford, Muggeridge, Gummer, Johnson, Joseph and eventually Thatcher (and undoubtedly countless other opinion formers, minor politicians, journalists, magistrates, town councillors, and general civic busybodies). For Johnson, with the colonial perspective of Christianity as a civilising force, the South Bank tendency pushing towards 'Christianity without Christ', 'no *ecclesia*',

Illustration 2.14 Poster for the Hornsey College of Art pornography debate in 1971, pitting the trendy against the parsonic. Published with permission.

'no factual truth either', and so on (Johnson 1977, 120), is a milestone on the journey of the sorry decline of Western civilisation ('the approaching catastrophe', to include 'our familiar culture [which], in its political, social, economic and creative aspects, is soon to perish'; ibid.: 1). Both Gummer and Johnson would find the answer and antidote to this decline in the coming to power of Thatcher, at which point both would work to articulate a Christian justification for the possession and use of nuclear weapons (Moore, Wilson and Stamp 1986: 26). Part of Eliza Filby's thesis, *God & Mrs Thatcher* (2015), arises from framing such strands of discontent as a possible or attempted interdenominational bifurcation of the Church of England of the 1970s – heightened tensions between liberal and traditional wings, or (as it would be known) 'the trendy' vs 'the parsonic'.

An ecclesiastic proxy target in this anti-permissive backlash was Michael De-la-Noy who, in 1970, was fired as the press secretary to the then Archbishop of Canterbury, when it transpired that he had written articles on transgender individuals and, for the semi-pornographic magazine *Forum*, 'The Un-Permissive Society'. The former sought to expose cross-dressing as anything but a new phenomenon, and scoped the sad existence of an elderly adherent – 'Roman Catholic public school and Sandhurst ... [Leslie] describes himself at his prep school as the school whore, and claims to have been buggered by about fifty boys' (De-la-Noy 1971: 99). The latter addressed the consequences of the Church's idiosyncratic unwillingness to talk about new sexual mores: 'If society was really geared to enjoying sex rather than equating it with sin, as our Judeo-Christian tradition has taught us to do, there might be less [*sic*] restless, frustrated nights in matrimonial beds; less unsatisfactory promiscuity for homosexuals and less unfulfilled fantasising, lying and deception for heterosexuals' (ibid.: 96).[27] Leech and De-la-Noy seem to present different readings of the challenge and opportunity of permissiveness to the Anglican Church: acceptance, for Leech, leading to a new communalism; or, for De-la-Noy, leading to less stuffiness about an individual's sexual activity and identity.

In total, then, for Holbrook, '[t]he strangest thing of all, perhaps, is that the individuals pushing this fanatical pseudo-revolution are seeking to harm us, and even destroy us, in our innermost being, at the very centre of life itself – yet we greet them with serious regard, gratitude and reverence, despite the sordidness of it all' (Holbrook 1072c: 97). Thatcher's tonic to all this was to be administered from a position of someone who knows best about the health of the nation, and Gummer anticipates such a patrician intervention.[28] Hence, in setting out the terms of his investigation into the Permissive Society,

we have found it hard to know where to draw the line. When does private action become public? How do we protect the young and feeble-minded – or do we protect them at all? How important is family life to the security of the State, and how is it threatened by public immorality? What about private immortality which puts a cost upon the State? Beyond all these questions are two fundamental ones. First, what duties can the State properly ask of its citizens; and second, do we need a total reappraisal of morality. (Gummer 1971: 7)

Gummer offers a 'voice of reason' to counter the times, finger-waggingly young-fogey-ish, and with virtually no references to data or literature to support his arguments. Gummer identifies (or feels besieged by) a 'European Marcusian Left' (10), the 'Pepsi-generation' (15), 'extreme feminists' (identified as the '"burn your bra" brigade'; 25), all of whom would seem to endanger 'Western civilisation [as it] is based on a community where the family is the most important unit' (60), sees trouble in both Denmark, and the United States, with their less restricted cultures of pornography (although also notes some areas of the latter uninfected by permissiveness; 8), and concedes that perhaps one copy of *Last Exit to Brooklyn* might be retained while the rest are given to '[m]agistrates in Britain [who] could have no hesitation in destroying large quantities of these books' (87). The books to be totally destroyed include, for Gummer: *Sin for Breakfast* by Mason Hoffenberg, *The Cult of Pain* by Edmond Dumoulin and *Lesbian Career Woman*, seemingly by Toby Thompson. Henry Miller's *Tropic of Cancer* can also survive as one copy, as can 'faded medical textbooks' (87). Gummer is unclear whether he is referring to stocks held at individual pornographic bookshops, or to the total UK holdings of these texts.

Finally, Gummer complains that the Christian churches have not done enough, and calls for a new spirit of community, based on an assertion of moral standards. Gummer complains – and this is a point conceded in Davies's study *Permissive Britain* (1975: 46–57) – that there was a reluctance on the part of the institutions of law to enforce the law. So there is (one can surmise) a crisis of the rule of law that is damaging the psychic well-being of the nation. Gummer's screed could be dismissed as anecdotal and slanderous, but he wrote this book while in office (he was elected a Conservative MP for Lewisham West in 1970; prior to this he was a member of the Education Committee of the Inner London Education Authority). An idea of what kind of theocratic solution was effectively envisaged in these kinds of positions, and as a logical extension of this kind of rhetoric, can be found in Pete Walker's *House of Whipcord* (1974), written by David McGillivray – with an opening on-screen dedication: 'to those who are disturbed by today's lax moral codes and eagerly await the return of corporal and capital punishment'.[29] Thereafter, a Pattie Boyd-like French model Ann-Marie Di Verney (played by actress and glamour model Penny Irving) is kidnapped and taken to an extrajudicial prison, referred to as an 'institution' – although the film subverts the moralism with 'women-in-prison'-style exploitation: nudity ('you are in this room to be bathed and checked for vermin before putting on your uniform – now get your clothes off! ... Since you are not willing to undress yourself, you will have to be stripped!') and whipping. The charge made against Di Verney, in a blacked-out courtroom with the banner 'The World for Christ', expresses the sentiments of elements of the anti-permissives:

> *You are here to serve sentence according to the proper moral and disciplinary standards, for conviction of a serious charge: for exposing yourself unclothed, without shame, for monetary gain, to a photographer in a public place ... for which outrage against public decency, a corrupt and permissive London court fined you £10 and discharged you.*

And, for sentencing:

> *This court, my dear young lady, exists outside the statutory laws of this land; it is a private court. And we are constituted here by private charter... to pass what we regard as proper sentence, on depraved females of every category, with whom the effete and misguided courts of Great Britain today have been too lenient; immorality [dialogue obscured by talk] must not be tolerated ... This, young woman, is a real prison. This is a proper ... house of correction.*

The relevancy of Walker's vision is twofold: on the one hand – like Ken Russell's *The Devils* (1971) – an attack on the hypocrisies and hysteria of organised (or, one could say, actually existing) religion as it positioned itself in relation to the bourgeois state. But, on the other hand, *House of Whipcord* seems to be the only British film of the 1970s that actually shows that which, via the Independent Inquiry into Child Sexual Abuse (IICSA 2018a) and the Commission of Investigation into Mother and Baby Homes (2021) reports, discussed below, is now known. The opening sequence of a distressed woman (muddied, bloodied, beaten, barely clothed, unable to speak), running alongside a road in the rain to escape her abuse, directly re-enacts scenarios of ritualised abuse and beatings in schools and church organisations, or of the victims of Savile. The film entwines these two aspects in a way that, at the time, would have been unthinkable as a realistic proposition – and so can be read as a righteous attack on NVALA, and general satire. Indeed, the natural inclination is to take the film as satire (although the satirical framing is hard to locate in the film). But considered straight, *House of Whipcord* simply delivers the workings of much anti-permissive activism of the time.[30]

If the crisis of Christianity in the 1970s was one of a sense of legitimacy and relevancy (to the young of liberal Western democracies), then clerics Trevor

Huddleston, Daniel Berrigan, Kenneth Leech and Michael Cleary would have represented solutions and even role models, while condemnations of pornography would have only pushed the Christian churches further into irrelevancy.

Indeed, it is possible to check back some years later – in fact, at the end of Thatcher's term as prime minister – from the perspectives of the unreconstructed moralistic, via the verbose 1990 collection *Christianity and Conservatism*, which opens with a Foreword by Thatcher herself, and closes with her address to the General Assembly of the Church of Scotland (Alison and Edwards 1990). The clerics and Tories assembled would seem to have been those happy with the informal historical affiliation of the Church of England and the Conservative Party (a 'discreet blessing', 4; the Church of England has occasionally been called 'the Conservative Party at prayer'), and still smarting from the 1985 publication of the report *Faith in the City: A Call for Action by Church and Nation* (Commission on Urban Priority Areas 1989), taken to be a direct attack on Conservative policy. As per Gummer's position in this 1990 collection, this strata within the Anglican Communion had gravitated to the idea that the Church of England hierarchy or establishment had become fashionably, and damagingly, left-liberal. Consequently, and perversely, the Church's then leaders, seemingly poisoned by tendencies around South Bank theology some years before (Gummer 1990: 313) had rounded on the idea of morality, including through attacks on 'the traditionalist view' (ibid.: 307). The concerns were poverty, deprivation, and pensive considerations of the ideological position from which the economy had been allowed to function unchecked. One of the volume's editors, despite claiming that the free market is one of God's gifts to mankind, even recommends that some checks and balances on God's seeming direct intervention into the British economy be imposed (Edwards 1990: 331 and 332, respectively). From this vantage point, it is difficult to avoid the conclusion that the idea of a Permissive Society had primarily functioned to allow for the very existence of those identified here, and loudly identifying themselves as, anti-permissives, rather than being able to articulate any coherent or pragmatic position for which they stood. This Pharisee tendency also explains why spiritual warfare was the preferred terrain of battle: obscurantist, ennobling for the dabblers, and transcending the need to engage with democratic norms.

The hardcore pornography that then represented extreme damage to national spiritual well-being should also reveal, via a close examination, the actual contours of the permissive mindset, and experience, that was deemed worthy of the ire of such opposition.

Notes

1. *Encounter* was only nominally progressive, as it had transpired, in 1967, that it was being funded by both British and American intelligence agencies, seemingly in an attempt to turn progressives (Fabians, artists, teachers, etc.) against communism, as part of the cultural front of the Cold War (Saunders 1999).

2. Long, who died in 2012, and whom I had known since the late 1990s, was in no sense cautious when discussing his career. He happily recalled his scrapes and scraps, felt no compulsion to defend films he had made that he believed were terrible, and saw only hypocrisy in the massed ranks of those arrayed against permissiveness. Long believed in direct and often immediate communication with his public enemies – a tendency that seems to have done little for his career but that enlivens his autobiography, co-written with Sheridan (2008).

3. For commentary, see Hewison 1981; on attempts by local councils to deal with the film, see Egan 2020.

4. For the Whitehouse correspondence on this matter of the shelf position of *Knave*, see Thompson 2013: 278–79. Huddleston was also a contributor to Longford's report. On Berrigan's radical ministry, from being 'on the run' for anti-war activism to eventual imprisonment, see Halligan 2018.

5. Holroyd offers an alternative theory to Johnson's: homophobic persecution as ostracising potential Soviet recruits with experience in Intelligence (Holroyd 1995: 706, fn 12).

6. For a selection of correspondence around these targeted films from Mary Whitehouse and her associates, see Thompson 2013: 209–35. On the BBFC's position on the release of Swedish exploitation sex education films, see Smith 2018: 34–51. 'White coaters' typically claimed a sociological bent, as evidenced with documentary-style voice-overs, and occasion doctor-type figures, sometimes both condemning the same things that the film shows at length – and so this commentary must be considered to be included in enormous bad faith. For a discussion of the BBFC's handling of the documentary aspirations of sexploitation, see Hunter 2013: 114.

   'White coaters' also had their literary equivalents too, which mixed sociology (sometimes sourced from the writing of notable academics) with detailed descriptions of sex. The paperback *The Wonderful World of Penthouse Sex*, for example, includes a pseudo-reportage section, of uncertain authorship, called 'Couples'. Across half a dozen case studies of couples, each partner describes their sex lives in turn ('Bob was the first man to ever touch my bare breasts. Would you believe that? I was nineteen. God, I'll never forget the thrills the first time he put his lips on my breasts'; Vassi 1976: 213), followed by 'Analysis' ('Now her relationship with Jack has freed her subconscious, sexual personality – as his has been freed – and his love has allowed her to give full rein', etc.; ibid.: 219). The book's cover promises: 'A manifesto for the erotically liberated – and everyone who would like to be'.

7. Lord Harlech (David Ormsby-Gore) was then president of the BBFC. One rumour as to Murphy's misfortunes concerned his poor eyesight: he would tend to demand cuts based on what he could hear of a film, rather than what he could see of it.

8. On *Growing Up* as a sex education film for schools, and the wider controversy surrounding it, see Limond 2008 and 2009.

9. Letter: Mulley to Whitehouse, 4 August 1976, held in, and courtesy of, the National Viewers' and Listeners' Association Collection. Special Collections, Albert Sloman Library, University of Essex. Further correspondence and press clippings in relation to this are also held. I have obscured the identities of those involved. More generally, I here draw on a number of

interviews I conducted with some involved in the screening (and who were unaware of NVALA activity around this matter at the time), and who have requested anonymity.

10. Letter: M. Whitehouse to [name redacted], 7 May, no year. Box 97. Courtesy of the National Viewers' and Listeners' Association Collection. Special Collections, Albert Sloman Library, University of Essex.

11. Document relating to Martin Cole. Box 97: Courtesy of the National Viewers' and Listeners' Association Collection. Special Collections, Albert Sloman Library, University of Essex. This document may have been drawn up between these years; the *Men Only* magazine noted was from 1973. Novotny's role in much of this remains obscure.

12. A former colleague, who worked in accounting at the University of East London, often recalled the educational highlight of his youth, at age 15, and from which he had seemingly never quite recovered. This was a school trip to the National Film Theatre to see the new Jean-Luc Godard film *Weekend* (1968), and walking home afterwards through a free concert in Hyde Park. There he observed groups of nude hippies sat under trees, wreathed in clouds of marijuana smoke, while the volume of Pink Floyd's engulfing 'Set the Controls for the Heart of the Sun' swelled as he wended his way through the psychedelic chaos and towards the group playing live, evermore convinced that these were the very final days of known civilisation. (He eventually continued home for his tea.)

13. Outside this timeline, two forerunners may be noted: Cecil Hewitt Rolph's 1961 *Does Pornography Matter?* and Wayland Young's 1965 *Eros Denied*.

14. Holden notes the Williams report in the context of a Whitehouse-engendered controversy around Jens Jørgen Thorsen's unmade *The Many Faces of Jesus*, later known as *The Sex Life of Christ*, to be shot in the UK and featuring hetero- and homosexual acts. The home secretary had the Danish film-maker arrested when he arrived at Heathrow in 1978. He was denied entry into the UK on the basis of his carrying the script for the film, and that his presence might lead to breaches of the peace (Holden 2004: 216) and see too (Wistrich 1978: 125–26). The film did not materialise.

15. These comments are heavily contextualised, or nuanced or even opposed, with footnotes in the 2014 edition, and with the suggestion of pornographic magazines in schools removed altogether.

16. Censorship in Denmark was abolished in Summer 1969 – a moment marked with a party/sex trade fair called SEX 69; see Stevenson 2009.

17. On Braun on 'Mike Hunter', see the Rialto Report (2015).

18. Court cites Siegfried Ernst's 1976 *Man: The Greatest of Miracles: An Answer to the Sexual Counter-Evolution* in support of this theory too (Court 1980: 58).

19. Robinson-Brown relates the lived experience of exclusion to Rowan Williams's influential lecture 'The Body's Grace' (Williams [1989] 2002: 309–21), delivered to the Lesbian and Gay Christian Movement. Robinson-Brown, reading Williams's position from a postcolonial and queer perspective, finds the matter of divine revelation as for the individual rather than the collective, so that 'for the black LGBTQ+ Christian, the invitation to transformation often presents itself as the requirement to leave your Queer body, with all its desires, at the door' (Robinson-Brown 2021: 106). Williams is the former Archbishop of Canterbury; for the reception of this contentious lecture and Williams's related writing, see Shortt 2008: 143–46.

   Whitehouse launched a 1976 prosecution of *Gay News* and its editor, Denis Lemon, for publishing James Kirkup's poem 'The Love That Dares Speak its Name' (with homoerotic illustration) on the grounds of blasphemy; see Nash 2017. Jonathan Smyth represented

Whitehouse (Graystone 2021: 2). Lemon received a fine and suspended prison sentence (quashed on appeal), *Gay News* a fine.

20. This was seemingly the sole publication from Jasmine Press, which was located in a residential block of flats in Penge.

21. The BBFC has no listing for a certificated film of that title (so Holbrook presumably would have had to have bought membership to the club to see it). Holbrook seems to have functioned as provider of theoretical foundations (vaguely sociological and theological, and with a distinctly North American holistic strain of psychoanalytical thought) for Whitehouse's positions, and she notes and draws on his work in *Whatever Happened to Sex* (Whitehouse 1978: 192–93 especially).

    For Holbrook's own take on cinema see (Holbrook 1972b: 191–98), which opens with the complaint, presumably in relation to *Films and Filming*, 'Why should film magazines, for example, more than any other journals, come to contain small advertisements offering exchanges of perversions?' (ibid.: 191). (On *Films and Filming*'s preference for nude males and the magazine's gay classified contact aspects, see Bengry 2011.) Holbrook thereafter notes 'hate' as the main structuring concern of cinema, as accommodated by a lackadaisical attitude on the part of film-makers – with evidence gleaned from interviews with Joseph Losey and associates.

22. On a Longford interview with David Sullivan and associates, Killick writes:

    Longford seemed more interested in giving them fatherly advice about their choice of career than in hearing their views on pornography. His first question set the tone of the interview: 'It's rather a weird choice, isn't it? I don't know what your parents would think of it'. ... Afterwards, Sullivan claimed that the whole interview was a wasted opportunity and Lord Longford had made no effort to obtain any information from them that could have helped his report ... '[T]he interview lasted only fifteen minutes. We thought we would be questioned by a panel but only Lord Longford was there. He seemed more concerned about a television appearance he was making that night than in what we had to tell him. He kept asking his secretary about it'. (Killick 1994: 17–18)

23. If Holbrook's comment regarding the sexual lives of the pupils refers to staff–pupil relations, then one would have hoped that Holbrook acted to ensure intervention rather than just complain; Dartington, of these years, features in Renton's overview of sexual abuse at public schools (Renton 2018: 274–76). Hickson notes a belated move to diffuse such problems: the 'debachelorization of housemasterships (evidenced in the "all our housemasters are married" presentations of several school prospectuses)' (Hickson 1995: 213). And, more generally on the culture of 'the candid tutor–pupil friendship' in boarding schools, see ibid.: 56–73.

24. I am acutely aware of the problematic nature of this observation, both in terms of assessing the documentary, and in terms of its inclusion in my argument. In her critique of Ellis's 'On Pornography' (1992), Claire Pajaczkowska opens with 'I am writing this article because of the anger I feel at the way that "women's pleasure" has been used as a concept in some current [1981] discussions of pornography' (Pajaczkowska 1992: 184). The documentary here seems to document Joensen's contentedness, at the moment of its making; whether this is accurate or false, and/or whether Joensen performed as much in a dissembling manner, or revealed as much truthfully, is not known. To deny the display of contentedness, if truthful, is also to further deny Joensen expression. As with Mary Millington (as noted below), Joensen's selfless love of animals seems to indicate a fundamental decency, which sets them both apart from the selfish majority of characters considered in this book. I will speculate that, just as Millington

channelled the financial rewards of her work to the cause of sick animals, Joensen too may have performed for pornographers to continue to enable her to love animals in all senses. Her eventual loss of her animals also seems to have led to her eventual loss of her life.

25. For the account of filming Joensen, see Kronhausen and Kronhausen 1976: 41–53; see too Stevenson 1994. On Joensen's filmography, see Stevenson 2000: 177–89; and on her life, 'The Real Animal Farm' episode of the Channel 4 documentary series *The Dark Side of Porn* (tx 19 April 2006), and Andersen 2012: 272–79. *Screw* magazine itself cast Joensen as an agony aunt, answering spurious letters from readers (Joensen 1974: 8, for example) – an unlikely arrangement. Joensen died in 1985, possibly from alcohol-related illness (although the rumour of suicide persisted), after some years working as a prostitute, and performing live bestiality sex shows. For a fuller discussion of the Muehl films (often ritualistic, incorporating enemas, bestiality, torture and coprophilic practices, sometimes in semi-laboratory conditions), see Halligan 2016: 132–37. *Bodil Joensen 'A Summerday'* screened as part of the 'Taboo' programme, from a 16-mm print, at I Mille Occhi in Trieste in 2007. For a transcript of interviews conducted during the filming, see Joensen 1973: 156–65.

26. Robinson gave evidence in defence of *Lady Chatterley's Lover* at the 1960 trial around the charge of obscenity, brought against Penguin Books, as did E.M. Forster.

27. De-la-Noy's commentary on his dismissal and the controversy that it aroused, along with a reproduction of the two articles and a general critique of the Church of England, were published as *A Day in the Life of God* (1971).

28. Gummer himself was to become a minister in Thatcher's cabinet, retaining, in Alan Clark's words, his 'demonstratively *churchy* and (unlike the Lady [Thatcher]) moralistic' side, and with this making trouble for a fellow minister exposed as having an affair (Clark 1993: 46; Clark's italics).

29. Walker had made a number of loops, such as *Top Models of the Year* (1959) and *Miss Britt Hampshire* (1967), that tended to film strip routines, albeit slightly enlivened by New Wave flourishes.

30. The other British film-maker of this period who consistently examined creeping totalitarianism without a mitigating sense of satire was Peter Watkins. But his films in this category tended towards considerations of the apparatus of state violence (in the name of ideological conforming) rather than individualised, sexualised violence (in the name of morality). They are: *Privilege* (1967), *Gladiators* (1969) and *Punishment Park* (1971). *The Devils* and *A Clockwork Orange* can also be associated with this strain, along with *Scum* (Alan Clarke, two versions of 1979).

PART II

The Hardcore

CHAPTER 3

The 'Connoisseur of Female Beauty' and the 'Curve Prospector'

Harrison Marks and Russell Gay

Some Views for Sale

In the scope of this study, Harrison Marks is the pre-eminent pornographer.[1] His rise, and falls, occurred in tandem with the most vibrant periods of British film pornography: its development was also his development. Marks began with still photography, and this remained a constant across his career – individual stills, magazines, and even an exhibition; Petronius recommends, to the London visitor of 1969:

> Harrison Marks: New Exhibition of the Nude in Photography, 4 Gerrard Street, W1. This is a more or less permanent show, with over five hundred studies ... featuring the work of one of London's leading figure photographers. (Petronius 1969: 34)[2]

Marks seems to have shifted effortlessly from the medium-shot murky nudity of silent black-and-white film loops, as per *The Danish Maid*, to extreme close-ups of engorged sexual organs, in glistening colour. He worked with the most notable model-performers of four decades (Pamela Green, Mary Millington, Linzi Drew, Paula Meadows), from 8-mm film reels to video cassettes to DVDs, from a cottage industry run out of Soho to the beginnings of David Sullivan's pornography empire, and its mainstream aspirations. And in Marks's work alone is a questionable, or even unwelcome, continuum between Victorian music hall and variety shows, to soft and then hardcore pornography – the very antithesis of the Thatcher resuscitation of Victorian values, not least in respect to Marks's alleged pimping.[3]

Marks audaciously promoted himself as a director and a brand (so that his name was, at one point, synonymous with pornography), and, in his liking for cameos and even supporting roles, he was seemingly unable to confine himself to keeping behind the camera. When seemingly afforded a measure of artistic freedom, he seems merely to have indulged his desire for threadbare recreations of antiquated slapstick comedy. The long musical number in the middle of his *Come Play With Me* (1977), 'It's Great To Be Here', with the bewigged Marks himself (now in his 50s and head-to-toe in unflattering thermal underwear), tirelessly leading the singing from the front of a swaying posse of nurses (that is, models in nurse stripper costumes) is unique to his particular vision, and British cinema in general. And, like so many other male European film auteurs of this period, life and art entwine, as crystalised in the erotic – so that the 'calling' is to both film- and love-making. From Marks's 'biography':

> *Marriage is of paramount importance to Harrison Marks. He is a difficult man for any woman to be married to by the simple nature of, if one may term it so, his calling. His life is women, some of the most beautiful women in the world. (Wood 2017: 65)*

Marks seems to have ghosted (as well as provided the Introduction to) his biography, which was published as *The Naked Truth: About Harrison Marks* in 1967, as authored by journalist Franklyn Wood (1925–1991). If Marks himself is to be believed, a deeper exploration of any libertarian or artistic impulse to his life's work (which, in the biography, seems to be a professional role of 'connoisseur of female beauty'; Wood 2017: 1) was set aside in favour of the serial pursuit of women, off-camera – fulfilling this, 'his calling'. And Marks, he would have you believe, was successful in this too – that is, assuming these are Marks's own words, from 1967:

> *Harrison Marks is 40, reasonably good-looking, black hair, a black moustache, tanned and fit. But really no Adonis and certainly not a film star image, say, in the mould of Errol Flynn or Tony Curtis. (Wood 2017: 7)*

> *Nowadays George lives, as he readily admits, quite a hell-raising life … All the vices are there: wine, women, and song in plenitude. … Still, he looks fit, bronzed, active, alive and very, very healthy. (Ibid.: 15)*

Despite the great expectations sketched out in 1967 – '[b]y the time this is read, there is every possibility that I will be in Hollywood making my first film there' (ibid.: xiii) – Marks would be bankrupt by 1969, which may in part account for his turn to harder material at this time. And this may explain why Marks's legacy is obscure; his distribution strategy was outside legal channels, and so rarely troubled film journals or magazines, or the British Board of Film Censors. Consequently, possibly hundreds of his films have been lost or are unidentified or beyond reach, or perhaps failed to make the transition from celluloid to a digital format. They may reside in attic tea chests of 8-mm reels, or are now buried in internet archives, title-less and origin-less, on specialist websites (mostly related to spanking).

It is certainly possible that, if Marks was shooting hardcore on film in the 1950s and earlier in the 1960s – presumably for private collectors or events – then my rough periodisation of Marks's work is quite incorrect. Young, writing in 1965, describes unnamed hardcore films, which he terms 'haptic-convulsive', in detail, even to the point of outlining the function of the money shot in them (Young 67–68, 305–6).[4] Therefore I cannot answer with any certainty a basic question of this study: when did hardcore first appear on film in the UK?

Marks seems to have worked flat out across the late 1950s and the 1960s in terms of producing pornography, as a photographer, magazine editor (founding *Kamera* in 1957, in close conjunction with model Pamela Green) and publisher, and director of 8- or 16-mm loops (from about 1958) – and with a profitable sideline (and convenient front) in cat photography.[5] Distribution of the films seems to have been mostly run through mail order, as advertised in the back of Marks's magazines, and with culled stills often doubling up as photospreads, or the loops sold 'under the counter' (i.e. by direct request to the shop proprietor) from sex shops and newsagents.

Peeping Tom details, in its post-opening credits sequence, just this ritual around the purchase of pornography from a newsagent – with windows crammed with ice cream and cigarette adverts, magazines, birthday cards, and photographs of women. The strong suggestion here is that a newsagent is mostly an outlet for the images from the studio immediately above it, with both run by the one proprietor. A distinguished-looking customer (played a furtive Miles Malleson, then in his early seventies) asks, in an officious tone, for *The Times* and the *Daily Telegraph* (two right-wing broadsheet newspapers) as a tentative preamble to buying Marks-style nude images. For this second transaction, he looks about the newsagents to ensure no other customers are nearby, leans in, lowers his voice, and says to the proprietor, 'I'm told by a friend that you have some views for sale'. When asked 'What sort of views, sir?', he replies 'Whuh? Well... huh. Err...'. As befits a well-to-do reader of such respectable newspapers, he seems able to shell out 4 pounds and 10 shillings for the whole folder of nudes, produced from under the counter, rapidly declines to be put on any mailing list and, in his excitement, forgets his newspapers as he exits. But the Malleson character may have chased such 'views for sale' for all of his adult life from such shops – as already familiar at the turn of the century, as per Conrad's novel of 1907, *The Secret Agent*: just such a shop, as noted above, and where customers included 'men of a more mature age ... [w]ith their hands plunged deep in the side pockets of their coats, they dodged in sideways, one shoulder first, as if afraid to start the [shop door] bell going' (Conrad and Mallios 2004: 3–4).

Marks only figures in passing in John Trevelyan's memoirs, in relation to the BBFC being wrong-footed by *Naked as Nature Intended* (1961), which was banned and then un-banned (Trevelyan 1977: 101), and not at all (at least, not directly named) in the Longford Report (1972). Such omissions illustrate the extent to which Marks, as prolific as he was, worked in a covert fashion in terms of standard methods of film exhibition – although skirmishes with the law sporadically occurred over sending 'obscene materials' through the mail. Marks's second major trial ran in 1971, although he avoided incarceration. The titles of his films seem like covert samizdat too: crass and indicative of the film to come, and yet succinct and distinctive enough to be rapidly communicated by the potential buyer to the retailer – just the name of the model herself, or (for example) *After the Show* (1960), *Gypsy Fire* (1961), *Brush with a Body* (1964), *The Lash* (1968) and *Apartment 69* (unknown). Harder Marks material was distributed, perhaps exclusively, in Scandinavia and the Netherlands by Color Climax. Erasing identifiable information from the films may have been a protection strategy.

The 1950s phase of pornography seems to have been relatively innocent: stripping and nudity, a shade beyond coy, but nothing seemingly too detailed or shot in close-up. In this respect, 1950s loops recall fairground peepshow machines, as with 'What the Butler Saw' mutoscopes from the turn of the century: the woman, in themed surroundings, is seen in the nude for a few dozen seconds. Marks's film work seemingly began with the naturalist film, which proclaimed (via voice-over) aspirations to sociological or ethnographic documentation, as well as his straightforward boudoir pornography – from *Nude in the Sun* (filmed in Cornwall in 1963) to *Strictly for Bachelors* (1968; 'Cindy Neals Shows You Why!'

promises the 8-mm box), respectively. But the relatively elaborate scenarios, and humour, indicate that more than the straight delivery of nudity was understood to be needed. In this there is a sense of an understanding of an audience with a taste for comedy – the fun balancing the furtive. 'It's Great To Be Here', then, could function as something of a constant theme across Marks's work (or even his motto): the promise, or illustration, of enjoyment that would ideally be collective (the 'here' with the others) – and to which an invitation is extended. And to accept this invitation, and arrive at this destination, only requires a stepping away from the middle march, and slightly off the beaten track, towards this siren call. And what then awaits? As a model, Green seems to suggest, in her health and youth and silhouette, a culture of leisure and comfort beyond war-time deprivations; the countering, or reset, of *Brief Encounter*'s Celia Johnson. Marks then projected the future – and a future that, in its freedom, and fun, and amoralism, can be read as in direct opposition to the notions of propriety and responsibility that fired the anti-permissives.

The *Window Dresser* (1961) featured a fully naked Green as a burglar who pretends to be a lingerie shop dummy to avoid the police, with Marks himself as the shop owner. *Sexational* (1965) sees a woman (Margaret Nolan) stripping in three different scenarios: on a bed (white underwear), in a dungeon (black underwear), and in a bedroom with a substantial drinks tray (black underwear, costume jewellery). *Vampire* (1964) sees a naked woman (Wendy Luton, 'Doll of the Month' for *Modern Man* magazine, of December 1964) hypnotised and transported from her bedroom to the castle of Dracula III (played by Marks).[6] Marks appeared again in the silent *Four Poster* (1964), as the hunchback hotel receptionist who first spies on his naked guest (Nolan again) through the cut-out eyes of a leering painting of Marks himself, hung on the wall, and who attempts to rob her as she sleeps, and then tries to murder her (a spiked ceiling is lowered onto the bed), only to be thwarted by a soldier who bursts in – they fight as a naked Nolan looks on, and Marks, unsteady on his feet, acts out knifing himself and collapses to the floor.[7] But the loop ends with the three performers taking a theatrical bow, then miming surprise at an imagined hostile audience reaction, at which point Marks holds up a card reading 'What do you want, blood?' The final shot is of Nolan's naked behind, with the words 'The End' written across it. All these loops are frontally lit, resulting in maximum body detail, and deep shadows across the small sets.

By the time of *Halfway Inn*, made in 1970, Marks seems to have moved on from showcasing nude models to scenes of implied love-making (that is, nude couples writhing and kissing). But even in this shift towards hardcore, something of Marks's erring towards a theme remains: micro-vignettes of narrative that establish the kind of *mise en scène* in which pornographic scenes can then unfold. *Halfway Inn* is fairly elaborate in this respect: a mid-1800s setting in which the raffish visitor to the inn in question is left in a state of exhaustion by continual sex with a maid (in a four-poster bed, say, or hidden in the inn's grounds by weeping willows). In fact, in this silent film's twist, the visitor's exertions are revealed to have been unwittingly doubled: identical twin maids have seduced him (played by Mary and Madeleine Collinson).

And yet, despite this shift into harder material, by the late 1960s Marks seems to have attempted to take pornography into the mainstream, via the feature-length films *The Naked World of Harrison Marks* (aka *The Dream World of Harrison Marks*) and *The Nine Ages of Nakedness*. And *Fornicon*, now seemingly lost, followed in 1971. *Naked World* had a 1967 US release and was certified X after cuts by the BBFC in December 1968. *Nine Ages* was released in the UK in 1969, and distributed by Tony Tenser's Tigon British Film Productions, which had channelled the commercial profits from *Witchfinder General* into a swinging Southport sex comedy with much-loved 1950s comedian Norman Wisdom, *What's Good for the Goose* (Menahem Golan, 1969) – the film that ended Wisdom's film career. Marks often talked about his work with Wisdom in his biography, as a portrait photographer – seemingly keen to place himself in that then-reputable strain of popular British comedy.

Marks led the pornographic auteurs in regard to directly articulating his worldview, as with the pseudo-documentary *The Naked World of Harrison Marks* (1967), and the dramatization of his, and indeed his ancestors', sexual sensibilities with *The Nine Ages of Nakedness* (1969). While *Naked World* suggests an enviable lifestyle for the titular protagonist, *Nine Ages* seems to be closer to what would later be known as the 'essay film': a personal exploration of themes and concerns, to explore or advance an argument or thesis. With a hesitant way and thick black-rimmed glasses, Marks presents or performs himself, as the character Mr Marks – a nebbish Peter Sellers-type who has found himself caught up in a moment of sexual liberation, and yet frustratingly lacks the confidence to capitalise on the opportunities that seem available to him, surrounded as he is by women.[8]

Exploring this sexual paralysis is the narrative engine (and indeed structure) of the film, with Marks as the unwitting ringmaster of the history of seduction of womankind: 'Well, to go back to the very beginning – there was my great, great,

great, great, great, great, great, great, great [i.e. nine generations] grandfather'. Thus the film intercuts between Marks talking to a Harley Street psychiatrist (eventually revealed to be a blonde woman with the voice of an Indian man) and vignette sketches of historical scenes that concern his ancestors and their failings and inabilities or bad luck with women. Marks confesses his problem, in a way that anticipates his (auto)biography:

> Marks: I even dream about them [women], you know – I just can't get away from them.
> Psychiatrist: Men all over the world must envy your problem! You're rich, famous, successful and you're in constant contact with Man's greatest love: beautiful women.

Marks – not a bad actor, and with a compellingly laidback presence – also appears in various roles across the vignettes, where he tends to paw rather than grope the women. His roles are grandly detailed in the film's credits: the Cave Artist, Egyptian Slave, the Mandarin, the Greek Philosopher, Harrison de Chandelier, the Great Marko, the Professor, the Poet. And the film also evidences an element of awareness of the contested role of sexuality or erotica in cultural history. In the Victorian sequence, which purports to tell the history of 'living statues' (seen to be advertised as 'The Great Marko presents … see with your own eyes 12 LOVELIES portray the great female figures of history', purportedly at the Palace Theatre in Mile End), a judge winds up ravishing and then performing oral sex on one, at least when daydreaming during 'the Crown versus Marko' trial – for which the Great Marko has been summoned for mounting obscene theatre performances.

Taken as a whole, the series of vignettes seem like a series of themed loops, built around models and nudity. The sequences have the same rhythm and ambience of loops: cramped rooms, and slow and performative nude women, and space made for the women to perform in – which comes to represent the highlight of each vignette. The vignettes also anticipate Marks's seeming shift from soft- to hardcore, at around the same time (from *Halfway Inn* onwards). So, in the Continental cut of *Nine Ages*, or at least one of the Continental cuts, there is Neanderthal male genitalia, and Egyptian lesbian cunnilingus in some detail, an erection and (mostly obscured) heterosexual fellatio in Ancient Greece, and seemingly actual intercourse in Civil War England.

In returning to Marks's grandfather (many times over) of the very beginnings of the given timeline, the film arrives at prehistoric times: a scene in a cave and topless women – a harem kept by (literally) Neanderthal men, although the group sex, long hair and sheepskin clothing suggests a time closer to the year of the film's making (1968) than 38,000 BC. Likewise, the arrangement of the topless women in Ancient Egypt recalls the Windmill shows of the 1960s, and 'living statues' of live nude women: in Classical Greece they are, at first, statues – only to then come alive with seductive performances. The science fiction ending results in the Neanderthals, now captured by women in bondage gear, transported via Moon Ship 17, and returned to a Cape Canaveral-like control room, manned by topless women. In this future all men have been destroyed bar one – 'he's in constant use', via a glory hole. Marks's vision of the future, at this point at least, seems to be one in which men will be subservient to women, and reduced to their sexual functioning alone – albeit, presumably, quite happy with such a fate.

This aspirant commercial/semi-respectable element of Marks's work would culminate in 1977, with the substantially budgeted, and commercially successful, *Come Play With Me.* (In December 1978, *Come Play With Me* achieved the record for the longest-running British film of all time, after eighteen months at the Moulin cinema.) Here Marks freely melds bordering-on-hardcore pornography, featuring very notable British glamour models of that moment (Mary Millington, Anna Bergman, Sue Longhurst, Suzy Mandell), with geriatric comedy, via the incorporation of a range of ageing character actors. The film, for which David Sullivan was the executive producer, was – after cuts – certificated X by the BBFC in January 1977, and was also distributed by Tigon. Reputedly some sex scenes were filmed as hardcore, with this footage going missing shortly after – although, for Killick, this story was just a PR ruse from the film's producer (Killick 1994: 27). The released version was cut to softcore levels but, at times, by only a few dozen frames. Two in-name-only sequels were released (in fact, just misleadingly retitled Swiss sex films), and a tie-in, anonymous 'Playbirds Novel Special' was published (Anon 1977). Marks directed a hardcore loop called *Cum Lay With Me* in 1977.

Come Play With Me swings between a James Bond spoof and a standard Marks boudoir strip scene in its opening minutes. The film concerns two thieves who, on the run from the law, lay low in a health spa (which seems more like a countryside brothel). Even in this, erotica, sexual adventure and pornography are associated with a collective experience – and hence the music, and the dancing. Joy is collective in this vision of the world, and inclusive (at least in the way that the film places the unlikely senior characters with the models).

A further clue to the collective conceptualisations of Marks's erotica can be gleaned from the 1975 one-off magazine *How to Give a Blue Film Party*, which featured softcore stills from Marks's hardcore loops, interspaced with sex education prose (albeit with titles such as 'How To Handle a Woman's Breasts' and 'Towards Bigger and Better Boobs'). The editorial notes that the magazine exclusively features Marks's work, which can be ordered via the back pages. One feature, 'How Adult Movies Helped Our Sex Lives', suggests the films for marital assistance and enhancement: from a party, to the home. As per expectations of such writing (and as with the *Forum* Readers' Letters), the article introduces a couple with limited sexual engagements. He is exposed to a Marks loop by a factory friend, after work, and realises that what he took to be the inflated fantasies of the erotic literature he had read (such as oral sex) had been documented and so evidenced as extant by Marks: 'I'd never seen a sex film before so I went along for a laugh! But I didn't laugh... I learned something instead!'[9] He reacts powerfully, pays to borrow the projector and films, returns home with them, and so engenders a similar response in his wife:

> At first she registered amazement as the guy started to fondle the bird ... 'I think it's disgusting!' she said, but she never took her eyes from the small screen, nor did she remove my hand [from her thigh]. When the bird sucked the guy's cock into her mouth, I damn near shot off in my pants. Alice was mesmerised by the scene, but she didn't say anything ...
>
> I started the film again, went back to Alice, this time undoing the front of her dress and caressing her tits. To my surprise she didn't stop me, instead she pushed her chest out as if she wanted more [etc. ...]
>
> The film flickered out.
>
> 'I'll put it on again', I said.
>
> 'We've made love once John, we never do it twice in the same evening'.
>
> 'Then it's time we did', I told her. (Anon 1975: 34)

The story concludes, after the beginnings of a regeneration of the couple's love life, with John buying a projector 'plus a few black-and-white Harrison Marks films', and enthusing his wife to hitherto unknown levels ('to my amazement she flung back the clothes, siezed [*sic*] my cock and put it in her mouth'; ibid.: 34).

From there, he plans a party: 'Not wife-swapping, I don't hold with that, but I wouldn't mind say a couple having it away at the same time as Alice and I. It would be like watching a film, wouldn't it?' (35) The figure of Marks re-enters the prose, with a note that his films are seen in 'many countries', and that even those who have developed beyond the limits of heterosexual coupling can still assist in the sexual education of the heterosexual couple – plus (and with an implied heteronormative limit to the 'limits' themselves) 'there is something strangely beautiful about seeing two girls making love' (35).

The next case study casts the female as the initiator of the Marks-enhanced marriage. And the article concludes: 'Two cases from among thousands that show sex movies being a help in sexual relations. All you need is a projector and you are away. Harrison Marks movies can be purchased easily, and even if your sex life is all you desire, you could get some new ideas from them' (38). This very idea of pornography (in the summary of the Report of the Committee on Obscenity and Censorship) 'implant[ing] in husbands the desire to engage in sexual experimentation which their wives found abhorrent, and which therefore introduced tensions into the marriage', is noted as a concern of Mary Whitehouse and the Festival of Light (Williams 1979: 87). Lawrence's figure of the impotent husband, of *Lady Chatterley's Lover*, articulates just this fear of wives becoming proactive in seeking pleasure – as the husband rages over the news that his autonomous wife has chosen to have sexual relations with a gamekeeper. There is a general sense, shared with Whitehouse then, that without the strictures of society, sexuality will degenerate to pure biological functioning, and for free use – as with the couplings of soulless animals. The accusation against Lady Chatterley is of the '*nostalgie de la boue*' ('nostalgia for mud'; Lawrence 1960: 274); that she has taken leave of propriety, decorum (including having a discrete affair with a member of her own class, as per her husband's approval) and even senses, and in this descended to a pure, unchecked sensuality. But the subtext is that of a sense of the greater potency of the labouring classes, and a greater freedom for them to be potent – as per *Maurice*, and for example (and as associated with Lawrence and E.M. Forster), the poet Edward Carpenter. In his *Towards Democracy* of 1896, Carpenter 'lie[s] abed in illness and experience[s] strange extensions of spirit' (68), and recalls social types, with the working classes (bi)sexualised: '[t]he bathers' who 'advance naked under the trees by the waterside, five or six together, superb, unashamed'; '[t]he thick-thighed hot coarse-fleshed young bricklayer with the strap round his waist' (69); '[t]he ragged boy with rare intense eyes not to be misunderstood – in the midst of much dirt and ignorance the soul through suffering enfranchised, exhaled'; '[t]he slut of a girl who has become a mother, the ready doubt among her neighbours [as to] who was the father' (70). This rustic potency reasserts an early gender dichotomy, with the woman as subservient, and then usable in terms of gaining experience, in Laurie Lee's *Cider with Rosie*. Lee, in a Lawrencian way, recollects life in a discursively sexualised (teenage fumblings, bestiality, incest, child abuse) Cotswolds village, just after the end of the First World War: females, then (and further to a thwarted gang rape attempt) warmly and nostalgically remembered as 'the little girls who had been our victims and educators, and who led us through those days' (Lee 1959: 261).

Sexual liberation, for Marks, seems to spread from the 'proletarian' below (the maids, the factory workers, the burglars, the nurses) – and becomes a collective endeavour rather than a matter of one individual's satisfaction. In this respect, Marks's vision of sexuality is antithetical to that of the anti-permissives: mankind moves forward en masse, in conversation, in mutual expectations, in threesomes or orgiastically. Any hindrance based on individual moral prohibitions seems doomed to marginalisation, or outright failure, against this tide. Mankind then is a communion of carefree sinners, rather than individual souls.

The Bachelor Gaze

Despite the commercial aspirations and sheen of *Come Play With Me*, Marks was producing grimy hardcore loops at a prolific rate, for private or Continental distribution, from the early 1970s. Marks would generally distance himself from hardcore film production, in print – perhaps simply to avoid prosecution. For example, from a 1971 profile for the pornographic magazine *Fiesta*, on 'Europe's Mr Sex': 'He hates shoddy hard-core porn, saying: "Technically it's abysmal and I hate crudity. I don't see anything beautiful in showing a great gaping cunt"' (Manley 1971: 24). And yet Marks's own *The Happy Nurses* spends some time delivering just such shots.[10] In *Die Lollos* (The Customs, 1970 – just such a Continental release), a customs officer inspects the baggage of female passengers, and finds one (Clyda Rosen) with multiple wristwatches – a scenario that ends up with a strip search and sexual encounters in a backroom.[11] This is initially with the customs officer but, after an interruption from Miss Durex of Custom Control ('What is going on here? Is that what you call a thorough search?'), then with Miss Durex herself. The female passenger returns home to her naked and masturbating boyfriend, with a consignment of Continental 8-mm loops in her suitcase (which the distracted customs officer had neglected to inspect). They watch one of these films while they make love. This time the Marksian twist is that the same boyfriend is also in the loop that they watch, with two other women – to the feigned, post-orgasm annoyance of his girlfriend: 'You could have waited for me!' The twist in *Sex Is My Business* (also known as *Sex Shop*, 1974, with Mary Millington and Marks's wife, Toni), which follows an orgy in the Lovecraft sex shop on Coventry Street, is the revelation that the customers had accidentally overdosed on one of the shop's products, an airborne aphrodisiac, which had been knocked to the floor.[12]

Other loops were not so imaginative. *Autogramm Stunde* (Autograph Hour, 1973), in which two groupies (one of whom is Rosen) meet and have sex with Randy Toole and a bandmate, seen in close-up and at length, closes with their selling a photograph of the naked musicians to a newspaper, which they have taken with Toole's stolen camera. *Dolly Mixture* (also released as *Vor Geiheit Kochen*, 1973) reworks Frankenstein – a woman (presumably the 'mixture' of 'dolls' of the title) is brought to life, and then makes love to everyone in the laboratory. *Dolly Mixture*, as with *Vampire*, and Russell Gay's *Blood Lust* (1979), elements of *Legend of the Witches* (Malcolm Leigh, 1970), *Virgin Witch* (Ray Austin, 1971), *The Wicker Man* (Robin Hardy, 1973) and, to a lesser extent, *Blue Blood* (Andrew Sinclair, 1974), and even José Ramón Larraz's British-shot *Vampyres* (1974), are indicative of a minor tendency: the pornographic extension of British horror, and particularly at the point of the waning of the popularity of Hammer Horror. Satanic sexploitation was not an unusual concern for 1970s pornography, as seen in sequences in *The Playbirds* (Willy Roe, 1978), which is set in sex industry environs. *Virgin Witch* and *Vampyres* both contrive, for example, to place naked women in country houses for extended scenes of witchcraft and vampirism, which are blended into love-making. *Legend of the Witches* recreates Cornish pagan ceremonies, with free love and nudity. Horror goings-on, as per Hammer Horror films, are taken as an access to female sensuality. For Gay, this horror template seems to accommodate BDSM (through the blood-letting) and hardcore pornography (for the heightened erotic content) as a kind of natural development to the sensuality of much horror of the time. In this respect, the pornographic films establish a dialogue, of sorts, with the more erotic quarters of respectable British film-making – and so position themselves with respect to an outlier horror adult audience, who want more.

All the film-making, and seemingly Marks's own physical state (as he often appeared in his films), deteriorated across the 1970s – far from the biography Marks of 1967 ('fit, bronzed, active and very, very healthy'; Wood 2017: 15). As he checks in to Bovington Manor Health Farm (in fact Weston Manor Hotel, near Oxford), in character for *Come Play With Me,* his voice sounds slurred. And by *Arabian Knights* (shot in two days in 1979 – twice as long as usual for a Marks loop shoot) one has the sense of an orgy haphazardly arranged by someone who was, nevertheless, not quite in the moment on the day itself, and perhaps remained slumped in a darkened corner throughout – leaving the performers to proceed to earn their pay without much thought or, crucially for a Marks film, performed 'fun'.[13] The film is nominally set in a harem in Persia (conjured up via plastic palm trees and clichéd music), but was in fact shot at the Hotel Julius Caesar in Queen's Gardens, Bayswater, with an orgy scene in the hotel's swimming pool area. A sheik and businessman converse, with champagne served by Mongolian-Scottish actor and wrestler Milton Reid (familiar from a number of James Bond films, and *Come Play With Me*), and women line up to be groped by the sheik as Reid stands behind them (and with one model looking genuinely shocked at the scene as it unfolds, and mouthing something to the woman next to her).[14] The sheik eventually choses two women (whom he pays with jewellery), and the businessman chooses one, while Reid continues to look on. That is – the women have been offered as payment for a business deal.

Busty Baller (1979)[15] lacks Marks's usual narrative mischief too; an upper-class woman (elaborate corset and jewellery, a flat opposite Bond Street tube station, and played by Nicky Stanton) fantasises about sex while masturbating alone, and when a window cleaner enters her apartment looking to fill his bucket with water they have sex. *Cockpit Cunts* (also known as *Aviator,* 1979) also features a single woman, masturbating in a bath, while fantasising about a foursome. But these films do seem to break free from the claustrophobia of upstairs Soho studios, and into the semi-public spaces of the metropolis. This anticipates later strains of public sex videos, such as Ben Dover's tendency to visit models in their homes for film-making in the years around the turn of the millennium, or the incorporation of video-making into public sex practices, as with dogging videos (which Dover also anticipates, in *Death Shock* of 1981, directed as Lindsay Honey, with its multiple couplings over a gold Ford Cortina in a woodland) – so reimagining spaces to erotic ends, as Public Sex Environments (PSEs), and with the attendant problems for those managing such spaces for the use of the public (see Byrne 2006: 29–31).

In Marks's case, this seems an evangelisation of sorts – taking the message of free love out into the world, and freeing the oppressed. This potential is everything that the anti-permissives feared.

There is seemingly a gendered distinction, to a degree at least, between the feature films and the hardcore loops. The feature films assemble the material in a straightforward fashion: women as the object of the male gaze, as per Laura Mulvey's theorisation of the structuring of the film text in relation to the visual pleasure of the male (1975), and so arranged or choreographed the stripping accordingly. Thus *The Naked World of Harrison Marks* documents Marks's work as a ringmaster of contemporary models (he picks up June Palmer for an assignment in his Rolls Royce under the opening credits), and *The Nine Ages of Nakedness* (1969) even works this notion into its framing device: a nervous Marks himself, under psychoanalytical observation, conjures up fantasies of desirable females, from the caveman era to the space age future, and many points in between. The hardcore loops, on the other hand, often seem to concern the fantasies of a woman, which are then seen to be fulfilled through a chance sexual encounter. So there is a doubling of narrative strands: the fantasising woman (narrative #1, often framing the loop), and the fantasy itself (narrative #2, which contains the majority of pornographic action). Here the fantasy may be imagined, or located elsewhere (as in *Die Lollos*, where it is the 8-mm film loop that the couple watch as they make love, or even the sex shown in a shop backroom via closed-circuit security monitoring, to startled customers, in *Sex Is My Business*), or just coming true (seemingly as per *Busty Baller* and *Cockpit Cunts*). In this conceit, one wants to note a degree of relative sophistication – seemingly, at times, in the attempt to 'get into' a fictional woman's psyche, and the suggestion then that narrative #2 represents the sexual desire of that woman. Therefore, in a way – perhaps even if in a facetious way – this conceit could be said to step away from the male gaze structuring of the typical loop, as with, for example, Margaret Nolan stripping for the camera, which cuts to leery close-ups from time to time, mimicking the male's changing visual vantage points – so with the (medium shot) whole woman reduced to the sum of her sexual 'bits', inspected in close-up.

But, firstly, this conceit could merely suggest that the women are complicit, or more complicit, in film-making that could be said to be exploitative, as the films are nominally about their outer and now inner lives – a suggestion that, during the 1970s, seems like a defensive reaction in its counter-positioning of the 'new idea' of female sexual desire and agency against any voices raised. The occasional film with a female voice-over delivers a story of the fantasy and sexual yearning on the part of the female – akin to readers' letters.

Secondly, this conceit suggests that Marks is the person to curate and present all this – doubly problematic, as the women are mostly mute, or just groan, and typically have performative intercourse, in the sense that allows for maximum exposure of their nakedness. And, at this point, for better or worse, there was no shortage of male experts who flaunted a degree of medical expertise in terms of their access to this area of female desire (as per Alex Comfort's love-making guides, discussed below). Marks's qualifications in this area would have been, one assumes, his experience in seduction, or the Soho culture of exalting and demeaning women. It is as if someone once outlined to a wide-eyed Marks, over a Cinzano in the early 1970s, the cliché of the 'essential' difference between men and women: men as aroused by images of sex crudely splayed before them, whereas women as aroused non-visually, by the 'idea' of sex. And this psychological insight then held good for the rest of Marks's professional life. While this is speculation on my part, something of this conception is evident in a segment of an interview given to *Fiesta* by Marks in 1971. In response to the question 'Have you ever been raped?', Marks answers:

> *Well, almost, I remember one girl [with whom I would work] ... She'd have a few drinks and then she'd have a terrible row with me, screaming that I was trying to make [love to] her, that I was always trying to get her – of course I wasn't. And eventually it always meant I had to screw her. And then she was great, ready for work. This sparked something off in her, it gave her something on the studio floor that she certainly didn't have before. (Manley 1971: 62)*

In this way, Marks posits himself as the explorer and liberator, and indeed beneficiary, of the mysterious workings of the female psyche, on his film sets.

Thirdly, the fantasy that then may be said to structure the pornography as seen is merely that of a woman being overwhelmed by sexual desire, and seeking fulfilment accordingly – to the benefit of, for example, the accidentally intruding Bond Street window cleaner, or the airline pilots of *Cockpit Cunts*. Philosophically, why would the condition of female sexual desire in itself be one that charges to fulfilment, in fairly short order – at about minute 8 or 9, with the money shot, which was the end of the loop's length? Such an idea interprets women as entirely available for men, and often dressed accordingly: cruising the streets or shops, or alone in their flats, and waiting for intercourse to happen with anyone, which – edging towards a rapist's interpretation – represents their sole interest in life. But in this respect, something of a difference can be detected between the straight-forward male gaze of the 1960s softcore loops (the stripped woman) and the male gaze of hardcore loops (the woman engaged in intercourse). The latter still structures and delivers the erotic spectacle, but re-routed: the woman frames (say, via voice-over) the spectacle as her fantasy. This, therefore, is a male gaze upon or into nominal female fantasy – which is their need of a man, or multiple men. So a fantasy narrative in a real world space is created in which the viewer can situate himself, imagining the potential of such female sensibility – and from here he surveys a wider world, albeit a world that unfailingly suggests women as being sexually available and in need. One could only really term the latter, pace Mulvey, with an acknowledgement of its roots in Marks's pornographic magazines, as the 'bachelor gaze'.

After the 1970s, Marks seems to have drifted into speciality and niche pornography. *Warden's End* (1981) sees the traffic warden in question (Linzi Drew) arguing with the manager of the Janus bookshop (40 Old Compton Street), follow him into the shop with a parking ticket, become distracted by the material on sale, and eventually agree to 'audition' for Harrison Marks himself (named, but not seen). This involves stripping, spanking and then caning, in front of the shop's counter. Marks's taste for everyday adventures, and humour, remains intact. But by the point of *The Cane and Mr Abel* (1984), the spanking films had become much as any other from that period – given over to unlikely scenarios of procedure, usually with authority figures (teachers, policemen, military types, prison wardens), with a close-up of the submissive woman's behind as she complains or wails about the punishment, and periodic comments on the way in which the skin has become distressed.[16]

The Cane and Mr Abel was shot on video (and sold on video cassette, at a very steep £50) – a new technology, which radically changed Marks's film-making: the erotic experience could be discursive and expansive, and no longer the hurried one-note and one-ambience of the loop. Indeed, pornography videos in the early 1980s often collected a number of loops onto cassettes, achieving variety by default. The real innovation, in respect to late 1970s/early 1980s videos of erotic content, could be said to be the *Electric Blue* series of 'video magazines' – and their imitators, such as the Red Tape or Red Tape International video series, with comedian Keith Allen as host (the first of which was released in 1981), and *New*

Look, 'A Video Magazine for Men', from Iver Film Services Video in 1983 (mostly clips from European softcore erotic films). *Electric Blue 001* (Adam Cole, 1979/80, and with a pre-certification video release) was hosted by Fiona Richmond, and included car-related footage, vox-pops, three strips (two models, and a 'reader's wife'-styled performer) culminating in fairly explicit masturbation, the cartoon *Snow White and the Seven Perverts* (David Hamilton Grant, Marcus Parker-Rhodes, 1973), some footage from a David Hamilton film, and a review and preview of *The Bitch* (Gerry O'Hara, 1979).[17] The Red Tape knock-offs included stripping, comedy-themed nudity sketches, and general interest material, such as hand-gliding footage, and were sold, at £30 per tape, from Video for Pleasure Ltd, on Carnaby Street. Allen was perhaps positioned to pull in new audiences from cultures he was then associated with (alternative comedy and punk) rather than a figure like Bernard Manning, whose engagements with X-rated releases, such as *The Great British Striptease* (Doug Smith, 1980), would have returned the erotic ambience into a 1970s culture of working men's clubs.[18] But just such videos existed too, complete with old school compères, as with *The Stag & Hen Video Night* (director unknown; New Crest Services, 1981; released 1982), introduced with the screen titles 'a bawdy entertainment for both sexes', 'blue humour, male and female strippers, plus [*sic*] drag queen', and 'this performance was filmed on location at Rockfords Nightclub, Essex'.

For Marks, the technology-enabled change was in relation to possible durations. And, indeed, duration is a component of BDSM and its rituals: practices that could not be so readily captured on 8-mm loops. *The Cane and Mr Abel* is twenty-five minutes in length, and with shots often in the region of ninety seconds – the choppy editing around erotic spectacles has gone. Now Marks seems to just film, and periodically switch camera angles to refresh the view, rather than feeling the need for a new set-up.

Roddick describes a film very similar to *The Cane and Mr Abel* in his writing on Soho pornography, as shown at the Spankarama Spanking Viewing Lounge (itself reviewed by Bob Diver for *Razzle*, 1983). For Roddick, the videos shown 'were of the worse technical quality of any I saw … but the "lounge" – a tiny, stuffy basement with 25 seats – was packed out at 1.30 on a Saturday afternoon' (Roddick 1982/83: 21). For Diver, the only positive aspect of Spankarama was that the seat he sat on did not collapse beneath him (Diver 1983: 6–7).

Margaret, a teacher (Linzi Drew), canes a pupil, Fiona (unknown performer), for spreading sexual rumours about her:

'No, Miss, please, please, please don't hurt me, Miss.'
'It's too late!'
'Please let keep my knickers on, please Miss.'
'This is going to sting your bottom, you know.'
The headmaster enters:
'What on earth is going on here?'
He further chastises the pupil:
'You have got off remarkably lightly, girl. If there's any more, I shall strip you of your prefectship as well.'
And he also spanks her.

Once the pupil has left, the headmaster turns on the teacher, on the grounds of irregular punishment and the potential for the involvement of the European Court of Human Rights in this spanking, and requests her resignation 'at the end of term'.

In scene two, the teacher is told to visit the headmaster for 'a very sound spanking' in his 'private room – at 7 o'clock tonight, suitably dressed, and there you will get a spanking that you will remember for a long time', whereupon he canes her. The second vignette opens with a close-up of a carriage clock on the headmaster's desk, slowly chiming seven. This seeming idiosyncrasy, in a film like this, signals the ritualistic nature of flagellation ceremonies – not least the tendency that spankings do not occur out of anger, or on a whim or in the moment, but are predetermined and prearranged. This indicates that the film-makers – and, one assumes, from his performance, especially the headmaster figure – were very familiar with the subject matter, and keen to reproduce with verisimilitude the particulars of these behaviours. On these characters, Paula Meadows, recalls:

George told me once that a woman in her late 50s had written to him offering to pose for the magazine. I later met this lady and she told me she had deliberately wanted to satisfy a long-held desire to be spanked. George put her into one of his videos and paired her with a man in his 60s, who had also written in to offer his services. While they were doing the scene, the lady became extremely excited and actually wet herself. Of course, George kept it in! Incidentally, this pairing worked out so well that the couple eventually got married. Kane had performed a valuable service.[19]

Gibson, discussing the rituals of the 'flagellant ceremony' (Gibson 1992: 267), draws on 'the huge mass of Victorian flagellant pornography' (281), but finds it still thriving – at the point of his writing in 1977 – in 'the porn marts of Soho today, [which,] like their Victorian predecessors in Holywell Street near Drury Lane, do a busy trade in "fladge"' (265–66).[20] Indeed, this genre of spanking pornography is one that, in a progressive move against ageism, seems to introduce senior figures, in not-directly-sexual roles, back into pornography. Although, with this, comes the reduction and infantilisation of many female participants to naughty schoolgirls or, seemingly mostly for 1970s variants, a sexualisation of family scenarios, with the daughter spanked by the parents.

Margaret, however, after five minutes of complaints, feels that she has broken through the pain barrier and decides she has enjoyed the experience – 'I think you're learning your lesson, Margaret', 'I think the lesson's just beginning'. Among the videos that followed were *Five of the Best* (1988), *Kane Assignment* (1991),[21] *Stinging Tails* (1992), *The Rules of the Game* (1992), *The Spanking Academy of Dr Blunt* (1992), *The Spanking Game* (1993), *French Maids Flogging* (1994), *Schoolgirl Fannies on Fire* (1994), *Spanked Senseless* (1995), *Stinging Stewardesses* (1996), and so on (among some eighty spanking titles). And Marks ended his days apparently compering live spanking shows. Paula Meadows recalls:

> *During the time I knew George, he was organising occasional live shows. I think he viewed them as a sort of Vaudeville show. The spanking sketches were mostly improvised, but they all had a dramatic context, most of it supplied by George's fertile imagination or the ideas of the participants – many of whom were involved with CP [corporal punishment] in some form or other. I think George may have taken part sometimes, but mostly I think he compèred. I only experienced one of these happenings.*[22]

'Vintage' films, that occasionally surface, of elaborate spanking scenarios, with a muzzy 1980s analogue video haze, seem to me like the work of Marks – but, shorn of credits or indeed any information as to their providence, and with the spanking videos lacking in Marks's old lightness of touch, it is impossible to say. I assume the *Spanking Party* series, with the on-screen credit 'filmed in the very early 1980s at a cabaret club in London', and indeed filmed in front of an audibly live audience, were Marks productions. Part one (of five) has two girls arriving on stage for an audition, only to be told that this would involve spanking; part two has two girls in boaters, seemingly caught bunking off school, and so forth.

I stumbled across Marks again, for the first time since mid-orgy in various loops of the mid-1970s, and then his bizarre presence in *Come Play With Me* (1977), in a surviving fragment of *Spanker's Paradise* (1992). This, like *The Rules of the Game,* is set in the fictional Brighton Hotel Derriere, where Marks himself seems to be working. Both hotel and Marks are solid, but have seen better days. He wears a baggy blue jumper, perhaps feeling the cold, but his gold is still there (watch, ring), recalling his flashy days of youth. And his voice is rich and resonant, his stance is welcoming, and his manner immediately friendly as he greets a German hotel guest in black suit, trilby and sunglasses. Marks is animated, still, by offering the promise of sexual adventure to others. He wags his finger in an ironic way at the guest: 'You're going to be working with a girl called Helen…' (he gestures as if clearing away all other opposition, and squeezes his eyes closed as if to emphasise this sensual opportunity) '… who is an absolute knockout'. He signals the way to the guest: 'Would you like to book in with the [searching for the word] … receptionist?' Then he beckons an obscure third man to follow him, gifting him a use in the evolving scenario: 'We'll go down and get those props'. Marks is able to exert soft control over an environment in which he directs others to engage in erotic missions – always presented, compellingly, as for their benefit and entertainment, and as unique opportunities. He stands at the centre of the highly unusual situations that he so unfussily orchestrates, channelling and satisfying desires of unknown others: the master pornographer of the last century, glimpsed in *Spanker's Paradise* for just a few seconds, still at work, in his last years. He leaves to collect the 'props' – completing a career that began in the dying days of the remnants of Victorian music hall, and ended on the cusp of online pornography. Marks's films then encompassed the entire spectrum, from suggestiveness to eroticism, soft to hardcore, and subcultural sexual practices, as they evolved across the twentieth century.

Russell Gay's Electrified Lust and Lesbianism

Russell Gay, who was already notable as a glamour photographer in the 1950s (on Gay as a 'curve prospector', see Spillman 1957: 4–9), had a career that paralleled Marks's. For Venus, in the early to mid-1960s, he made a number of loops: *Bard – To the Skin!* (backstage dressing room stripping); *Decorator's Dilemma* (changing clothes for home decoration); *Margaret's Big Splash* (gauzy petticoat, stockings, paddling pool); *Peeping Prohibited* (voyeurism of upper-class woman's boudoir; fully nude with camera movements deftly dodging genital exposure); *Picnic – For*

Two! (two women picnic and, counterintuitively, strip); *Terry's Night In* (a woman undresses and goes to bed, but a phone call summons her out, so she redresses and leaves; from the title card: 'Voluptuous Terry just can't get an early night'); *What the Doctor Ordered* (stripping for medical inspection; 'Even an apple a day could not keep the doctor away from glamorous Joy') – and probably very many more. From this, there is, firstly, a tendency to narrative reasons to undress twice; secondly, a preference for the kind of women that Spillman describes. Gay published *Knave* magazine, owned Mistral Films, and seems to have continued to made loops across the 1970s. But he seems too to have attempted to advance the Marks blueprint in a number of ways, pushing the idea of the sexually possible into the aspirational, with 'classier' hardcore pornography. Gay's films looked better: less murky than Marks (and John Lindsay), even to the point of being brilliantly lit, and of television advert quality, with performers who look like professional models, seem better dressed, and with more money spent on sets. For *Beach Orgy* (year unknown; 1970s), Gay constructs a beach within a small studio, and the male lead seems to be a bodybuilder; for *Rock Around the Cock* (year unknown; 1970s), the setting is a 1950s diner, with endless cutaway shots (fruit machine, Pepsi and Coca-Cola signs) to evoke this.[23] The sex is more performative, especially in respect of prolonged shots of kissing with extruding tongues, and slightly 'cleaned up', in the sense that ejaculation shots (at least in the films viewed) are not seen – without this resulting in suspicion that the sex is merely simulated. This occupational hazard was such that Marks even spoofed the dangers of projectile semen at the end of *The Happy Nurses*, with the fez-wearing foreign dignitary (in blackface), in a hospital bed close to the action, caught in the crossfire.

In addition, relatively substantial amounts of time seem to be devoted to men performing oral sex on women, and the sex is presented as mutually pleasurable, and seems more sophisticated in its execution than the hurried coupling found in other loops. It is possible that Gay's thinking was to attend to the fabled (and probably non-existent) couples' market, rather than supplying material for exclusively male viewing.[24] And the settings are private, seem newer (rather than run-down), and are contemporary (albeit of a 1970s vintage – of shag-pile carpets, moustachio'd men, elaborate suspender belts), and recognisable as homes. Across a number of films, Gay suggests an expansion of the norm of coupling: heterosexual at first, and then with the introduction of another woman or women, and then possibly with the return of the even-further-aroused male to the lesbian scenario. *Hot Vibrations* exists in two parts. In the first part, a door-to-door salesman of marital aids visits a single woman in a summer dress. She makes tea, examines his wares, and they make love. The end credits for the film loop promise just this development: 'Another satisfied customer... But the real action comes in Part Two when our salesman sets his equipment buzzing and works his way through no less than three girls in a totally uninhibited orgy of electrified lust and lesbianism'. In Part Two, the salesman encounters two further women in two further houses, and one then uses the marital aids on the other, in a hippy crash pad, and the salesman then returns and joins in. The standard jokey punchline is that, after his exertions (and walking with a stiff gait and wiping the perspiration from his face), the salesman offloads his briefcase of wares to a random passer-by in the street, with a pat on his back – he seemingly was not a salesman after all. And the passer-by then runs into one of the houses, presumably for his turn (or maybe he was meant to be a returning husband).

The pattern is repeated in *Open for Anything* (unknown year; 1970s): a couple enter a clothes shop, she and the female shop assistant have sex in a changing room while he, feigning ignorance, spies on the action. Then the couple have sex in the changing room while the shop assistant spies and masturbates, and eventually winds up naked on the floor – at which point he comes out, they perform oral sex on each other and then have penetrative sex, whereupon the female returns and a threesome ensues. And in *Beach Orgy*, one woman seduces another's boyfriend away from her. The injured party then dons a wig and suspenders, oils herself up and masturbates, and then seduces the intruding woman.

The expanded sexual sensibility also occurs in terms of the perception of sexual fantasy, as shared between females and males. In *Wet Dreams* (also known as *A Tramp in Paradise*; unknown year), an elderly man follows schoolgirls home and peeps at them through the windows of their house while masturbating in the bushes. At this point, Gay cuts to a fantasy sequence, which is seemingly that of both the tramp and the sleeping girls: now he enters the house, in a cape and top hat, and is greeted by the two nude women. He also turns up in their dream, watches as the women make love, and then partakes too. But, as expected, the gender weighting is invariably in the male's favour: a masturbatory female threesome can occur in Gay's *Shower Lust* (year unknown; 1970s), but heterosexual norms dictate against comparable combinations with two males and a female.

Gay's notional expanded sexual reach suggests that all women are bisexual – but this attribute does not foretell autonomy or independence (as per 1970s feminist imagining), merely adds a layer of intrigue and pleasure for the attendant males, which can be capitalised on, in plain view, but remains a secret to the general public. *Open for Anything* ends with the three asleep in the changing room, exhausted from their exertions, while a new shopper enters, unawares and unsuspecting. The events of *Hot Vibrations* are confined to their moment: as soon as the fake salesman exits, no one else will be much the wiser. And sequences of women masturbating and fantasising can be taken as private (unless a prelude to, or interrupted by, actual love-making). But this suggests Gay carves out a discrete and safe space for 'transgressive' imaginings – of a type that would later be described as bi-curious – offering an interplay of fantasies that therefore enliven the mundane heteronormative existence of his protagonists. *Response* (1974) strictly compartmentalises its fantasy and reality elements, which seems to allow for an expanded range of imaginative possibilities; the protagonist is free to safely fantasise. The film opens in an office, seemingly of a pornographic magazine. A blonde woman (Mary Millington) behind a desk talks to a red-haired woman, who is called away by her partner for afternoon sex:

> *'Can you come around?'*
> *'Right away?'*
> *'Well I really want to see you very much.'*
> *'I'll see you soon – bye.'*
> *And then, to Millington: 'Men – they're all the same!'*

But as they make love, her mind drifts: she imagines a lesbian encounter with Millington. Gay runs these two love-making narratives simultaneously – the actual heterosexual coupling, and the fantasy homosexual coupling – so deepening the sense of erotic possibilities with the fantasy of 'different' sex during standard sex. The sequences occur in two different ways. Gay films the heterosexual coupling from above, down onto a double bed (the typical Marks angle), and she eventually becomes bored with this perfunctory missionary sex and, raising her arms above her head, allows the male to press on as he sees fit. But the homosexual coupling is shot more cinematically – unhurried pans up and down the vertical bodies, disrobing and exploration (tongues and fingers), and a concentration on (explaining the casting) the contrasting pubic hair colours. In this, Spillman's observation of some years before is quite correct: Gay's close concentration on the undulations of these (non-bruised) bodies does cast him as a 'curve prospector'. Pastoral music plays, and groans increase; the lighting is revealingly bright but sympathetic, the clothes are fashionable, the make-up seems applied by a professional.[25] For this latter narrative, Gay shoots from the same level as the coupling (the typical Lindsay angle) – as if a part of this, rather than above it. And while Gay intercuts the simultaneous climaxes, the film's preference is clearly for the fantasy narrative. The fantasy remains a fantasy, because once the red-haired woman has returned to the office, she delivers some papers to Millington without any indication of anything unusual. But *Response*'s twist is that, once she has left the office, Millington looks at her as if suddenly overwhelmed by a lesbian yearning of her own. *Response* then reverses the standard female/female/male dynamic identified across this study: here the female/female encounter is exalted in itself, and not relegated to pre-phallus foreplay.

I speculate above that Gay may have attempted to tap a couples' market or, in relation to Roddick's comments that couples were highly unusual in Soho cinemas (Roddick 1982/83: 20), to generate such a market. And in this respect, his expanded sexual reach is, tellingly, not expanded beyond what already seem to be established relationships. Gay's hardcore loops seem eminently grounded in reality: this is what could be, with some rearrangements and open-mindedness to already existing networks – a measured leap in the permissive imagination.

This then is the development of Marks's project (or, at least, some of it): Marks liberates the nebbish, and even stands in for that man himself, or dwells amongst them – as if a visiting saviour, showing mankind the way to sexual salvation. Gay then educates the liberated (and possibly his partner or partners) – further pitting the fun, fulfilment and adventure of the permissive revolution against the straitened lifestyles advocated by the anti-permissive bloc. In this light, Marks and Gay seem to suggest an imagined audience wishing to step into, and advance, the conditions of possibility of the permissive age. The pornographic artefacts are only a part of that process. And the ambiguities over gender power dynamics are telling in this respect: for crucial stretches, the female seems to lead the way, or (in the context of the time) is given leave to lead the way. Even Marks's final BDSM phase can or could be folded into this position (albeit with numerous caveats): spanking scenarios that first necessitate a negotiation, on equal terms, in terms of who is dominating whom, in the play-acting. John Lindsay, on the other hand, seems entirely pragmatic over visionary: what the permissive age can actually deliver, in terms of basic sexual opportunity – and how to go about getting it. It is within this line of thought that Mike Freeman's films then take on some significance. On the one hand, and especially with the switch to video and the relaxation arising from the use of that easier technology (as evident in the films' longueurs and technical failures), the films seem inconsequential, if unpleasant. In *Sex Slave* (1979), two men break into a house and rape a woman, who then seems to enjoy the encounter and reciprocates – one assumes the scenario is presented as play-acted. In *Sex Lessons* (presumably 1979), three women as schoolgirls discuss their A-levels and are then spanked by their headmaster, and group sex follows. As with *Truth or Dare* (1980), discussed below, the films simply and tediously present consenting adults, in rooms, engaging in sex. Elements of 'deviancy' (BDSM and rough and group sex, and homosexuality in *What a Gay Day*) suggest, or are even presented as containing, some kind of libertarian, liberating edge. But this provocation (bar the homosexuality) is already familiar from Marks, Gay and Lindsay.

However, at the dawn of the 1980s, and with the homophobic language and then legislation of the incoming Conservative government, Freeman's approach, consciously or otherwise, seems more nuanced.[26] The very freedom for those consenting adults to do as they wished, and as evidenced as existing practices in these films, in these small domestic spaces, also provokes. Is neoliberalism liberal enough to tolerate these liberations? And here, one can note that 'Freeman' is the nom de plume of Mick Muldoon: Muldoon, freed from prison, declaring himself a free man, and (with the Irish ambience erased) an Englishman.[27] Freeman's continued trouble with the police and the seizing and destruction of his films suggest that the hardcore provocation was too much – or now (with Thatcher in power) unwelcome. Freeman (whose films are discussed later), in terms of the distribution of his videos in the early 1980s, is essentially outside the scope of this study. By this point, Marks, Lindsay and Gay had all taken their leave from hardcore. Marks, as noted, moved to BDSM – films that may not include actual sexual activity, and so are difficult to prosecute. Lindsay had given up; Millington's suicide might have contributed to an acknowledgement that a prosecution culture would not be lifted. Gay seems to have left the UK in a hurry in the early 1982; Pemble recalled: 'Russell left unexpectedly, although I don't remember there being an official explanation. However, we later heard he'd moved to Monaco, and its reputation as a tax haven might be pertinent' (quoted in Campbell 2014: 41). Gay's UK business operations presumably ended at that point, which might account for the obscurity of his work and his name. Color Climax also seemingly reigned in their catalogue, and tried to remove paedophilic material. The Video Recordings Act was pending, which would have impeded the transfer from 8-mm to video.

In this light, Tory moralism would seek to police inside the homes that so many Freeman films are set in, and intrude on the privacy of consenting adults. As discussed, this impulse was completely counter to the libertarian reading of the Permissive Society – and suggests Thatcher's tipping of the balance in favour of a constant of heteronormative Victorian values, and with a threat of legal action to follow.

Notes

1. Marks, also credited as George Harrison Marks, lived 1926–1997; he was referred to as Harrison Marks, but friends would also call him George.
2. The scenes with model Pamela Green, in Michael Powell's notorious Soho-set serial killer film *Peeping Tom* (1960), were seemingly shot in the 4 Gerrard Street studio. Marks acted as a consultant for Powell with respect to the locales and milieu in which *Peeping Tom* was set.
3. On the young Marks and music hall, see Wood 2017: 11–12, 41. On Marks arranging additional sex work for his performers, in the 1970s at least, see Tutti 2017: 194.
4. The 'money shot' is visible male ejaculation, which verifies the non-simulated nature of the sex seen – at least, for the male, and at least when not faked; for discussion, see Williams 1991: 93–119. Dworkin sees in this the demeaning of the female – 'on her, not in her. It marks the spot, what he owns and how he owns it. The ejaculation on her is a way of saying (through showing) that she is contaminated with his dirt; that she is dirty' (quoted in Moore 2007: 84). Heather Berg also reads this authentication in terms of evidence of labour (i.e. the task of bringing about orgasm in another) – albeit labour that, in a way familiar to feminist thinking, seems to need to pass itself off as a 'natural' female preoccupation. Thus 'authenticity is both a form of labor and a discourse that conceals labor' (Berg 2017: 689). And, for Berg, this is particularly present in 'porn work' and the 'market for authenticity'. This is why the idea of payment for sex and Mary Millington, jars, and why John Lindsay seemed able to volubly blame the failing 'tools' rather than the female 'workmen' for on-set problems, both noted elsewhere in this study. At the same time, Lindsay is crudely straightforward in some of his films: the interaction is clearly one of exploiter and exploited, of prostitution, and not, say, the supposedly frustrated female housewife, overcome with lust at the visiting milkman, losing control of her behavioural norms.
5. Marks's annual cat calendars were reputedly very popular, although the cats in his studio often made appearances on his loops too. It is possible, as with contemporary techniques to quell tension (for prisoners awaiting sentencing, or students their exams, for example), that the cats functioned as a therapeutic distraction for otherwise nervous models.
6. Seemingly later released as *Dracula the Vamperve*, 'filmed on location in Sohovania'. The creative contributions of Marks's long-term set designer, Tony Roberts, are very apparent in films such as *Vampire*.
7. The hotel room, with the garish 'period' painting of Marks, four-poster bed and the false wall of the rotating bookcase, was seemingly filmed in Marks's own house.
8. Sellers, of films such as *The Millionairess* (Anthony Asquith, 1960) and *Only Two Can Play* (Sidney Gilliat, 1962). However, *Nine Ages*, in its structure and variations of punchlines around sexual frustrations, seems to owe more to *Bedazzled* (Stanley Donen, 1967).

9. Petronius also notes the propensity for factory workers – 'not foremen' – to arrange 'blue film-shows between or even during shifts' (Petronius 1969: 247). It is possible that this can be explained by the use of 8- and 16-mm projectors in factories, for industrial training films. Certainly, this technology was used at this time to screen radical and militant films in occupied factories across Europe (see Halligan 2016: 106, n13).

10. If it was made at the same time as the softcore version, *Goodnight Nurse*, then *The Happy Nurses* can be dated to late 1972.

11. An English dub also exists of this film, and it was seemingly first filmed in black and white, and released as *Unaccustomed As I Am*.

12. The film seems to exist in a softcore, albeit full frontal version – but it is difficult to think that a hardcore version does not also exist.

13. Paula Meadows recalls the end of this trajectory: 'In his last years he drank heavily and this altered his demeanor. The lively, warm-hearted, easy-going George descended during the course of the day into a morose, dissatisfied soul. If he happened to be directing a video, the shooting would start off in an organized way, but come the late afternoon, everything started to descend into chaos as he became more and more drunk. Luckily he had a very efficient cameraman who had worked with him a long time and understood him; he managed to subtly take over, without it being too noticeable, to make sure all the scenes were properly completed.' Personal correspondence, 14 April 2021.

14. Reid was ostracised from the film and television industries after the *Sunday People* newspaper ran an exposé on his involvement in *Arabian Nights*; he died in uncertain circumstances in 1987 (Sheridan 2011: 269).

15. The softcore version was called *Busty Ravers*, as a giveaway with the pornographic magazine *Peaches*.

16. Mainstream British BDSM of this period might include *The Penthouse* (Peter Collinson, 1967), *If....* (Lindsay Anderson, 1968), *Performance* (Nicholas Roeg and Donald Cammell, 1970), *Sleuth* (Joseph L. Mankiewicz, 1972), *The Brute* (Gerry O'Hara, 1977) and *The Wicked Lady* (Michael Winner, 1983). *The Brute* combined both country house and white coater strains, discussed elsewhere, and casts Bruce Robinson as another variant of the *Blow-Up* photographer.

    Actual school corporal punishment in the mid-1980s – a practice then in its last few years – was in fact also equally given over to ritual and process: the time to arrive arranged in advance, the wait to be summoned into the office of the teacher, an executive summary of offences prior to the beating, the suggestion that this is the lesser of two evils (that is: caning over expulsion), the numerical organisation of the strokes (typically 3 or 6, even reputedly an exceptional 12, 'of the best'), this often interrupted by instructions on the positioning of the hands or the behind, something of a moral at the end (along the lines of '... and let that be a lesson for you'), followed by the customary thanking of the one who had administered the punishment. And, after, the redemptive sense that these few minutes of terror and, at times, actual pain, had closed the file on whatever misdeeds had first occasioned them, allowing the recipient a sense of the potential to start afresh. My thanks to the late headmaster of Winterfold House, and occasionally his late father, for these insights. Further commentary on the headmaster's use of the 'whack', also recalling the present author as a co-recipient, can be found in O'Brien 2020: 15, 54–57. This process had barely changed in centuries; the detailed descriptions of as much at Stonyhurst College by 'One of the Boys' (pseudonymously Percy Fitzgerald), recalling 1850 from the vantage point of 1867, would hold good over one hundred years later. This was true with respect to the confusing experiences of partaking of a meal while knowing that the final course would be followed by the scheduled beating, which 'somehow seemed like the breakfast the condemned man "partakes of heartily" before going up to the scaffold' (One of the Boys 1867: 46; for the general outline, see 43–50), and having to directly request the thrashing too ('Please, sir, would you give me twice nine?'; Fitzgerald 1895: 33).

Sir Rhodes Boyson, noted elsewhere in this book, saw and promoted corporal punishment as ideally intrinsic to Thatcher's return to Victorian values: thrashing established respect in the schoolboy, and so the 1984 abolition of the practice brought about 'a weakening of the close relationship between pupils and staff' (Boyson 1996: 67). And this laxness had created wider problems in society; speaking in 1976 on 'the morals of our young' who 'have been brainwashed by mindless sociologists', in relation to coverage of a case of 'young girl prostitutes' at the time: 'We need more policemen and fewer social workers ... we need to get back [sic] towards the Victorian days of discipline' (cited in Brown and Barrett 2002: 169).

17. Pre-cert videos are those without a BBFC certificate – something possible prior to the 1984 Video Recordings Act. As no submission to the BBFC was legally mandated, films were often released in an uncut form, and with lurid covers. A sense that matters had got out of control fed into the Video Nasties moral panic, and the banning of various (mostly horror) films; see Wingrove and Morris 2009.

18. Released on video cassette as *An Unbelievably Dirty Evening with Bernard Manning – 16 Young Strippers* in 1986.

19. Personal correspondence, 14 April 2021.

20. Although the back-cover copy of Gibson's book includes an endorsement from *Janus* magazine, so Gibson cannot have been too critical of this modern manifestation of the, as he terms it, 'English vice'. Such a crossover is hardly novel, however; correspondence on whipping one's maid, from the *Englishwoman's Domestic Magazine*, popular with middle-class women in the 1860s, was reproduced verbatim in pornographic publications of that time (Marcus 2007: 140–41).

21. This featured Paula Meadows, who had worked with Mike Freeman on *Truth or Dare* (1980) and which she had found (presumably in contrast to the precise arrangements of BDSM matters), quite chaotic: 'Others involved [one would assume Ben Dover] with the project didn't take it seriously enough; they didn't follow the script' (quoted in Bayldon 1991: 51). See Meadows (1992: 25–31) for an impressionistic outline of the BDSM subculture and pornography across the 1980s.

22. Personal correspondence, 14 April 2021.

23. The Gay films discussed here all had 1981 pre-certification UK video releases, from Mistral Films – seemingly two loops per video, and presumably sold through mail order and via sex shops. Gay seems to have made at least a few dozen films, shot in Kilburn, but the majority remain unavailable or lost. The films viewed (sourced from Super 8-mm) were silent, but conceivably sound versions exist, as there are talking sequences. Some video volumes of compilations of softcore cuts of loops appeared in the early (pre-certificate) and mid-1980s (with BBFC certification), such as *The Rustler Connoisseur's Collection*. Anecdotally, Gay and Marks, initially fierce rivals, became friends – not least through a (consecutively) shared ex-wife.

24. However, rumours at the time in the *Knave* office had it that the hardcore films were directed by one of Gay's wives. This might, at the risk of reductionism, account for their more sympathetic accounts of love-making in respect to the female experience. Much to the

detriment of this study, with the absence of opinions from any female film-makers, I have not been able verify this rumour.

25. A former colleague of Gay's from the magazine *Knave* remembers secretaries asked to supply orgasmic 'squeaks and groans' to beef-up the lacklustre soundtrack for at least one of the films (private correspondence, January 2019). This could well have been for *Response*.

26. This legislation is read as an 'intimidating ideological attack' (Ardill and O'Sullivan 1989: 126). Section 28, designed in 1986 and implemented in 1988, forbade engagement with the subject of homosexuality in schools. On Section 28, in context, see McManus 2011. Operation Spanner, resulting in mass arrests for BDSM-practising gay and bisexual men, and with a homemade videotape of such practices seized and used as evidence for a police hunt (including the assumption of murder), would begin in 1987; see White 2006. The Conservative Party would apologise for Section 28 in 2009 but only, Monahan notes, in the context of 'two discourses: the pink pound neo-liberalising of gay identity; and the seeing of marriage equality as supporting the traditional institution of the family' (Monahan 2019: 144).

27. Mike Freeman lost equipment and tapes to police raids, and lost his personal liberty. As Michael or Mick Muldoon, his late 1960s career with Climax Films ended with incarceration relating to the death of his minder – sometime porn performer, Gerry Hawley – whose body was dumped in Epping Forest in Essex, a death which even took Mad Frankie Fraser aback in its intensity (see Fraser and Morton [2001] 2007: 90). Muldoon re-emerged as Mike Freeman in the late 1970s, shooting on U-matic video and founding the Videx company during the pre-certification phase. On Muldoon/Freeman, see Carter 2018.

CHAPTER 4

Erectile Dysfunction and Societal Dysfunctionality

The John Lindsay Loops

John Lindsay was, across the 1970s, the most visible maker and distributor of, and outspoken spokesman for, hardcore pornography in Britain. The films themselves were as unmistakably blunt as Lindsay's own media persona as a no-nonsense Glaswegian, lacking the humour of Marks and the homely ambience of Gay, and typically extremely quick to get down to the business at hand. Sheridan notes (although the source is unclear) that Whitehouse referred to him as the 'Devil's Ambassador to England' (Sheridan 2011: 29 and 258).

Lindsay briefly appears in Long's *The Wife Swappers* (1970) too, albeit seemingly inadvertently. Lindsay had originally worked as a still photographer for Long in the late 1960s, after a stint as a photojournalist (including, apparently, as an official photographer for a Buckingham Palace ball; Sheridan 2011: 29). And Lindsay was also involved in the making of a number of feature films: *The Love Pill* (Ken Turner, 1971; Lindsay has a co-writer credit); *The Hot Girls* (co-directed with Laurence Barnett, 1974; a documentary concerning nude modelling, which seemingly also exists in a hardcore version); and *I'm Not Feeling Myself Tonight* (Joseph McGrath, 1975; as co-producer – a credit that was removed by the production company in response to Lindsay's legal troubles). Lindsay wrote *The Sexorcist*, regarding his legal trials, possibly later reproduced in magazine format.[1]

For his hardcore loops, and even for the few of his films that moved beyond the 8–10 minutes duration, scene-setting was broad and curt – a hospital, a boat, a bus shelter, a school, a dinner party, the milkman arriving, outside Euston rail station, school showers and so on. And, thereafter, Lindsay filmed, often in close-up to extreme close-up and with full and mostly unforgiving illumination, in forensically gynaecological or phallic detail. The camera is at times so close to the manually stretched vaginas that the images seem in danger of blurring into abstraction – particularly once the films were transferred to video.[2] However, this framing makes complete sense when watching the films on 8-mm or, particularly, Super 8-mm (as first intended): the proximity seems calibrated to the size of the projection – close enough to render sufficient or requisite detail. And the typically slower-than-life film speed does not degrade the quite astonishingly vivid quality of the Super 8-mm image, particularly for the colour films. This pre-digital technology makes for a luminous aesthetic realism, complimented by, rather than offset by, the slight slowness: Lindsay has captured and delivers these scenes of intimacy, and their colour and detail meet the expectation of close attention.

In terms of audio: the noises of urgent squelching and sluicing are mixed so loudly in the dubbed soundtracks that a naive viewer could only assume that the vaginal or anal passages themselves had been mic'd for the occasion. At other times, the dubbing lags substantially, or has wound up in this way through processes of duplication. In *Gypsies Curse* (unknown year), a woman seems to talk in an unimpeded way while performing fellatio. And the sex acts themselves were typically strained: fully splayed vaginas and anuses, and often, on the part of the male performers, a seeming biological urgency to reach climax, speeding the whole narrative forward. In the evidence presented in a 1974 trial, Lindsay was noted as presenting sexual intercourse 'in its rawest and nastiest fashion' (quoted in Whitehouse 1978: 189). Lindsay does not seem to have cared for the films he made: 'I found them [either his films, and/or pornography in general] to be dull and boring, without exceptions ... What always amazed me was that they were evidently purchased by people who were perfectly capable of performing the sex acts depicted, so why look at pictures of it?' (quoted in Kerekes 2000: 194).

This unadorned basicness seems redolent of the particular besieged situation for hardcore British pornography production in the 1970s. Legal concerns and social and moral stigma seem to have curtailed time and drained money from sets, resulting in a furtiveness and urgency to get to the climax, with no concomitant quality control deemed necessary. Conceivably too, in terms of urgency, there was a need to generate a large quantity of product. The enormity of Lindsay's output suggests a substantial market for his films.

Lauret's above-mentioned essential difference, in terms of sex cultures, between the UK and Denmark (Lauret 1970: 6–7, 24), is also the difference of the quality of desire: Denmark allows for desire and dreams, whereas London only offers sordidness and a possible threat of violence. Marks and Gay could be associated with the former, and Lindsay's and Freeman's films – without casting a value judgement in this respect – are of a piece with that particular sordid ambience. Marks and Gay suggest the possibility of the anonymous souls of the city being enlivened, socialised, made whole, beyond the confines of marriage. And whereas Lindsay signals to as much in *The Pornbrokers*, the films seem unable to deliver anything beyond soulless bodies.

A Lindsay loop that is particularly true of this ambience is *Euston Capture* (1972).[3] *Euston Capture* seems to riff off a common story of the time that concerned pimps waiting to talk to lone young women or men alighting at central London train stations – those who have just left or been ejected from their homes, head to the capital without resources but with a sense that opportunities await, and so can easily end up being recruited into prostitution. For example, from Harris's study of male prostitution, regarding Euston 'at the beginning of winter' and a newly arrived sixteen-year-old: 'Huddled in the station, he was approached twice by men, who offered to put him up for the night, informing him discreetly what they expected of him in return' (Harris 1973: 30). Daly records as much too (Daly 2018: 89–90), as organised by Roger Gleaves – and with sequences in *Johnny Go Home* directly showing approaches made by Gleaves and associates, with steaming urns of soup, to the cold and disorientated young in Euston Station. And Savile's own associates seem to have been in operation in Euston – taking runaway children back to a flat, where they would encounter Savile, who would then convey them to parties for sexual abuse; Davies dates this to 1967 (Davies 2015: 233–34). Astonishingly, Savile's autobiography boasts about his taking sexual advantage of just such runaway waifs, in full view of the Leeds police (Savile 1974: 51). But Don Chaffey's 1957 film *The Flesh is Weak* dramatizes this trope too: Italian ingénue arriving at a London train station, sped into prostitution in Soho (via a brief stint as a nightclub hostess), and left standing in the rain while anonymous men circle. *Euston Capture* then capitalises on this 'erotic' possibility – with 'capture' presumably originally intended to mean some kind of slyly executed pick-up. The two women, who when first encountered seem lost (standing outside the station, looking at a map) would seem to evidence the consensual nature of the sex that follows with their eagerness to drink and disrobe once back at the flat. But in a film without sound, it is possible to think that the men just offered much-needed money rather than whisky and company. Either way, the film channels the mythology of Euston as a hunting ground for the vulnerable. And the plying with drink, as in *Girl Guide Rape* (Lindsay, year unknown), is also presented a stratagem. The Euston victims of Gleaves and Savile were all approached on the basis of an offer of the warmth, food and shelter that they needed.

Illustrations 4.1 and 4.2 Euston pick-up scenes from John Lindsay's hardcore *Euston Capture* (1972), and Euston pick-up scenes of Roger Gleaves from the documentary *Johnny Go Home* (John Willis, 1975). Screenshots by the author.

Lindsay seems to have had a tendency to shoot parallel to, or just below, areas of genital interaction – even to the extent that performer limbs seem to have been positioned to allow access to the camera. This contrasts to the more conventional filming of sex in the hardcore loops of Marks from the 1970s, where the camera is often placed above (at standing height) and then angled down onto the genital interaction, as with *Bistro Bordello* (1972).[4] There may be a pragmatic reason for this difference in terms of filming: more ejaculation seems to occur in Marks's hardcore films, as he typically initiated full orgies. Conceivably then there could have been a danger of the camera or cameraman being sprayed in ejaculate, as per the twist of *Happy Nurses*, and hence the distance being kept. For Lindsay, the filming is typically a more sustained engagement with one interaction at a time, climaxing in one ejaculation, allowing time for the film-makers to take cover via a set-up.

Firstly, the effect of Lindsay's preference for, at times, being in such close proximity to the coupling, and with the performers shifting legs and stomachs to allow for this presence, is that the viewer is positioned as if an active or imminent part in the couplings, and for whom this space is reserved (i.e. the third, or fourth, person in this tangle of limbs). A later variant of this effect, for the contemporary category or genre of 'POV porn', seems less sophisticated: in POV ('point-of-view'), in general, the gaze of the viewer is aligned to the passive male, who is only partly seen, and the focus is the genital interaction managed by the fully seen partner. The partner may even directly address the passive male / viewer, with rhetorical dialogue ('You like this, don't you?', 'You've been a bad boy, haven't you?', and so on). In this POV arrangement, a narrative unfolds leading to an event occurring – typically either a climax or, say, with a dramatic flourish, the partner's absent husband arriving back home from work early). In Lindsay's proto-POV, the narrative does not account for or try to accommodate the imagined presence of the viewer in the action, and the close proximity seems to work to just present a series of sexual possibilities at any one moment, which may then be the basis of the viewer's own fantasy imaginings. Indeed, the sustained shots of uninterrupted genital interaction may act as effectively dismissing any scene-setting narrative and elongating the actual action, so that fantasy imaginings can take over in parallel to this film: a kind of 'pause' button facility when such a thing (in a cinema club) may not have been available. And this proximity and non-conventional angle results in, secondly, a sense of exploring or testing or charting rather than just showing (as with Marks) the genital interaction – that *this* is what it looks like from this position, or with this kind of touching or penetration occurring.

The loop titles (announced via illustrated title cards) tended to bluntness too: setting / personnel / act, as with *Juvenile Sex* (1974), *Boarding School* (1976), *Sex Lessons at School, Sex After School, Wet Nymph, Triangle of Lust, Sex Kitten, The Kinky Vicar, Hot Sensations, Naughty Schoolgirls, Juvenile Sin, Girl Guide Temptations, End of Term, Jamboree, Sensuous Introduction, Sweet Sixteen, Dr Sex, School Teacher's Orgy, Hippy Orgy, Schoolgirl's Pussy, Schoolgirl Seduction, 100% Nymph*.[5] Across such a substantial body of work, and seemingly with much of it unavailable and long since unseen (or possibly destroyed), it is difficult to make generalisations as to thematic consistency. But the one aspect that does emerge in Lindsay's films was apparent to Stanley Long: 'he had a thing about jailbait fantasies' (Long, with Sheridan, 2008: 148). Lindsay films also seem to have shifted freely between a power dynamic of narratives that would seem to suggest fantasies about forcible coercion or rape (as with *Euston Capture, Anal Rape, Girl Guide Misfortune*, or *Girl Guide Rape* of 1976, or *Danger Route* with a male seen to be raping a female he has knocked unconscious with bottle), to narratives that suggest female initiation of sexual encounters. In *Danger Route* the raped female awakens to find the male now making love to her friend (and fellow thief; they had faked a car accident and robbed the male), and then joins in, for a threesome. The latter tendency, of female initiation, can be seen in three substantially longer (that is, in excess of 20 minutes) Lindsay films, which are, tellingly, set in an upper-class milieu. In *Health Farm* (1975), which includes an upper-class voice-over and a character called Lady Samantha, a client of the health spa calls a waiter/trainer up to her room under the false pretence of wanting fresh orange juice – commenting, partly inaudibly, as she masturbates in anticipation of his arrival, that she already has plenty of juice. In *Desire* (1971), the newly released aristocrat, the 'jailed playboy' Peter (Timothy Blackstone) seen in a newspaper headline that opens the film, returns to his home in his chauffeur-driven Rolls Royce to find an orgy in full swing – the viewer having previously seen a group of four women arriving for 'the party' and talking of how they will ensure that this party is a 'good one'. The playboy, removing his morning suit, exclaims: 'Lovely – all ready, willing and able. I haven't had a fuck in eighteen months and I'm raring to go. Come on you two, let's get at it!' (and, later, 'Blimey, darling – I'm going to shoot my lot!'). And in *Sexangle* (1975 or 1976) a 'Madam', Lady Samantha, the owner of a country manor, is visited by two interior decorators; meanwhile, a chauffeur in a soft-top Rolls Royce picks up hot-pants-clad young women.[6] But this latter tendency is also apparent in loops too: *Man Hunters* sees two women aggressively preventing a male from leaving their flat once he takes fright at seeing that one is without underwear under her miniskirt.

The idea of such an open and fecund 1970s hardcore culture is difficult to compute in the British context. Lindsay seemed to disregard prohibitions without apology, at least in relation to that portion of his work that was visible in the UK – visible in the sense of public rather than private screening and distribution. The films were for sale as 8-mm loops (and shot in 16-mm) and later as videos, and could be viewed in his London cinema clubs: the Taboo club in Great Newport Street and the London Blue Movie Centre in Berwick Street. These 'clubs' were effectively a street doorway leading up to a room in which the films were being shown, with advertisements around the door that left little ambiguity as to what was being shown – quite different to Marks's relative discretion.

From the late 1960s onwards, Lindsay produced, he claimed, thousands of loops (cited in Sheridan 2011: 258). The Duncan interview claims six thousand by 1978 (Duncan 1978: 70), which would necessitate around twelve new loops each week for the duration of his then circa ten years as a film-maker – and with the majority shot in the UK. This would have been possible from a few well-organised days shooting per week, and with a high percentage of film exposed actually used in the loops – and the intensity and speed of such work would explain Lindsay's nemesis: erectile dysfunctionality on set, potentially bringing the entire production process to a halt. There are seemingly about forty to sixty loops in digital circulation, and an unknown number that seem to only exist on celluloid. Lindsay films, on DVD transfers from 8- or 16-mm, remain on sale in sex shops in Soho. Some look like they were sourced from the early 1980s, pre-certification video releases of Lindsay films – as with the two 1982 'Teenage Series' videos (VHS and Betamax, distributed by Taboo via mail order): *Girl Guide Misfortune*, *Sex Kitten*, *Schoolgirls Joyride* and *Teenage Sex, End of Term, Boarding School* and *Naughty Schoolgirls*.

Even with ruthless police efficiency, it seems unlikely that thousands of further Lindsay loops would have vanished. The editing, and individual title cards, and sound work, suggests that some care, at least, was needed in preparing each for release. Kerekes notes that by 1974, Lindsay had made one hundred 'short features', of which a third had been shot in the UK (Kerekes 2000: 10). It is possible then that Lindsay's 'thousands' referred to the numbers ordered. What does seem to be missing is a bulk of films from the latter half of the 1970s and even early 1980s. The dramatic increases in the number of obscene items seized by the Metropolitan Police in the years 1976–78 (as per Table 1.1) might account for this. However, with so many films undated, it remains difficult to comment with precision.

Even his first arrests and court appearances did not seem to stem the flow of pornography. After being cleared of 'conspiracy to publish obscene films for monetary gain' in 1974 (which Whitehouse [1978: 188–89] notes as two trials, the first inconclusive, and that a defence was in part mounted along the lines of the therapeutic nature of pornography), an additional opening title card was added, at the top of each film, as seen in *Jolly Hockey Sticks* (1974), which proclaimed:

> This is a John Lindsay Production.[7]
> I, John Lindsay, was prosecuted in Birmingham Crown Court in 1974, and at the Old Bailey, London, in 1977, under the Obscene Publications Act 1959, and 1964.
> I was acquitted in both cases, and the jury found my films not to be obscene.
> [followed by Lindsay's handwritten signature]

Geoffrey Robertson recalls that, after the 1974 acquittal, Lindsay 'opened a [Soho] shop which only sold those films [that had been] the subject matter of the

Birmingham indictment', repackaged the films to note their legal difficulties on the covers, and decorated the shop with posters made from relevant newspaper cuttings regarding the trial. And, after the second trial, which was an unusual and failed attempt to re-try Lindsay for the offences considered in the first (he was cleared in 1977; Sheridan 2011: 258), Lindsay placed the contentious films on continuous show (Robertson 1979: 77 and 84). His magazine adverts for the films contained a similar formulation, and at times even a picture of Lindsay himself: his seeming earnestness, pinched features and functional glasses did not suggest the never-satiated imbiber of carnal pleasures. I remember coming across these adverts in the back pages of a cache of film magazines (film in the sense of 8-mm and 16-mm) that I had bought for £2 from a jumble sale in, I think, summer 1979 or 1980, attracted by covers that promised coverage of *Star Wars* (George Lucas, 1977) and *Superman* (Richard Donner, 1978). Even at 8 or 9 I had a suspicion that it could not be the case that such things were permissible, and that somehow the spectrum of film entertainment surely did not stretch from spaceships and superheroes (on the cover, in the first few pages) to explicit sex (8-mm loops to purchase, as advertised at the back). Kerekes reproduces one such magazine advert, from 1974:

> *I, John J. Lindsay... GUARANTEE YOU THAT FILMS OF THIS* [sic] *EXPLICIT SEX NATURE HAVE NEVER BEFORE BEEN OFFERED OPENLY FOR SALE IN GREAT BRITAIN...!*
> *... I risked my freedom to give YOU the right to buy them...!*
> *... I GUARANTEE delivery of every film ordered or will return your money without question...! (Kerekes 2000: 195)*

Jolly Hockey Sticks and *Girl Guide Rape* add another opening title to this effect: 'The film you are about to see is a genuine uncut copy of the film cleared in the above court cases'. Kerekes reproduced trailer commentary for *End of Term*: 'See schoolgirl teenybopper Jane tend daddy's chauffeur in a mind-blowing orgy of Lolita lust' (ibid.: 196, fn 4).[8] Of this strain in Lindsay's work, *Classroom Lover* (undated; perhaps 1973/74), notoriously, was filmed in a Birmingham comprehensive school, during the holidays, and featured the return of the actual former headboy (David Freeman) and school caretaker (Colin Richard) for an orgy (ibid.: 195).

It seems adequate to say that using boaters, school uniforms and hockey sticks was enough to suggest a catering to a certain clientele, as Long also observes – and perhaps this was understood more in terms of a sexed-up *St Trinians* tendency, rather than – should one want to draw a distinction – the pederast market. Indeed, Petronius notes 'St Trinian girls' as a London 'type' – 'enchanting creatures' – in the section of his guide to pleasure in the capital concerning 'Nymphs and Nymphettes' (Petronius 1969: 96).

But it was not to be the case that such brazen themes were seen to be permissible: Lindsay's 'risked my freedom' gambit was third time unlucky, and he would be jailed after a 1983 raid. On the other side of a twelve-month stretch, now in his mid-40s, and pursued by the Inland Revenue, he would sell up and move on. Lindsay seems to have maintained that the police planted evidence – videos of violence and homosexual rape, that he himself would have felt deserving of criminal conviction (see McGillivray 1992: 119–20) – in order to make good on a vendetta against him. By this point, he had reissued his films on video, in the days before the BBFC began to certificate video releases. Chibnall (2003: 46) notes that Lindsay was in the habit of paying off the police – McGillivray (1992: 119) records Lindsay had received at least one tip-off of an impending raid – and perhaps bribe-related disagreements had reached a head. It is possible that Lindsay was less pliable than other pornographers, and he had something of the protection of a public profile and a taste for legal showdowns. Kerekes notes Lindsay's intention of submitting a film to the BBFC, with a view to fighting any subsequent ban and so humiliate the organisation (Kerekes 2000: 196).

A 1981 Thames Television documentary, *Soho: People Live Here Too*, produced by Ken Craig, includes an interview with a duffle-coated Lindsay, conducted by Allan Hargreaves in the street, after a sequence showing a jovial police raid on his Taboo sex shop:

> *Every film that I have, or had, prior to the raid this morning, has been acquitted of all charges of obscenity by a Crown Court jury ... The police – not the police who conduct the raids, and are nice enough blokes; they are only doing their duty – but whoever is ordering the raids is completely disregarding a High Crown Court jury's decision. I will restock, and I will be raided again, with legal films. So they're obviously determined to close me down – not through due process of law, but through hitting me financially.*

The foremost erotic star of British 1970s cinema, Mary Millington, whom Lindsay had 'discovered' as a waitress (Kerekes 2000: 192–93) when she was merely Mary Maxted, and who featured in his early hardcore loops (seemingly four: *Oral Connection, Betrayed, Oh Nurse!* and *Miss Bohrloch* of 1970), would also cite police harassment in her suicide notes of 1979. Rumours have persisted, which may have been smears planted in the press by intelligence agencies hostile to the Harold Wilson government, and drawing on the Keeler experience, of her connections to high profile figures. Her personal volatility, discussed below, and connection to Lindsay – an outspoken figure who had been legally tested ('Lindsay was a man without fear' [Long 2008: 148]) – would have potentially given cause for concern, particularly then, with an uncertain balance of political power. So campaigns against Millington and Lindsay could have been credibly motivated, just as standing down investigations into other political figures in respect to their behaviours seem to have occurred at this politically volatile time (for example, see IICSA 2018b).

Lindsay seemed to have reacted to police pressure, which he viewed as part of a wider state conspiracy against sexual well-being, by documenting his own practices. *The Pornbrokers*, co-directed with Laurence Barnett, spends a third of its time at a Lindsay shoot (for *Wet Dream*), before taking the viewer off for an autumnal tour of the 'red light' quarters and sex industry environs of some North European cities – finessed with a paternal voice-over: 'This is a blue movie being made in Denmark. This is called pornography, and as such [is] not to be seen by anybody'.[9] The narrative includes Lindsay meeting a young model (Maureen O'Malley) in his office, herself prompted to book this appointment with him via contact information from a friend, whereupon he talks about his own backstory to her, of moving from fashion to glamour photography. This is an illustration of how Lindsay 'discovered' models, although reputedly he would approach them on the street (albeit the streets of Soho) rather than wait for them to come to him. He jots down her details, including age and measurements, and then they move to a photoshoot – by the end of which she is nude and masturbating. During a cigarette break, Lindsay discusses 'film work':

> *Lindsay: Let me tell you a bit more about the whole business, you know. I cover everything, and the most important thing you've got to realise [is that] a pretty girl like you, if she's clever, can make a lot of money … What are you doing next week? Are you free at the moment?*
>
> *Maureen: I've left school. Haven't got a job.*

At all points Lindsay is polite and non-insistent, and does not hide behind euphemisms or gild the nature of what he asks his models to do, as if part of assuring full consent is demonstrable clarity as to what is expected. Even during the *Wet Dream* shoot when a male performer, Brian, is unable to perform, he is asked whether he minds if his girlfriend, Janet, 'a very pretty little thing', now 'works with another guy'. But it is difficult to accept that such scenes are, as they purport to be, actual documentary.

The profile of a willing 'starlet' working with Lindsay was published in *Knave*, relating how she had entered the twilight world of the blue movie scene, why she does it and why she enjoys it. For example, she needed money for a holiday with her sister; is from an 'Irish Catholic background'; was initially reticent about the idea but '… when I got there, I really enjoyed myself. Everybody was so nice and friendly; I had a lovely week on location'. Her various films are described, but I do not recognise them from the given plots; the familiar Lindsay complaint about male performances is voiced. Once back home, Chrissie ('not her real name') liberates her boyfriend and others, and feels sorry for 'so many friends who work a 40-hour week in offices and hate every minute of it' – one of whom, suffering from depression, was not inclined to take up Chrissie's offer of introductions, whereas Chrissie finds the life itself therapeutic, prompting her to make further films. And a union for sex workers would be useful as '[n]ot everybody's like John Lindsay' (Duncan 1978: 70–71). *Knave* concludes:

> *And with that [final comment of Chrissie's, she] went home to her flat in North London, a practical girl who sees herself as a worker in a fantasy factory. And, like John Lindsay, she sees no need to justify it, because she enjoys herself. More power to her pussy, we say. (Ibid.: 71)*

> *We [Knave] extend our regrets to that noted reformer of erring sinners, Lord Longford, who will be denied the pleasure of reforming Chrissie, because she does not want to be reformed … She is one of the sexual radicals that our post-war, 'permissive' society has brought into being. (Ibid.: 70)*

Long documented another Lindsay film shoot for *Naughty!* (1971), which looks considerably more miserable than the one Lindsay filmed himself directing, for *The Pornbrokers*. In *Naughty!* one of Lindsay's young performers, shooting hardcore threesome loops, is interviewed after a sequence in which Lindsay lists what he expects her to do, and when. She says that she performs for the easy and quick money, and that she wishes she had a 'normal' career. And in Cosey Fanni Tutti's recollections of working in the industry at this time, including with Lindsay (even though this 'performative' work was eventually to form part of the notorious COUM Transmissions 'Prostitution' exhibition), expectations of sexual encounters with pornographers 'off camera' were quite typical, as was the 'risk of the unknown', in relation to denizens of the underground.[10] And, after the brief phase of being the desired model or performer, and with one's star waning, invitations to 'private "parties"' and direct offers of prostitution work (in one instance, through Harrison Marks) were the next logical step (Tutti 2017: 194). And, indeed, this seems to have happened for Mary Millington too: 'On a promotional tour for *Come Play With Me* she blatantly worked as a high-class class girl' (Killick 1994: 29; see also Petley 2001: 214). In Dworkin's critique, this holds no surprises, and is captured in her diagram 'The Circle of Crimes against Women' (Dworkin [1978] 1988: 225). The seeming 'power' invested in women, to be able to sexually excite men (including by political progressives, who see this as a matter of individual autonomy), then results in women existing only in this respect, and in effect being guilty for all violence visited on them further to this excitement. Thus:

> *Going back to the whole model ['The Circle of Crimes against Women'] – the circle, the pornography at the center of it, the all-encompassing wall of prostitution that circumscribes it – it does not matter whether prostitution is perceived as the surface condition, with pornography hidden in the deepest recesses of the psyche, or whether pornography is perceived as the surface condition, with prostitution being its wider, more important, hidden base, the largely unacknowledged sexual-economic necessity of women … Each has to be understood as intrinsically part of the condition of women – pornography being what women are, prostitution being what women do. (Ibid.: 226)*

The Lindsay footage from *Naughty!* could then represent a point at which pro-sex feminist positions seem to falter and common ground is found, unexpectedly, with the anti-permissives. Germaine Greer, at the Wet Dream film festival in Amsterdam, noted that the troubled backgrounds that may propel women and girls into making hardcore pornography seemed only too apparent on the screen, as Gorfinkel (2006) records. And this too was Keith Joseph's identification of a progressive blind spot, noted above, of an 'accept[ance of] the exploitation of women by pornography' (quoted in Denham and Garnett 2001: 262). Thus, Caulfield is emboldened to note that, further to the unsuccessful attempt to prosecute a 'blue-film maker', and Mary Whitehouse and the NVALA 'stepp[ing] in with a demand that should appeal to every women's liberationist' – that juries should be gender-balanced – that '[h]ad Germaine Greer or [*sic*] some such woman called for fifty per cent of women on *all* juries, the idea would have been greeted with enthusiasm. When Mary Whitehouse put forward this plea on behalf of women, she was suspected of trying to extend the right to exercise censorship' (Caulfield 1975: 122; Caulfield's italics).[11] Lindsay himself is careful to note the autonomy of his performers; it is they who go looking for him (rather than vice versa), they are typically middle class and enjoy supplementing their incomes, and one element of evidence of this freedom of choice to perform is that they 'would make better money as prostitutes if that was what they were after. I'm convinced that they get a lot of pleasure out of it. I've never used a girl yet who didn't enjoy it' (quoted in Duncan 1978: 70).

'Simply Job-Descriptive Sex'

Two aspects emerge from *The Pornbrokers* concerning Lindsay's conception of pornography. Firstly, as voiced to Maureen, and if Lindsay is to be taken at his word, he seems to hold disdain to the point of near-contempt for the consumers of his films – 'the nutters who buy these films'. Man is, he tells her, essentially 'the weaker sex', and so can be exploited by Lindsay in conjunction with the wily women with whom he works: 'Men are real idiots when it comes to sex'. When this position is later put to Lasse Braun in the documentary, in relation to his opinions of the viewers of his films, he seems unable to answer, and then claims that he never thinks about 'the customers'.

This position regarding man as the weaker sex seems to extend to Lindsay's being plagued by failing erections – lengthy discussions concern as much, and the pre-sex pep talk to the male performers hones in on the issue, one would think counter-productively. Lower payments were made to those with erectile dysfunction.[12] Lindsay even notes that, irregularly, the film-maker himself was obliged to intervene in the heat of the moment: 'If I had a problem with the geezer – the stud – and I'd shot half the movie and now needed a prick that was hard to stick up the girl, [then] sometimes I had to stand in myself, but only because I didn't want to waste the

Illustrations 4.3 to 4.8 John Lindsay loops on Super 8-mm: *Man Hunters, Temptation, Triangle of Lust*. Photographs by the author.

film' (quoted in Sheridan 2011: 258). This might explain Lindsay's relatively extensive work with Timothy Blackstone, the Rugby School-educated actor and unlikely porn performer, whose nickname was 'the Non-Stop Spunker'. But even then, during the *Wet Dream* shoot, the application of fake semen is seen at length – as if the males could not even be trusted to deliver the literal substance of the required money shots. Many films end with a cartoon logo of a drooping penis, under 'The End', sometimes flopping through the porthole of a boat – a la 'la petite mort' – as if illustrating that this occurrence denotes the closure of the narrative, the end of the action, and thus the end of the film.

Secondly, and more particularly – as this aspect underwrites *The Pornbrokers* – the idea of pornography is considered in relation to societal dysfunction. Lindsay posits two regimes of images via an opening montage of iconic shots of atrocities and executions, mostly war photojournalism. Such images are revered. The second regime, on the other hand, which involves images of love, is forbidden. In this montage comes, although neither party would approve of the comparison, a direct dramatisation of the Church of England's contextualisation of the obscenity of pornography as nothing compared to the obscenity of 'war, famine, poverty' (Board for Social Responsibility 1970: 14).

The models later discuss the 'morality' of pornography, and the Longford Report is mentioned too – in some ways, *The Pornbrokers* can be taken as a direct response to Longford (and, in other ways, would be well suited to a double-billing with *The Wife Swappers*, as both deal with new forms of etiquette and processes around sex with multiple partners at the same time). One model blames the Catholic Church in Northern Ireland for 'fear and ignorance' and the 'screwed-up society', and seems to suggest that her role in the porn shoot is part of a cathartic response to this, for reasons of self-healing. However, the high number of Irish models she says she encounters on porn shoot sets reflects how widespread this damage has been.

It would have been historically conceivable that former inmates of Magdalene Laundries / Magdalene Asylums are being referred to here. These included those who had children out of wedlock, and who wound up incarcerated in abusive (including sexually abusive) workhouses – the child either adopted (typically with no records maintained of the biological mother or parents) or 'disappeared' (mass graves were later discovered); see Grierson 2017 and, for the final report, see Commission of Investigation into Mother and Baby Homes 2021. That is, that these sexually active 'fallen women' discussed may have been traumatised victims who had fled from the crimes of the Catholic Church in the Republic of Ireland. Indeed, some then seemed to have worked in London as prostitutes. One archived survivor's narrative, detailing the way in which working as a dominatrix eventually allowed her to obtain a new persona, through which she was able to control, ritualistically, abusive situations, echoes just such an idea. For this, she offered credits to 'the nuns' – seemingly for the ability to work in such extreme situations, situations that they had first propelled her into (O'Donnell, Pembroke and McGettrick 2013: 128).[13]

While Lindsay seems a hippy libertarian, there is a sense that bad-mouthing his performers and articulating amazement at the material rewards he is reaping, in *The Pornbrokers*, then passes for a critique of commercial exploitation. His frustrations, more generally, coalesce around two dysfunctions in the 1970s: erectile (hampering his film-making, indicative of man's failings) and societal (hampering his film-making through counterproductive censorship, indicative of mankind's tendency to violence and warmongering, offset by moralism). The former perhaps explains the duration of erection shots in his films, as Lindsay, mid-shoot, filmed what he could, and overshot on the basis of his pessimism – to the extent that some online commentators have speculated that the film-makers had a preference for aroused males. While I do not wish to uncritically accept their explanations of their work in order to read that work, pornography can be so one-dimensional that any orientation around a wider context can be useful. And what emerges in *The Pornbrokers*, with still another ten years of film-making left for Lindsay, is a certain imperative: the need to achieve the mechanics of love-making in order to show how the mechanics of a better society are already physiologically present (in the realms of love and sex). This was not a particularly new idea, and 'free love' was widely equated with, or simply understood to be, direct action against oppressive ideologies, often drawing on the writing of Wilhelm Reich, around 1968. And, perhaps, Lindsay was opportunistically voicing such a position just to justify his film-making, and redeem any sense that he was an exploiter. But Lindsay's actual pornography, through the *mise en scène* strategies noted above (the broad and curt scene-setting), sought to push this action – in the sense of sex, and in the sense of anti-authoritarian positions – into domestic and everyday settings. The Permissive Society was happening at home, or on home territory. Lindsay located the liberatory power of the orgasm as present on, say, the top deck of a double-decker bus (for *Schoolgirl Joyride*), as well as in free-love happenings, understood at least, as *The Pornbrokers* suggests, to be occurring elsewhere between 'manning the barricades' and engaging in anti-war activism.[14]

But Lindsay's audience, it would be reasonable to feel, were not a revolutionary-minded proletariat, striving, on the side, to liberate sexual expression further to overturning state institutions and structures. Rather, they were presumably men discretely masturbating in a dark room at 37 Berwick Street (the London Blue Movie Centre), or at Lindsay's Taboo chain of cinema clubs around Soho. And, likewise, Soho was no British version of a free love commune, germinating non-capitalist lifestyles, as with Freetown Christiania in Copenhagen. So Lindsay's films can be understood as a rearguard action: a crack squad of hippies working to roll out the Permissive Society into the suburbs – or, at least, capitalise on this opportunity, and seemingly for no particular ends other than financial. And, for that operation, there needed to be full disclosure in terms of aesthetics: no more teasing intimations or BBFC-calibrated shooting around the subject – this was, rather, the time to see everything. And it is for this reason that male arousal is so central: not only in terms of enabling heterosexual couplings (because Lindsay seemingly only dealt with heterosexual or lesbian couplings), but, as a function of this, also showing the actuality of extant sexual occurrences. The project, then, is the sexual remaking of modern life – to a wider degree than *The Wife Swappers*, as Lindsay moves beyond the metropolitan centres, and out into the cul-de-sacs and commuter belts. And in this context, it is possible to see the 'jailbait', as per Long's observation, as indicating not only a pandering to a pederastic sensibility, but also indicative of the next generation of sexualised citizens. These young people can freely adopt the liberation achieved in the late 1960s, and allow it to be embedded in their day-to-day lives for the 1970s. And this ever-present eroticism suggests the idea of a certain fantasy of total availability of any and all desirable women encountered – something shared with the deplorable gender politics of virtually all middle-of-the-road television comedies of the time.

But it is easier to claim this in terms of the historical existence of Lindsay's work, rather than see the furtive members of the London Blue Movie Centre as recipients of, let alone propagandists for, such enlightened knowledge. One of the precious few traces that there was an understanding of the import of Lindsay's work, on the part of the film-makers, comes in an anecdote from Long. He had lent his apartment to Lindsay for a photoshoot, belatedly realised his naivety and, indeed, upon returning from holiday, found a film crew and a copulating couple:

'What the fuck is going on?' I demanded.

'We're filming!' the stranger retorted, 'and we need absolute quiet'.

    Looking beyond the man's right shoulder I was startled to see what was happening on my Afghan rug ... I stormed into my living room and saw a cameraman and a group of what can only be described as hippies standing around, eyes intently fixed on the naked couple.

'Excuse me! Who the hell are you?' asked the cameraman.

'I just happen to own this fucking flat!' I shouted. 'Who gave you permission to film porn here?'

'We're from the BBC,' said the cameraman, like it explained everything.

    Thinking that the scene hardly looked like an episode of Dixon of Dock Green, I grabbed the camera and told the crowd to leave my home immediately.

(Long with Sheridan 2008: 149; Long's italics)

When confronted, and after Long had viewed the confiscated and then developed film and discovered the extent of the use of his flat, Lindsay presented a novel reason: 'I lent your place to the BBC. The Open University wanted to film a couple of my actors for a sociology documentary' (quoted in Long with Sheridan 2008: 149).[15] Long's disbelief was dispelled when he received a formal apology from the director of the BBC's Educational Studies Department, and an assurance that the educational programme would be shown in the early hours of the morning, without press listings, concluding: 'In those days anything was possible and everybody was dabbling in porn, even, it seemed, the Open University' (ibid.). It is possible that Lindsay was asked to film something for the Open University, but used the occasion to turn out a few more loops – sending the institution some mild offcuts.

    This general position with respect to sexual freedom puts Lindsay in a particular, and perhaps even contradictory, position. On the one hand, the films simply need to dramatise or illustrate, or even advertise, the joys of uninhibited sex. But, on the other hand, the films are sometimes grimy and depressing – and the stark and unforgiving lighting heightens this – the couplings perfunctory, and the lack of synchronised sound adds a layer of insincerity (as arising from this evidence of performance and fakery) to what is seen. Cosey Fanni Tutti, recalling her work in the hardcore pornography industry in the early/mid-70s, including with Lindsay, noted: 'I performed the sex well enough. There was no pleasure, love or desire involved; it was simply job-descriptive sex' (Tutti 2017: 169). To adapt

Alex Comfort's volume title, Lindsay's oeuvre seems more concerned with the 'Joylessness of Sex'. Erotic frissons are mostly founded solely on the biological evidence at hand, in close-up, and the sense that this activity is freely available. But what is freely available is presented reality rather than fantasy: Lindsay, even when clearly creating fictional narratives, documents, nonetheless, the actual biological or physiological happenings – as evidenced, in the classic style, by the money shot. The rearguard action mentioned above also denotes the limits of Lindsay's project: coupling as an end in itself. The radical import afforded to other areas of sexually explicit material suggests more than this: documenting taboo-busting on the way to ever greater collective freedoms, with the films as critiques of, and in defiance of, state/judicial censorship. But Lindsay's comparable stance, in the opening title card quoted above, is merely a guarantee of quality from a salesman – that this product goes further than other products.

So, to turn to *Miss Bohrloch* (1970), which is probably Lindsay's most widely seen film: the narrative concerns two men, who look like blue-collar workers, hiring a prostitute.[16] What is sold successfully, in this context, is Millington's appearance as an ideal type, both in terms of conventionally attractive looks and sexual confidence and gusto; the type Lindsay identifies (above) as '[i]nnocence ready to be seduced' and as 'what the average man wants' (quoted in Duncan 1978: 71). But the sexual offer here is utterly functional: that of hiring an available prostitute. Elsewhere, in domestic settings and arrangements, what seems to be on offer is merely the availability of sex: the man or men arrive, find lesbian encounters underway, and then shift the narrative to straight encounters as they make love to the women (as in *Oh Nurse!* and *Betrayed*); or a common set-up, such as friends invited over for a dinner party (for *Anticipation*, date unknown), results in couplings. But these couplings are strangely conventional in Lindsay's world (particularly for the hippies that seem to predominate in his films) when compared to Gay's work: lesbianism often gives way to heterosexuality, as if lesbianism is merely an exotic form of foreplay for a more fundamental sexual act. This ordering or hierarchy is seen in Lindsay's *Live Bait*, where two females have sex by a river bank, and then a male, who has been fishing and smoking, joins them, at which point the 'real' sex begins; it can also be seen in his *Tourist Surprise*, in which a female tourist returns to the flat of a local woman she meets and they have sex, only to then be joined by a male – possibly a husband. And in *Betrayed*, the men take charge with suitably direct dialogue, once they have returned from the pub and discovered their girlfriends making love with each other, in order to realign the sexual encounter to heterosexual norms: 'You can't trust these girls for five minutes! Come here, darling!', 'Right – let's get rid of that vibrator!', 'Right – get your mouth around this!' And here the 'glamour' continues in respect to the bright hippy clothing, and the red nail varnish of the title character (played by Mary Millington), offset against close-ups of masturbation and fellatio. Or, for *Oral Connection*, the glamour is aligned with aspiration: the flat ('Hey man – nice pad!'; the same flat seems to have been used for *Anticipation*), the flowers that are brought as a gift, the underwear that one woman reveals, and perhaps even the easy-listening soundtrack. The *mise en scène* is compelling elsewhere, as noted above: in *Health Farm* (a fairly plush spa), *Triangle of Lust* (a modern apartment with spacious shower; perhaps the least unpleasant of all Lindsay films), *Desire* (a well-appointed living room), *Sexangle* (a country mansion), and even *Safari* (presumably an African safari park, via a Land Rover); now it is the turn of the animals to look on bemused as the humans copulate in front of them. But this seems to be the exception – and it is possibly confined to earlier work. *Temptation* is an exemplar: the loop moves from train station to taxi to high-rise council flats, with a solid 120 metres or so of lesbian love-making with the taxi driver, who has failed to depart having carried his passengers' bags up, masturbating furtively in the shadows – before joining in.

And, while female/female/male set-ups are not unusual in Lindsay (as with *Gypsies Curse*, *Triangle of Lust*, *Danger Route* and *Fruits of Sin*), the male/female coupling is more typical. Where two couples make love simultaneously (and Lindsay tends to edit to synchronise climaxes), even in the same room or space, the couples are seldom seen together, or share the same shot. Where this does occur, such as in *Oral Connection* and *Ship Ahoy!*, there is a sense that just one vagina is insufficient for a Lindsay loop: a doubling of vaginas, afforded their own screen time, seems to be needed, as if underwriting Lindsay's sales pledge. When compared to Braun's loops, Lindsay's seem particularly straightforward. Braun's *Prostitution Call Girl* (1971; the loop box suggests it may have been shot in London) is artily edited to near abstraction. For Braun, the possibilities of a threesome (two males, one female – and so with a fumbling bisexual frisson that would be alien to Lindsay) is rendered as a confusion of limbs and angles, decentring the act of love-making from the one moment of climax.

Such a tendency away from the mixing of organs of the orgy suggests that access to sexual pleasures is a near-individual matter. Even in the orgy of *Desire*, women outnumber men, with Blackstone presented as able to afford a selection of women rather than overseeing (in the manner of *Bistro Bordello*) a full-blown and shifting series of encounters, initiated by all present. This, combined with the tendency noted above to place lesbianism or female bisexuality in a secondary position, suggests that the sexual revolution in the suburbs has been subsumed by the extant matrix of sexual relationships – essentially, couples coupling – and this as extended quantitatively (more one-off encounters) rather than qualitatively (couples joining other couples joining other couples, and so on, as per Marks and Gay, and Braun). It is for this reason that the failing erection is a disaster for Lindsay: it puts pay to the possibility of the encounter within those tight terms – other erections are unavailable in the tight sexual fantasies of John Lindsay on screen (despite the body-double operation seen in *The Pornbrokers* of talking about partnering the girlfriend with another male when the boyfriend in unable to perform; such a mid-coupling conversation is, in itself, problematic in terms of porn production). And erectile dysfunction even further suggests that this sexual encounter, as is documented, is somehow intrinsically not as exciting as would seem to be necessary to justify the excitement understood to reside in the pornography, or even to provide Lindsay with the (seemingly libertarian) ethical position, or unrestrained free love, from which he justifies his taboo-breaking and risk-taking.

Jolly Hockey Sticks, which remains the most notorious of Lindsay's films, contains a narrative shift that illustrates just such a limitation. The narrative moves in a picaresque linear development rather than through an increasing intensity and deepening of action. Two nominal or supposed schoolgirls are seen in two different scenarios. Firstly, we see a teacher showing the girls how to play hockey, and specifically the 'bully off' – and eventually having sex with one of the girls ('Oh Jane, my dear, your young body is lovely!'). The two girls, one with a distinctively middle-class name (for the time) of Priscilla, then proceed to a council flat where they have sex with their boyfriends. So the loop suggests a series of possibilities at different junctures within the same ambit for the characters: at school (with a teaching giving in to sexual temptation) and then bunking off school (to 'slum it' for sex with some locals 'roughs') – that is, they simply have sex twice rather than have better sex.

Compared to the expansive notion of free love, that one would think would inform Lindsay's view of sex, this is a conservative impulse. A parallel is apparent in Alex Comfort's seminal sex manual, *The Joy of Sex: A Cordon Bleu Guide to Lovemaking*, first published in 1972. Comfort, whose languid and hip writing style seems to owe something to R.D. Laing's public persona, grapples with ways of addressing sexual liberation and, very briefly, feminism (as 'Women's Lib'), and not wholly successfully. The section on swinging and orgies (Comfort 1972: 180–84) is stuck uneasily between liberal advice to experiment if one wants to, concern that women may be psychologically vulnerable to the dangers of partner-swapping (unless 'they are adult, well-adjusted and storkproof'; ibid.: 181) or uninformed enough to be taken advantage of, and a general position that seems moralistically against such a phenomenon, articulated mostly in relation to the dangers of boredom and sexually transmitted diseases.[17] The 'issue' of bisexuality (in the 'Problems' section of the book) also arises in relation to matters of partner-swapping and orgies, as a potentially accidental occurrence for men in the thick of action. Comfort seems less concerned about female bisexuality ('women exciting each other are a turn-on for males'; and concludes '[s]traight man–woman sex is the real thing for most people – others need something different, but their scope is usually reduced, not widened, by such needs' (ibid.: 223). And there is further class-based confusion too: the orgy needs 'martini-lubrication' (180) and yet can be 'ruined by liberal intellectuals who invariably end up talking rather than doing – and fall to the ground still talking' – so the best class strata for 'orgiasts are the prosperous upper-middle class, minor jet setters, and showbiz' (181). In this way, Comfort seems to be attempting to define, index and explain a new sexual culture, and unapologetically dives in head first to do so, but in this embrace illustrates elements of a conservative impulse at which, even in the early 1970s, proponents of free love would have scoffed. Lindsay's modelling of a sexual culture of the 1970s effectively functions in just such a way too.

If this is a conservative impulse, it is also one that, in general, marks the way in which sexual liberation can be re-enacted in the suburbs: through privacy, and the increased ability to do as one wishes within the confines of living spaces. In this context, even wife-swapping seems essentially timid: a couple exchange the wife with the wife of another couple – and then presumably return to the standard domestic arrangement. This tendency also suggests individualism and a reward for those who step out of their comfort zones (that is, that one sets out on an adventure, as with the interior decorators of *Sexangle*), and the ability to have an individual access to then-considered-different or 'other' social strata (mostly, here, in relation to class, but one notes too that interracial sex is not unusual in Lindsay's films).

This is not free love a la 1968; coupledom 'ownership' remains in operation. And sexual access often suggests opportunism, or even value for money (i.e. what can be got by money) rather than the value of money (i.e. finessing access to more upmarket erotic ambiences, as per Paul Raymond). Freedom then is a commodity, and Lindsay's sexual world is that of a radical or libertarian conservative, rereading the Summer of Love – or demanding a belated access to it, even spreading out to the suburbs, with the buses and the commuters, even if cash for services rendered is required. In this context, senses of value for, or value of, ultimately make little difference: Lindsay's long Summer of Love is a monetarisation of the gains of the counterculture (for, presumably, his business, and legal bills – but as writ large in the films too, for the viewers). Lindsay's is a countering of the counterculture. And it was just this sort of countering that then formed the basis of Mark Fisher's incomplete theorisation of 'acid communism': the 1970s as a decade of state soft subversion against the gains, and dreams, of 1968 – or a 'hostile takeover of a new collective consciousness' by 'a burgeoning neoliberal order' (Fisher and Colquhoun 2021: 6). This subversion, in particular, headed off the terminally dangerous potentials of a working-class embrace of hippiedom, through a moving against (for Colquhoun) a culture, and its artefacts, 'that built new bridges between class consciousness and psychedelic consciousness, between class consciousness and group consciousness, but which [then] was smothered or abandoned before its time' (ibid.: 5). So this countering, in the 1970s, is the very reverse of Stalin's conception of the role of the artist of the 1930s: Lindsay as not so much the 'engineer of the human soul' (Gorky et al. 1977: 25–69) but the dismantler: Lindsay's blueprint of the individual's hedonism in prolonged hippiedom, and sometimes psychedelic clothing, fractures class and group consciousness.

The pornographic film *Boys and Girls Together* (Ralph Lawrence Marsden, 1979, for David Sullivan's Roldvale company) offers context, or a control experiment, to Lindsay, in this respect. The film is uniquely progressive in what it shows (heterosexual couplings, and gay male and female couplings, as well as interracial couplings), but seems especially middle class (in terms of its characters: students and foreign visitors), arty and tasteful (with a sunny David Hamilton style), and communal (closing with a bisexual orgy on Hampstead Heath): in short, an extension of the Summer of Love. Hampstead Heath is jarringly different to the indoor spaces of Lindsay love-making, or even the tight framing of the outdoor spaces: a place to journey to, and with surprise (rather than inevitability) awaiting. The Heath was later assumed to be exclusively a gay cruising zone, but Houlbrook notes its heterosexual history too, so that the film appropriately moves to this transitional phase, as juxtaposed with the miserable scenes in Soho earlier on, for an ill-fated attempt by one character to pick-up a call girl (Houlbrook 2006: 52–54). *Boys and Girls Together* could be taken as the 'long vac' of a film like the Oxford University-set *Morning in May* (aka *May Morning*, Ugo Liberatore, 1970), with its sexually experimental undergraduates ('I didn't see you at the love-in in Port Meadow') vaguely aligned to contemporary political radicalism ('students are trying to overthrow the system all over the world, and you're still discussing whether gowns should be worn at dinner'). And in this respect, as also aping Lindsay's work, *Boys and Girls Together* falls into that category of defanged psychedelic artefacts, in a line between (for Colquhoun) 'the surrealist abstractions of a bourgeois Pink Floyd concert, repurposed nostalgically and apolitically for today' and 'the average BBC Radio 4 listener's dream of a quiet Sunday that never ends' (Fisher and Colquhoun 2021: 5, 6).

This idea of access or spread is the dynamic of *Euston Capture*: the film moves from the public outdoors to the private indoors, with the two women first encountered as lost tourists, and then seen as naked sexual partners – from no connections to intimate connections. The lesson is clear and pragmatic: sexual encounters as realisable. Even a grinning passer-by, waving at Lindsay's camera as the four get into a car (or, later, a penis slipping out of a vagina), unwittingly lends a cinéma-vérité verification of the realisable nature of this kind of sexual event: this is the everyday, and these are usual-looking people, among many other usual-looking people – tourists with their map and bags, young men kicking their heels around Euston, and then to a bare flat with a small record player and a few bottles of alcohol. The single-mindedness of the narrative then locks this lesson, and dynamic, and these 'types' of people, into a bigger concern: this is the inevitable (and so, too, eminently realisable) sexual activity of this unremarkable demographic – that is, the 1970s working class. In this sense, Lindsay effectively works to pander to an assumed idea of some kind of erotic destiny for the everyman, as a turn-on for his cinema club audience (who would have been watching, not so far away from Euston). And in this is a countering of so much of the patrician concern animating anti-permissive thinking. This scenario is everything the anti-permissives had warned about: possibility, experimentation, amoralism, the 'ruining' of women, and men unable to repress urges. And this class, to use Communist terminology, is a 'coming class' for Lindsay, and therefore enacting an (erotic) destiny, and even enacting their function.[18]

Of course, the problematic power dynamics of *Euston Capture* here point to the way in which liberation does not exorcise exploitation, so the films seem drawn from the condition of misery, as much as, or just rather than, joy. And in this dynamic of erotic destiny, as coupled with the focus on genital interactions (rather than anything much else), the final proof of Lindsay's conservatism is apparent: the money seemingly needed by his performers is available in the counter-vortex of the Permissive Society – the step into the 1970s where that which has been made permissible can now be bought and sold. John Lindsay's performers therefore seem to be the collection of their organs alone – bodies without souls or, pace Fisher, consciousness.

Notes

1. I have been unable to locate the publication (closer to a pamphlet or booklet than a book), or any bibliographic record of it, although Kerekes cites it and reproduces the cover (Kerekes 2000: 191–96), and gives a 1974 publication date. The cover reproduces various newspaper articles ('Cleared, the Blue Movie Freedom Fighter', 'Sex Film Debut of Head Boy', 'Blue Films Man in Court Shock', etc.). There is a Lindsay loop of the same name. A later heavily illustrated magazine-type profile publication on Lindsay, attributed to Norman Diamond, appeared in 1976 in *Sexplay*: 'If ever a man was born who could effectively snuff out the flames that illuminate the Festival of Light, that man is John Lindsay' (Diamond 1976: unnumbered).
2. On the decay of the image quality when repeatedly reproduced on video formats, particularly in respect to pornography, see Hilderbrand 2009: 66–72.
3. I surmise the date from an advertisement briefly seen on Euston Road, announcing the coming release of *Mary, Queen of Scots* (Charles Jarrott, 1971), which was in early 1972.
4. The film, also known as *A Night at the Bistro Bordello*, which was shot in Marks's Farringdon studio, and now seemingly only exists in the West German dubbed hardcore version, under the title of *Zum Knutschkeller*.
5. Unless otherwise given, the years of release are unknown for these films.
6. Some of the dialogue in *Sexangle* is so bad that I surmise it may be intended as ironically humorous. The film also features Blackstone, and Cosey Fanni Tutti, of COUM Transmissions and Throbbing Gristle.
7. The legal victories may have emboldened Lindsay, since a nom de plume had seemingly been in operation prior to this: Karl Ordinez.
8. For a general discussion of paedophilic themes in popular culture during the Permissive Society of the 1960s, and changing perceptions around the same, see Jones 2007: 112–31. I re-engage with this concern in the discussion of David Hamilton, below, whose work is more appropriately read in terms of the 1970s phase of the Permissive Society.
9. *The Pornbrokers* exists in soft and hardcore versions, at one hour (for a 1977 release, seemingly for North America and Australia) and one and a half hours respectively. The hardcore version was consulted for this discussion, but the distribution history is uncertain, and the BBFC holds no record of certification.
10. Tutti notes she was interviewed as part of the 1975 investigating into the unsolved murders of Eve Stratford, who worked at the Playboy Club in Park Lane, and Lynne Weedon (Tutti 2017: 169–70).

11. This incident would seem to be in relation to private film clubs showing *Deep Throat* (Gerard Damiano, 1972), despite its lack of a BBFC certificate (see Wistrich 1978: 48–49).

12. General or indicative levels of (one-off) sexual performance payments in November 1970 are given in Cox, Shirley and Short 1977: 165–66: £20–30 per film for females (nearing the average weekly wage in the UK in 1970), £10 for males. Longford's report notes 'housewives and others' (as in a 'made very cheaply' arrangement) getting £10–15 per film, and that '[l]ittle acting ability is required' (Longford Committee 1972: 35–36). For female hardcore performers for John Lindsay, in 1978, 'fees of £100–150 are not uncommon' (Duncan 1978: 72).

13. Peter Mullan's dramatization of the story of two such victims, for *The Magdalene Sisters* (2002), ends with two escapees dressed as outgoing and self-possessed young women, as typical of the late 1960s. Their appearance, now out of laundry uniform, is seemingly only in part subterfuge: to dress attractively, the film suggests, is their way of recovering their subjugated and violated bodies, and so is a vital beginning to recovery.

14. On the perceived revolutionary import of free love in the 1960s, see Halligan 2016: 120–38.

15. During these years, the Open University would broadcast educational programmes throughout the night for those undertaking degree study at home. From the look of the interiors of *Desire* – oil paintings, rugs, fireplace, chaise longue – it is certainly possible that this was filmed in Long's apartment.

16. The film was shot in West Germany, and has also gone under the names of *Miss Bawlock* and *Miss Bollock*. The film won the Golden Phallus Award at the 1970 Wet Dream Film Festival in Amsterdam.

17. Elsewhere, he uses the term 'bird' for women (Comfort 1972: 180), and advises, in a section on rape: 'Don't get yourself raped – i.e. don't deliberately excite a man you don't know well, unless you mean to follow through' (ibid.: 248). Sheila Jeffreys, in an overview of the sexual revolution, spends some time critiquing Comfort: 'It is a handbook [that] will teach women their new role in the sexual revolution, the serving of male sexuality actively and not just passively' (Jeffreys [1990] 1993: 120), and are therefore effectively 'surrogate prostitutes' (ibid.: 121).

18. On the 'coming class', see Samuel 2006: 176–79.

PART III

The Softcore

CHAPTER 5

Derek Ford in Essex

1970s Vistas of Aspiration

To contextualise his praise for Pirelli calendar models, raffish British leading man David Niven complained, in 1975, that 'anything on shiny paper can pass for sophisticated, and erotica is all too often an unpleasantly bulbous woman in Wellington boots' (Niven 1975: unnumbered). Sophistication, for Niven, and the Pirelli calendar-makers, meant tasteful (in the sense of nothing bluntly displayed) and arty or artsy (an aspiration to aesthetic beauty per se, with the nude woman as only one contributing part of this) – and, for variety, sometimes also 'exotic' (non-white models in non-Western garb; beaches, boats, baskets). The issue, for Niven, is that local or home-grown erotica is or has come to be insufficiently fantastical, and photographer/film-maker David Hamilton can be read as starting from this point too, in terms of his conception of erotica. The British model in a waterlogged woodland or, if a Reader's Wife, in front of her husband's prize shrubberies in a secluded suburban garden (hence the Wellington boots), is a far cry from the beaches of Saint-Jean-Cap-Farrat or Mustique. But if British aspirations are limited to the near possible rather than the distant improbable, these aspirations were also a determining factor in the kind of erotica produced: local products for a local market – the possibility of what could be available next door. This is, as argued, the tenor of Lindsay's pornography. The concern, in 1975, may have been that Lindsay and his ilk were, in the context of the activism and pressure from the anti-permissives, endangering an entire culture of eroticism, then at a crucial juncture. Sophisticated erotica, such as *Playboy* magazine of this moment, was jostling on the top shelf next to the tawdry, notable models next to readers' wives, sophisticated reading matter next to shameful reading matter, Hugh Hefner's Playboy Mansion in Los Angeles next to David Sullivan's Birch Hall in Essex, and lifestyle aspirations next to evidence of the downward mobility of various former models.[1] There is a strain of Niven-calibrated porn: the 'Mayfair

Film Society' (i.e. *Mayfair* magazine) 8-mm loops are colourful, entirely softcore, 'fun' in terms of narratives, and feature *Mayfair*'s favoured models: *Groovy Girl, Miss Mayfair, Girl Friday, The Girl from MayAir, The Secretary, Country Girl* (directors unknown, 1970 – circa 1975). Nudity is accidental, and so invariably arises from the models spilling drinks on their clothes, in offices or trains, or getting muddy, or through work as exotic dancers (as with *Miss Mayfair*, which is set backstage at the Latin Quarter, a Soho restaurant). A little subtlety, and a little more upmarketness, might allow the culture to continue to grow, discretely and unimpeded – perhaps to a British equivalent to the cause célèbre reception, or dinner-party-talking-point, of *Deep Throat* (Gerard Damiano, 1972) in North America, and its wider 'Golden Age of Porn'. Perhaps, in a comparable British porn renaissance, other areas of erotic practice and preference could find articulation in British film-making – as, indeed, would prove to be the case with Derek Ford (in relation to swinging) and David Hamilton (in relation to pederasty). As to a British renaissance of mainstream, risqué erotica: the Anglophilic British ambience of *Caligula* (Tinto Brass, 1979), and once respectable actors such as Denis Price and Anthony Steel, on their uppers, adding a touch of bleary-eyed class to 1970s Euro porn and horror (or directors: Robert Fuest's *Aphrodite* of 1982), or even Niven's dry handling of the appearance on stage of a male streaker while presenting a segment at the 1974 Oscar ceremony, suggested that something might be possible. But the actual result seems to have been mostly via a sexualisation of unremarkable period dramas, post-*Women in Love* (Ken Russell, 1969): from *The Awakening of Emily*, directed by Lord Henry Herbert, the 17th Earl of Pembroke, in 1976, to Michael Winner's *The Wicked Lady* (1983). Films in this vein with some character, such as José Ramón Larraz's *Symptoms* and *Vampyres* (both 1974), or *Erotic Inferno* (also known as *Adam & Nicole*, Trevor Wrenn, 1975), are exceptions. But even the remake of *Brief Encounter* (Alan Bridges, 1974) added a modicum of swinging, with the married couple now cautiously confessing their attempted infidelities, without triggering accusations of betrayal or even particularly emotive reactions. (John Smyth's labyrinthine house, which was also a location of abuse, doubled-up as the family home for this remake; Graystone 2021: 12).

The Awakening of Emily, which in the UK showed in a double bill with *Emmanuelle*, illustrates the tropes and limitations of such classy erotica – throwing the (8-mm) grain and stark explicitness of unclassy erotica into arguably favourable relief. Sex sequences are clearly simulated, 'daring' revolves around some light lesbian interactions (topless and kissing, or in a shower), the mother's lover chases the daughter, the house servants are drawn into erotic encounters, and the narrative soon falls into a series of *Benny Hill Show*-style vignettes, albeit without the humour.[2] In terms of ambience, the light is diffused, the clothing aligned to the mid-1970s revival in Victorian fashions (as per Laura Ashley), and the period setting ('Made on location in the South of England' – in fact, shot around Wilton House) is one that posits a bohemian free love carry-on in a series of posh settings. The whole has an aspiration to D.H. Lawrence, but replaces the harshness with cliché (orgasms are occasions for the swelling of music, not the 'crisis' moment of *Lady Chatterley's Lover*) and rustic lyricism (the theme song, 'Sweet Emily', for example, contains the lyrics 'coming home in summer / for as a flower can be / ready to bloom … / Blooming soon / Sweet Emily'; 'Watching her climb / from a child to a woman / Watching her stretch and grow / Prettiest girl I know'). The British experience fails to achieve the sophistication that Niven espouses, and finds in Pirelli: there is no British *Emmanuelle* of this period, if this is a reasonable reading of Niven. But there is a suburban sophistication, coupled, in Ford's case, with a very British, semi-comic, stumbling upon or into eroticism.

Derek Ford (1932–1995) seemed to believe more in a form of karma in which the ingénue is forever manoeuvred, by fate itself, into swinging – and fate, in this, seems to be attempting to bring about the next step of human evolution: the swinger of and for the 1970s. This suggests a force of fate that, for a secular age, is making up for time previously lost to superstitious sexual repression: the 1970s phase of the Enlightenment. A 1971 pseudo-documentary of Ford's, *Secret Rites*, which follows 'King of the Witches' Alex Sanders and his Notting Hill coven as they initiate new members, functions in just such a fashion. Unlike *Legend of the Witches* or *Disciple of Death* (Tom Parkinson, 1972), the rites of *Secret Rites* are relatively straightforward: the simple framing for nudity. However, the film could be said to fall into the classic Ford trope: one is invited to a social gathering, ostensibly by the documentary-makers, and innocently attends, only to find that it is effectively an orgy, and some of the other attendees, now naked, also happen to have worked in British hardcore pornography. And this secret gathering is going on in an outwardly quiet and respectable area. And to or within this could be added another Fordian element: Sheridan notes rumours of hardcore versions of Ford films appearing as early as 1971, from *Secret Rites* onwards, (Sheridan 2011: 86; see also 30–31). And Ford's collaborator Stanley Long recalled this tendency of melding film-making with life: 'Both men's [i.e. Ford, and David Hamilton Grant] sexual preferences off camera had eventually seeped into their movie-making activities … making hardcore versions of his "harmless" British sex comedies soon became an obsession ... I heard stories that after a long day's filming, Derek's "regular" cast would go home, only for a bunch of models to turn up and start having real sex in front of the cameras. Derek would then prepare two completely separate versions of his movie ... Derek's peculiar fetishes drove his work' (Long with Sheridan 2008: 164–65).[3]

'His Prey: The Housewife'

In terms of familiarity, a recognisable and 'local' location is essential. Ford's *Suburban Wives* (1972) opens with dull shots of cul-de-sacs, empty roads, identical houses and grey skies, and closes with credits imposed over maps of London's suburbs, seemingly culled from an *A–Z*, with 'directed by DEREK FORD' emblazoned over Putney. But this is not to say that Ford and associates were producers of softcore working-class pornography. The tension here is not between the jet-setting, playboy lifestyle of Niven and his circles, and that of the blue-collar worker stuck back at home – although this divide may be quite correct in terms of *Suburban Wives*: Ford noted that the film consists of stories told to him by his wife, relating to other married women (Anon 1973b: 45). In *The Wife Swappers* (Ford, 1970; co-written with and produced by Long) the tension is, rather, between old money and new. A surprising number of Rolls Royces flit through British softcore films, and house boats are common, as well as the standard indications of the relative wealth of the 1970s (no wife seems to work, furs and living room corner bars, working environments and cultures are relaxed and well refreshed, and au pairs seem commonplace – even employed by married couples without children). This is the new money that underwrites the erotic world of Derek Ford.

The city flat of the debutant swinging couple of *The Wife Swappers* is spacious, modern, and tastefully decorated. The couple dress well, their drinks tray is in order, the ashtray is marble, and books are neatly stacked on their bookshelves. Posters suggesting foreign travels, along with oil paintings of their children, hang on the walls. Love's lush and languorous LP *Forever Changes* (1967) and a lava lamp are prominently displayed. The film's tie-in paperback adds a Curriculum Vitae detail:

> *In general, swingers and swappers come from the ranks of white-collar groups –*
> *the blue-collar worker in swinging is a rarity [... which] can be attributed to the*

fact that the white-collared, college-educated individual will be more likely to have a rather liberal outlook on sexual promiscuity; the lesser-educated man and woman will still be clinging to more puritanical attitudes. (Caron circa 1970: unnumbered [33–34])[4]

The couple's evident boredom with their lifestyle can only be predicated on an excess of leisure time, and an awareness that in the metropolitan centre in which they live (the film opens and closes with panning shots along the River Thames, specifically locating this new phenomenon of wife-swapping in central London) monogamy is considered passé in some quarters. Indeed, the film was marketed directly to curious couples as a risqué night out – 'If you're over 18, and married, you MUST see this film!'; 'Take the wife too!' – and with some measure of success in this endeavour, according to Long (Long with Sheridan 2008: 24–25). *The Wife Swappers* is a vista of aspiration: both sexual (the possibility of encounters with the swinging set) and financial, with these two aspects grounded in a vision of a certain new and enviable hedonist lifestyle.

Suburban Wives pushes this logic further. Here swinging is not just a pastime or weekend matter, or exclusively in the domain of the bored housewife, but goes to the heart of professional relationships surrounding the marriage, and new moral conundrums that then arise. Once a sexually frustrated wife begins an affair with her husband's manager, the husband is himself promoted (as a by-product of this happier working environment), whereupon he gains confidence and a renewed sexual drive to the extent that he feels able to leave his wife for another woman. In this respect, the swinging seems little more than de rigour for the hearties of the permissive era – infidelity now nearly an open rather than clandestine operation, and with sophisticated couples outgrowing possessiveness and embracing this expanded freedom. For David Lodge, 'adultery was being institutionalised as a party game' (Lodge 1980: 115). In just this way, when wife-swapping comes to the popular television comedy *Whatever Happened to the Likely Lads?* (for the 1974 Christmas Special), it is a possibility for the upwardly mobile and game Bob (Rodney Bewes), misbehaving during a swinging Christmas fancy dress party, rather than an amoral indulgence by his friend the blue-collar Terry (James Bolam), accidentally consigned to work as Bob's taxi driver for the evening.

The 'white coater' spoken commentary of *The Wife Swappers* is precise in this respect: 'Our wife-swappers are, in the main, drawn from that very strata of our society [that] has previously been considered the backbone of respectable urban life: the affluent, professional middles classes'. But the commentator still fulfils the classic role of the sexploitation moralist: wife-swapping, 'a new kind of novelty', is initially lumped in with 'gambling, alcoholism, drug addiction, pornography, and every conceivable kind of sexual licentiousness', not least in that the exponents of wife-swapping egg each other on ever further into addictive behaviour, and are now vulnerable to blackmail and susceptible to mental breakdown. In this respect, alone, it is as if Ford and Long have made a film exactly for the wavering NVALA member – perhaps finally steeling themselves to see what all the fuss has been about – and, surreptitiously attending a screening of *The Wife Swappers*, they would have been amazed to hear commentary that could have been straight from the Whitehouse or Longford discourse, and a mirror of their own gender politics too (these are wives swapped, not husbands). The commentary exudes disinterest and, in its different (that is, non-British) inflections, suggests a remoteness from the phenomenon now under pseudo-scientific scrutiny, with the weary professionalism of a public information film narrator.[5]

Of all these listed ills, blackmail is the most problematic: gambling, alcoholism, drug addiction and mental breakdown are all quite normal within Ford's strata of the 'affluent, professional middles classes' (and indeed these vices are ways of accessing this strata), and the film does not trouble itself to illustrate them. Blackmail, however, represents financial danger and class insecurity – as it had in the years prior to the decriminalisation of homosexual relations in the UK. This matter was illustrated in *Victim* (Basil Dearden, 1961), presented as a social issue film, in which the life of a respectable lawyer is turned upside down by a threat to reveal his homosexual liaisons. But heterosexual blackmail can occur too, as it potentially suggests an ejection from the 'affluent, professional middles classes'. And this concern was illustrated in *Not Tonight, Darling* (Anthony Sloman, 1971), which, being a conservative tale about the importance of fidelity in a loveless marriage (despite its substantial nudity, and the fact that the film also seems to exist in a cut with a few minutes of hardcore inserts) complements *The Wife Swappers*.

The film concerns a young couple, with one child, living in a modern London flat – he, a busy lawyer, has a long commute; she shops alone during the daytime, grows sexually frustrated, and stares at a male mannequin sporting red underpants in a shop window. She is ignored by her husband, both evening and morning (he reads novels in bed, and newspapers at breakfast), even when she takes to wearing lingerie around the house. A supermarket assistant, sensing a lonely and vulnerable woman, spies on her through her bedroom window (which he refers to as 'birdwatching', and this voyeurism is delivered via point-of-view shots) and a wager is struck, back at work, to seduce her – which then occurs. When she then tries to fellate her husband (a habit she has seemingly picked up from her affair) he is aghast, making her promise never to repeat such an attempt, as he stands cautiously back from their bed, in his striped pyjamas. And the subject comes up again at breakfast the next morning: 'I'm sorry I spoke to you so sharply last night, but whatever came over you? ... All our married life our love-making has been the same, and suddenly you try something like... that!' After he leaves for work, a photograph, covertly taken of her unfaithful love-making, arrives in the post, and soon she is blackmailed into joining a swingers' group. Meanwhile the husband accompanies a business client to a strip club where a hardcore loop with the very Marks-like title 'Willing Flesh' is shown (and indeed the court case they discuss concerns a figure called Harrison). The star of 'Willing Flesh' is, of course, his wife. But while he is even further aghast, she has entered a sensual world that includes naked woman-on-woman massages at a sports club. The film eventually ends with the suggestion that the rituals of the family unit itself will offset the hurt over infidelity, and restore the couple. As with *Sex Farm* (also known as *Frustrated Wives*, Arnold Louis Miller, 1973), the ignored wives need only travel beyond the fringes of suburbia (to a health spa) to find sexual adventure with willing males – and even a modicum, prior to a full orgy, of 'unusual' practices: bodies smeared in food, interracial lesbianism, BDSM, and gerontophilia. The film opens with two sets of suburban bedrooms and domestic scenes: one wife has her sexual advances spurned, and eats chocolates to compensate, while the other is treated to perfunctory sex, brusquely completed before her orgasm. And this engenders a domestic argument:

> 'You're having a bit on the side, aren't you? That's where you're going to spend your weekend! "Business trip" indeed!'
> 'It's strictly a working weekend.'
> 'I'd like to know who'd have you anyway – I mean, just look at you! You're getting more and more tired and old and passed it.'
> 'I hadn't noticed you rejecting sex with me.'
> 'But only when you want it. I need all I can get, you know. I'm a healthy girl. Once a week just isn't enough. And that's usually on a Saturday night when you're too tanked up [drunk] to do it properly anyway.'

'You cow! Instead of thanking me, all you can think about is sitting back and taking it easy. Or lying back, should I say, and wanting it easy. And that's just making you flabby, like an old pro.'

'Well at least a pro enjoys herself and isn't useless, like you!' [Throws pillow at exiting husband].

Thus it is male failings (and, indeed, their infidelities) that set the 'frustrated wives' on a quest to sexual fulfilment.

Blackmail occurs at length in *Suburban Wives*, with the offender eventually revealed to have been jailed for extorting money from the suburban wife he has persuaded into a racy photo shoot. His 'in' is via photographing her infant child, without permission, and the sequence then works as a 'how to' for a Readers' Wives shoot. The protagonist is presented as a new social type – in voice-over: 'His name in Stephen. He is a hunter. His hunting ground: the suburbs of our cities. His prey: the housewife' – and takes over the voice-over narration himself, explaining the art and ease of his deceptions, and illustrating the use of technology and media (photography, colour magazines) to personal, sexual ends. For the housewife, this encounter with the photographer offers the possibility of financial gain (money from the pictures of her child modelling) and sexual diversion – both alleviations from the humdrum weekday existence. In these respects, blackmail is the cancer on the Permissive Society: the metastasis of moral condemnations of sexual freedom, shifting from the tut-tutting of the censorious to the petty criminal or spiv underworld. But the offence seems even greater than this: if the permissive era is first achieved in the Summer of Love and then maintained, for better or worse, through consumer power (the libertarian conservative position), then such blackmail is the perversion of that progression – ushering shame and guilt back in, and verifying an anti-pornography sense that the women displayed may not be present under their own will. In this way, the existence of blackmail threatens to overwhelm the entirety of pornography, through the re-emergence of the very unglamorous figure of the spiv.

The Wife Swappers opens in a rebarbative fashion for its pre-credit sequence too: seemingly a daylight kidnapping, on Westminster Bridge, as a leather raincoat-clad woman is bungled into a car, blindfolded, driven into the countryside, stripped, and made to swim across a lake to a moored boat. The film's title card appears with the sound of a scream – seemingly the woman's reaction once she has entered the boat. The contrast between the Mod-y roughs and the quiet demeanour of the woman, and her motionless complicity in the – presumably – playacting, suggests a BDSM scenario is being enacted, filmed or perhaps even documented at close quarters. The scenario is then rerun, but now presented as a (possibly) more socially acceptable practice, and without the scream. Now a couple are seen driving to a wife-swapping event, with the wife pondering the wisdom of attending, as a 'stream of consciousness' voice-over. This prompts an extended flashback to the couple's home life, which begins in their flat, with the lava lamp and *Forever Changes*. The swinging allows a rapid ascent of the social ladder: after an initial session with friends of the husband, who visit the flat, the couple now find themselves in a country house for an orgy, with a sizeable and mostly unknown crowd.

Here, point-of-view shots lock the sequence into the present, but more generally the events portrayed up to this point remain at several removes: flashbacks, illustrated personal recollections, recreations or dramatic recon-structions, and reportage. The ontology of the film is uncertain, and this pushes *The Wife Swappers* away from any conventional documentary-made-in-bad-faith (as typical of the sexploitation genre) and towards a state of absolute ambiguity and atemporality. Long's account of the making of the kidnapping sequence, in his autobiography, only further confuses matters: 'We decided neither to condone nor condemn the subject matter,' he inaccurately recalls, 'but just to present it as dramatised "fact"'. Long then identifies the initial aim of making 'a piece of socio-documentary', directly after noting that the 'members of the public [interviewed] at Trafalgar Square... were all actors we'd hired for the morning' (Long with Sheridan 2008: 20, 21). More usefully, Long then describes the film as Puritanical in nature, but without a recourse to moralising, so that '[b]asically, *The Wife Swappers* is a titillating cautionary tale' (ibid.: 22). Such confusions seem to have arisen over the need to present both the titillation and sexual spectacle as a matter of found reality, and to mount a condemnation of this reality. But, without recourse to moralising, the condemnation invariably comes in the form of the psychological ills that are said to result – so there is a need to run the footage along with a number of voices raising continual objections: the dispassionate commen-tator, and the mea culpa of the swingers who find themselves badly out of their depth.

Consequently, rather than assemble something as unfolding in the present tense, as per standard for any documentary presenting itself as dealing with contemporary matters, the film-makers of *The Wife Swappers* do quite the reverse.

The film, with all this narrative ambiguity, is more akin to a dream or hallucination. The wife seems in a trance as she is led, from one location to another, and without a visible trace of the turbulence of raging emotions that she describes in voice-over. A further framing device then emerges, in parallel to the prurient and unseen narrator. These events are also, it transpires, curated as material for (and at times then introduced by) a psychiatrist. At one point, he even opens a folder to examine written details of the marriage. And then, it turns out, some of these events are declared to have been re-enactments, presumably in the interests of general adult education and medical science (two causes always claimed by sexploitation): the initial kidnapping is later identified in this way.

But a further, anecdotal problem emerges: Long notes that the re-enactment sequence was done without permission, and that the reactions of the genuine passers-by were essential to the moment (Long with Sheridan 2008: 20). The psychiatrist, Long recalls, was an actor who was paid £20 to read out a script written by a camera-shy 'old professor' – 'contacted [via] a mate of mine who was chummy with a Harley Street psychiatrist', and this done in order to get the film certified for release by the BBFC after their initial refusal (ibid.: 23). The BBFC seem to have lost their records on this matter. Long's *Naughty!* is relatively straightforward in comparison: the recreations, of Victorian scenes of family hypocrisy, are clearly signalled as dramatic licence.

In these ways, the swinging events of *The Wife Swappers* are a matter of recollection, and entirely at one or more remove. The dynamic that is then established, between the familiar (the empathy-inducing voice-overs, the everydayness of the erotic content itself, orgy notwithstanding) and the strange (sudden sex with strangers, as the seemingly unavoidable consequence of being invited to swing), across moments of uncertain veracity, seems more than just the 'fascinatingly impure, hybrid and often haphazard style of realism' of, for Hunter, the 'sexploitation documentary' (Hunter 2008: 8). It is, rather, a kind of modernist collage, although more idiot savant than avant-garde – not least because *The Wife Swappers* conforms admirably to Long's final guidance in his 'Ten Tips for Making a Successful Low-Budget Movie': 'Always keep it simple! You can't afford to fiddle around with experimental new techniques' (Long with Sheridan 2008: 247).

The structure of *Commuter Husbands* (directed and written by Ford, 1973/74) is equally disjointed, and revisits the vignette form of *Suburban Wives* – the titles alone suggest an exploration of either side of the modern marriage. This time a framing device is introduced: Gabrielle Drake, visibly braless in a shear blouse, as

'The Storyteller', and talking directly to camera from inside the plush surroundings of the Penthouse Club, will narrate six tales of modern sexual woes. These will reveal the male psyche – which she posits as shaped by the battering of the ego from attempts to suppress the male hunter instinct in contemporary society: the opening music is 'Man Is a Hunter', sung by Samantha Jones. This thesis is tested through a scrutiny of 1970s men, in relation to the idea of a contemporary crisis of masculinity – a situation found in commonplace but, nevertheless, emasculating scenarios. And the film also implicitly offers a solution to these problems shown.

The first vignette concerns a businessman. He fakes business engagements for a weekend of infidelity, while his wife does the same. Yet, as chance would have it, they have both booked into the same luxury hotel, where the Storyteller herself is spotted enjoying a massage. The businessman and wife reunite, while their 'on the side' partners enjoy an extended liaison in one of the hotel rooms. Then we move to the story of a plumber who is called to urgently fix the sauna of a model, with whose work he is familiar. But her plush flat is hosting a psychedelic swingers' party (at which his oil-soiled boiler suit is mistaken for an avant-garde costume), which seems to incorporate actual love-making, including a threesome, involving uncredited extras. All this is filmed with a handheld camera, circling the bed – that is, from the point-of-view vantage point of someone who is part of the scene, or about to join them. Here, the culture of swinging is so open and welcoming that even the blue-collar worker can find a place (albeit once he has had a bath).

Such ideas of possibility are then offset by the stories of fantasies. Next, a bored commuter dreams of stealing a motorcycle, and a rapid montage follows of sexual scenes: women in biker leathers stripping, male bikers in a farm barn making love to women, the naked women encircling the commuter, and a point-of-view shot of a naked woman being chased through the woods. Much of this seems ritualistic, with supernatural undertones, and this imagery and ambience anticipates Ford's later *Diversions*. The next story concerns a wife who has manufactured, unbeknownst to her husband, his quarter-decade-long visits to a prostitute, for tea and company, followed by his spying on the work of the prostitute next door (who wears a facemask), to satisfy his Peeping Tom tendencies. When the spying is revealed, he is sent packing by the prostitute. Another businessman story follows, this time concerning the lusting after a French host during a trip to Amsterdam.

The final story, as with the first two, concerns the ease of the step, or even unwitting step, into swinging. (This, then, is quite different to swinging as envisaged by Caron's circa 1970 study, where arrangements need to be carefully and proactively made, often after some deliberation, as per Alex Comfort's guidance too.) But the seriousness with which Ford approaches this final vignette removes it from the standard sexy comedy with a throwaway punchline. Drake herself plays Carol, whose husband's manager asks him to hire two girls (rather than prostitutes) to entertain a client. Carol is annoyed that her husband should suggest asking a close single friend of hers, and so makes that request herself and then accompanies the friend herself to the rendezvous. They will be the two 'good time girls'. The husband is shocked when he sees Carol: 'What the Hell are you doing here, and where did you get that dress? ... It makes you look like a tart'. Carol's rejoinder: 'I thought that was the idea'. Inevitably, the husband is mesmerised by the blonde friend, who performs a dance lifted from ... And God Created Woman (Roger Vadim, 1956). This prompts Carol to perform a more seductive dance, for the client. The upshot is that while the husband fails to seduce the friend, there is some uncertainty as to what Carol has done with the client behind closed doors: she denies anything, but then winks at the viewer.

'I trust that these [stories] have contributed something to the knowledge of the male', says the Storyteller. The moral of the stories seems to be that sexual fulfilment can only be achieved outside fidelity, and such straying, while jarring at first, is soon understood to not be an issue – or, if it is an issue, swinging can continue on the sly (it may be possible that one's other half is already indulging anyhow). Not to swing is the way to being sexually unfulfilled, and even a dupe. The fantasies, which could be taken as elements of unfulfilled yearning, seem to be further evidence of a natural inclination to make love widely, or to be in the vicinity of those who do. And 'those' are ordinary men, not the rich, famous and decadent; they are the residents of cul-de-sacs, and Ford's emblematic Putney.

So to make his case for suburban sexual revolution, Ford needed to call upon the evidence of fantasies (as if case study-indicative of psychological needs), the evidence of the street (the omnipresence of the sexual society – even if at one remove; behind bungalow lace curtains, say), the entrée into closed society, the authority of the documentary form (with its informed narrators and expert presenters), and even the witness of history itself (as discussed below).

Where sexualised flights of fantasy occur in comparable fictional films, they are generally limited to just showing scenes of the wishful erotic imaginings of the protagonist – wishful and perhaps comedic, because they cannot always be made into, or found in, reality. This is true of If... (Lindsay Anderson, 1968), Bedazzled,

Intimate Games (Tudor Gates, 1976) and another of the films that Leon Hunt terms as, along with *The Wife Swappers*, 'suburban reports' (Hunt 1998: 94), and that is *Au Pair Girls* (Val Guest, 1972). The plot of *Intimate Games* – following Oxford University students working on assignments recording the sexual fantasies of themselves and others, which in turn drives their distracted lecturer into such a sexual frenzy that the film concludes with the arrival of an ambulance – is structured around fantasy sequences. And the fantasies playout in flashbacks, or give rise to seductions in the present tense. For *Au Pair Girls*, one of the male protagonists (Richard O'Sullivan), excited by secretaries and the au pair he meets from the airport, becomes distracted and even tormented by such imaginings. This film gaily moves from one humorous instance of sexual assault to another, effectively confirming the maxim of radical Second Wave feminists that all men are potential rapists (and the film suggests men can be reduced to helplessness by their desires – a legal defence, in the sense of diminished responsibilities, not uncommon in the 1970s). The narrative of *Man about the House* (John Robins, 1974), again with O'Sullivan as the bashful, frustrated letch, seems entirely constructed around sexual conspiracies, via coercing others into strip-poker, or taking advantage of a bathroom door that does not lock – as aimed at his two female flatmates. At least the occasional bad faith position of sexploitation is that the matters at hand are a cause for concern, or guidance is offered into a realm of erotic possibility, rather than serial predatory gamblings. The 'naughtiness' of *The Wife Swappers* is mitigated by the constant chastisement of the commentator. And even those who get their comeuppance seem to have done so after the consolation of consensual sex. The film comes to function, then, as a literal confession: sins committed, narrated aloud (placing the viewer, in the dark of the cinema, as akin to a Roman Catholic priest in the dark of the confessional), due punishments, and lessons learned. On the latter facet, the films themselves come to function as a penance: the work of film-making as a warning to the curious, and of allowing unseen viewers to learn from the mistakes of others. Likewise, *Suburban Wives* features a narrator who is implicated in the text: a female investigative journalist, seemingly of a feminist bent and warning against the dangers seen in the film, and to whom the film returns between its vignettes – and who then confesses that she too suffers from 'suburban syndrome'.

This framing, and pseudo-condition, even holds good for Ford's fully fictional *Diversions* (1976): a foundational sense of an extreme boredom induced by the suburbs-to-the-vanishing-point horizons, as seen again and again by the protagonist Imogene (Heather Deeley) as she escorts a handcuffed prisoner on a train journey. The diversions that follow – extraordinary sexual scenarios that 'cast' the other and unknown occupants of the train carriage, and (female) prisoner, which she partly narrates in voice-over – then seem to be directly reacting to these cosmically dull surroundings.[6] The scenarios slide from daydream to nightmare, but draw on concerns that illustrate a fantasy of rebellion against conformity, albeit of a seemingly hysterical mind. And Imogene at first seems to be the prisoner, and so the assumption can be made that the fantasies are pathological in nature, but then must be seen as the norm once she is revealed to be the figure of state authority: a prison guard.

Now the uncertain narrative status of the fantasies may not be so much ontological (as caught ambiguously between reality and dreams) as epistemological: are such rebarbative imaginings of submission and degradation willingly dreamed? To what extent does one have autonomy over such revelries? They seem to exist as a psychic altermodernity to the suburbs seen – and in this respect, overlap with the imaginings of British punk, frequently read in this way, and also dated to 1976 as the year of inception, and which likewise playfully appropriated and sexualised Nazi iconography. Sex with a man on a couch (Timothy Blackstone, the Lindsay regular) is interspaced with flashbacks to the gang rape of Imogene by soldiers. She then repeatedly stabs a man with a dagger, masturbates with its handle while spreading his blood over her body, re-erects the seemingly dead man only to castrate him, fellates the dismembered member, and dresses in a PVC catsuit to bury the body, which she transports in a golf cart. As with avant-garde, sexualised 'happening' tendencies in film-making, which seek to challenge the viewer in extreme ways (as with the commune films of Otto Muehl, or Don Letts's documentary *The Punk Rock Movie* of 1978), *Diversions* seems to intimately document and even witness, as much as dramatise, obscure and taboo-breaking rituals intrinsically opposed to the status quo. Unlike Muehl, however, and *Bodil Joensen 'A Summerday'*, *Diversions* arises from conditions of authority and impending imprisonment, not aspirations to non-capitalist freedom. This pervades the film's dynamic: the prisoner in transit, the prison-like train carriage, the cells and prisons of 'Nazi' sex scenes, the restraining during rape, and the surrounding suburbs as a gilded, living imprisonment. In contrast to the ideological positions of Muehl (Marxist–Reichian) and the makers and subject of *Bodil Joensen 'A Summerday'* (anarcho-Green), *Diversions* charts the trajectories of sexual fantasies of nation-state capitalism, as inextricably bound up with authority and suburbia, freedoms of sexual choice, even, with the scenes around Piccadilly Circus, the pervasiveness of prostitution, and a past (the war scenes) that is seemingly understood as a struggle for these freedoms. But the fantasies in Ford are so often those of the female. It is her interior life that seems to concern his films – or, as per my conceptual framing of this material, the *imagined* female interior, as imagined by Ford in anticipation of his male viewers; that is, the male perception of the male audience perception of the female. What reading of the female then emerges? Or: what is woman?

But it is here that the second feminism/pornography collaboration or co-option occurs. I note above the unease with which feminists found the common cause had been made with the anti-permissives, in the joint crusade against pornography. In the same way, pornography, via or drawing on feminist thought, is able to posit the eroticised figure of the pro-sex woman: modern, liberated, autonomous, shameless, guilt-free, and in touch with her sexuality – the initiator of sexual encounters. Here feminism effectively collaborates with (or finds itself in collaboration with, or co-opted by) pornography.

Sexual Evolution for the 1970s

Around the time of his final film (*Urge to Kill*, 1989), Ford wrote a novel, *Panic on Sunset*, and co-wrote a study, of sorts, of Hollywood sex scandals, called *The Casting Couch: Making It in Hollywood*. The latter was written with Alan Selwyn, who had written *Keep It Up, Jack* for Ford in 1974, briefly appeared in Ford's *The Sexplorer* (1975) as the proprietor of a porn shop, rapidly arranging for a perusing woman to hook up with a photographer friend of his ('if you've got what I think you've got under there, you'll make a very good career out of it'), and indeed actually worked recruiting performers for hardcore pornography for Harrison Marks and John Lindsay, according to Tutti (2017: 169), and presumably for Ford too.[7] *The Casting Couch* is credited to a joint nom de plume: Selwyn Ford. A related video-released documentary, *The Casting Couch*, directed by John Sealey, produced by Selwyn and presented by Susan George, followed in 1995. The book breezes through a few decades' worth of sex scandals, purporting to offer hard historical facts rather than speculation or urban myths (all unsourced, and related to subject matter old enough to ensure no legal comeback), and is a pale shadow of Kenneth Anger's *Hollywood Babylon* books. But *The Casting Couch* contains an enlightening equivocation, and a reading of cinema that perhaps also speaks to Long's recollections of Ford, the man, noted above.

That reading is quite blunt: cinema seems to exist, in its essential parts, 'off screen' – that is, the way the promise of fame, or just a career, allows for a spectrum of opportunities from casting couches to full-blown orgies. Thus Erich Von Stroheim achieved status in Hollywood by moving from pimping 'willing young ladies' for D.W. Griffith's delectation to 'supervis[ing] the resulting orgies' (Selwyn Ford 1990: 32). The authors then suggest – the wording is carefully ambiguous – that Von Stroheim later filmed actual orgies involving all of them, as unreleasable out-takes from his major productions, and these were presumably for private consumption (32–33). Later, sentimentally, the authors sum up a consideration of David O. Selznick's extended hunt for an actress to play the female lead in *Gone with the Wind* (Victor Fleming, 1939) thus:

> *The less proud record of* Gone with the Wind *was Selznick's cynical nationwide publicity stunt which raised such hopes in hundreds of thousands of young girls and ruined a goodly proportion of them. Just how many of today's grandmothers secretly, possibly bitterly, remember a small-town hotel room in which they dreamed of playing Scarlett O'Hara? (Selwyn Ford 1990: 121)*

This sentimentality, about 'possibly' bitter and 'ruined' women, is the equivocation of the study itself. On the one hand, the authors suggest a motivation to vaguely expose such behaviours along the lines of '[s]ex in exchange for career advancement' (ibid.: 10), albeit mitigated by the thesis that the casting couch was, essentially, the film industry, from its earliest days (as it was in the theatre) (10–11). And the origins of this are located in working-class London, via the impresario Fred Karno (and the origins of Charlie Chaplin and Stan Laurel) rather than California (14). But on the other hand, for the authors, there is the discursive question of who is exploiting whom in such arrangements. The book's epilogue concerns '[o]ne lady who spoke candidly and openly', and offered just such a revision:

> *Now this casting couch thing. Do you have any idea how sexually attractive those men [producers] were to us? Forget what they looked like. Listen, there's no more powerful aphrodisiac in the world than a man with power. Especially when it's the power to make your dreams come true. I don't think many girls were dragged kicking and screaming to bed! (Selwyn Ford 1990: 217)*

And further specifics, relating to her case, then follow. Ford's novel (styled as a Jackie Collins-style 'bonkbuster'), *Panic on Sunset* (1988), concerns the same: a Shirley Collins-like Hollywood starlet (a world-wise 'fifteen-year-old daughter of a whore', 16), propelled to stardom by a manager in the 1920s. He later talks with a British woman he encounters in a brothel, who had initially hoped to make it as an actress but wound up as a prostitute who imitates the starlet:

> 'So you're an actress?' he salvaged from this thoughts.
>   Aileen smiled and nodded. 'It's ironic, really. Everybody I went to see in London had this one idea of how the interview should end – me on my back like an upended turtle. I even grew the shell to go with the imagery. I played their game, and even started to enjoy it. Trouble is, it's addictive.'
>   'Sex?'
>   'Playtime sex. ... It never occurred to me that I was whoring. ... Don't you think it's ironic to start out as an actress playing the whore and end up as a whore playing an actress?' (Ford 1988: 54)

The sentiment then is identical to that of the epilogue of *The Casting Couch*, but with the dramatic sophistication of a collapsing of the roles of actress/prostitute, essentially along pragmatic lines (in that the women are seemingly still compelled, albeit willingly compelled, to sleep with the film-makers). And this scene itself occurs in Ford's softcore comedy *What's Up Superdoc!* (1978). An extraordinarily fecund sperm donor (who had fathered 837 male babies) is besieged and pursued by women beset by mass nymphomania in his presence, and fearful that – as per a twist familiar from many Benny Hill sketches – he might 'get raped': 'They're after my blood!' he confides to a nurse; 'I don't think it's your blood they want'. After a stint in the Raymond Revuebar, hiding in the audience of a strip show, he escapes into the bedroom of a Soho prostitute, when chased by Paul Raymond's models. 'Do you work late?' he asks the prostitute. 'Well, I enjoy my work', she responds, and after they make love, followed by some confusion as to the exchange of money, she pays him, with 'come as often as you can, Doctor!'

Early on in *The Casting Couch*, the authors note that such arrangements of sex-for-employment are themselves historical: 'Today's changed values mean that the [sexual] action is more likely to be extended into an "affair" rather than a close encounter on an office couch. Today's hopeful will expect dinner or, at least, some semblance of social sparring' (Selwyn Ford 1990: 14). If this is presented as advice for 'today's hopeful', the latter sentence seems doubly problematic: 'some semblance' is needed nowadays, but otherwise business can carry on as usual.

Such a position, in fiction and pseudo-history, and in film, seems entirely in keeping with Ford's modus operandi: film-making as utilitarian – both enabler and by-product of social encounters organised for sexual ends, and hardcore out-takes from official releases that may or may not be seen (in terms of Continental releases, or perhaps a subculture of out-takes shown in Soho clubs, or for private orgies – it would be difficult to believe otherwise, but nothing seems to have ever been in commercial circulation). And that those hired to grant the sexual favours may have edged towards seeing this as advantageous, even pleasurable, rather than a matter of their exploitation. And perhaps with the 'dinner' and 'social sparring' now expected as something of an advance on the demands inflicted on the generation of their grandmothers, *The Casting Couch* thus articulates Ford's reading, enlightened by cynicism, and pragmatic philosophy, of cinema.

And this also explains the centrality of Ford's status as an Essex film-maker: that relatively wealthy portion of the UK, often drawing on and drawing in a formerly working-class (i.e. as per the cliché, less morally restricted) populace. They are then spread relatively thinly across a substantial suburban/countryside landmass (i.e. with fewer opportunities for urban entertainment), and with generously sized houses and gardens, plus an edge against the sea, so that the 'miniature gaiety of the seaside' (as Larkin put it in 'To the Sea'; 1974: 9), of caravans and boarding houses, cheap restaurants and sunbathing, is also available – that semi-sexualised culture, redolent of Donald McGill's 'saucy' seaside postcards. And that culture included the showing of films such as Ford's, and various film versions of television series, for the holiday chalet-occupying, and so television-less, tourists.[8] One thinks of the sexualisation of the Essex countryside of Ford's *What's Up Nurse!*, shot in and around Southend-on-Sea. There is the naked hero squelching through mud while pursuing a frog (a subplot involving psychosomatic medical treatment), or chancing upon a group of gallivanting nude females in a clearing (and being set upon by the 'anti-peeper patrol'); and town life disrupted by a runaway ambulance stretcher, with the patient sporting a large pole inserted into his anus (for another medical subplot), as he rockets down the high street; and a boat party, with a nurse stripping, and older men mixing aphrodisiacs into the drinks of unsuspecting women; and, towards the end of the film, the young doctor absconds with Felicity Devonshire in an orange MG, speeding across the flat Essex countryside, only to wind up in a wet cement quagmire in a new development. From a 'suburban syndrome' perspective, the new development seems in part propelled by this emergent 1970s swinging culture: more hinterlands for more mischief or naughtiness – the dream, in a way, of the protagonists of *Brief Encounter*.

Permissiveness for Ford seems then to occur as directly mapped onto power relations, in the light of an understanding that women's own sexual desires have been freed and can freely be enflamed. And these desires are not merely outside the categories of containment (celibacy, marriage), but have done away with a sense of exploitation and use as allied to prostitution. It is as if Ford has heard two evolving messages from 1970s feminists – firstly, that the failure to acknowledge women's sexual independence is a calamity; and, secondly, that loveless or materially dependent marriage effectively turns the housewife into a kept prostitute – and fully endorsed them, albeit without realising that these are criticisms rather than causes for celebration. Ford's self-declared sophistication seems to have been in sifting through women accordingly: those he deemed sexually attractive, and those with 'spark' (which can compensate, for Ford, for lack of sexual attractiveness), which allows for another vantage point on them. Talking of Gabrielle Drake in 1973, he commented: 'It's not necessary to undress every girl … [p]articularly if she's as good an actress as Gabrielle. You must remember, 99.9% of women have to be sexy every day without taking their clothes off' – although he adds the cryptic comment: 'Anyway, I've got something special in mind for Gabrielle' (Anon 1973b: 49).

So what kind of ideal woman, then, do Ford's films envisage, within this imagining of sexual relations? The answer arguably comes in Ford's best (indeed perhaps only) remembered film: *The Sexplorer* (also known as *The Girl from Starship Venus*, 1975). This sex comedy begins as a pastiche of *Star Trek* (in voice-over: 'Space – the infinite frontier'), with an alien woman called 'the Surveyor' (Monika Ringwald, the 'interstellar traveller of love' as per the soundtrack) assuming female form to explore Earth at the behest of her UFO line manager, whose instructions are heard across the entire film. The film seems to knowingly invite the audience to laugh at it, rather than with it, in its terrible humour. The UFO lands on Eros (the fountain and statue in Piccadilly Circus), allowing for immediate access to a massage parlour, where the Surveyor notes gender differences, thereafter straight on to Soho – a sex shop, a porn cinema, a sex show, and a photo shoot (where she observes love-making). The Surveyor eventually winds up 'sexploring' herself (that is, masturbating), with her UFO handlers, swerving into anti-permissive-speak, advising that this is 'dirty', risks blindness, and so forth. In a Reichian manner, the alien uses eroticism and orgasm to take control of herself, and to be herself for the first time – and so able to refer to 'my body'. As per the film's title song, 'she's turned on to permissiveness'.[9] Orgasm itself (once she has switched off the electric current that runs through her vagina, to the literal shock of another admirer) persuades her to retain her human form, forfeiting alien immortality, and abandoning the UFO.

The Surveyor is, at first, blank and wide-eyed, even when stumbling in on a man masturbating in a booth in Selwyn's sex shop, or peering at the genitals of another man in a public urinal, or stumbling around the fleshpots of Soho. She cannot be hung-up about any of this since she has no preconceived basis for judgement, and so seems the perfect swinger, in the sense that she is unshockable. When men make love to her, she initially lies still, as if detached. Female lust would seem to hold the potential to disrupt a complete and free access to her by males, as it would add selectivity and then preferences of practice. But when lust belatedly arrives, as enabled via an embrace of a permissive atmosphere, she finds herself, and becomes herself. And the men who initially left her unmoved (in a parallel to *The Casting Couch*'s older, leery producers) suddenly become objects of desire: aphrodisiac alchemy.

From the perspective of his films, Ford seems to mount a complex operation that points towards a new subjectivity, allied to unstoppable progress and change in the cultures of suburban lifestyles: a psychic desire to transcend the humdrum via an unregulated and unashamed sexualisation of life, and with swinging as the mechanism through which this can be achieved. This is different to Marks, and his expanded sexual spectrum. For Ford, this seems a matter of the evolution of society and humanity, across the 1970s.

The suburban cul-de-sac is not so much a *Brief Encounter* dead end but, for the noveau riche, the privileged enclave-Penthouse that becomes the loci of personal freedoms. Ford explored this via reportage, comedies of manners, and fantasies (from the standard to extreme) – both human and (imagined) alien, and from a majority female perspective. How is such a new subjectivity then to be read as a wider social current of the 1970s? For this, it will be necessary to keep following the new money. Ford seemed to film the Essex petite bourgeoisie of the everyday, while others filmed the bourgeoisie proper, for aspirational pornography.

Ford's vision was one for a secular society (despite the occasional dalliance with Satanic elements): his souls yearned for pleasure alone, from Soho side streets to sophisticated suburban orgies, with pallets expanded through swinging. So sexuality in Ford is not a 'hotbed' of licentiousness in the sense of a generator of new, objectionable or subversive cultures. Rather, this is the literal bed – the destination bed of 'hot' action: the king-size bed, or waterbed, the ruffled bed skirting and soft furnishings, scatter cushions, wicker furniture (a la *Emmanuelle*), lamps with dimmers, strategically placed mirrors, easy listening LPs, and the ashtray on the bedside table.

Notes

1. On *Playboy*'s targeting or creation of a certain lifestyle, see Preciado 2014. For a brief survey of pornographic magazines, as they evolved into various identities in the late 1960s, see Freeman 1967: 31–39, and on their readerships, see Williams 1979: 250–57. The shift into 'recognizably modern pornography' is dated to 1964 by Collins (2003: 134) and, thereafter, a strain of British porn magazines seemed to want to climb the social ladder, from their titles alone: *Mayfair, Park Lane, Penthouse, Knave, Club International, Sportsman* and *Debonair*. Again, Niven offers guidance: 'Right behind came the tide of hairy-chested magazines with gruntingly monosyllabic names like "Thrust" and "Poke", and the girls were of such pneumatic plasticity that they looked as though one touch would reduce them to a burst valve and a pool of silicone. Worse, they were almost all called Dolores' (Niven 1975: 13).

   Killick's biography of Sullivan, the Welsh business magnet whose fortune was made from pornography (operating out of Forest Gate in East London, and then in the Essex/London suburbs between Gants Hill and Ilford), who 'impudently' (Williams 1979: 41) named a pornographic magazine *Whitehouse*, after Mary Whitehouse, and who produced *Emmanuelle in Soho*, and thereafter (and after a spell in prison), sought respectability, opens in rural Essex (Chapter One: The Man Who Collects Women): 'Birch Hall is Britain's newest stately home. It stands in its own grounds just outside the little village of Theydon Bois ... the opulence of Birch Hall is a calculated gesture of defiance aimed at all those who have tried to stop him over the years ... [h]is achievements are now, literally, set in marble and stone' (Killick 1994: 1).

2. Indeed, *The Benny Hill Show* seemed to function as a halfway house between the British porn industry (even hardcore) and the models needed for the 'naughtier' elements in mid-evening light entertainment at the time, most notably in *The Two Ronnies*. At least one of John Lindsay's performers would later appear in a small role in *Are You Being Served?*

3. Long here also details Ford's 'clandestine business practices', and his company of 'some pretty shady people'. The *Secret Rites* film seems to have been part of Sanders's attempted media blitz of the early 1970s, and a tie-in paperback was published, with stills and quotes from Sanders (Ford and Sanders 1972).

4. *Wife Swapping* may not have been an official tie-in, and the text seems sourced from North America, but the cover makes the connection explicit, and the book is UK published. Caron is presented as the editor of a series of fieldwork investigations by Hugh and June McKuen, swinger sociologists, that have resulted in transcriptions of interviews, including detailed sexual narratives (backcover: 'In vivid detail, delivered to the reader with the impact and interpretative

skill that only experience can attain'; 'Factual accounts in the most descriptive detail'). Of this methodology, they write: 'Feeling that it would be eminently unfair to discuss wife-swapping without detailing the acts of the swappers themselves, June and I have taken our memories – if not our tape recorders – into the bedrooms of some seven or eight other couples with whom we have had sexual intercourse, either separately or together, within the past year. We have emerged with this book' (Caron circa 1970: unnumbered [9]).

5. The commentator was David Gell, a Canadian Radio Luxembourg DJ, who also provided the commentary for another pseudo-reportage event in 1970: the Eurovision Song Contest.

6. The softcore British cut, called *Sex Express*, runs nearly half an hour under the Continental cut. But this Continental cut, *Diversions*, lacks the urolagnia element in the Nazi orgy that one finds in the West German print, which is also called *Sex Express*.

7. One of the nudists encountered in the film, played by Lisa Taylor, had been a regular hardcore performer for Lindsay – appearing in both *Juvenile Sex* and *Jolly Hockey Sticks* from 1974, in a David Hamilton Grant softcore production (*You're Driving Me Crazy*, 1978), Derek Ford's *What's Up Nurse!* and *What's Up Superdoc!* (both 1978), as well as Marks's *Come Play With Me* (1977). Her last official credit was *The Great British Striptease*. Taylor's presence in British softcore and hardcore films therefore illustrates something of the porous boundaries, and shared personnel, between them.

8. As these were cinema releases, they tended to be less coy in terms of nudity, more violent, and with riper language, and often involved, empathetically, the familiar television characters going on holidays that test their patience. They were (excluding the various Morecambe and Wise, and Tony Hancock, film vehicles): *Till Death Us Do Part* (Norman Cohen, 1969), *Dad's Army* (Norman Cohen, 1971), *On the Buses* (Harry Booth, 1971), *Please Sir* (Mark Stuart, 1971); *The Alf Garnett Saga* (Bob Kellett, 1972), *Bless This House* (Gerald Thomas, 1972), *For the Love of Ada* (Ronnie Baxter, 1972), *Mutiny on the Buses* (Harry Booth, 1972), *Ooh! You Are Awful* (Cliff Owen, 1972), *Steptoe and Son* (Cliff Owen, 1972), *Father Dear Father* (William G. Stewart, 1973), *Holiday on the Buses* (Bryan Izzard, 1973), *The Lovers* (Herbert Wise, 1973), *Love Thy Neighbour* (John Robins, 1973), *Never Mind the Quality Feel the Width* (Ronnie Baxter, 1973), *Steptoe and Son Ride Again* (Peter Sykes, 1973), *Man About the House* (John Robins, 1974), *The Likely Lads* (Michael Tuchner, 1976), *Are You Being Served?* (Bob Kellett, 1977), *Porridge* (Dick Clement, 1979), *George and Mildred* (George Frazer Jones, 1980), *Rising Damp* (Joseph McGrath, 1980), *The Boys in Blue* (Val Guest, 1982) and, less directly, Kenny Everett in *Bloodbath at the House of Death* (Ray Cameron, 1983). These then could play, in increasingly ragged prints, across rainy summers, from Colwyn Bay to Canvey Island, and from Blackpool to Westward Ho! This substantial body of spin-off films, many of which were some of the most popular in their years of release, has been almost entirely ignored in histories of British cinema.

9. 'The Girl from Starship Venus', by Don Lang (written by Bruce Graham and Alan Selwyn, presumably after the lewd drinking song 'The Good Ship Venus').

CHAPTER 6

Tory Erotica

Sexual Fantasies for the Nouveau Riche

'The Porn Crowd'

An early Derek Ford sexploitation film, *Groupie* (also known as *I Am A Groupie*, 1970), could be said to dramatise the back cover of *The Madcap Laughs*, as discussed above: scenes of casual hedonism around post-psychedelic rock cultures, dandies and their crash pads, women wandering about naked at parties and, as usual for Ford, protagonists chancing upon a swingers' party. *Groupie* begins with Sally (Esme Johns) stowing away in the back of a touring rock group's van. Her story then moves from consensual sexual encounters with the group to her rape at the hands of the police investigating a fatal car crash – with the police able to blackmail the group into complicity with their knowledge of the group's culpability in the crash. In this respect, the film holds together, paradoxically, and by now in a familiar way, the two standard tropes – sexploitation and moralism: offering the viewer both the sex, and the story of the comeuppance for those who seek it. And *Groupie* also speaks to the concerns of Ford's writing, as another behind-the-scenes, sex-centred exposé of the woman who mixes herself up in show business – and, indeed, the scenario in which the woman remains silent about her use or abuse, seemingly on the grounds (for Ford) of her acknowledging her own foolhardiness or even responsibility for this, via her forwardness. In a limited way, then, *Groupie* seems to aim to end inconclusively, but with a note of dramatic complexity, with a contemplation of the story of (and possible future for) Sally – if the viewer buys into this kind of objectionable blame/comeuppance narrative. (Ford's use of a point-of-view shot, from Sally's perspective, at the start of the rape indicates that an essential sympathy for her is being suggested.)

In its closing minutes, Sally leaves a small country manor – the scene of a party and then the rape – in the dark. But Ford cuts to morning light, and she is still walking in the grounds. The sense is of a 'morning after' ambience, where the bright light of day has somehow failed to expel the memories of the night before – something that happens twice in Federico Fellini's 1960 *La Dolce Vita* (during the Trevi Fountain sequence, with a jump-cut to daylight, and at the film's close, after a similarly abusive party, with the partygoers stumbling out onto a beach). In *Groupie* and for the Trevi Fountain sequence, the cuts contradict the standard expectation of film grammar: other or additional shots are expected to show that time has passed, typically a fade. A member of the rock group pulls up in his car and offers Sally some money, before driving off – yet another Fordian trope, of women unwittingly becoming prostitutes. The film's theme, 'You're A Groupie Girl', by Opal Butterfly, returns, and with the multi-tracked male voices suggesting a chorus of men associated with, or thinking of, this sole female.

And Sally continues to walk, into the woods, on her own, through an autumnal *mise en scène*: semi-bare trees, seemingly after a rain storm, and maybe with the light fading again. Irrespective of the horrors that have befallen her, the film seems to want to say, consider this ending (in its own underwhelming way, it recalls the similar final shot of Carol Reed's 1949 *The Third Man*), with the woman of experience now setting out, again, into the world. And contrast this with the film's opening: an anonymous urban street, with kids hanging around, and so the stowing away seeming to be the solution to that closed vista of possibilities – taking off with a rock group (no matter how third rate) as the only exit strategy from a life of servitude and inconsequence. And fate, for Ford and writer Suzanne Mercer, has delivered: Sally is now in the environs of a country house, and of a cultural and social scene, and her undoing has been, after all (in the film's rebarbative conception) predicated on her new-found desirability. Sexual excess has led to social access. The model Flanagan (who engages in an extended fight with Sally earlier in *Groupie*) exemplified this too, as detailed in her memoir *Intimate Secrets of an Escort Girl*. This follows the Keeler and *Wife Swappers* template of the innocent girl whose exuberant sexuality results in invitation into rarer environs. The memoir opens on the London underground, and her awareness of commuter interest:

> Not that I was surprised. I'd put on my shortest skirt to achieve just that effect.
>   With a ripple of my shoulders and a wriggle of the hips, as though adopting
> a more comfortable position, I managed to hitch my hemline even higher and
> felt a real glow of satisfaction as the top of a Guardian inched down to its

reader's nose. Overwhelming success, I mused. Even appealing to the intellectual class of voyeur. (Flanagan 1974: 7)

Groupie suggests a different reading of sexuality to that found in Lindsay. Availability and fulfilled access to sex are not the end points of this kind of erotica. Rather, availability and the fulfilment of access are placed in a larger evolved scenario – the scenario in which a certain social scene enables availability, and works to embed the constant condition of availability (of desirable females) within a new lifestyle. These closing moments of *Groupie* retrieve something, perhaps unintentional, from an otherwise shallow ambiguity: Sally is walking in the right grounds (a country manor), has hard cash offered to her, has sexual experience and the access that comes with that, and so has the language and understanding, and look, to move on to the next scene. And her framing in the countryside seems to clear away the concrete of the opening minutes, and differentiates her from the other now forgotten teenagers, to allow her alone to dominate the screen. *Groupie* then signals to lifestyle erotica, where money shots seem to give way to a straight sense of money.

Mary Millington's True Blue Confessions (Nick Galtress and John M. East, 1980), made and released in the immediate aftermath of Millington's suicide, directly correlates swinging with successful upward mobility. In reflecting on Millington's short life, the film suggests that the correlation is a historical fact, so that the lifestyle advice of Ford has indeed, with Millington as exemplar of sexual liberation, come to pass – shifting from Maldon to (as the voice-over commentary puts it) 'the heart of the stockbroker belt, in Surrey, [specifically on a road] leading to the former home of Britain's leading sex star: Mary Millington'. Her enviable new-build house is shown as a place of orgies, in bizarre sequences that suggest themselves either as flashbacks, since the present time frame is one of mourning ('[n]ow the house stands still and neglected – a memorial to Mary'), or as present-day recreations of the once-swinging scene (certainly some of the models move as if on a catwalk – as if fully aware that they are performing). Thus the sentiment that it is 'strange to enter this house now, so still and silent, when once every room reverberated with the sound of music and frivolity; when Mary threw a party, it was something to be remem-bered' is illustrated, at length. The recreation of Mary's pill-strewn deathbed, seemingly using her actual bed and, via an actress, Mary in a coffin, follow shortly after.[1] But the correlation cuts across any melancholy: to have attained this lifestyle Mary is presented as an entrepreneur in her own right:

'In hard porn pictures, scenes like this were the prelude to orgies. Mary recalled that she did the first one for love, and the next one for £300 a day'. And the media that is curated, jarringly, around such sequences (her suicide note, modelling and holiday photos, newspaper cuttings and headlines, along with porn industry 'names' recalling Millington in interviews) serve both as an obituary that borders on the hagiographic, and evidence of Millington's business philosophy and acumen, founded on her libertarian beliefs.

The position of the film is that it is striking, in an appropriately titillating manner, that such Bacchanalian events go on behind closed doors in a wealthy and therefore respectable suburb. And, in this, producer David Sullivan seems to have up-scaled the films that Ford envisaged. John Lindsay's *Desire* (1971) also fits into this orgy-in-the-manor model, as does Michael Winner's *The Wicked Lady* and the culmination of the Joan Collins soft-core thriller *Nutcracker* (Anwar Kawadri, 1982), with an orgy following a ballet performance at a ballet school, in between copies of *Tatler* and *Country Life*. The other such setting of the time, in terms of a semi-squatted free love zone, would have been the semi-abandoned Georgian or Victorian abode, chaotically repurposed as a crash pad – as seen in *The Servant*, *Blow-Up* and *Performance*, and, later, *Withnail and I* (Bruce Robinson, 1987) and *Mad Dogs and Englishmen* (Henry Cole, 1995). And yet, particularly in *Mary Millington's True Blue Confessions*, the very condition of the germination of this free sexual culture is the wealthy suburb. The house is new, spacious and private (unlike *Performance*'s): new money rather than old. People arrive to make love rather than finding themselves in a location where people are making love.

An influx of the newly wealthy into the British aristocracy of the 1960s and after, such as actual rock stars of that time (unlike *Groupie*'s), had turned to *Country Life* magazine for mansions, country estates and farmhouses. The estate grounds or remoteness were effective at slowing the approach of police cavalcades, the labyrinthine buildings ideal for stashing drugs and people, and acting the role of the gentleman farmer or countryside steward was a good strategy for gaining outward respectability – although this had not been effective at the point of the police bust of the Rolling Stones and friends, allegedly mid-orgy, at Keith Richards's Redlands Farm in February 1967 (see Collins 2019).[2] And an erotic ambience had also pervaded such a *mise en scène* too: as per the gatefold inlay of *Beggars Banquet*, discussed earlier, or the availability of stable hands and barns (as with Lasse Braun's 1977 *Country Life*, or Lindsay's *Riding Stable*, year unknown), or the public persona of the swinging aristocratic hippy, such as Alexander Thynn, the Seventh Marquess of Bath.[3] Thynn had allowed his stately home in Wiltshire, Longleat, to be used as the setting for the film adaption of his own psychosexual novel *The Carry-Cot*, as *Blue Blood* (Andrew Sinclair, 1973), and starring Thynn's model/actress wife. In this transition, a sophisticated hedonism becomes a force of modernization for the old aristocracy, and their haunts.

For Millington and Ford, housing becomes a democratization of such advantages – and with more practical solutions to the pragmatics of orgy-convening. Modern amenities allow for discrete, rather than entirely secret, play – and hence the swimming pool, Jacuzzi, soft furnishings, spacious bedrooms, large sofas, and supply of curious neighbours, primed for a Fordian finding-yourself-in-situ-at-an-orgy experience. The central heating required for an orgy, especially during the winter months, would preclude many country manors. And modern housing would allow for the easier inclusion of new technology, particularly film-making technology. In this way, *True Blue Confessions* does not so much sexualise financial gain – the film is not particularly ostentatious – as suggest the psychic sexual condition of wealth, at the cutting edge, with these 'beautiful people' (to use the commentator's term). The anti-permissives seem to have understood this too: the condition of wealth, for certain opportunist class-shifting types (given over to 'colour-supplement living'), feeding a culture of sexual experimentation: '[T]hose who, having emerged from an upper working-class or lower middle-class upbringing within the last twenty years to enjoy the butterfly existence of an "executive", are now only satisfied with double garages, company Jaguars and wife-swapping parties' (Caulfield 1975: 5).

And this emergence was to have been the basis of Millington as a crossover star – ushering the erotic into the expectant mainstream, in the company of popular and respectable actors such as Windsor Davis, Kenny Lynch and Glynn Edwards for *The Playbirds* (Willy Roe, 1978). *The Playbirds*, which was the sequel to *Come Play With Me*, stepped back from the sozzled Harrison Marks atmosphere, and into the genre of a police procedural (even techno-) thriller, and with enticing sex industry settings – and meeting and matching such ambitions with its budget. (Ostensibly, Millington works as an undercover policewoman tracking a serial killer of models, further to auditioning, as one of three candidates for this job, via stripping – 'first we'll have to find a policewoman who will look good without her clothes on'.) The film suggests luxurious living across an alternative network of power and pleasure in various settings: in Soho, where even a sauna seems to have been subject to a deep clean before filming; at the horse racing track; and stopping off in plush apartments overlooking the Thames (champagne and marble ashtrays) and at a mansion with an indoor swimming pool. The latter prompts one police inspector to comment to another, as they watch Millington stripping by the pool: 'Fine villa; the porn crowd aren't ashamed to be ostentatious anymore'.

This observation is quite correct. The bounty of *The Wife Swappers* did as much for Long, who was as unapologetic in this as his Essex counterparts:

> If I'd made the sort of films John Trevelyan had wanted, I'd still have been living in a flat and driving a rusty Mini… I wasn't yet 40 and I had made my first million quid, helped in no small way by selling sex to the masses. I was rich beyond my dreams, and it suddenly dawned on me just how far I'd come from my very humble beginnings. *(Long with Sheridan 2008: 27)*

Long also lists the purchases he made with the money earned – all of which seem in keeping with the narrative of the film: a Hyde Park penthouse, an Aston Martin DB6, and an upgrade for his aeroplane (ibid.); and, cited in a profile some years earlier, 'a nine-foot-square waterbed' (Anon 1973a: 37).

Such rising potential is also the tragedy of Millington's life, as editorialised by *True Blue Confessions*: she was an insider rather than an outsider, and those who ought to have protected her, seemingly from threats of blackmail, in fact betrayed her. The implication is made that the 'protection money' she paid to the police only led to further extortion. And this backstory occurs in *Queen of the Blues* (Willy Roe, 1979), starring Millington, where a 'gentleman's drinking club in Mayfair' is targeted by criminals (including Milton Reid), seemingly free to demand protection money as they like, without police interference.

The figure of £300 a day, which may be a reference to Millington in Lindsay's early films, jars in the context of the film: it undoes the suspension of disbelief in aspirational pornography. The payment of the models would equate them, certainly in a legal sense (and particularly post-Keeler), with prostitutes. But, in an erotic sense, this knowledge endangers the fabric of the film: the naked, giggling women, running around the house, are presented as free, pleasure-seeking and modern – not as those hired to simulate pleasure and mime good times. The aspiration on display is to have a *Playboy* lifestyle in Surrey, not to have to pay prostitutes as poor compensation for having failed to realise that lifestyle. A new subjectivity resides with the former (the legacy of free love), old vices with the latter (further exploitation of the working classes). Fudging the issue of the actual status of women performing could be said to account for the comfortable surroundings of many of the films discussed here: a mitigation of the expected shabby milieu of prostitution, so that the 'glamour model' is not in fact desperate, or seen as 'a semi-whore' – Shelagh Delaney's precise term in her 1958 play *A Taste of Honey* (Delaney 1989: 7) – or as a woman taken straight from the street or plucked out of a Soho erotic cabaret or 'knocking shop'. But there remains an ontological ambiguity in terms of the women presented. The giggling and sex automatically raise questions of performance and motivation. Are they there freely, or for pay, or under duress – or a mixture of all three?

'The Powers Attributed to Musk and Ginseng'

There seems to have been a conscious, if flailing, effort to ensure that Millington's death did not rob the industry of a sense of a star attraction: the regeneration of Millington, via Roldvale and Tigon's X-certified *Mary Millington's World Striptease Extravaganza* (Roy Deverell, 1981). John M. East, as compère, addresses the film viewers directly, with a clip ('I'd like you to have a look at...') from *Queen of the Blues*: 'Mary Millington, who died tragically a few years ago, made a profound impression as a stripper ... the fact her films are so successful all over the world, even now, shows our need for legends and our bizarre talent for creating them'. What then follows is initially quite confusing: typically, two women strip at once, introduced (by another compère, Bernie Winters, this time with a clipboard), Miss World-style, in respect of their respective countries ('the lovely Christine from Holland. And from Greece... Elena!'). Shots of some audience members making notes are seen, and 'semi-finalists' are eventually mentioned – the procedure is a competition, for a prize, announced as £1,000, a film contract and a holiday in Jamaica. One of the 'Roldvale Girls' suddenly jokes in voice-over that she had better win, after having performed fellatio on the judge the night before – which is then seen in flashback (which adds the detail that she had invited another woman to join them).[4] Without this (compromised) competition element, one could reasonably assume that *Mary Millington's World Striptease Extravaganza* was just another film in the cheap early 1980s subgenre of films of strippers and strip clubs – as with *Female Foxy Boxers* and *Hellcat Mud Wrestlers* (both David Sullivan, 1983), filmed in a pub in Croydon and with East as the interviewer, and part of the *Electric Blue* video magazine series. But perhaps the film should be taken literally:

a proactive attempt to find the next Millington; or rather, and in her very locale, an attempt to regenerate Millington via the medium of another stripper so as to carry this strain of erotica boldly forward into the 1980s. The setting, with its detail-revealing (especially in close-ups of gyrating bodies) brilliant brightness, the lull of the non-diegetic easy-listening disco music, and an unseen Sullivan presiding as the executive producer, seems primed for such a conjuring. And the spell is entirely capitalist: competition via monetary incentive as sifting and sorting until the strongest candidate, worthy of further financial investment, has emerged.

In the modes of wealth and pleasure projected in some of these films, a decisive meritocracy is envisaged. Even in *The Bitch* (Gerry O'Hara, 1979) – which could not be further from seedy hardcore ambience in its setting of a gilded palace of sin and privileged spaces of wealth and beauty – this realm of the fantastical is accessed by the everyday protagonists. Fontaine Khalid (Joan Collins), a middle-aged socialite nymphomaniac living in luxury at the expense of her absent husband, is chauffeured around London in a Rolls Royce, wearing lingerie under an enormous fur coat, from one sexual encounter to another. And, eventually, she extends sexual favours to her driver, seemingly as her fallback option. The trope returns for *Nutcracker*, with Collins as the grande dame of a Covent Garden ballet school, conducting an affair with a male dancer that is so strenuous as to eventually render him impotent. She moves from a massage in her bubble bath from her homosexual PA to a four-poster bed for a sequence reminiscent of David Hamilton (as are other moments: ballerinas waking up in the morning, and later showering).

But beyond this instance of cross-class intercourse there is a more general penetration of the everyman into this rarefied, champagne-bottle-strewn world of discotheques and exclusive clubs: working-class figures, where they have a use, now exist on the margins, or, as fledgling nouveau riche, can be glimpsed at its centre. Indeed, the creation of this tertiary industry, of the classy entertainment of upmarket night clubs and discotheques, as per *The Bitch*, is understood to require both taste and finance, and barrow-boy hard sell. *The Bitch*'s prequel, *The Stud* (Quentin Masters, 1978), opens with working-class protagonist Tony Blake (Oliver Tobias), after a one-night stand, prepping and preening himself for the day ahead, and exclaiming 'You handsome bastard!' as he catches himself in the mirror. His flat looks like a cut-price version of Khalid's – who, then, is exerting a centrifugal force of embourgeoisement over this world. And for fellow travellers,

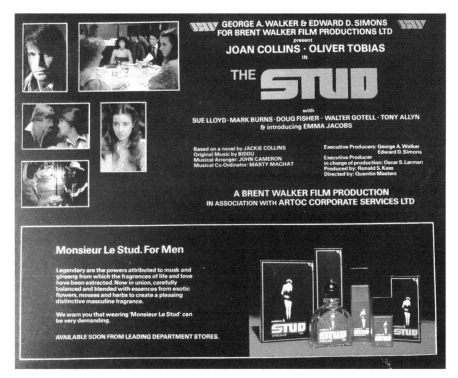

Illustration 6.1 Musk, ginseng, exotic flowers, mosses and herbs – essence of Le Stud: aftershave advertisement from the vinyl soundtrack of *The Stud*, released by Ronco in 1978. Gatefold detail shot by the author.

or those who wished to smell like Tobias, a tie-in aftershave was also released – Monsieur Le Stud – with adverts reading 'Legendary are the powers attributed to musk and ginseng [etc.] ... we warn you that wearing Monsieur Le Stud can be very demanding'.

Later, a member of their circle talks of the clientele of their disco, and quips, in passing: 'They ask for comics and a bag of sweets [and] you give 'em *Penthouse* and amyl nitrate'. In such ways, in order to renew and sustain itself, this fantastical realm seems to need an influx of the lower orders, even at an impressionable age, and those not born into privilege – a fillip for those who are first in line to take advantage of the invite, as with Khalid's chauffeur (or more problematic for those whose innocence is soon lost after an initial step into this world). In *Nutcracker*, this even seems a front in the Cold War, with a convoluted plot concerning a defecting ballerina, seeking refuge in the ballet school, and an investigative journalist in pursuit.

And, for the privileged, this fantasy becomes one of having 'a bit of rough': the construction of the working-class figure as sexual interloper – a demeaning sexualisation of the uncouth labourer, whose underdeveloped superego allows him to neglect polite rituals of socialisation, with the id running riot, jettisoning discretion in terms of sexual encounters, or even failing to confine himself to politer sexual practices. *Lady Chatterley's Lover* includes a passage of what seems like heterosexual anal sex, with Lady Chatterley herself then pushed into an experience – 'different, sharper, more terrible that the thrills of tenderness, but, at the moment, more desirable', where 'the shame died … [s]he was her sensual self, naked and unashamed' (Lawrence 1960: 228) – that she would not necessarily expect from gentleman suitors. And it is along such lines of class-ridden preconceived ideas that even Long's *Adventures* films can be read: a reinforcing of the clichés of the kind of blue-collar worker – the taxi driver, the private eye and the plumber's mate (1975, 1977, 1978 respectively) – that would be needed in (and so encounter) the middle-class milieu. In that these workers are not working as hard as they should or could, as sexual adventure seems to be a greater priority, one can also detect the patrician critique of the anti-permissives too: the Protestant work ethic giving way as the distracted worker sinks further into hedonism, egged on by the imagined pervasive culture of pornography. One thinks again of Lauret's pilfering, unionised postman (Lauret 1970: 64), viewing another's Danish porn.

This also suggests a reading of Michael Winner's *The Wicked Lady* (1983) in relation to the complexities of inter-class desire and relationships in the Conservative 1980s context. In the original *Wicked Lady*, a Gainsborough period melodrama (Leslie Arliss, 1945), the suggestion of sexual adventure is allied to boredom with bourgeois and married life, and its pursuit is linked to criminality. Barbara Worth (Margaret Lockwood) becomes a highwayman, passing herself off as the notorious Captain Jerry Jackson (James Mason). When they actually meet, they begin an affair; she then betrays him in a fit of sexual jealousy, but he escapes the resultant hanging and, locating her, rapes her once she rebuffs him. In this way, what is 'wicked' is genuinely criminal and with such brutal outcomes. Winner's film retains this plot, but in many ways this element of wickedness seems incidental to the general eroticised bonhomie of the *mise en scène*. Within the first quarter of an hour alone, four instances of stumbling across couplings behind closed doors occur, and thereafter Winner and his cinematographer Jack Cardiff use deep focus and depth of field to cram as much deep cleavage into the frame as possible. Now the erring wife is a straight nymphomaniac, and other women fantasise about being robbed and manhandled by Captain Jackson (Alan Bates), with one actively trying to arrange her own ravishment. At the climax of the film, Jackson's post-escape mistress engages in a public whipping match with the erring wife, in a prolonged sequence of lashing, screaming, blood, hysteria and increasing nudity – essentially a classier (for example, Tony Banks of Genesis composed the soundtrack) *Hellcat Mud Wrestlers*. The baseline assumption across both versions of *The Wicked Lady* is that a greater freedom for women has given rise to stratagems of shameless seduction. While this behaviour is unusual and wicked (in the sense of evil) in 1945, by 1983 it merely seems to allow an enhanced male access to 'wicked' (in the sense of lustful and naughty) women. Both films ostensibly revolve around the cuckolded Sir Ralph Skelton who, enticed by the sudden appearance of the wicked lady, dumps his fiancée for her, at the start of each film. But while he is a tragic figure in 1945, undone by this one mistake, by 1983 he seems to be at the epicentre of a vista of the sexual fantasies of 1980s middle management.

The film could be taken as a series of weekend breaks in country pub hotels, with a trophy wife in tow: marriage troubles and illicit evening activities, boisterous entertainment with friends, business arrangements with the extended family, and all while the estate workers (home help) defer to the lord of the manor (line manager). The middle manager himself takes some liberties with the letter of the law where necessary, and possesses a general ease of access to an endless array of women, all dressed up in a sexually provocative manner, and is often very refreshed. *Nutcracker* seems, inadvertently, to outline another locus of power and pleasure: the ballet school. Like a 1970s school for troubled girls, familiar from the IICSA reports, it includes a political dignitary (William Franklyn, as Sir Arthur Cartwright), presumably a governor, able to resolve various day-to-day problems and lend respectability, and in return is seemingly serially seducing ballerinas with the full knowledge of the headmistress.

Essex Man, 1979

In their discussion of the emergent 'Essex man' – as representing or personifying that demographic of the newly wealthy who, as Keith Joseph intended, ditched their traditional working class allegiance to the Labour Party in favour of voting for

Thatcher's Conservatives in 1979 – Biressi and Nunn (2013) track the economic case and geographic particularities for this development.[5] Essex man was understood as vulgar and crass, self-centred and materialistic, lacking in culture and education, and yet newly rich – not in spite of but, to some measure, thanks to, such personality traits. He was, in this sense, the creature of deregulation: of a freeing of the desire to make money from old mores and societal norms, and even legal restraints. The newness of these newly rich was both in the sense of breaking with previous modes of financial accumulation, and in the generation of new money and the founding of a new culture. The Conservative Party in power, across the 1980s, has been read as being itself increasingly orientated to this particular strata: a 'strategic choice to favour an electorate that desired to be "upwardly mobile" … allowing a part of the working class to climb up the social ladder, not always as far as education or occupation were concerned but in terms of wealth and self-image' (Haigron 2009: 142). And their heartland – or, at least, the county that lent its name to the social type – Haigron notes, was Essex. Thus this strata is understood to have moved (in the mind of political strategists at least) from the 'working class' to the 'aspirational class', switching their voting allegiances from the comradely (i.e. the parties of the workers) to the deferential (i.e. the parties of the establishment); ibid.: 146–47.

Bastions of the British Establishment reacted accordingly, and Biressi and Nunn note the distaste or, at best, the highly guarded admiration, expressed by commentators on the right, and the satire of this culture by those on the left. The latter could be said to include two non-pornographic films that critique this coming culture: *Abigail's Party* (a television film, Mike Leigh, 1977) and *The Long Good Friday* (John Mackenzie, 1979/1980). *Abigail's Party* forensically details the spiritual paucity of the middle-class aspirations of those who saw in Thatcher a chance to realise their goal, while *The Long Good Friday* sees the redevelopment of the Docklands area of East London as an entrenchment and legitimisation of criminal cultures.

For the 'highly guarded admiration', and some rearguard reassurances see, for example, Nicholas Coleridge's 1986 *Spectator* piece 'The New Club of Rich Young Men' (Coleridge 1989: 101–6): BMWs, company Visa cards, annual bonuses, multiple holidays – but fundamentally the stockbrokers encountered are decent, polite and cultured. And, crucially, 'the majority of highly paid city boys are not *nouveaux riches* at all; they are traditional upper-middle-class pinstripes' (ibid.: 103). Tension then arises because, firstly, '[t]he new young rich have highlighted the plight of the educated, middle-class poor. A junior expert at Christie's [auction house], aged 27 with an Oxbridge degree, may earn £8,500. His City flatmate, quite probably stupider, may earn £116,000. Only a deeply philosophical or insane person could avoid a rush of panic and jealousy'. And, secondly, 'I can think of several families that struggled a bit to put their children through public school, only to find that eight years later their standard of living is considerably lower than that of their sons' (ibid.: 104–5).

But Biressi and Nunn's approach, and indeed that of Haigron, does not stretch to a consideration of psychic condition of this development, beyond the occasional and incidental glimpse: the 'Essex woman' of a quoted *Times* report from Billericay is seen reading Jackie Collins – Joan's younger sister, and the writer of *The Stud* and *The Bitch* – breaking off to agree with her husband's reactionary sentiments (Biressi and Nunn 2013: 32). Sherman is less condescending, in terms of Thatcher's female constituency: those 'women on council estates who aspired to something better' (Sherman and Garnett 2007: 86). The development of this new subjectivity, across the 1970s, in terms of lifestyle and gain, finds a nuanced expression in the softcore pornographic vistas of aspiration. And porn in this respect can be read as an aspect of the prehistory of Thatcherism, and an affective agent on the mindset of the coming nouveau riche. Indeed, Thatcher's proclaimed return to Victorian values can be read not only as a matter just for public consumption, at least on sexual grounds (the 'new moralism'), but as a way of, paradoxically, finessing such more-breaking shifts. Weeks notes that various reactionary stances were not supported at the level of policy, as also noted above (along with Whitehouse's realisation of as much). And, for Jenkins, Thatcher's moral concerns were more to do with the political economy and its 'immoral' enemies (chiefly welfarism, as endemic among those lacking a work ethic or entrepreneurial spirit, and so on; Jenkins 1988: 66–77) than the direct legacy of the 'permissive age'.

The picaresque happenstance of the countercultural period ('falling into' sexual encounters), and the dangerous proximities of the first half of the 1960s (as with the Profumo scandal; Soho and Westminster; erosions of class barriers) were struggles from an earlier time. Modernisation – at least, on heterosexual grounds – occurs via promiscuity, as social mobility. Eroticism becomes a kind of hermeneutics, through which the old Establishment is remade. Thus stories identical to Fontaine Khalid's, of furs and Rolls Royces and secret encounters, but applied to Princess Diana, circulated privately, and sometimes in the tabloid press, shortly before her death.[6] Whether this was via hack journalism or proxy-planted Palace slander which lazily lifted the ambience and the imagining (of the desperate woman, feeling herself over the hill, and opportunistically on the pull to stave off boredom and breakdown) from *The Bitch*, or *The Bitch* that accurately portrayed such a condition as typical of a certain social culture around the Chelsea, Kensington and Knightsbridge areas of London, is difficult to tell.[7] The same trope appears in *Lady Chatterley's Lover* too: 'She heard the catch of his intaken breath as he found her. Under her frail petticoat she was naked. "Eh! what it is to touch thee!"' (Lawrence 1960: 114). And 'fur coat and no knickers', and 'Essex girl' would later become common pejorative terms.

Eroticism was only one element of the radical remaking of the old Establishment along such lines, but it was one that struck to the core: eroding the tight circle of families who perpetuated their elite via breeding, with *Country Life*, with its monthly 'Girls in Pearls', offering a preview to prospective suitors. In jettisoning the detritus and codes of taste and tradition, of morals and propriety, the Thatcherite nouveau riche was born. Power is to be gained on democratic and meritocratic lines, through sheer financial ambition and accumulation, so that vulgar displays of 'new money' were now a sign of vigour and desire for progressive change. This is why the porn film reorganised people and places: it was not a matter of buying a passage to an exotic locale to seek sexual adventures, or an entry into a permissive zone (the brothel), but that sexual adventures can occur, and are seen to occur, back home – even in the actual (that is, un-recreated) houses and flats of the aspirant classes. The sexual revolution of the 1960s was readily found in urban centres; it is its slow wending out into the suburbs and backwaters, after 1968, that represents a real entrenchment of this liberalisation (and hence the concept of 'the long 1960s').[8]

Such a development could not occur in the centre, and exert a centrifugal force over the suburbs. Rather, the suburbs became the incubator for – in a correctly neoliberal manner – thrusting innovation outside the stagnant institutions of the centre (political, media, religious and civic), unencumbered by the centre's bureaucracies and legal accommodations, and their public school / Oxbridge staffing. This project of modernisation was devolved to the suburbs. The coming economic freedoms of the Thatcherite 1980s, after deregulation and the partial dismantling of the state, were mirrored and matched, personally and sexually, in sexploitation's aspirations: freedom within marriage, freedom to partake of the gains of the sexual revolution, freedom to reinvent the dull 'suburb-scape' as a place of sexual promise, freedom to make gains. This was the making of, to paraphrase E.P. Thompson, an English erotic class.

Notes

1. This scene was arranged by John M. East (see Sweet 2005: 313), whose strip club requiem for Millington is noted below. Killick notes that this moment was, unsurprisingly, considered 'particularly offensive by her friends' (Killick 1994: 30). Millington ended her life with gin and paracetamol on 18 August 1978, after being arrested for shoplifting. She wrote, in a suicide note to Sullivan, 'please print in your magazine how much I wanted porn legalised, but the police have beaten me' (quoted in Petley 2001: 212). She suffered from police harassment (of her and her pet dogs) and problems with the Inland Revenue over unpaid taxes, and from paranoia amplified by cocaine use and kleptomania. Despite this, Millington had become a crossover star and raised money from appearances for her favourite charity, the People's Dispensary for Sick Animals. I want to note her selfless involvement with this charity as significant – especially in the context of a book that includes a fair number of unpleasant individuals, and encounters a fair number of miserable or wrecked lives – given the escape that animals offered to victims such as Bodil Joensen. On Millington's life, see Sheridan 1999, and Petley 2001: 203–17.
2. A threat to the continued existence of the country house and estate was indeed a theme for British Conservatives (of the one-nation, patrician type) across the 1970s, particularly as articulated through the Victoria and Albert Museum's 1974 exhibition 'The Destruction of the Country House 1875–1975', overseen by Roy Strong (see Strong, Binney and Harris 1974; and Strong 1997: 139–40, 142); on the exhibition's political effectiveness, see Adams 2013. Such impulses of modernisation, with new ownerships and new types of social gatherings, would have been understood as a considered response from the old aristocracy, keen to be seen to be conceding ground to upstarts, even if only to safeguard their own positions. And this concern is articulated in the introduction to Harold Acton's book on Tuscan villas: 'Since more and more of the great country houses are disappearing and doomed to disappear – unless they be preserved by National Trusts in an age of expanding penal taxation ...' (Acton and Zielcke 1973: 9). It also became the basis of the plot of the BBC's *To the Manor Born* (1979–81), with the manor bought by a non-British, nouveau riche businessman, displacing the widow of the manor's owner to a modest lodge on the estate.
3. *Country Life* was also released as *Land Leben* and *Lolita's Anal Orgasm*.
4. The other odd element is an audience shot, recycled from *Queen of the Blues* (which showcases distinguished, often suited, audience types), of a woman groping a sitting man. Is this 'product placement', for the not-too-bleary-eyed viewer, indicating that the actual club is also functioning as a knocking shop?
5. On the successful Conservative gain from the 'middle ground' of both Labour and Liberal voters, so that swathes of voters are read as moving towards a 'dealignment' from parties of the working classes, see Särlvik and Crewe 1983. Eric Hobsbawm had anticipated such a fracturing some years before, in 'The Forward March of Labour Halted?', which then informed the Labour Party's own reorientation in the light of Thatcherism (see Hobsbawm 1978: 279–86).
6. A trace of this gossip of yesteryear can be found in Heawood 2014. Diana herself used a 1995 BBC *Panorama* television interview to articulate her awareness of a campaign of gossip and slander against her, which included a leaked recording of an intimate telephone conversation from the late 1980s – the so-called 'Squidgy tape' – of obscure provenance (see Campbell 1998: 212–15). Rumours deemed printable at this point also included news of a leaked video of a 'romp' between Diana and James Hewitt – in *The Sun* (8 October 1996; first five pages)

as 'Di Spy Video Scandal' (see CNN 1996). Hewitt's attempt to communicate his side of the story may be read as a validation of Diana's declaration of much-needed love (as noted in Campbell 1998: 215), in the Mills & Boon-style *Princess in Love* (Pasternak 1996). In this way, a counter-narrative of dignified and discrete romance seeks to dispel any permissive sense of an out-of-control harridan, or lust in plush surroundings, fermented in the popular imagination by '[m]y husband's department' (quoted in Campbell 1998: 215), and as somewhere between the performances of Timothy Blackstone, or Backstairs Billy's Clarence House rent-boy orgies, and the coming age of tawdry amateur or housewife pornography, as per Ben Dover.

The mid-point between Joan Collins and Diana, in terms of cars and furs, is David Bailey's 1987 Volkswagen Gulf television advert, with model Paula Hamilton, looking very similar to Diana. She storms out of a Mews house in the early hours, ditching her ring, pearls, and fur coat – but retaining the car, and patting the steering wheel as a mark of its trustworthiness and constancy.

7. Long recalls a sequence along just such lines that he could not afford to include in *The Wife Swappers*: a woman, naked but for her fur coat, flies to Manhattan to deliver a letter to a businessman: 'The letter had "Please fuck this slut" written on it, so the businessman did just that over his desk… Despite this being a genuine story, I didn't feel [that] the public would believe it' (Long with Sheridan 2008: 21).

8. As I have argued elsewhere, the subsequent forms of sexual liberation across the 1970s – particularly in feminist and queer cultures and subcultures – became a matter for swingeing critique from those who tracked the shift from hippies to yuppies with increasing bafflement and alarm (see Halligan 2014).

CHAPTER 7

David Hamilton and Uranian Aesthetics

This erotic English class, however, could be said to be in need of an aspirational outlier: not what was available (John Lindsay), or what more could be done sexually (Harrison Marks and Russell Gay), but an exoticisation of eroticism – sexuality beyond the (Fordian) suburbs. This was delivered by David Hamilton, and represents the ascendency of eroticism into the mainstream; in this sense, it is a measure of the Permissive Society culture across the 1970s. However, this project – in Hamilton's work – was particular to one aspect of the Permissive Society: the case for just-pubescent or even prepubescent sex. In this way, the 'most' legal, and most mainstream, of pornographers considered in this study was also the one who extended the most problematic element of the Permissive Society.

Hamilton's erotic world was consistently concerned with young females – those seemingly either side of the age of consent, and so in a bracket that would seem, or look, to be across the years of 14 to 17. The sexualisation of these young girls, in terms of their presentation in Hamilton's feature films and (albeit a secondary consideration here) his photography, may have been Hamilton's authorial work, or may have been a matter of documentary-like, if obsessive, observation of a dawning sexual awareness on their part. Either way, this presented sexualisation is, at times, tremulous and, at times, emboldening. So the very question of autonomy on the part of Hamilton's models (which is an immediate response to his work) is sidelined in favour of a preference for presenting young girls in a way that displays their uncertainty about their changing feelings and changing bodies. The British quad poster for Hamilton's 1977 *Bilitis* ('Bilitis is a young girl') offers the slogan 'That exquisite moment of a girl's sexual awakening', while the US poster offers 'I don't even know how to kiss... yet'. And the British poster for *Laura* (1979) has the slogan 'The moments of fleeting beauty... between innocence and womanhood'. All this encapsulates Hamilton's work. The films hone in very precisely on this moment.

Bilitis, Hamilton's first full film, is nominally based on or inspired by Pierre Louÿs' collection of odes to lesbian love, *Les Chansons de Bilitis* (1894).[1] The film centres on a summer spent by the young girl Bilitis (Patti D'Arbanville) at the country house of family friends: bisexual Melissa (Mona Kristensen) and her mostly absent and philandering husband Pierre (Gilles Kohler). Bilitis rejects the positive responses to her initial romantic interest in a local photographer, Lucas (Bernard Girandeau), in favour of a sexual encounter with Melissa. When at home, Pierre is aggressive toward Bilitis, and rapes his wife (who, on one occasion, exhibits an eventual enjoyment of this assault) – prompting Bilitis to find a new partner for Melissa: Nikias (Mathieu Carrière). So Bilitis, who has feelings towards Nikias herself, must therefore make something of a sacrifice in denying herself the chance to lose her (heterosexual) virginity with the one man she happens to like.

The location of the film's setting is unannounced and unclear although, to an extent, such confusion may simply be collateral narrative damage from the at-times somnambulistic English dubbing. At a stretch, it could be the English South Coast during a high summer, but is more suggestive of a part of the South of France reserved for the holiday homes of the moneyed middle classes. And yet the setting is so verdant that it could equally be read as a colonial outpost, perhaps in Indochina, with an inward-looking huddle of displaced Westerners insufficiently defended from the temptations of 'going native' through a shaking off of their Western sexual inhibitions. The timeframe is also ambiguous, not least through the use of classic tailoring – Pierre in Cerrutti 1881, Nikias in Renoma, and Melissa ('Mona Kristensen's dresses from her own personal collection', noted in the end credits) in 1930s-styled afternoon dresses. But the disco-fied and melodramatic score, by Francis Lai, at times pulls against this, suggesting a more contemporary, if by now seemingly totally atemporal, setting.

Hamilton's *Laura, les ombres de l'été* [Laura: Shadows of a summer] (1979), concerns the reacquaintance of a sculptor, Paul Thomas Wyler (James Mitchell) with his former lover, Sarah (Maud Adams, in Chanel), now married – but not before he has first set eyes on her schoolgirl daughter Laura (Dawn Dunlap), during a ballet lesson. After much discussion as to whether the daughter will pose nude for a sculpture, or whether the sculpture will be made only with reference to photographs of her (a curious daughter's and a jealous mother's preferred options, respectively), a studio fire results in Paul losing his sight. Therefore, in order to execute the sculpture, he runs his hands over Laura's naked body, at length, during a clumsily contrived climatic sequence, as she visits to bid him farewell. They then make love. The film is credited as based on a story of Hamilton's own devising.

It is now difficult to approach Hamilton's work: the content seems deeply déclassé. Yet no resort to legal guidance is possible: in the UK, the films were commercially released, played in respectable cinemas, and continue to circulate commercially without BBFC cuts. And no quick sampling of the films seems possible. Their aestheticism is so absolute, and so overwhelming, that Hamilton's *mise en scène* requires an 'are you in, or are you out?' response. The viewer either rejects the entirety (perhaps on the immediate grounds of the Hamilton film experience as being so hackneyed, or just dull) or surrenders to it, ideally on the heavily signalled grounds of Hamilton's unrestrained artiness. The light-saturated *mise en scène* presents itself, self-consciously, as in a direct aesthetic continuum with Impressionist painting. And further obfuscation follows in this wake: it is hard to know exactly what is being looked at, and why. The film's focus is clearly towards exposing substantial expanses of unclothed young female flesh in detail, and the models/actresses are ultimately and repeatedly deployed to just that end. But a reading of Hamilton as a straight pornographer is difficult to make stick – and hence the ways in which his work seems to have existed in the mainstream as tasteful softcore erotica with little trouble and little comment, at a time when John Lindsay was in court over questions of the age of models in his films, which had to be shown in private – plus, Lindsay's models seem to have been older than Hamilton's. As naff as Hamilton's aestheticism is, it somehow dissipates the idea of anything so crude as pornography operating beneath it to deliver the nudity and simulated sex. And yet that delivery is, nonetheless, made – repeatedly and centrally, and with narratives constructed in the manner of pornography – as a series of weak excuses for more of the same: they evolve around climatic scenarios of nudity and love-making. These narratives are so incidental and underpowered that Hamilton has denied the viewer the guidance of some kind of unfolding story through the sun-bleached, breeze-rustled, honey-skinned sprawl. And the narratives retreat ever further into the background with each film – so that his final film, *Summer in St Tropez* (1983), virtually eschews narrative (and dialogue) altogether. And technical proficiency is, then, at the fore – albeit with the evidence now more visible in Hamilton's published photography collections than his films (which exist in poorly scanned, worn, scratched, and haphazardly dubbed prints).

And Hamilton's films remain unwatchable historical oddities. Perry R. Hinton, in one of the only substantial academic engagements with Hamilton to date, frames much of his argument around the striking observation that Hamilton has gone from omnipresent in the 1970s ('one of the most successful and famous photographers in the world'; Hinton 2016: 11) to nearly completely forgotten by the time of writing. And a 2001 *frieze* article on Hamilton ('aestheticism out of control', etc.) begins by describing the author's inability to locate a copy of *Bilitis* in Hamburg – both in regular video rental stores and in the sex shops of the 'red light' district.

That omnipresence is remembered in terms of Hamilton's still images: for posters on bedroom walls, in the published collections of nudes (as art books, or as stills from his films in softback, effectively approximating a pornographic magazine), and also via Hamilton's shoots for many fashion magazines. Even images that were not Hamilton's – such as Martin Elliott's 1976 shot of a tennis player exposing her posterior in early morning light, as reproduced on Athena posters and calendars well into the 1980s (McDermott 2011) – seem entirely redolent of a Hamilton mindset, or from a Hamilton acolyte. Soft and sunny light, almost to the point of overexposure, a light but warm colour pallet, and models at their ease, occasionally from unusual angles, were the chief components of Hamilton's style. But Hamilton's approach, just as Hamilton himself started to vanish as a name image-maker, seems to have exerted substantial influence. And this influence illustrates a redemption of Hamilton's 'low' concerns, and that Hamilton's imagining of sexuality was something acceptable within the mainstream, from the topless, naive and innocent young girl-next-door look favoured by the British tabloid newspaper *The Sun*, to Royal portraits from Lord Snowden.

This finding of eroticism in the everyday, and the normalisation of as much, points to a continuum of British nudity that goes nowhere near Hamilton's preference for early Renaissance frescoes (Hamilton 1993: 296). Could it not be said that Hamilton's real predecessors were Stanley J. Long and Arnold Louis Miller, in respect of their naturalist/nudist work of the early 1960s – most notably *Take Off Your Clothes and Live* (Miller, 1963)? The premise is not dissimilar to almost all Hamilton films: friends going to the Côte d'Azur. And the film strategically or opportunistically mixes the harmless (interminable sequences of Crazy Golf and dancing the Twist), the suggestive (the jiggling of beach ball games and trampolining) and the erotic (the naturalism, via sunbathing and swimming, although thongs remain on for both sexes). There is a determining use of colour and shading (here via Long's cinematography), which renders the locales sunny and enticing. And there is a sense of access to a society of liberated females: the flirtatious voice-over dialogues that run throughout the film include the comment from one of the holidaymakers, Heidi (Hedy Borland), introduced as 'the truly perfect secretary', and speaking on behalf of 'we girls' at the outset, concerning the determination 'to get away from dear old wet London'. In these ways, *Take Off Your Clothes and Live* functions as a sexier variant of travelogue B-features of the time, and connects to, or even evolves, a post-war mythology of sunny holidays abroad as inculcating a permissiveness in the working classes. And all this requires forward movement: away from the UK, and towards foreign environs.

Snowden also shot images that are near indistinguishable from Hamilton's, both in terms of diffused light and content. Snowden's group shot 'HRH The Prince and Princess of Wales with Prince William and Harry, 1991', for example, contains all the familiar elements. A wide aperture allows the natural light to flood in, white clothing and blonde hair is fully illuminated by and enhances that light, and the arrangement of the four figures is via natural (albeit studiously natural) poses. And fertility, or the potential of fertility, is seen as resonant in the foliage and wildlife overrunning the background, while the Edwardian-style knick-knacks posit a certain temporal confusion, or timelessness, which here perhaps mitigates or limits any burgeoning sense of eroticism. While this aestheticised vision offered something quite different from 1960s realism (the brutality of photojournalism or the street reportage of paparazzi images), Snowden nonetheless leaves in the easy or informal glamour of those strains or tendencies.[2] Snowden seems to find that – as if in contrast to 1960s photographers – people are inherently beautiful. The lightness of their attire and appearance, capitalising on the light that he affords these aspects, suggests an angelic quality. His figures seem removed from, or unsullied by, the pollution of the world: grime, poverty and pain are seemingly unknown experiences. A young, naked Rupert Everett, framed behind the glass panes of a window, gazes calmly at the foliage seen reflecting in the window panes, which casts a gentle and dappled light across his skin (Snowden 1983: 5). His insouciant expression and smooth, tense torso, which suggests a hired male call boy waiting to be summoned to perform, does not seem to darken the image.

But Snowden, to an extent, tames and dilutes Hamilton's aesthetic. Hamilton crushes the depth out of his images, sometimes with zoom lenses – 'I try to work with a fully open lens aperture in order to obtain a characteristic flatness, without perspective, similar to the frescoes at the beginning of the Renaissance' (Hamilton 1993: 296) – and allows light (typically sunny yellows and oranges) to wash across them, or sometimes filters his light through gauzy materials such as tents, canopies, mosquito nets, nightgowns or hair. This flattening and diffusion, combined with a tendency to wide shots, positions the resultant films at the opposite end of the spectrum to typically pornographic aesthetics – of shadows, or direct and unforgiving artificial light, and more often than not in small (private) spaces. Snowden, as befitting a portrait artist, restores realism, and maintains the ease, but also channels something of the eroticism to more conventional (i.e. married) ends. But even such a use of eroticism in this regal context – compared, for example, to the unsexy regal-ness of Cecil Beaton's royal figures – is a modernising impulse.

This capitalising on Hamilton's aesthetic by others – from Athena, to fashion photography, to *The Sun*'s Page 3 models, to the Royals, to the early years of MTV – eventually hijacked Hamilton's film-making altogether. For his final film, Hamilton seems to have shifted towards the idea of the ambience of fashion shoots as enough in itself. The near dialogue-less *Un été à Saint-Tropez* [A summer in St Tropez] (1983) seems merely to run through a number of sequences that frame women in certain clichéd settings: horse riding, girls showering and then drying each other, girls kissing in a field, sunbathing, and so on. At one point, six naked women run along a beach in slow motion, crashing waves mixed into piano/synthesiser accompaniment, followed by their slow-motion pillow fight in negligees, and then they pick flowers in a meadow. In distilling his typical concerns and visual motifs (such as mirrors), coupled with his idealised female types (tanned, long-limbed and lithe, free-flowing hair and make-up free) into narrative-less vignettes in this way, *Un été à Saint-Tropez* seems to suggest nothing less than Hamilton's vision of a secular/hedonist utopia or heaven – that is, experiential segments that seem to exist only to impart pleasure to the viewer, for a shared, albeit finite, moment. Indeed, when the film opens in a dormitory of sleeping women (one fully nude and sucking her thumb) who will soon all awaken to sunlight and warmth, it suggests a vision not quite tactile, or slightly beyond reach, as if these figures are waking into a better realm of existence. The point-of-view of this moment is, disconcertingly, that of a silent intruder who has broken into the dormitory to observe the girls. Perhaps the suggestion is that Hamilton will guide the viewer into this heavenly realm by stealth – as present, even in intimate moments, but unseen. Reputedly, however, the film was shot in Hamilton's own house: in this respect, they are the 'intruders', invited into his realm, for naive play-acting. The stratagem suggests something of Harold Acton's 'legendary garden' of Villa La Pietra in Florence (Strong 1997: 100): maze-like, with high hedges, barns, alcoves, benches, and summer houses. This was the very *mise en scène* for witness-free discrete seduction of local youths under starlit skies, and with fountains for post-coital ablutions, all far from the gossip circuits of the UK, or with ready excuses if need be: taking the night air, strolling around the grounds and reciting the rosary, showing the visitor the garden's statues.[3] The vague historical-setting impulse of Hamilton's, as noted, also seems to function as if to exert mitigation over these sexual scenarios. It seems too pat to just account for this interloper sexual tendency as seeking historical justification for the eroticisation of youth. Perhaps it is a matter of the predator repositioning himself – in a bygone age, in which consequences would not be understood as they would be today, or the populace was bolder in imagining youthful sexuality.

Historicisation can work to render ritualised sexual fantasies as removed, and so perceived to be safe. I recall a friend telling me, of his time in prep school, of a pastime for a rota of two or three boys invited to join a certain teacher for his weekends on his barge, navigating canals. As dusk fell, the boys were given bedcaps and long, white, flowing nightgowns to wear – in a Victorian or Edwardian style (but probably more derived from illustrations of Dickens's Scrooge). The boys would then walk beside the canal in the failing light, as if apparitions from the past, as the barge silently floated by, with the teacher inside – the culmination of this semi-secret, lone ceremony. Likewise, the character of Montague Withnail (Richard Griffith), of Bruce Robinson's *Withnail and I* (1987), nostalgically dwelling on his 'sensitive crimes in a punt with a chap called Norman, who had red hair and a book of poetry stained with the butter drips from crumpets' while an Oxford undergraduate. And, in the present tense of the film (of 1969), Monty is further given over to strategies to seduce the film's young protagonist, Marwood (Paul McGann), despite his loud objections and later arming himself against such an eventuality, and seemingly on the grounds that Marwood does not necessarily comprehend what is in his own best interests. Monty's Lake District cottage, Crow Crag, seems to have been his countryside seduction pad since at least the reign of King George V (1910–36), whose framed picture is on the wall, so that Marwood's positioning there transports Monty back to this earlier time and strategies of seduction, with long country walks, a roaring log fire, camp chatter over games of cards, chaises longues, and a substantial wine collection.

Hamilton's St Tropez recalls the template imagining of young sexuality and St Tropez – of Brigitte Bardot in *... And God Created Woman*, of twenty-five years before. Yet in Bardot, sexuality seems to disruptively break surface, turning the world upside down. In *Summer in St Tropez*, sexuality seems to exist, and remain, beneath that surface. In this way, sexuality can be readily observed in the everyday realm for those who know where to look (so casting Hamilton as a kind of optician for voyeurs): glimpses of breast through a negligee, or of underwear as a girl reclines under a tree at a picnic. But this gateway perception then spreads, reworking or reinterpreting otherwise non-erotic contexts. So *Cousins in Love* (1980) opens with a montage roll call of the film's characters – cousins and other relatives, parents, lodgers, chambermaids, the stable boy, and so on – who almost all seem to fall into the erotic scope of the film in the ways in which they are presented: mid-action, sunbathing, semi-dressed. But the very title of the film suggests the condition, and zenith (or nadir) of reworking or reinterpreting to stretch the boundaries of possibility of eroticism: cousins should not be in love. However, this all-encompassing eroticisation in *Un été à Saint-Tropez* gives rise to no great advancement: the *mise en scène* seems merely to be that of aspirational lifestyle advertising. To that extent, this vision of heaven is nothing new in itself, and yet very different from grim 1970s experiences of porn. But to a larger extent, and hiding in plain sight, what is different about Hamilton's heaven is that the focus of sexual desire is the young girl – and this focus is achieved fairly seamlessly. Perhaps the familiar language of advertising allows for a familiarisation with the imagery that, in turn, effectively normalises this difference. And, as discussed above, Hamilton's approach was one that had the potential for a reassuring familiarity for those whose work exhibited his influence: Snowdon could be 'sexy', but was never shocking; *The Sun*'s models were wholesome not wanton; the tennis player was merely naughty rather than a chronic exhibitionist. Whether consciously done or not, such a strategy on Hamilton's part works in conjunction with other attempts to normalise young sexuality of this moment – that is, for Hamilton: unclothed females just over, and occasionally prior to, the cusp of puberty – or straddling a visually ambiguous interzone between the two (where, for example, a certain camera angle alone can suggest which side of the 'line' the subject is on). The two Hamilton films principally considered in this chapter were initially passed uncut by the BBFC: *Bilitis* was certificated as X in December 1977, and *Laura* was certificated as X in April 1982, and they remain in circulation.[4] The films remain legal, in the sense that they are not clearly catering for paedophilic desires with under-aged models. But whereas tarrying in such an ambiguous interzone, with the blessing of the BBFC, was once perhaps just a particularity, now such explorations would seem entirely questionable.

Yet a certain philosophical position on sexuality seems to emerge in Hamilton's work, and it is the particularity of the articulation of this position that results in the way in which the films seem to effectively be, or achieve the status of, legalised paedophilia. This is not meant as a singular criticism: commentators have noted general tendencies towards the sexualisation of such young girls in terms of commercial coverage of sport matches (especially tennis at Wimbledon) or, for Whiteley (2003: 53), the predominant paedophilic construction and presentation of the young girl in the mainstream of popular music of recent decades. Prior to this, the sexualised young girl seemed more an adornment in permissive aesthetics, and psychedelia – as with, for example, the nude child cover image of Blind Faith's 1969 eponymous album, by Bob Seidemann.

The philosophical position in Hamilton's work arises from two tendencies: firstly, the use of landscapes and nature, and secondly, the way in which the totality of the films seem to exert a force on perception, in order to return the viewer's gaze time and again to one fundamental image. These tendencies are apparent through straight textual analysis. But the particularity of the articulation is one that Hamilton himself, in a reasonably forthright manner (in the introduction to a retrospective book of his photographic work), elucidates:

There exist among young girls, within a clearly defined age group, some rare beings who are able to exert a powerful erotic attraction upon certain much older men. It is a kind of magic, a fleeting charm which touches such men, of whom I am one, in a secret part of their sensibility. By means of my photographs I make a sincere confession that few men, bewitched as I am by the forbidden desire, will dare to make. (Hamilton 1993: 268)

While Hamilton here freely notes the illicit (i.e. 'forbidden') nature of the desire that he finds in himself, albeit a nature accommodated within the rareness of his connoisseur's soul (the 'sensibility'), this 'sincere confession' is one that speaks to the reasons underlying his use of technology. One could surmise that photographic reproduction allows for the only access to this forbidden sensibility by the outside world – offering familiarity to those other 'few men' with whom Hamilton shares this sensibility, and something of an education for others yet to be bewitched. The challenge is that this position casts the viewers (bar those 'few men' already in the know) as awaiting a bewitching, as Hamilton's film form is effectively evangelical about the erotic joys of young girls.

At a risk of continuing to allow Hamilton the leave to explain his own films, the question of rural landscape is, itself, presented as formative to his psyche and later artistic work. Hamilton's own recollections frame feelings and sexual awakenings in terms of the countryside. His earliest memories involve being evacuated from Kennington, in London, to the Dorset countryside (which he notes was geographically close to Thomas Hardy's *Tess of the D'Urbervilles*), where he remained for the duration of the Second World War. So the acute, even sensual contrast is established from a 'dreary, grey London to a life in the countryside and a boyhood spent climbing trees, bird-nesting, fishing and swimming', and that the balance would disadvantage him: 'my return to London at the end of the War was not at all pleasant. I had not missed the city' (Hamilton 1993: 9). The first sexual memory offered is outside the urban environs of Kennington where, '[w]ithout understanding why, the eroticism of the incident affected me profoundly' (ibid.: 10). During a bike ride with friends through Dulwich Park,

> I saw something fleetingly, which made a lasting impression on me. Two boys
> and a girl were on the grass. One of the boys had pinned the girl down, and the
> other boy had pulled up her dress and was sliding blades of grass and daisies
> between her knickers and her skin … I made no comment to my friends, but the
> scene and the feelings it aroused remained with me. (Ibid.)

It was only years later, discovering the 'earthly paradise' of St Tropez, that this feeling seems to have found a new wellspring. The town is described by Hamilton as a 'sublime setting with beaches where people sunbathed in the nude', so that '[i]t was a world that was completely new to me, and nothing, during my youth in England, or the life I had led until then [1962] had prepared me for it' (Hamilton 1993: 242). In these ways, the encounter with the world is sensual, and shot through with utopic ideas of life in tandem with unspoilt, rural environs. *Frieze* (2001) concludes that the context for understanding Hamilton's 'frozen idylls' and 'artificial heaven' is his conscious hanging on to the spirit of the Summer of Love of the 1960s, in opposition to the militancy of the counterculture beyond 1968. But Hamilton's frame of reference seems earlier: a freer Edwardian society, as perhaps preserved in rural Dorset, as echoed in the glimpsed scene in Dulwich Park, and for which war-time deprivations, and the inner-city squalor of Kennington, would have been unknown. The fact that Hamilton, like Peter de Rome, seemingly had to go abroad to find an access to this ideal suggests that the exiled pornographers are, in fact, the truest to an erotic imagining of Britain. And North America, for de Rome – and indeed for the artist David Hockney, or David Bowie in the mid-1970s, or Genesis of *The Lamb Lies Down on Broadway* (1974) – seems to offer possibilities of an expanded erotic consciousness, rather than just expanded sexual practices. Memory then becomes the referent for the *mise en scène*, or effectively acts as the storyboard, and finds further freedoms through distance and artistic licence, so that fantasy takes on more resonance than reality. Such a dynamic is found too in Robert Browning's poem 'Home Thoughts, from Abroad' (1845): while in Northern Italy, Browning seems to have to work hard to imagine an idealised and missed rural England which, in April, would have begun to bloom. The difficulty for Browning, as apparent in tension and competition between various images, is that the imagining is in the teeth of intrusive thoughts, indicating that the countryside, as he knows, is not quite as pleasant as he recalls it. What is missing from all this is the intrusive sense of the anti-permissives. Hamilton and de Rome have simply abandoned the grounds of contestation. And the legality of Hamilton's films, and their Niven-calibrated artiness, may have removed them further from the firing line.

For Browning, the act of idealisation is one that is able to strip out the unpleasant elements of the reality referenced. Indeed, the idyll seems to need to be a Garden of Eden, free from the harshness of the world outside. And this relocation (reality to idyll) is something particularly transformative for the question of sexuality, where acts are so fully invested with, and remade by, the judgements and censors and prohibitions of the outside world, as manifest in guilt and misunderstandings and trepidations. Only permissiveness can seemingly overcome these issues: being in that 'anything goes' zone, total freedom is taken as read; and being isolated from the outside world, it no longer seems to trouble anyone in the zone. So the idyll can only remain an idyll on the basis of mutual consent. *Frieze* draws parallels with *Bilitis* and *Emmanuelle* – the latter caused something of a sensation when shown in Britain (cut and X-certificated in September 1974) – but it is clear that, aesthetic similarities aside, the films are quite different in their imaginings of the world. Emmanuelle's (Sylvia Kristel) concern is reigniting or reawakening eroticism, and with this comes a series of seeming dangers (including her rape in an opium den). For Hamilton, who notes that he was initially asked to direct *Emmanuelle* (Hamilton 1993: 268), the awakening needs to occur for the first time – for, at least, the central narrative concern of his films. Secondary characters often play the parts of those who, now older and jaded, vicariously or voyeuristically live through their first sexual awakenings. And the central young female protagonist emerges from a pack of similar girls (school friends in *Bilitis*, ballet school colleagues in *Laura*) – as if to suggest that this individual is that 'rare being' who bewitches, as per Hamilton's observations (ibid.), and that the nearly comparable beauty of the others, corralled and referred to in the closing credits of *Laura* as 'Et Les Demoiselles d'Hamilton', has been filtered out by the eye of Hamilton. That 'rare being' quality, in Bilitis and Laura, also comes from the way in which the girls seem slightly set apart from the pack – preferring their own company, and finding the space to explore the sexual curiosity that begins to awaken; and so, in partial isolation, they are available for encounters with those who then come into their orbit. Indeed, Hamilton's formative memory of Dulwich Park is one of tentative experimentation on the part of the girl (assuming that she was consenting to the encounter; it is not clear in his writing) – perhaps with two boys from the nearby boarding school Dulwich College, who had sought out a local girl (that is, a lower-class girl, perhaps from nearby Peckham or Brixton), who would be more readily available for erotic exploration than their immediate 'well-brought-up' counterparts. Hamilton is clear about the relationship with a certain type of burgeoning, conscious or barely conscious beauty, the ostracising side effect of this, and the space that then becomes available for dreams and fantasies – presumably prepping the young girl for a situation in which such fantasies can become realities.

> *These young nymphs who fascinate me often shun the avid gaze of the public, which reflects an awareness of the beauty that they themselves are trying to ignore ... This transparency of the skin and eyes, extreme fineness of hair, excessive fairness which blurs the eyebrows, projecting cheekbones, high forehead, the movement of full lips, and the snub nose, like a tender pink muzzle, earns them, at school, the curious, envious and sometimes jealous thoughts and glances of their classmates. And if, by chance, in the changing rooms, their classmates observe that the sensual moulding of the face is also revealed in more intimate parts of the anatomy, then they have to live with teasing or envy, like symbols of segregation. Thus, often solitary and silent, these young girls take refuge in dreams which they have wished to bring into reality. (Hamilton 1993: 281)[5]*

Cat Stevens, in songs about Patti D'Arbanville (his girlfriend of some years before *Bilitis*), had first expanded on just the qualities Hamilton identifies, and which presumably resulted in her casting by Hamilton. D'Arbanville has a kind of exiled regal countenance in *Bilitis*. And, for Cat Stevens, she is or was someone set aside, and almost not of this world – a vision rather than a cause of action, as someone unable to be possessed. For 'Lady D'Arbanville', the singer seemingly observes her sleeping, is disturbed by her stillness, quietness and coldness, but comforts himself thinking about spending the next day with her, and then imagines (or, perhaps, this is already the truth of the matter), that she is in fact dead and buried. For 'Wild World', the singer regrets his lover leaving him (reputedly also Patti). The world waiting outside their relationship (or, pace Hamilton, outside the idyll) holds the potential to strip her of her innocence and harden her, a sentiment or warning that Stevens delivers (sings) with unusual passion and drama, his voice overwhelming the music – in sharp contrast to what seems to have been a protective, idyllic relationship with the singer. He notes, on their parting, '[a]nd I'll always remember you like a child, girl' or, conceivably (as the delivery is ambiguous), 'a child-girl'. And for 'Hard Headed Woman', the singer yearns for a female (again reputedly also Patti) who is not given over to the fickle nature of the times (that is, who is not one of the many known 'fancy dancers' or 'fine feathered friends'), and in whom he can lose himself, and in so doing will seemingly be pushed out of emotional complacency.[6] But D'Arbanville, born in 1951, would have been aged about 19 for Cat Stevens, and 26 for Hamilton. Hamilton strips a decade off her age, though, in his presentation. She initially seems like a somewhat reigned-in and sulkier Brigitte Bardot, with her blonde hair, worn loose, as if chafing against her schoolgirl status. (Hamilton's preference was for waif-like Nordic blondes with high cheek bones, pinkish complexions and arrested-development physiques; Hinton notes, of this, a certain bourgeois preference in operation; Hinton 2016: 5). This is schoolgirl sexuality as per Larkin's *Willow Gables* or, in comparably mainstream film terms of this time, Jenny Agutter in *Walkabout* (Nicholas Roeg, 1971), Helen Mirren in *Age of Consent* (Michael Powell, 1969), Linda Hayden in *Baby Love* (Alastair Reid, 1969), Susan George in *Lola* (aka *Twinky*, Richard Donner, 1969), Nastassja Kinski in *To the Devil... a Daughter* (Peter Sykes, 1976), or the schoolgirls of *Picnic at Hanging Rock* (Peter Weir, 1975). But any imagined concern about the nudity and sex scenes of someone on the edge of puberty in *Bilitis* is met with the unavoidable image of thick pubic hair. However, this is not necessarily to contrast one idea ('forbidden' prepubescent sexualisation) with a corrective other (defiantly pubescent or post-pubescent): as per digital image manipulation, composite figures are possible, and indeed are also grounds for legal action, and this seems to effectively be how Hamilton has managed D'Arbanville for *Bilitis*: physical aspects of each for his 'child-girl'.[7]

Landscape, in Hamilton, functions as a kind of naturalisation of the events that are shown. To be precise: when one thinks of pornography in urban settings, there is often a heightened denaturalisation of what is shown – the sexuality becomes part of the general degradation, or enabled by the abrogation of legal or social norms in the zones of inner-city squalor. Each environment (rural and urban) offsets, and is seen to enable, and even colour, the sexual activity that is then seen to occur within it. And nature, in the case of Hamilton, intrudes into sexual activity – but more than just in terms of incidentals (as per the blades of grass in Dulwich Park, or the French Riviera of *Take Off Your Clothes and Live*). In *Bilitis* the eroticisation of the entire world seems to occur, albeit for the viewer: the erotic spectacle, at the outset of the film, of the girls who cycle, strip and swim, is seemingly not understood by them as sexually sensual, but merely naturalist-like sensual in its tactility. But that realisation then dawns on them (or, at least, Bilitis, as the outrider of this group) – so that the viewer, as with the pederast, has foreknowledge of the coming sexualisation of the sensual, and the new experiences that await the young girl. It is as if the viewer knows what will arouse her before she does, and can potentially utilise that foreknowledge as a self-justification for seduction; or as if the viewer understands that the young girl retains the pretence or come-hither appearance of innocence, even once she has stepped into, or anticipated a step into, experience. This dilemma is illustrated in one of Hamilton's photos of a reclining blonde, hands over her head, and who gazes fixedly at the camera. There is a knowingness in her eyes that seems substantially in advance of her years, or is even positively sexually jaded – as if this look, combined with her reclining, is an invitation to sexual intercourse. Her smooth features and puppy-fat-soft face, in contrast to the eyes, suggest prepubescence. Her elaborate silk nightie is hiked up to reveal her stomach, and the photo crops the image prior to revealing her vagina. The cropping poses a question for the viewer – who is the recipient of the come-hither look: does the lack of clarity around pubic hair indicate prepubescence? Would a response be a 'yes' or a 'no'? Even to scan the image downwards (as is unavoidable, with the arrangement of the image – in which the viewer's eyes first meet the model's eyes) is, in a way, self-implicating, in terms of flirting with the idea of a 'yes'. And Hamilton assists the idle viewer with this mystery: the image (reproduced in Hamilton 1993: 33) is titled 'False innocence, South of France, 1986'. The image is strongly reminiscent of the notorious photography of young girls in coy and seemingly sexualised poses by Lewis Carroll, although Carroll's models seem even younger. For Robson, who avoids the painful and seemingly irresolvable 'interpretive dance' around Carroll's intentions and actions, Carroll was a major figure, but only one figure, in the 'peculiarly Victorian obsession' of 'the nineteenth-century phenomenon of girl worship' (Robson 2001: 138 and 192). 'False innocence' recalls Carroll's image of Xie (Alexandra) Kitchen at 7 or 8 years of age, lying on a chaise lounge ('Xie Kitchen, 1872'). Here, the dress (white cotton rather than Hamilton's white silk) has been pulled back from the shoulders, down to just above the nipples (and, seemingly, a blanket has been kicked off). Thus Carroll, like Hamilton, poses the same teasing question. But Hamilton's model, unlike Carroll's, has open eyes, and her nipples are dimly visible through the nightie. And Hamilton's aesthetic, while seemingly Victorian, is one of invitation: the warmth of the colours, the openness of the arms that invite an embrace, and the sense of motion from the ruffles of the nightie and the disarray of the hair. The stillness of Carroll's sleeping child would prompt one to tiptoe away: the image as if an intimate domestic scene – albeit with the sexual charge (consciously or otherwise), perhaps then even more troublingly (i.e. incestuous), intact.[8] Unlike Carroll's German counterpart, Baron Wilhelm von Gloeden, whose preference was for photographs of Sicilian boys, outdoors in pseudo-classical and come-hither poses, seemingly taken in the early 1900s – 'sometimes merely naked, more often embellished as though they were the catamites of ancient Rome enacting mildly erotic *tableaux vivants*' (Sewell 2011: 309) – Carroll remains observational. He even remains, from today's vantage point, partly ethnographic: domestic scenes, peasant scenes, and everydayness. The difference, then, is one of permissiveness: Carroll's images a few paces back, and the thrill arguably derived from a voyeuristic basis; Hamilton's images as aspiration, or showing a potential sexual gain, and so suggestive of paces forward. Von Gloeden's 'Head of a Sicilian Boy' (1890s) or 'Three Nude Youths' (circa 1900) could suggest very particular actions – or simply be ethnographic studies with classical pretensions. 'Head of a Sicilian Boy' presents a garlanded youth, possibly with rouged lips, and sporting a sullen expression, turning his knowing, even world-weary, eyes directly to the onlooker – as if waiting for a move, or as if a study of the hard life of such non-cossetted youths. The 'Three Nude Youths' are arranged around a fountain – two nude, muscular backs to the viewer and behinds visible, and a third (seemingly botched by Von Gloeden: the figure is blurry and his eyes closed), holding a sheet around his waist. The fountain, which includes a female statue (as if to offset the male nudity), is found at a small woodland crossroads, with three different paths. The elevation suggests that the viewer is standing, as if now needing to make a decision: one has to choose one's direction, and possibly to take one or more of the waiting boys along, or merely to stand and note, as if a missionary, the uninhibited nudity of the heathens.

But it does not seem to be a matter of suggesting that the transition from Victorian images to Hamilton's contemporary ones is that transition from the purity of inaction to the impurity of action: Carroll, von Gloeden and Hamilton all present images that, for the viewer, suggest a blurring of the two. And, indeed, this blurring may be a technological matter: to create such images already suggests actions have been taken (boys arranged, nighties pulled). In this respect, achieving that aesthetic is a permissive matter: a process that requires actions and imagination. And such an aesthetic seems to draw on a pederastic tradition of idealisation, going back to the 'Uranian' appropriation of classical ideas of beauty.

'Sensitive Crimes'

The Uranian poets, in d'Arch Smith's analysis, reveal a number of principal themes and philosophical positions in terms of their mostly highly sexualised imaginings of boyhood, all of which can be seen to be in action in Hamilton.[9] For d'Arch Smith (1970: 163–96), these are, in my summary:

- The fleeting days of youth
- Guilt (on the part of the poet/voyeur)
- Peeping (on the part of the poet/voyeur)
- Lost youth (that is, the lost youth of the no-longer-youthful poets themselves)
- The angelic vision (in contrast to the unpleasant actuality of the 'real boy, grubby, ink-stained, insolent, uncomprehending of Uranian passion and rebuffing its smallest manifestation'; d'Arch Smith 1970: 174)
- The supremacy of Uranian love (which, for Kaylor, saw the Uranians as taking themselves as 'the inheritors of a "more authentic" Western culture than their contemporaries understood' – a Hellenic tradition; Kaylor 2006: 379)

- Sexual love (albeit that '[p]hysical passion in Uranian verse is rarely in evidence'; d'Arch Smith 1970: 177)
- The ways of evasion (by which the poets sometimes buried their problematic concerns beneath surface engagements with more acceptable themes)

D'Arch Smith's final identification is with, as he terms it, 'The Prince and the Pauper': a class-bound 'longing for an attachment to a boy either of a far higher or, more often, of a far lower social rank', with the latter possible because 'such [working-class] boys possessed a sexual frankness and uninhibitedness which allowed them to withstand the man's strong erotic desire' (d'Arch Smith 1970: 191). And this pauper, in the context of beauty and desire, is transformed into a prince in the eye of the beholder – seemingly, though, only for the fleeting duration of his youth. And this time-limited experience is one that then comes to excuse or justify pederastic or even homosexual desire, or even interactions. D'Arch later reflected (1986: 246) that these unusual, wayward and indeed criminal (if acted upon) relations cannot persist, in a disapproving society, and so, in a sense, are not really fully sexual (in a heterosexual way, by which such relations would then be accommodated within society via marriage and parenthood). This would account for the lack of a comparable literature concerning young girls. But this position itself would have been specific to a non-secular age. Hamilton, for the permissive age, is able to make this extension to young women, who are free to act, freed from a sense that their action then determines that social destiny.[10] One could add the freer availability of contraception, and increased acceptance of relationships outside marriage. If Uranian passion was understood as purer than heterosexual passion (as heterosexuality invariably terminates in marriage and procreation), and so exists abstractly (as self-sufficient and 'in the moment') and cannot be considered within the matrices of relationships (as the younger party is too young to make such adult attachment), then the advances in family planning some one hundred years later would spread that abstraction, somewhat, to heterosexual passions.

The problem with a Uranian context for Hamilton is that Hamilton's light films cannot bear the weight of Uranian preoccupations (which were aesthetic, classical, and theological) – or, only, perhaps, in relation to the most hackneyed poems from Uranians. D'Arch Smith's 'ways of evasion' prompted the development of a kind of erotic samizdat. So yearnings of an erotic nature could be displaced, unconsciously or otherwise, onto religious intent – i.e. a theological structuring and rewriting or re-enacting of erotic desires. The entirety of the Oxford Movement, for those who would see in it a kind of homoeroticisation and homosocialisation of high Anglo-Catholicism, would seem to exist at this juncture. This reading is not just confined to more recent academic writings, as with the overview of various interpretations offered: by Janes in respect to (Anglo-) Catholicism's closeting and, simultaneously, sacramentalisation of non-heterosexual urges (Janes 2015: 19–20); or that which Hanson refers to as 'an atmosphere of homoerotic exuberance' (Hanson 1997: 25); or Bethmont (2006), who finds in Anglo-Catholicism the fusing of religion to the senses, as the body is given a role in worship and spirituality, and hence the sensuality of Anglo-Catholic, and generally Catholic, practices. Hilliard quotes Waugh's *Brideshead Revisited* (1945), and the advice offered by Charles Ryder's slightly older cousin in the first days of Ryder's time at the University of Oxford in the early 1920s (Hilliard 1982: 18) – '[b]eware of the Anglo-Catholics – they're all sodomites with unpleasant accents' (Waugh 1945: 25) – and similar strains in English literature concerning the same, as 'subtly permeated with hints of homosexuality' (Hilliard 1982: 18–19).[11] And it allows Kaylor, with an expansive and canon-forming impulse that seeks to transcend d'Arch Smith's penchant for bad poetry, to find in the Uranians, or an expanded Uranian heritage, a renewal of poetic traditions, which became (mostly via the reception of the proto-modernist poetry of Gerard Manley Hopkins) a major tributary into modernism itself. To do this, and in the tradition of 'queering' readings, Kaylor rereads the Uranians and seeks to decode the obscurantisms or unpick the metaphors. Thus a few lines of a ditty found in his papers after Hopkins's death in 1889, nominally about archery, are taken to be a fantasy, seemingly idly inspired by the sight of bathing schoolboys, about their engaging in rough buggery with each other – something gingerly dismissed as an unintended meaning, or denied altogether, by previous scholars (Kaylor 2006: 96).[12] Or, for Roden, Hopkins's transition from Anglo-Catholicism to Roman Catholicism replaced the sense of queer desire as sublimated into nominally typical friendships to a freer state of fantasy, in which 'love' and 'desire', through the vector of the figure of Christ, become a central concern of his thinking and poetry (Roden 2002: 84–85). So '[t]he queerness of "going over" made the process of conversion a kind of "coming out"' (ibid.: 93). But in these biographical discussions, and more so in the poetry, sermons and writing, Roden rereads the prose as infused with hidden (from the public, and/or from Hopkins himself) gay or queer desires. So the analysis is one of scrutiny of metaphors, and subtextual excavations, albeit bordering on the explicit. Roden quotes Hopkins seemingly on (for Roden) 'man [himself, who] would sodomize Christ': Hopkins writes '[i]f only God could be put into the position: the mortal sinner would have his way with him (the men of Sodom, Judas, and Caiaphas are three typical cases) ... if the sinner defiles God's image so he might God's person if he could; if he takes the limbs of Christ and makes them members of a harlot, so he would Christ' (Roden 2002: 96; the quote is from one of Hopkins's torturously awkward sermons).

Freed of the need for evasion, and seemingly free to push against the boundaries of acceptability (in terms of the seeming youth of the desired figures) in this freer zone, Hamilton can plough into directly erotic concerns. To watch a Hamilton film is to be part of a process in which boundaries, then, are in a constant state of expansion. But this is not just a matter of showing more, or expressing more, early revealings of intimacies. Rather – and perhaps in this Hamilton is delivering a female-equivalent of the Uranians – it is a constant harking back to a moment of awakening: the first realisation of erotic feelings on the part of his young protagonists.

Hamilton's chief concern is that dawning: a charting of the affective moments of the wind in the hair as the girls cycle in *Bilitis*, or the little crawling turtle kept in the pocket of one of the schoolgirls, or the sliding down the staircase rail, or the tentative touching of each other's breasts, and then full-blown lesbian experimentation. And the clutter of nature in the frame undergirds this dawning: in the clichéd sense, the girls blossom and come to fertility in parallel with nature. Thus, to deny or censure the young girls' burgeoning sexuality is to go against the fecundity of nature, irrespective of ideas of propriety or laws of ages of consent. (There is even a homophobic current in this: lesbianism read as an exploratory halfway station, or rite of practice, before the full shift to adulthood and heterosexual intercourse, or simply as the outlet for sexually frustrated heterosexual women – Bilitis's first substantial lesbian engagement comes after her declaring that she loathes men.) But Hamilton goes one step further in terms of the role of nature. Bilitis learns of love not only from the example of other adults (from watching the host couple, and indeed her being naked at night comes about through her imitation of the stripping she has seen). She also gleans sexual feelings from nature itself. In her voice-over words:

I undressed and climbed into a tree. My naked thighs embraced its smooth, damp bark, and my sandals walked on its branches. High-up, among the leaves, sheltered from the heat of the night, I sat aside the spreading fork of a branch, my feet hanging free below. It rained, and drops of water fell and ran along my skin [a pan up Bilitis's naked body takes in her now erect nipples], my hands were green in the moss and my toes red from crushed flowers. And [I] felt the beautiful tree vibrate with the wind's passage, and so I tightened my legs around it and pressed my open mount against the long, downy neck of the branch.

As seen (including on the back of the soundtrack LP cover) and described: the vibrating branch stimulates Bilitis's clitoris while the wet bark reciprocates the saliva of the kiss. The subsequent sequence, of swimming in the sea, leads to a lesbian encounter with Melissa. In these ways, blameless, amoral nature first awakens sexuality. The agency for the age of consent then is with creation itself, as if the laws of nature, rather than opportunistic legal bureaucrats who seem to come after the fact. And nature, for the viewer, even comes to act as a kind of lighting designer: the nudity of Bilitis, offset at one point against a pitch-black night sky, is sharpened and defined. *Tendres Cousines* [Cousins in love] (1980) and *Premiers Désirs – Le derniere été d'une jeune fille* [First desires – the last summer of a young girl] (1983/84), as with *Bilitis*, also include scenes in which the young girls watch adults make love as a prelude (and guide to) their own such engagements. And *Tendres Cousines* ends with the protagonist slapped by the girl with whom he has argued and made love: sensuality giving way to the sting of the grown-up world. (The religious ritual of Confirmation, which historically included a slap for the young Catholic – the welcome to the world of adulthood, from which faith can now be freely confirmed by the individual – is denoted by just such an unwarranted blow, with no retaliation permissible.)

This use of nature means that the sadness that pervades *Bilitis* is not necessary something understood as being owed to any one person or concatenation of interactions with the other characters in the film. The film is bookended by a present frame in which Bilitis looks wistful and pensive, and then upset, as she reflects on the experiences that make up the majority of the film. It is the process of life itself, and perhaps the kind of sadness that Cat Stevens reflects upon: the imminent loss of innocence, through and for the harder world outside, that awaits the woman who takes leave of him, for the 'Wild World'. Or, for the *Tendres Cousines* variant: the film's 1939 setting allows for a carefree pre-war bohemianism – so the societal space for the free love that is shown would soon be lost, as indicated by portents of impending disasters into this world (Hitler's voice on the radio suddenly interrupting a dinner party, for example). *Bilitis* opens with a montage of shots, often still, that are presented as snapshots from Bilitis's recollection (they are intercut with shots of her remembering): characters, places and events that will make sense as the narrative, as one long flashback, then unfolds after this pre-credit sequence. This first casts the narrative as immobilised too (via freeze frames, as if caught in amber), as if via a bittersweet nostalgia, as Bilitis thinks back across a period that saw her loss of innocence, and the shift from girlhood to the threshold of womanhood. And the shift from still images to moving images also signals a kind of animation of Hamilton's photographic work – while keeping to the essence of his concerns. In thanking Henri Colpi (as producer and editor) and Bernard Daillencourt (director of photography) for making *Bilitis* 'a charming film', Hamilton notes that the film is one 'in which the audience could find and enjoy the atmosphere of my photographs' (Hamilton 1993: 286).[13] But it seems to be more than this: the technology of film brings with it the ability to bring still images to life, shifting reproduction to an engulfing immediacy. *Laura* also begins with still images, but this time sketches, and prints of paintings, of nudes. And Laura is often presented with slow fades in and out, from a fixed camera position, as if the line between still and moving images is one that can oscillate at Hamilton's behest. That line is presumably understood to be the one between object of fantasy (the young women: the object then of a narrative of the imagination, from the viewer or possessor of the still image) and the fantasy itself as played out (Hamilton's narrative, the nude and love scenes as shown on the screen, and so on). This ability to stop and start time, mobilising a still into life and, once shared with the viewers (and repeatedly too, for additional viewings), as a mechanism for enacting paedophilic fantasy, then positions the apparatus of cinema as a way of overcoming one of the classical issues for the paedophile: that time is the enemy – the object of desire will lose his or her youthful beauty, and grow into an adult. So, in this, Hamilton freezes those fleeting days of youth, and somewhat then recovers those lost days of youth – to return to two of these aspects of the challenges for paedophiles, as demarcated above with respect to d'Arch Smith. The period settings suggest an essential difference between Hamilton's erotica and the pornography discussed elsewhere in this study too. Hamilton functions nostalgically and historically, charging memories with sexual frissons. Pornography otherwise looks in the opposite direction: what could be, or might be, in this present and the near future, charging sexual possibilities with sexual frissons.

However, the films still remain a matter of 'in which': that is, that the audience invariably find themselves immersed in the totality of the experience of a Hamilton film. Components seem to interlock with each other, and the drama-turgical flatlines of *Bilitis* and *Laura* means that there is almost no way out: so little seems to happen that no pit stops or pause points present themselves. The films merely continue, rather than develop. How does one exit? It is in this way that the totality of the films seems to exert a centrifugal force of perception: the immersion is total, and affectively aligns the experience of the world of the film, which is one of eroticism, with the immersion. In this respect, the vague or ambient philosophical position or positions of the films become unavoidable. And the very representation of this state of total eroticism can be taken as an aspiration on the part of Hamilton, or the raison d'être for his art or artiness. It is a representation of total freedom, and what then transpires in this state – and how different that is from, and healthier than, the dysfunctional relationships that represent the norm of today. For this, it is necessary to step aside from the found or known world: extant reality does not yield up sufficient beauty to enable this process. In Uranian terms, this is d'Arch Smith's tension around the 'angelic vision' (d'Arch Smith 1970: 174): one has to look elsewhere, even into imagination, to achieve sufficient beauty. This is underscored by the oddness of the out-of-place location of the films, as noted above. And this explains, or accounts for, Hamilton's own exiled status: to look to a state of exile, as if to the distant angelic plateau, and so to look away, or leave or abandon, the rough and disappointing (that is, unerotic) figures of known reality. Perhaps it is only in exile that this remaking of British eroticism is possible: exile away from the rainy isles, and exile from the stringencies of laws around age of consent, and the anti-permissives. The difficulty then is whether this is a matter of the representation of the fantastical, or of a known, but perhaps secret, as illicit, society. Does Hamilton (a) parallel reality, with an enhanced and angelic vision, or (b) offer an exposé of what could be and may already be? Even the ambiguities surrounding the death of Hamilton seem to speak to this question: a strong denial of accusations (of sexual assault and rape) made against him by former models, followed by suicide by asphyxiation (see Willsher 2016).

Hamilton's films then reduce the viewer to a kind of naive and seducible figure. The films offer an education for him or her: you may not expect erotic frissons from an unlikely group of females, but expect the unexpected – and with that an initiation into, or at least a dalliance with, the illicit. What is implicit in this is that Hamilton knows more, and maybe even knows better. So this is not a matter of knowingly catering to already-existing bases of tastes, but of pushing those tastes, of expanding the pallet, and in so doing helping the viewer to lose his or her innocence. The perception of the imagined viewer in Hamilton's films is of the adult male wishing to be enlightened into paedophilia or even the child wishing to be groomed, through exposure to such films. In just this way, in a fictionalised commentary on the experience of watching *Death in Venice* with a sexually predatory teacher, as a prepubescent boarding school boy, see Golding 2001: 313–16 (I assume this refers to the BBC2 broadcast of 23 September 1976, at 9pm). For the teacher, the film 'was elevated to the status of a cult, and adopted with messianic fervour by melancholy inverts everywhere, [such as] men quite old enough to know worse' (315), as with 'the imperturbable countenance of our director of music, [which] is, can you believe, stricken with tears' (316). The film galvanises the narrator of Golding's book to end his relationship with the director of music in question.

Freedom of expression in respect to a fuller access to emotions and feelings, particularly at the crucial juncture of a coming of age, is or was the pivotal point in pro-paedophilia writing and conceptions during the decades of Hamilton's film-making. And d'Arch Smith's presence as a coda to Warren Middleton's 1986 academic collection, which sought to delineate and gradate paedophilic desire (the book *Betrayal of Youth: Radical Perspectives on Childhood Sexuality, Inter-generational Sex, and the Social Oppression of Children and Young People*), can be taken as working to directly relate contemporary thought and indeed activism from this quarter to the Uranian models of the previous century. Likewise, Hamilton's aesthetics also seem to seek to place the concerns of the films in the context of the 1800s. But such aspirations or indicators potentially obscure the otherwise very clear context of Hamilton's films – as part of a discourse around adult sexual desires focused on the young or underaged. Hamilton's films can be read as, firstly, an illustration of the principal arguments that emerge from this discourse, so an 'expert witness' in the pro-paedophile cause. And, secondly, Hamilton's films can be taken as, effectively, the imagining of such a discourse: a laboratory in which such desires can be re-enacted or recreated for later analysis. The ideological import of this endeavour emerges in the context of a brief review of pro-paedophile thought in the 1970s and early 1980s, which follows shortly. And

Hamilton's position is essentially conservative, in that he aligns his eroticism with hetero-pederasty rather than homo-pederasty ('boy love'), which would take on an additional payload of protest, around, or coming to be associated with, or arguably hidden within, gay rights activism.[14]

Such questions were being asked at the time of Hamilton's films: a final frontier of the 'long 1960s' in which the moment may have come to push further boundaries of sexual freedom or, for Middleton in his Introduction to *Betrayal of Youth*, to identify and help those persecuted sexual minority groups – not least via a theoretical front of dismantling the perceived misconceptions concerning paedophilia. Reviewing a number of prosecutions prompts Middleton's foundational question, 'Just what is this witch-hunt, and why all the hysteria?'; and it has framed the edited collection as an attempt to provide an answer, and as partly aligned with the persecuted group the Paedophile Information Exchange (PIE).[15] He notes the paedophile is in a line of scapegoats ('replacing gays and blacks'), and so is prey to state 'head hunters', operating '[u]nder the guise of "child protection"', and that such a movement is bolstered by the establishment, the church, and indeed parents who, wary of increased personal liberties, fear losing control over their children, and so 'are reasserting their "rights" over them'. For this '[c]ontrolling children's sexuality is the trump card they hold and wave in the maintenance of this oppression' (Middleton 1986: unnumbered). And, sure enough, Mary Whitehouse had escalated the group to a major target by the mid-1980s, and gained political traction for this – even reproducing a PIE leaflet in full in an appendix in her *Mightier than the Sword*, and proposing outlawing the group and all its literature (Whitehouse 1986: 152–53).

Tom O'Carroll's *Paedophilia – The Radical Case* (1980) assembles a base-line argument that 'children may be sexually attracted to adults… [and] that there are adults who genuinely love children, and who are sometimes able to form positive erotic relationships with them, despite all the social prohibitions' (O'Carroll 1980).[16] To deny such thinking is therefore, from this perspective, to deny or repress feelings among children – typically then considered to be a human rights issue, and one that stretches to other areas too, hence, as Jeffreys (1993: 206) notes, the campaign against corporal punishment for schoolchildren. For Middleton, 'the myths of childhood innocence and the asexuality of children continue to survive … [t]his is not to say that childhood sexuality isn't recognised; it is, but it is not accepted in sexophobic cultures like our own' (Middleton 1986: 141). And this is in keeping with Peter Tatchell's conclusion to his chapter in *The

Betrayal of Youth, which questions 'moral values left over from the Victorian era' and suggests rethinking the idea of 'children' in favour of 'young citizens':

> *In a fully democratic and egalitarian society, there can be no question of adults usurping the rights of young people by keeping them in a state of ignorance, fear and guilt, or by resort to arbitrary and autocratic laws [that] deny them responsibility for decisions affecting their lives, especially about their own bodies and emotions. (Tatchell 1986: 118)*[17]

And the oppressive situation of a moralistic, Victorian mindset, or denial of childhood sexuality, also places the paedophile adult in a psychologically impossible situation – one that then leads, in a kind of 'stage two' (where 'stage one' is abiding by legal codes of behaviour), to a degeneration that endangers everyone involved. O'Carroll illustrates this by drawing on his own history, further to a 'dangerous state of mind' after he had lost his teaching job:

> *[it pushed me to] something as close as I have ever been to sexually predatory behaviour. Released from the rules that [had] bound me in the teaching profession – released from having anything to lose by breaking them – I was determined to find a boy, or boys, for what I assured myself would be mutually pleasurable and affectionate sex. I would spare myself the hopeless, romantic yearning I felt for [his former pupil] Chris, and instead just concentrate on giving the child a sexual turn-on, by masturbating him. All I had to do was pop out to the nearest canal bank, or swimming baths, or park and start chatting up boys. I'd soon find those who were into it, if only I had the guts to actually talk sex. (O'Carroll 1980: Chapter 1)*

Elsewhere, O'Carroll outlines the acceptable or ideal 'step-by-step' process of seduction, for 'each stage is "negotiated" by hints and signals, verbal and non-verbal, by which each indicates to the other what is acceptable and what is not – a process of mutual education' (ibid.: 49).

Stephen Fry sought to articulate such sentiments, situated in a prep school environment, in his 1980 satirical play *Latin! or Tobacco and Boys*. One teacher, detecting another is in a sexual relationship with a 13-year-old boy, forces a confession and offers his silence (and thus complicity) via blackmail: demanding BDSM sessions from the pederast, as if the two practices are comparable. The defence of paedophilia, as with PIE literature, and indeed as with Golding's (2001) willing – even forward – youth, is framed in an entirely Uranian way:

> I struggled through [the University of] Cambridge and emerged a bruised and faded violet. Pleasure for me lies between the thighs of a young boy, under fifteen, blond and willing, or between the pages of a romantic poet, sighing in verse for lost love and lost beauty … But I came upon my Halcyon days though – I discovered [the pupil] Cartwright, the Kingfisher. He is delightful … delightful. A shining sun, whose very smile ripens fruit and opens petals. I cannot begin to describe the outstanding hard work, initiative, flair, dedication and conspicuous gallantry he displayed in order to earn those House Points. (Fry 1993: 450–51)[18]

But once news of the corrective rewriting of the boy's Common Entrance exam to Ampleforth College breaks, the game is up, and teacher and pupil flee to Morocco (the play closes with the rest of the pupils following suit). Fry seems to intimate that a life of a catamite in Morocco is preferable to the brutal fate awaiting Cartwright in the Catholic college of Ampleforth – 'Pity really,' the BDSM teacher quips, 'he would have gone down rather well at Ampleforth' (ibid.: 463).[19]

This maelstrom of feelings and moving towards possibilities is one that could be essentially different to the Uranian period – although Middleton explicitly notes the Uranians 'as forerunners to PIE' (Middleton 1986: unnumbered). From this contemporary perspective, sexual occurrences seem to occur, or remain viable outcomes. It is possible that the Uranians, or some of them, would not have thought of such an outcome; repression, or self-policing, or even denial, perhaps in tandem with piety, would have dispelled such action. But a commonality remains, and O'Carroll introduces this through two intermediary figures: the authors T.H. White and Iris Murdoch – White in terms of (seemingly) his life and feelings for boys, and Murdoch in relation to her 1958 comic novel *The Bell*. In both examples, for O'Carroll, an affection for innocence is presented as the fundamental or a priori psychological impulse of the paedophile. And, for Murdoch, the condition that allows affection for innocence to fuse with illicit sexual desire for the innocent is religion – Anglo-Catholicism in the case of *The Bell*. Here, a highly strung but essentially well-intentioned religious retreat is disrupted by a botched gay pass on the part of one of the retreatants to another. But the point is not that this is somehow irregular. The pass is, rather, organic and all too human. So, for O'Carroll, '[l]ike White, I see no inherent contradiction between the sexual nature of my love and the affectional aspect of it' (O'Carroll 1980: Chapter 1). Indeed, this is a levelling event – one of a founding of equality, moving beyond the repressive societal dynamics of the adult/child. For Warren Middleton, writing in *The Betrayal of Youth*:

> *The key to a successful paedophilic relationship often lies in the adult's ability to forgo power and become again, in effect, the child he/she once was. The younger partner's consent is usually a sign that trust is present and that the adult is attuned to the same wavelength: that he/she has been prepared to meet the child on the child's own terms … [whereas] the grown-up who is simply on a power trip will get nowhere fast, unless he/she is prepared to use threats or force, in which case he/she could be correctly termed a child abuser. (Middleton 1986: 154)*

The fundamental position then for this form of sexual expression is trust, founded on a relationship of understanding, recognition of feelings and mutual benefit. The media coverage of paedophiles effectively removed any such fanciful nuances between the welcomed-initiator and the child abuser from the public perception of paedophilia.[20] Thus, towards the end of *Betrayal of Youth*, Middleton suggests the imperative of 'changing people's attitudes through a comprehensive, systematic re-education programme of the masses, which will encourage individual awareness … to raise levels of consciousness', noting the importance of feminists and homosexuals as fellow travellers in this project (ibid.: 166).[21]

Just such consciousness-raising then can be said to occur in Hamilton's films, and from the safety of the softcore mainstream. And, despite Moody's objections, one could reasonably argue that an acceptance of young-girl sexuality, in a heterosexual context, would then have been a step towards an acceptance of young-boy sexuality, in terms of a man/boy context. Hamilton, perhaps via relocation to France, or his aesthetic embrace of historical (that is, now safely bygone) settings, is able to mount a consciousness-raising experiment, and to sample the fantasy, substantially removed from the debates about legislation, institutional critiques and so on, and indeed from the prosecution and imprisonment that occurred for many PIE members. Perhaps, then, it is only the contemporary elements of Hamilton's approach, like the disco soundtracks, that work to raise the contemporary relevance of that which is being said. Other than that, the utopian fantasy is one that works, via nostalgia, to return the viewer to the position of 'the child he/she once was', and from there to rebuild a sense of adult sexuality afresh. One measure of the success of this strategy, and the seeming legitimacy of Hamilton's work, is the existence and availability of his films uncut and certificated. From this perspective, John Lindsay's schoolgirls seem merely to bluntly present what could be on offer or available in a somewhat recognisable, and entirely drab and unappealing, environment. Lindsay delivers something closer to the 'power trip' that Middleton condemns.

Perhaps David Hamilton's final line of defence is that the erotic world into which he intrudes does not seem to register his presence. The recurrence of the mirror is noted above, but its use in *First Desires* is particularly apt for the world of Hamilton. There are several shots of the film's female protagonists (escapees from a boarding school summer camp; they borrow a boat and, after being caught in a storm, wash up on a Mediterranean island) looking into mirrors admiringly, exploring their own appearances and bodies. This allows for a sense of auto-eroticism, rather than the woman as directly presented for male delectation – both in narrative terms and in terms of the idea of the viewer, who could best be termed 'the onlooker'. So the position of the viewer would seem not to be the one from which the nude girl is objectified. Rather, the viewer – in this line of thinking – seems to be enabled to share in the admiration of natural beauty, or is conceptualised as such: an erotic connoisseur, as per PIE's imagining. Hamilton's imagery is at times that of the reflection: how the girls would see themselves, aware of themselves in transition, in a slightly scuffed mirror. The sense of autonomy is meant to remain with them. In terms of even a basic understanding of the mechanics of cinema, such ideas are, of course, ridiculous. But in terms of the documentary-like aspirations of pornography, this position would seem to be more dignified – and with that dignity, Hamilton seems to have been able to join those who then wished to explore and question the idea of an age of consent, with a view to an expanded eroticism, as one legacy of the Permissive Society.

Notes

1. Hamilton has an earlier credit as one of three directors of the documentary *Hildegard Knef and Her Songs* (1975).
2. For a reproduction of Snowden's (Antony Armstrong-Jones) image, see Derrick and Muir 2005: 258–59. In terms of Snowden and Hamilton similarities, see, for example, the 1981 shot of Snowden's daughter as a bridesmaid (Snowden 1983: 31), which offsets the whiteness of her dress against the greenery entwining the pillars of a veranda, or a *Laura*-esque 'The Royal

Ballet School' of 1981 (ibid.: 44–45; see also 52, 53, 56–57). These photos are not particularly representative of Snowden's work as a whole. It is possible that Hamilton provided a model for Snowden and other society photographers who may have felt beset by fashions flowing from punk and post-punk in the early 1980s. And Snowden's images seem to be recalled in the informality of Mario Testino's images of Princess Diana, and then of William Windsor and Kate Middleton (marking their engagement): ease and informality predicated from a sense that the subjects' natural beauty is sufficient to carry the images, and a generous use of natural light to illustrate as much.

For Snowden and Princess Margaret watching pornography at a party in 1967, and the hardcore gay fantasy *Un Chant d'Amour* [A love song] (Jean Genet, 1950), with the comedian Peter Cook improvising a chocolate commercial voice-over over it (as per the Cadbury's 'Flake' chocolate bar, whose adverts, also Hamilton-like, mimicked fellatio), see Lahr 2001: 79–80. Her nephew, Prince Charles, would go on to lend support to the Festival of Light – or, rather, find that his return note to the organisers, acknowledging the rally, was read out to the attendees as an endorsement (see Capon 1972: 70, 73).

3. See Acton and Zielcke (1973: 149–50) for illustrations of the garden, Strong (1997: 100–101) for the louche party culture of the villa in its heyday, Green (1976: xv–xxi) for the quieter years beyond, and Plante (1995) on Acton's sexual proclivities, and the villa in his declining years and after his death. Cleves (2020: 194) notes that Acton, unlike his friend and travelling companion Norman Douglas, was not 'sexually inclined towards young boys'.

4. *Bilitis* lost 25 seconds for a 1987 release (whether at the hands of the BBFC or the then UK video distributor, Xtasy Video, is unclear), which were restored for a 2005 DVD release.

5. Hamilton goes on to note Nabokov and *Lolita*, and the experience of Bournemouth beach in 1966 (and encountering a Hamiltonian architype in someone called Mandy), shooting for Yves St Laurent in the Canary Islands (whereupon, Mona), and a young girl he first saw in a telephone booth in Zurich (Heidi).

6. 'Lady D'Arbanville' was released as a single in 1970 and is also on the album *Mona Bone Jakon* of the same year. 'Wild World' was also a 1970 single, and is on the album *Tea for the Tillerman* of the same year, as is 'Hard Headed Woman'. The similarities in perception by Hamilton and Cat Stevens suggest that the songs might have effectively led Hamilton to cast D'Arbanville who, although New York-born, was on the London scene as a model in the early 1970s.

7. *Tendres Cousines* seems more problematic, despite its BBFC certificate (1983 for cinema release): the protagonist is presented as a boy of fourteen and a half (and the actor seems to have been not much older), and is seen making love to a both an older woman and a young girl. The latter is implied, and the sequence is framed above the waist.

8. Robson points out, however, that Carroll's images cannot be taken as spur-of-the-moment snapshots of domestic scenes, and other studies of Carroll's photography (and photography of this period) have made this error. The technology of this period was such that very lengthy and motionless poses would have been required to render these seemingly natural scenes (Robson 2001: 130–31).

9. Most of the poets have long since been forgotten, bar Lord Alfred Douglas and Digby Mackworth Dolben, but more for their associations with Oscar Wilde and Gerard Manley Hopkins, respectively, than for the quality of their writing. Wilde and Hopkins are included in a later study of Uranian poetry (Kaylor 2006), but do not figure in d'Arch Smith's canon. The earliest substantial study of the field was Arthur Lyon Raile's three-volume, privately printed *The Defence of Uranian Love* (1928–1930).

10. For a further consideration of d'Arch Smith's summation of tendencies, see Taylor 1976. Taylor argues that the poems reaffirmed such feelings among members of this tendency, rather than, as d'Arch Smith thought, sought to hide such feelings, as sublimated into classical or religious terminology and ambiguities.

    In terms of the idea of a Uranian cinema – something that has not, at the time of writing, been explored – the work of Lindsay Anderson, and various Italian auteurs working with English cast members come to mind: Luchino Visconti, Federico Fellini (for *Fellini-Satyricon*, 1969) and Franco Zeffirelli (for *Romeo and Juliet*, 1968). Anderson's Uranian sensibility is arguably implicit in a number of early documentaries and films, whereas Visconti's *Death in Venice* (1971) is explicit: the quintessential English screen presence, Dirk Bogarde, obsessively but chastely admiring a young Polish boy frolicking on the beach outside his hotel. The film was programmed in the 1984 NAMBLA (North American Man/Boy Love Association) Film Festival, and the power dynamics of its making were questioned in the documentary *The Most Beautiful Boy in the World* (Kristina Lindström and Kristian Petri, 2021). (For a queer commentary that also conceptualises the film as one offering the chance '[t]o touch the sublime!', see Tyler 1993: 122, 118–22.)

    Uncle Monty of *Withnail and I* (1987) would seem to have been a second generation Uranian, having been born around or just before the turn of the century. Jackson, in his study of the film, notes Monty's dialogue, both in terms of luxuriant pronunciations, and the endless literary allusions, and mangled or borrowed quotations, as indicative of an Oxford 'literate Uranian' (Jackson 2004: 62). Monty's seduction techniques seem historically accurate too – see, for example, Hanratty's recollections of other aspirant 'uncles' in the mid-1960s (Hanratty 2016: 20–1). The young, feminine looks of the protagonist of *Tendres Cousines*, Julien (Thierry Tevini), also nudges this film towards Uranian concerns, whereas the use of schoolgirl types by Lindsay, Freeman and Lasse Braun (*English School Girl*, 1977) just seems crudely aimed at catering to those preferences.

11. The 'unpleasant accents' may be a reference to social climbing on the part of those young and attractive Anglo-Catholic aesthetes who wished to bag a wealthy, elderly protector at Mass.

    Harold Acton (1948), often cited as one model for the character of the pederast aesthete Anthony Blanche (from, for Acton, 'malicious mutual acquaintances who insist on identifying me with the more grotesque of his characters'; 127; for Waugh himself, this 'aesthetic bugger', across a number of his novels, was two-thirds Brian Howard and one-third Acton – '[p]eople think it was all Harold, who is a much sweeter and saner man'; cited in Carpenter 1989: 407), suggests the young Waugh himself experiments with Catholicism and homosexuality while at Oxford. Acton refers to Waugh as a 'prancing faun ... wide-apart eyes, always ready to be startled under raised eyebrows, the curved sensual lips, the hyacinthine locks of hair ... [drawn to] a circle of Chestertonian friends, to Christopher Hollis and robust wits already steering for Rome. They assembled in his rooms for what they called offal' (Acton 1948: 126; for Hollis on Waugh and Acton, see Hollis 1976: 72–93 and 94–113 respectively). On Waugh's characters as composites, see (Brennan 2013: 83), and on homoeroticism in 1930s Oxford more generally, see (Brooks 2020).

    Acton complains of his reputation as a 'scandalous debauchee' (Acton 1986: xiii): 'I had evidently become a sinister figure in European eyes', rumoured to be enthralled to 'some secret vice, some enslavement of the senses' (Acton 1948: 380), which had seemingly barred him from Intelligence work during the 1940s. The second volume of his memoirs characterise the first as 'written in self-defence', as 'it was easy to believe that an Oxford aesthete of ephemeral fame had settled in China for the purpose of wallowing in vice' (Acton 1986 xiii; Hollis also notes such 'unsavoury and libellous private reports'; Hollis 1976: 108; see, more particularly, Plante 1995). But such 'vice' was seemingly nothing more than homosexuality, on Acton's part. In this second volume, Acton notes his familiarity with Uranian culture (Acton 1986: 317), and his close association with the writer Norman Douglas, who had fled the United Kingdom following prosecution for sexual abuse of a teenage boy – a tendency that was his lifelong preoccupation (see Cleves 2020). Acton and Douglas published privately a translation of the scandalously explicit memoirs of the Grand Duke of Tuscany, Gian Gastone de'Medici (Acton and Douglas 1930). And Douglas's 1917 novel *South Wind* features in *Brideshead Revisited* as required reading for the acclimatisation of the newly arrived undergraduate (Waugh 1945: 26). It is possible that Uncle Monty's fabled Norman (his Oxford punt co-conspirator in 'sensitive crimes', recalled in *Withnail and I*) draws from ancient gossip about Norman Douglas; certainly, the experimental homoerotic culture was no secret – as per Terence Greenidge's exposé, *Degenerate Oxford?* (1930) or, for pre-university boarding school years (and from Evelyn's brother), Alec Waugh's *The Loom of Youth* (1917). Green positions Acton as essentially a dandy of the 1890s, and, through the mutual friend of Charles Ricketts, connects Acton near-directly with Oscar Wilde.

12. Although even these dismissals are telling, because they seem chronologically not so distant, as first articulated, from the point at which Hopkins's poetry was known; Vincent Turner SJ writes in 1944 of recalling such discussions, and such references in an uncited manuscript – a contention he quarantines, in a footnote, as 'astonishing', but feels compelled to record nonetheless (Turner 1975: 138).

13. Hamilton's other collaborator was Catherine Breillat, who has a writing credit for *Bilitis*, and whose own films as director could be seen to be in direct contrast to Hamilton's: the messiness, even ugliness, of first sexual experiences. Breillat's *Une vraie jeune fille* [A real young girl] was made in 1976, but controversy delayed its release (substantially in some countries) – the film follows the sexual awakening and fantasies of a 14-year-old girl at boarding school.

14. Some pro-paedophile activists saw their position as exclusive to man/boy sexual relationships, so that my merging of the two (man/boy, man/girl) would be a fundamental error or 'convenient falsehood' (see, for example, Moody 1986: 122 and 126 respectively). On the other hand, Mieli reads the failure to differentiate male to female, or male to male, or male to female and male, paedophilic preferences as redolent of a discourse that casts the paedophile as a 'monster' (Mieli [1977] 2018: 29). Likewise, I may be eliding differences and nuances in equating the positions in *The Betrayal of Youth* with those of the Paedophile Information Exchange (PIE).

   Reasons for this exclusively gendered position included the idea of consequence-less sex (that is, without danger of pregnancy, which would then push the paedophilic activity into a new vector from which the battle may be lost altogether – Moody's chapter is subtitled 'How to Make Paedophilia Acceptable...?'). And, looking back to Uranian sensibilities, the idea that 'deviant' male/male relations were somehow not legitimate from the outset, in the sense of their not being ultimately procreational, and so therefore do not fall under the moral or societal censure and regulations regarding 'normal' sexuality, is also a given reason. Moody notes too that heterosexual understandings or assumptions about the use of the penis in sexual relations are misleading and indeed slanderous:

> The general assumption that a man-with-a-penis will respond to a boy-with-a-penis in a similar fashion as to [a] girl-with-a-vagina, [and] that the adult in a gay relationship will

> *generally use his penis as historically his gender has done with women, is not true. In actual fact, paedophile men rarely penetrate young boys, or even desire to do so, and it is certainly true that boys penetrate men more seldom. Here we see a prime failure to regard people as being free to decide their expression of desire without it being dictated by biological gender. My point is not that it is easy to reject the social dictates of gender, but that frequently paedophiles have neither tried, nor even seen the need, to do so'. (Moody 1986: 127)*

In this respect, this paedophilic sensibility would not necessarily be shared with the Danish 'Lolita' and 'Loverboy' films, assuming that they merely showcase sexual acts.

15. In retrospect, the group does not seem to have been so marginal. Its concerns were within the orbit of libertarian, socialist and feminist ideas, united through a critique of the patriarchy, and in the early throes of the development of identity politics, particularly around fighting the oppression of minority groups, especially where that minority status is predicated on sexual preference. Moody and Middleton state this strategy explicitly in terms of fighting for paedophile rights: 'The clear identification of homosexual paedophilia as a gay and feminist issue' (Moody 1986: 130); and 'It is now up to feminists, gays and socialists to decide which side they will take in the coming battles for children's autonomy' (Middleton 1986: 151). For this reason, some hostility occurred at the time (and more after) when it was felt that a pro-paedophile strategy to tag along with gay liberation groups was an effective opportunist lurch towards undeserved respectability, endangering those gay liberation groups. The group seemed entrepreneurial, and worked to open up new lines of communication, in tapping into new areas of leisure. And yet, through members' connections to establishment-friendly organisations and institutions (schools, including boarding schools, churches, social care providers, the BBC and the Boy Scouts among others), PIE seemed distinctively middle rather than working class. Likewise, PIE sought to effect a cultural shift, to exert political pressure, to create social groupings, and to talk about change rather than engaging in direct activism – a characteristic very typical of middle-class protest groups (although various members seem to have held that intergenerational sexual relations, in the context of the times, were effectively activism). Such ideas were not particularly unique to the UK, and are found too among post-1968 critical ('continental') theorists; on as much in France in these years, see Bourg 2006.

16. This quotation comes from paragraph one of Chapter 6. My references for O'Carroll need to remain incomplete; accessing a printed copy of the book has proven impossible – copies were seemingly purged from libraries around the times that O'Carroll became caught up in legal trouble, or remain under restricted access. Scans of the book, which contained no images, have been available online. Likewise, some pages are listed as unnumbered for *Betrayal of Youth* – another imageless book that has been difficult to source.

17. Tatchell noted in 2017 ('Underage Sex: Statement of Clarification') that he had been 'tricked' into contributing to *Betrayal of Youth*, and his chapter contained endnotes that were not his. However, Tatchell's position is useful to this discussion precisely because he raised questions, further to his wider critique of sexual mores, without providing dogmatic answers.

18. 'Kingfisher' – the prep school House of the unfortunate pupil – may allude to Gerard Manley Hopkins, of his 1877 poem 'As Kingfishers Catch Fire'. More generally, *Latin!* seems to seek to dive deeper into, and mine for further comic potential, the paedophilic subplot of Waugh's *Decline and Fall* (1928), in which pupils seem to conspire to deliver a pupil to an enamoured predatory teacher. The two-act play is reproduced in Fry 1993: 435–70, even as Fry goes some way to distance himself from it (431–32).

19. On sexual and physical abuse at Ampleforth, including at this time, see IICSA 2018a. In this reference to Ampleforth, Fry either suggests and extends the Oxford Movement continuum (Anglicanism to Anglo-Catholicism to actual Catholicism – and then to Islam), or attempts to balance the reactionary anti-Islamic element of the play with anti-Catholicism.

20. In the most complete overview of PIE to date, Basannavar (2019) argues that PIE's activism essentially created the mass media figure of the paedophile; prior to this, the figure was conceptualised in quite different ways. For an example of such a shift in perception, even in recent years, see Cleves (2020) on Norman Douglas. Many commentators have noted a 'Savile effect' in this shift: the public revelations regarding Savile emboldening victims to engage with a legal system that now seems more inclined to offer them a fair hearing; Graystone contextualises accusations against John Smyth and other Church of England leaders in this causal way too (Graystone 2021: 137). This sheds further light on the functions of the championing of Savile and other sex offenders by Whitehouse and the anti-permissives.

21. For an outline of how this strategy played out in feminist circles, see Jeffreys 1993: 188–210; she notes feminists as railroaded (197), filibustered (202) and affronted (205). Jeffreys, however, is a toxic source: the section on the 'Failure of Gay Liberation' includes shocking attacks on trans communities, as well as on cultures of sadomasochistic practices.

    Whitehouse also identifies, in 1977, paedophile activism as mixed into gay rights groups, and that the gay and minority sexualities support and counselling group, the Albany Trust, had been compromised by paedophile infiltrators – who in turn used this respectable front to secure funding (Whitehouse 1978: 71–72). It is not clear from where Whitehouse was gaining this information.

Post-Permissive Pornography

CHAPTER 8

'Fucking Bang Me Like a Slag!'

Men with Men after Thatcher

This coda considers the aesthetics of a production and distribution company, Triga Films, that make films that are overwhelmingly downwardly mobile in their ambience, and so exist as a polar opposite to the majority position, of aspirational pornography, discussed thus far. Indeed, in their matching aesthetic paucity, they run counter to the anticipated homosexual turn or phase of the Golden Age of Pornography, with comparable glitz and star power – as per Parker Tyler's 1972 discussion of gay porn, concluding in the prediction of a forward movement 'up and on' (Tyler 1993: 208). In this, the films amplify a class element to sexual imagining, as still aligned to a sense of the lower classes being more sexually available, and sexually freer. But this characteristic falls into the problematic category of 'scally porn' or 'chav porn'. I wish to position these films, via an engagement with a couple of them, as post-Thatcher pornography: the films made after the Thatcher era, and which also reflect the post-Thatcher era society.

This leap forward by a couple of decades swerves the entirety of the Conservative government that was in power from the election of Margaret Thatcher on 3 May 1979 to the ousting of John Major on 1 May 1997. Triga Films have been in operation since 1997 too, distributing their films through licensed sex shops, and now via their website. This leap means that my final critical engagement with British pornography will not end at the point of its marginalisation: that is, firstly, as targeted by the Conservatives as part of a wider purge of 'home entertainment', which first culminated in the Video Nasties scare, with new legislation following; for McGillivray, in his pioneering study of British pornography, clearly, '[i]t was the Conservatives who were directly responsible for the death of the British sex film industry' (McGillivray 1992: 83); and, secondly, with home video technology resulting in the disappearance of cinemas and clubs showing pornography to the public, and the eventual ending of that Soho culture. One could add that, thirdly, the exile of David Hamilton (in the sense of making films abroad, and his exile from the 'underground' porn culture, to the mainstream) indicates the effective victory of the anti-permissives – at least for a while. So what happens after 1997, in terms of a post-Thatcher porn culture, and at the point of the anti-permissives in abeyance?

The Triga films can, on the one hand, be read as loosely engaging with the industrial and social legacies of Thatcher and Thatcherism, in the sense that they are styled as broadcasts from those parts of the country, and social groups, that the Conservative Party immiserated and abandoned. They have the *mise en scène* that, in any other films (particularly those of Ken Loach and Mike Leigh) is read as a critique of Thatcherism. This then is a return to the ambience of Thatcher's Britain. 'Fun' seems strained, even desperate – which has not, historically, been the case with various other strains of 'gonzo' film-making from the turn of the millennium, from Ben Dover (the inheritor of Mike Freeman's mantle) to dogging films. These all represent a quest for sexual fulfilment, in the journey to the suburban cul-de-sac to meet the housewife, or the public park to join the swingers. On the other hand, the Triga films are also post-Thatcher in the sense that they came after the phase of the anti-permissives, and their champion coming into power – although, as noted above, the hoped-for clean-up did not thoroughly occur. After a renaissance of latter-day and explicit 'white coaters' had been certificated for release – starting with *The Lover's Guide* (Simon Ludgate, 1991) – the BBFC position on banning (almost) all hardcore imagery was over. The policing of the content of films sold in sex shops seems to have become less important and, at any rate, was a losing battle with the circulation of video bootlegs, openly sold on streets, the unregulated channels accessible via satellite television (as Whitehouse had predicted) and then beyond that the internet as a mechanism for distribution, and finally the entrepreneurial homemade pornography.[1] In this latter respect, Triga films came at a time when substantial freedoms were granted, including the depiction of homosexual sexual activity, thus allowing for maximal – let us say, wall-to-wall – pornography. So while Triga are post-Thatcher, they are also post-permissive in that the permission granted can be taken as read (pro-permissive rather than anti-permissive) rather than as a matter for contestation. Therefore, although this engagement with Triga sits outside the timeline that structures this study – from the Summer of Love to the coming to power of Thatcher – Triga nonetheless seem appropriately considered in the light of this period, and hence this coda. My engagement with Triga also

Illustrations 8.1 and 8.2 Men having sex with men in an avowedly heterosexual milieu; Triga's *Young Offenders* and *Thievin' Robbing Bastards!* (James Carlyle, 2009 and 2012). Screenshots by the author.

allows me to marginally correct the heterosexual imbalance in this study. But, as argued below, I need to talk of homosexual activity rather than gay film-making; those practising homosexuality protest that they are not fundamentally homosexual.

This identification of an immiseration *mise en scène* is not fanciful. Triga seem to work hard to promote and further their particular character (the films are 'A Council Films Production' and 'A Closed Curtain Production') and service (a DVD logo suggests the viewer can 'wank @ our website'). Their longevity is such that the 'chav' and 'scally' phase, which Paul Johnson noted, in his article 'Rude Boys', was then commonplace in gay consumer cultures (Johnson 2008: 69), seems to have come and gone during Triga's lifetime, with Triga's concerns with the underclass remaining consistent. In terms of Triga and the BBFC, the BBFC online archive notes issues with a small number of films, beyond cuts necessary to 18-rated (rather than stronger sex-shop-distributed R18-rated) films. Cuts were requested for: *Thievin' Robbing Bastards!* (James Carlyle, 2012) 'to remove all suggestion of lack of consent as men are grabbed and forced onto a bed, held down and forced to engage in sex, and where the men protest and struggle'; *Hard Top Skinheads* (Anon, 2012) in relation to 'harmful breath restriction during sexual activity'; and *Football Orgy* (2001) 'to remove scenes of urolagnia ... and scenes of violence in a sexual context'. In this respect, Triga seems in part to operate at the edges of the legally permissible, and produces films that – as circulating online – hold out the promise of extant 'harder' action in versions different to those found in shops, such as Prowler on Soho's Brewer Street.[2]

'Chav', which is reputedly an acronym for 'council housed and violent' (that is, living in minimum standard, state-provided housing, usually on an estate of local council-owned houses), became common currency in the early 2000s, and is typically taken as indicative of a dislike or fear of the disenfranchised white working classes – and a term, for Jones, resonant with the 'demonization' of this strata (Jones 2012). The foundational myth is that unchecked waves of newly arrived immigrants aligned themselves with the opportunities of a supposedly classless and meritocratic society, as engineered during the years of Conservative government, and later upskilled via an expansion of the university sector, resulting in an influx of 'outsiders' (by class, nationality or ethnicity) to better-paid jobs, and upwards mobility. Those who were once firmly ensconced, across generations, in blue-collar working conditions and cultures, found their way ahead to financial betterment blocked – whether such a comeuppance was deserved or otherwise. And the status quo, in terms of job availability and security, was further damaged by the outsourcing of much factory and call centre work to the sweat shops of the Global South. And yet those who did retain their jobs – so this narrative goes – behave with bad grace: lazy, inept, disinterested and always ready to pilfer from clients or employer.

The 'chav' strata of this British underclass – without hope and politically disorientated, in part because they had long been abandoned by the traditional workers' quarter of the political establishment, the Labour Party (and particularly from 1997, by New Labour) – were left to sink into entropy. Their culture was perceived, on the political right, as one of 'sponging' off the state (that is, claiming financial support) for money that would go on cigarettes, alcohol, fast food, satellite television, and possibly recreational drugs, and that their children, unattended and lacking in education, became 'feral'. The 'scally' is understood to be a North of England variant on the 'chav', typically associated with a city that has been slandered both by Conservative governments and the right-wing tabloid press: Liverpool. The scally, finding himself in the council house 'sink estate', is an unreconstructed petty criminal. To enable such a lifestyle, the 'hoodie' (i.e. hooded tracksuit top) look became essential, as it shielded the face from closed-circuit television cameras – and, for the political right, it created a parallel with another undesirable group: anti-globalisation activists. The young scally and the young hoodie became interchangeable, and thus class and criminality also became closely associated. For the middle classes, such cultures represent imminent physical danger (one thinks of the trope of television detective series with the enforcers of law finding themselves, mid-chase, in the council estate: risky, filthy, and maze-like, where all residents can be assumed to be on the side of the fleeing suspect). As the UK inner city riots of 2011 seemed to indicate (particularly in London, Manchester and Salford), such danger, and this class, were not always confined to ghettos; Tyler notes the casting of the rioters as the underclass as a hysterical affirmation by the printed media (both tabloid and broadsheet) that the discontents were strictly Other (Tyler 2013: 179–82).

'... with Gushing Gallons of British Builders' Piss and Not a Mug of Tea to Be Seen!'

Triga's immersion in this supposed social milieu seemingly verifies and complements the prejudices and distaste that has contributed to the construction of such stereotypes. The blurbs for the films fully subscribe to such purple prose of the right. I reproduce the following sections of descriptive prose as found. For *Dads 'n Lads Council House – Extra Dole*, for example:

> *Tuesday afternoon and as per [usual] doing fuck all! ... a couple of pals coming over to smoke some weed 'n knock back a bargain pack of Special Brew! ... In down 'n out social benefit fucking mix of Dads 'n Lads Council House watch as Jason takes it right up his young tight arse.*

Or, for *Van Fuckers Extra Fuel*:

> *Those horny van men we see all the time on British streets – swearing, swerving, red-light jumping, crotch-scratching cunts most of 'em. They're always in a hurry, cutting you up and speeding down your 20 mph zone – and our lot ain't any different! Filthy fittie Daniel and his mate Jimbo are your typical gob shite van drivers who like nothin' more than parking up their battered old Transit somewhere quiet for a crafty smoke and seein' if there's any randy lads about to suck their big fat cocks*

For comparison, the Millivres Prowler DVD of Bruce LaBruce's *Skin Flick* (also known as *Skin Gang*, 1999) quotes National Film Theatre (now BFI Southbank) programme notes and a Peter Tatchell (of the pressure group OutRage!) endorsement on the back, and promises a film that is a 'controversial and outrageous offering', and which also takes in 'two bourgeois gay men'. Unlike Triga, LaBruce's film has artistic aspirations – the sound collages, the pastiche of bad 'porn acting' and clunky dialogue, the use of grainy black-and-white images reminiscent of No Wave film; the film even opens with an early Terry Richardson photo shoot – then an edgy 'porn chic' gadfly (see Halligan 2017). For *Builders Piss Up*:

> *The builders are in, and some of the lads are having a beer break … [a]fter a bit of argy-bargy between Dave the cocky Manchurian [presumably 'Mancunian'] and Chris the scouser[,] Dave puts his money where his mouth is and dares him to taste his big dick… And what with all the beer they've all just necked down, the lads are bursting for a piss … with gushing gallons of British builders' piss and not a mug of tea to be seen!*[3]

In this respect, the frenzied homosexual activity that is outlined, and that promises to be 'excessive', 'tasteless' and 'disgusting' – the key attributes for the depiction of the working classes for Skeggs (2004: 99–105, 107–10) – seems part and parcel of a degenerate social layer as described. Triga's Lawrencian association of an 'untamed', even different (incorporating the female anus) sexuality with the working classes suggests a homosexual variant on the eroticisation of the working class. The working-class male is understood to be virile, not beholden to social niceties, and happy to exact revenge on his social betters by being a forceful 'top' (i.e. active rather than passive in sexual activity). But this historical perception still effectively affords a level of dignity to the 'simpler' man. In the Triga universe, the chavs and scallies, and unprofessional workmen and amateur sportsmen, are presented – both in blurbs and in the films viewed at the time of writing – as disenfranchised and deracinated to the point of the loss of such dignity. This is even a matter of health: for Lawrence, in *Lady Chatterley's Lover*, the groundsman was rough and coarse but supple and strong. The Triga protagonist is sallow and skinny, pale and blemished, displaying the kind of pumped-up physique one associates with steroids, and a leathery skin associated with excessive sunbed use. The bodies seem indicative of ill health, and the endangering of health, rather than vigour or vitality. This is not aspirational pornographic fantasy but an orientation to a rebarbative reality – the opposite of that Uranian flight from that 'real boy, grubby, ink-stained, insolent, uncomprehending of Uranian passion' (d'Arch Smith 1970: 174).

However, it is from this perspective that the question of sexual availability, and indeed sexual difference, can be approached. The prospect of 'dead time' in the lives of the unemployed protagonists is one that adjusts the bar (difficult to say 'raises' or 'lowers') in terms of whiling the hours away with the free activity of homosexual practices. Such pastimes, in fact, are understood as a way to kill time – or even to allow for the psyche, freed from the demands of paid labour, to spur one on to self-knowledge. This, by now, seems a common theme: first for the anti-permissives (where the strikes of the 'Winter of Discontent' were indicative of social breakdown in general); then as a phenomenon imagined by Lauret in the pilfering, unionised postman (Lauret 1970: 64); and now with unemployment opening up the opportunity for homosexual redeployment (for Triga's imagining). And this tendency makes for part of the premise of Selby's *Last Exit to Brooklyn* – noted above as talismanic in debates around censorship: a striking union official, with time on his hands and finance misappropriated from union funds, explores previously suppressed homosexual instincts. Closer to home, however, such dead time historically also occurs during holidays for the young British working classes, which then become erotic picaresques in the popular imagination – from popular British cinema of the 1970s (see, for example, the discussion of naturist films and the *Carry On* and *Confessions* cycles in Kerry 2012, and my filmography of seaside tie-in films, above), to 1990s urban myths surrounding package holidays to Ibiza, Tenerife and Majorca, and so forth, as aired in prurient or celebratory television documentaries. Such sunny zones of liberation – far from prying eyes and judgemental positions of those 'back home' (hence the maxim 'what happens in Ibiza, stays in Ibiza'), and away from the strictures of society that condemn and inhibit sexual 'excess' – allows for a testing or even transgressing of the boundaries and mores. And stimulants such as drugs and alcohol finesse such explorations; as an old joke has it – 'What is the difference between a straight man and a gay man? About four pints of lager'.

But this killing of time, which is invariably done with 'mates', is one that here, in narrative terms, seems to push light-hearted joshing into group and then mutual masturbation, and then further. A wider consideration of Triga's substantial output would be required to verify the sense that arises, in terms of the brevity of viewing that constituted the research for this writing, that the sexual experimentation occurs strictly within the discourse and confines of white working-class heteronormativity. The protagonists do not present themselves as gay or queer, or talk in a straightforward way of gayness or queerness: indeed, a kind of hetero machismo, initially in relation to crude talk and comparing sexual organs, typically then initiates the sexual action. It is as if the self-awareness necessary to understand the 'deviancy' and difference of such sexual activity is not present in such a strata: that sexual ease and lack of discrimination (as the slogan has it: 'any hole is a goal') goes hand in glove with a general philosophical position of taking what is available in the immediate for quick gratification. It is as if sexual interaction is swiftly snatched, on impulse – but a paradoxical occurrence, nonetheless, of what seems to be frenzies of intense homosexual activities arising between avowedly heterosexuals.[4] Triga's performers perform with gusto and without bluster, unencumbered by any sense that their activities define them.[5] It is a modus operandi familiar from stories of illicit intimacies achieved in public: rushed and furtive encounters, made in an awareness that the limited privacy afforded by, say, smashing the light bulbs of a public toilet with one's shoe for the purposes of cottaging, or an empty car park for dogging, barely offsets risk. Discussion and comfort have no place in these practices, and no drawn-out ritual of suggestion and seduction is enacted: speed is allied to the primary need to act on bodily impulse. This anal sex is quite different to that of *Lady Chatterley's Lover*: not the desire to push further on into expanded erotic realms, but merely to discharge into whatever is available and readily to hand. And it is quite different to the same in *What a Gay Day* (Mike Freeman, 1979), which enacts the standard template and narrative: visiting workman to a lower-middle-class couple's house, eyeing up and suggestive banter, and then a threesome, which is predicated on desire and then presented as sexually satisfactory for all involved. The camera errs towards a middle-class perspective on the working-class genitalia too (i.e. it is looked *at*, as if sharing the curiosity and desire of the middle-class protagonists). Indeed, Freeman's perspective – acknowledging first that the very existence of *What a Gay Day* is noteworthy from a number of positions – is the same as his heterosexual pornography, suggesting a standard modus operandi, with characteristic use of the living room sofa as a near constant. In Freeman's *Truth or Dare* (1980), a woman (Paula Meadows), overwhelmed by the differences between her native Basingstoke and London, articulated in an ingénue voice-over, visits BDSM-orientated rock star Tony (Lynsey Rod Honey) she has met at a party – naked from the point of answering the front door, and onwards.[6] They proceed to have sex as a forfeit after a game of cards (although they both lose one game each) – with Tony instructing her to strip, and in this identifying her middle-class background: 'Oh my God – get those Marks and Spencer's knickers off!' The film was discussed later in terms of class: 'an innocent young girl who meets a wild guy who exposes her middle-class hang-ups and opens her up to all manner of new sexual experiences' (Bayldon 1991: 52), and the woman seems to articulate something like this at the end of *Truth or Dare*, as the moral of the story: she had been 'bunged up to my eyeballs [?] with middle-class inhibitions', and had previously only had quiet sex in the dark. The 'new' mentioned included exhibitionism, as Tony encourages her to stand by an open window as they make love. And, duly empowered, she then takes the opportunity – having being abandoned by Tony in her underwear in the countryside – to engage in a threesome with the first couple she meets. (This sequence looks like it was filmed in the same house as *What a Gay Day*.)

But this inter-class occurrence in *What a Gay Day* speaks to Healy's reading of the erasure of the working-class homosexual: 'Consider the tautology here: working-class men had no access to gay identity. Why? Because "gay" is a middle-class identity. Why? Because working-class men had no access to gay identity' (Healy 2014: 30). And so '[w]e need to ask ourselves why the belief that rent boys are really straight is so persistent, even today' (ibid.: 31). Thus, the middle classes, albeit in this living room, 'out' not so much the homosexuality, as the working-class aspect of homosexuality.

There is typically a minimal 'setting of the scene' in the Triga films. For *Job Seekers Allowance: 'Extra Fuckin Benefits'* (Jamie Carlyle, 2013; also titled as *Jobseekers Allowance*), the setting – in terms of narrative – is virtually nothing more than a preamble. After shots of a job centre, a group of men are seen attending a session to help them to successfully gain paid employment. They are clearly marked as underclass (in tracksuits, or uncomfortable-looking in shirts, many with visible tattoos, even incomplete ones) and, despite the formality of the session, they joke and laugh; a few adopt a 'cheeky chappy' persona. When this goes too far, with the instructor given grief by the group for his delivery of the training (which seems to be full of useful ideas), the instructor begins to lose his temper. This initially results in some stand-offish exchanges:

> *(To the instructor): Fuck you, you cunt! If I had a job here, I would sack you!*
> *(In response): Hey, you cheeky twat!*
> *You haven't got a job, have you? You're fucking jobless, you twat!*
> *You fucking baldy prick!*

But, beyond this, the instructor invites the chief offender to stand at the front – where he is pushed against the whiteboard, has his trousers removed, and is spanked by another member of the group of unemployed men. Once stripped below the waist, an orgy ensues, with participants performing oral sex on each other, followed by anal sex, and bukkake (several men ejaculating on one person). Some have trouble becoming erect, and there is little or no kissing. During the sex, talk is confined to the odd and often rhetorical interjection: 'You fucking like that', for example. The sequence eventually shifts to men performing 'solo' – just for the camera: sat down in the job centre's chairs and masturbating, often looking bored or tired (the orgy lasts a screen hour – probably close to its actual duration, as the sequence is mostly delivered via long takes). For *Straight, Northern and Broke: Extra Tax Edition* (Carlyle, 2014), three youths, seen in a council flat playing games on an Xbox (closed curtains, cheap sofa, beer cans and cigarette detritus littering tables) are interrupted by a suited visitor requesting back rent on behalf of Manchester City Council. For this, he is dragged into the flat and undergoes sexual assault (to the point of being stripped – 'I'm going to pay your arrears via your fucking arse' – during which he counters 'You're still getting evicted'; beyond this he proactively reciprocates), leading to an orgy, culminating in the council representative being urinated on in a bath. As he provides oral sex to the tenants, he continually interjects in respect to the missing rent (which is eventually waived: 'You've got free rent 'til fucking Christmas'; 'Fuck the eviction, pay what you like'; 'I'll just tell the Council that you're not in'; 'You've got free rent for a year') and talks frequently, mid-sex, of Manchester City Council. The tenants are marked as local drug dealers; one notes that a contact in Prestwich owes him £30 'for a bag of sniff', and a later long sequence concerns one protagonist rolling a spliff (marijuana, or a variant) – and indeed spliffs are a major topic of conversation during the film.

After these opening sequences, both films shift to individual couples. For *Jobseekers Allowance*, these later scenes seem to visit the sites – in fact, building sites – of the house decoration jobs now being undertaken. For a later vignette, a clipboard-wielding employment instructor seems to have visited an unemployed man's home, which is only partly finished, and has large St George and Union Jack flags hung on the walls (as if an allusion to far-right politics and militancy).[7] The talk of a job 'selling pasties' (seemingly an allusion to the bakery chain Greggs, also understood to be a favourite of the underclass) leads to general talk of 'you want a job', where 'job' is recalibrated to imply 'blow job', which then occurs. The dialogue during this sequence, and often elsewhere, is more a matter of instruction and guidance ('Is that good, fella?'; 'That's it, lad!'; 'That is proper fit!') rather than empathy. Very occasionally a sudden and jolting difference of approach is apparent, between those who mechanically proceed with the sexual activity, as if disinterested, and seem to mostly look at the genitals of others, and those who seem to want to connect with other participants, and so seek eye contact and affirmation that their sexual skills are appreciated and that the experience is mutual. This sudden intrusion of empathy seems, in the context of Triga, outlandish.

Straight, Northern and Broke, as its title suggests, contains no dialogue concerning gayness or queerness. In fact, the film goes out of its way to introduce the characters as heterosexual: 'Where's your bird at?'; 'She's back in Liverpool', 'My bird fucking loves [the Xbox gaming console]', followed by talk of visiting a brothel. Dialogue prior to sexual contact in a bedroom later on in the film, decorated with images of female models from 'lad's mag' *Zoo* ('Who puts the birds up? I'd smash ["have vigorous sex with"] her') and footballers and team flags, is couched in terms of changing room observations rather than come-ons or verbal articulations of desire. And during homosexual contact, this heterosexual norm persists: talk of girlfriends during mutual masturbation, 'I've had girls beg me to fuck 'em', a solo performance from a protagonist while watching heterosexual pornography on his iPhone, cries that one protagonist's exposed anus is like a vagina, and the instructions 'Take it like a bitch!' and 'Fucking bang me like a slag!' The heterosexual machismo is seemingly not dented by such contrary behaviour; at one point, a protagonist's ejaculation is met with 'Well done, mate!'. Although instructions are given, often in explicit detail, and kissing also occurs in *Straight, Northern and Broke*, these processes are not acknowledged as sexually different from hetero norms, as embodied in the performers. The one slightly effeminate performer (with red hair, and sporting a bracelet of varnished wooden squares with kitsch religious pictures on each; a fashionable club wear accessory in about 2013) goes to further lengths to talk of his absent girlfriend. Likewise, Mercer notes, of *Saturday Nite Special* (Anon, 2014), the introduction of a female sex doll, and its use for demonstrations by a drinking and straight porn-watching group of male friends, leading to a gay orgy (Mercer 2017: 158–59).

In all sequences in *Straight, Northern and Broke* and *Jobseekers Allowance*, lighting seem to be crammed into one ceiling corner. The spray of white light across the room illuminates a high degree of detail, and casts sharp shadows. Sound is recorded live, and close-mic'd, and so is difficult to discern at times. And the vantage point of the cameraman is very much from within (that is, in the middle of, but seemingly not participating in) the sexual activity, as with the films of Harrison Marks. The camera is handheld. Sometimes the camera breaks off to look at an individual, or couple, before returning to the fray. Often cutting (by Paul Scouse, for both films discussed here) is simply to change angle on the same view, and without clear narrative motivation – although one could surmise a technical explanation (battery changes, light adjustments, or a break for the performers).

The bodies (if not the faces) are full of character for *Jobseekers Allowance*: relatively old for gay porn (men seemingly in their thirties or forties), built-up and muscular but often far from toned, and predominantly white, with distressed and patchy skin. These are masculine gym bodies rather than metrosexual bodies. The bodies of *Straight, Northern and Broke* are somewhat (but not much) younger, and blemished, skinny and sallow. One performer seems to have a degree of cognitive impairment. Body language is aggressive.

Camera movement is predominantly vertical rather than horizontal, and (or because) the performers perform 'vertically': standing up or sitting on a chair, rather than lying down. The camera surveys up and down, often with the ground- or base-level aligned to the genital–mouth/anus activity, and narrative then evolves in relation to looking up at the 'top', or down at the 'bottom' – the dominant and passive roles. Indeed, such roles are heightened in this: the top is towering, the bottom is fully on his knees. Often, during anal intercourse, the angle chosen is from between or below the legs of the 'top', looking steeply upwards.

The problem with this presentation of the underclass is that the presentation itself, while boasting of and showcasing elements of verisimilitude, even to the point of deploying neo-realist techniques of film-making (real locations, 'real people'), is a presentation allied to a discourse of the fantastical and fearful slandering of this underclass from the right-wing media. For that subscription to stereotypes, Triga can be condemned: Johnson twice uses the term 'pernicious' (Johnson 2008: 78, 79) for this wider 'chav porn' tendency, which he views as the imposition of a 'symbolic reality' in which the dominant middle class seeks to shore up its 'belief in its superiority and legitimacy' at the expense of those 'beneath' it (ibid.: 78). This vantage point includes middle-class homosexual cultures, especially around the 'pink pound', and as exemplified by *Attitude* magazine, a publication that, in Johnson's discussion, effectively positions working-class homosexuality '"outside" … normative gayness' (ibid.: 76). Jones notes the complementary political process in this matter of assailing public perceptions: those at the bottom are effectively dehumanised and so, crucially, become a stratum with whom 'it is more and more difficult to empathize' (Jones 2012: 249).

This is not to say that an approach such as Triga's necessarily precludes what could be taken as an actual immersion in this actual stratum – although this tendency has, since Triga's founding, been colonised by amateur documentarians and enthusiasts, capitalising on online distribution networks. But the framing itself, in terms of the fantastic, reactionary discourse, suggests that at best the films exemplify a middle-class perspective on the working classes – even to the point of the arguably muddle-headed recreations of the working classes, who then become, or are presented as, items of desire back to the middle classes (as noted by Brewis and Jack 2010: 252, 258). This criticism was levelled at British Free Cinema and the British New Wave cinema too: working-class heroes as imagined, and even eroticised, by young Oxbridge film-makers.[8]

However, this underclass *mise en scène* in Triga, irrespective of its contested epistemological value, is not just an add-on, or modishness, or some local colour. The films construct a universe of desire in which that desire is first run through the vector of the fevered conception of this alien underclass, by those who seemingly would not know any better. Indeed, an imagined understanding of what the underclass gets up to is the very situation in which sexual fantasy can occur. It is not a matter of, Eliza Doolittle-like, scooping up the unfortunate from the streets for a limited time of luxury in new surroundings (in the sense of, say, the rent boy suddenly finding himself in a plush house when hired by a wealthy punter). Rather, it is a matter of vicariously journeying out into the environs on the part of the unseen consumer of the films. And who is this figure that Triga films seem to anticipate and cater for? Without field or marketing data, it is difficult to say. Firstly, one assumes that queer members of the actual underclass would be either tickled or repulsed by their representation in these films – to the extent, at least, of failing to become buyers of them. Secondly, to actually buy such a film costs a relatively substantial amount: nearly all retailed, as of 2015, for about £25 each, whether DVD or download; and by 2021 for £30 a DVD or download (i.e. consistent with actual prices for pornographic video tapes in the early 1980s), or £50 for a bundle of six films.[9] Perhaps the fearful imaginings of the underclass, then, are repurposed as a dangerous sexual thrill for those who simply do not know. Or perhaps the fantastical nature of this imagining is something that, in itself, is a matter of recherché amusement for those who know better, because they have broken free, having entered the orbit of the upwardly mobile, on the fringes of the upper working class and lower middle class, perhaps via education or wealth, and so have long since departed the underclass environs of maybe their parents or grandparents. And these detached layers are understood to be the actual consumer group of underclass homoeroticism, by Johnson and by Brewis and Jack.

This suggests that the sexual dynamic, in terms of the imagined consumer of Triga films, is one that is also best understood as a matter of class distance. The thrill of the films is not only in their pornographic content, but also in the unapologetic and unreconstructed 'wrongness' of the ways in which they imagine the underclass. The underclass becomes a sexually charged fantasy, and one that is both removed from reality but still recognisable in terms of reality.[10] The longing for this circumstance – a rough or aggressive orgy with the gay underclass – is based on an acknowledgement that it could just happen, with the right people, in the right part of the city or town, as per John Lindsay. The relationship between the imagined consumer and the action is vicarious: these are supposedly the characters of a class that has been left behind by the consumer, and these characters are free to continue to behave in a way that would not be tolerated in the more socially upwardly mobile environs in which the imagined consumer now finds himself. It may then be fake, or wildly implausible, but the erotic desire for these characters, as predicated on possibility, is one infused with David Hamilton-like nostalgia – thinking of and missing something lost forever. Thus, the films effectively, in terms of my discussion here, project this assumed consumer.

The Scholarship Boy

What is to be made of the user of such homoerotic nostalgia, understood as structured in terms of class, and of this pornographic and vicarious access to certain imagined strata that have been lost? This ambivalence is typified in the figure of Richard Hoggart's 'scholarship boy', in his seminal 1957 critical study of the remaking of post-war working-class culture, *The Uses of Literacy*. Through 'a strong critical intelligence or imagination' (Hoggart 1971: 292), the figure of the scholarship boy is propelled out of his modest circumstances on the grounds that he is being educated and so equipped for his own variant of *Great Expectations*. However, for Hoggart, the process stalls, and results in a permanent stationing in a deeply unsatisfactory interzone of sorts: he is no longer of the working class and yet not innately middle class, nor at all at ease with that stratum. Hoggart notes that these, the 'uprooted and anxious' (ibid.: 291), can include 'psychotics' (292) but more usually those who wind up as excellent administrators rather than finding themselves thrust into visible positions of power and responsibility. When the scholarship boy tries 'to be "pally" with working-class people, to show that he is one of them, they "smell it a mile off". They are less at ease with him than with some in other classes' (ibid.: 301). This is a condition of exile that can be read across a variety of terrains – including sexual desire. Getting 'pally' is a reasonable reading of the homosexual activity that seems so reluctant to speak its name in the Triga films discussed here. But this orgiastic palliness is an occurrence that excludes the scholarship boy. In this context, he is the self-pleasuring consumer/ viewer, nostalgic about the imagined homo-habitus, as it were, that has been denied to him as he bettered himself. He remains 'a mile off', and so is only able to enjoy such company as an onlooker, from that safe distance.

But the nostalgia is questionable; as noted above, it is unlikely that an actual scholarship boy, with direct experience of the classes that Triga gleefully slander, would dally much with these imaginings. A resulting faux-nostalgia is more properly considered as a yearning: to have only been part of that group, or had some access to it, however slight or finite; or to find oneself within that group; or to perceive that group as a preview (or recollection) of the male prostitute trade available, especially for, as Reed (2014) notes of the business in recent years, a bourgeois penchant for rough street rent now bookable online.

A part of being set aside from their own classes can result in the 'delay' in scholarship boy's 'sexual growth' (Hoggart 1971: 298). And, although Hoggart shies away from the stereotypical association then much in vogue (when 'too close to his mother' became a euphemism for the dangers of a boy growing up to be, or turning out to be, homosexual), this process of becoming different may come about through the juvenile rejection of the world of men in favour of the world of women:

> *The boy spends a large part of his time at the physical centre of the house, where the women's spirit rules, quietly getting on with his [school] work whilst his mother gets on with her jobs – the father not yet back from work or out for a drink with his mates. The man and the boy's brothers are outside, in the world of men; the boy sits in the women's world. (Ibid.: 295)*

Leo Abse, in a 1966 House of Commons debate on the Sexual Offences bill, advances the same line:

> It is clear from the number of homosexuals who are about that, unfortunately, little boys do not automatically grow up to be men. Manhood and fatherhood have to be taught. Manhood has to be learnt. The only way for it to be taught is by example. It is true that there are dangers to a boy – a sophisticated House [of Commons] knows it – if an over-possessive mother ties her son to her with a silver cord so that the boy is enveloped in a feminine aura out of which he is never able to break and assert his masculine independence. (HC Deb 1966)

The delay in sexual growth can also be accounted for in terms of the difficulties in first recognising sexual difference in oneself, and coming to terms with it: a willed delay accommodates or finesses suppression. But, years later and on the other side of the class divide, the re-engagement with the world of men offers the promise of an access to that which was sacrificed (in order to access the scholarship escape route). What is arresting about Triga is the fact that men pile on men: sexual congress is a world of men in an enclosed space, where the two hands, mouth and anus of each at the very least quadruples opportunities for sexual interaction. Sexual interaction becomes the entirety of communication: uncomplicated, blunt, immediate, and given over to bodily rather than intellectual responses. The uprooted (the imagined consumer) can dream of being in their midst, rooted back into the imagined underclass, top and/or bottom, pally again and – with no need for talk or empathy – freed of social anxieties. In this, the post-permissive conception is not of visual/erotic access to another's body, but of a restorative reconnection with one's own body, and soul.

Notes

1. For a historical overview of this period of attack and tactical retreat on the part of the Thatcher government, and immediately after, see McGillivray (1992: 83–101) and Matthews (1994: 239–89).

2. See www.bbfc.co.uk. For further on Triga's place in the gay porn industry in terms of networks of distribution of media, see Johnson 2008: 80, note 5. And, for another commentary on their work, see Mercer 2017: 157–61.

   I will use the term 'underclass' as the least-objectionable shorthand to denote the social grouping at hand, despite the nuancing offered by Joanna Brewis and Gavin Jack (for

'Consuming Chavs: The Ambiguous Politics of Gay Chavism') of the difference between 'underclass' and 'chavs' (Brewis and Jack 2010: 251–52). The actual group are those reliant on pitiful levels of state benefits, which do not alleviate a poverty existence, as employment prospects are minimal or precarious, demeaning in nature, and with insufficient pay to escape from the cycle of poverty, for themselves or their dependents.

'Underclass' is the immediate predecessor to 'chav' in many respects – Imogen Tyler even dates the switchover to the new pejorative term to 2002 (Tyler 2013: 154) – although debates about this strata, in the early 1990s, typically centred on single-parent families; see, for example, Murray, Field, et al. 1990 and Murray, Alcock, et al. 1994. There is also an ontological problem in some of the writing cited here in terms of critiquing the representation of the 'chav' while contending that such a type does not exist. The term 'scally' can be heard as an exalted cry during sex ('Scally boys!') in Triga's *Straight, Northern and Broke*, as discussed below, and 'thievin' scally bastards' are promised in the cover blurb for Triga's *Thievin' Robbing Bastards – Extra Loot!* Such imaginings, pre-Triga, can be found in gay skinhead subcultures, which Healy identifies in the early 1990s in 'porn mags, illegal videos and ads for sex chat lines' (Healy 2014: 8).

3. It is difficult to tell if the Triga cover copy is genuinely semi-literate. Johnson notes advertisements for gay telephone lines that seem much more artily composed in terms of mimicking a vernacular: 'bet you'd luv to 'ave sex wiv a rough chav wot's gaggin fer it'; 'me scally gang have a group wank outside the offy' (quoted in Johnson 2008: 68).

4. This could be read as pansexual or of fluid sexuality, unintentionally manifested in gay or queer porn. But that would assume that the protesting protagonists are being truthful in their declarations. In her study of US 'hetero-erotic encounters [that] occur between men' (Ward 2015: 189), Jane Ward finds this tendency more typical of the upper middle classes (181) – which would also be true of the Oxbridge experience discussed in this book, and has subsequently been classified as 'MSM' ('men who have sex with men'). Western European traditions around as much, particularly in Italy, may skew differently in respect to class strata. But it is also true of bourgeois tendencies to excavate homosexual subtexts (and sometimes to elide paedophilic ones) in otherwise respectable cultural artefacts – as with Barlow's introduction to the catalogue (which also elides) of the 2017 Tate Britain exhibition *Queer British Art, 1861–1967* (Barlow 2017: 11–12). To respect the stated verbalised preferences of the performers, I use here the term 'men with men' rather than forcing an identification as queer, gay or homosexual, or even MSM. Mieli notes such a 'double males' tendency, which he also associates with opportunist heterosexual male prostitutes engaging in gay sex (Mieli [1977] 2018: 166).

5. The performers themselves, although named or pseudo-named, are unknowns. They are perhaps drawn from the ranks of rent boys (some Internet forums contain messages from those seeking to locate and hire the performers for sexual services, displaying an understanding that this is far from unusual), or via Triga's own website, which invites applications: 'Want to be in one? Send Us Yer Pix'. The application form notes the possibility of 'an unpaid trial session', and requests a level of contact information, as well as physical details ('any applications featuring just cock shots or half blurred faces will be deleted'; www.trigafilms.com). The voluntary model was also in operation for Marks, who would invite disciplinarians from BDSM groups to engage in spanking for his films. The occasional story in the news media throws further light on the origins of some of Triga's performers; see, for example, Gleave 2013.

6. This may be incorrect: the plot is difficult to discern because of the inept mixing of the extra-diegetic and diegetic soundtracks – the voice-over obscured by music, and so on.

Honey, later known as Ben Dover, seems to have modelled himself on 1970s glam rockers at this point, and had himself been in a number of rock groups, one of which was associated with Ian Mitchell, briefly of the Bay City Rollers. *Truth or Dare* even contains a moment of product placement for The Ian Mitchell Band, and Mitchell himself would later appear in the Honey-directed porn film *Rock 'n' Roll Ransom* (also known as *Rocked Shadow*, Lindsay Honey, 1982).

On gay porn distribution at this moment, Roddick notes that Soho gay cinema clubs played US material, on silent 8-mm: 'The Spartacus Gay Cinema Club was perhaps the most depressing visit of all. In a tiny backroom behind a notional bookstore, with a £4 admission charge and a membership register containing only first names, it boasts a mere 16 seats (several broken), but [it] held, late Saturday afternoon, upwards of 25 men, mainly standing at the sides' (Roddick 1982/83: 22). Gay film programming – artier, or trashier and camp – was occurring at the Scala cinema in King's Cross from the mid/late 1980s, where the toilets (known as the 'Lions' Den') were also used for cottaging by the clientele during all-night gay movie marathons, or 'Blue Mondays' (see Giles 2018: 25).

7. On the historical crossovers between far-right skinheads and homosexual or queer cultures, despite the militant homophobia of groups such as the National Front seemingly mitigating against such a figure as the gay skinhead, see Healy 2014 (particularly 179–92).

8. Allsop, in his rightist attack on Lindsay Anderson, says: 'This phoney idealisation, this bogus "common man" identification done in a corduroy cap and with a private income, is exactly the sort of "sincerity" Orwell loathed, for it has all the stink of that guilt-ridden period of cocktail party Communists and Mass Observation Balliol men with an uneasy "pleb" accent' (Allsop 1958: 126). On the previous page, in a homophobic quip, Allsop hints at the bad faith of the homoeroticisation of the working-class bodies, which can also be found in Anderson's documentaries, disguised as the progressive call for cross-class solidarity with the workers. But a problematic or even transgressive tendency towards passing off slack recreation as assumed actuality seems to have been present on the 'chav club scene' of the mid-2000s: of middle-class homosexuals attempting to seductively present themselves as underclass homosexuals (via sartorial dressing-down, talk of their council estate homes, choices of drink, and so on). Johnson concludes that the relevant club nights had become a kind of masquerade (Johnson 2008: 72). For Brewis and Jacks (deploying problematic terminology and associations), this is 'a form of class transvestism' (2010: 261), a 'short-lived transgression for the professional middle classes', and for 'carnivalesque middle-class sex tourism' (ibid.: 264).

9. The films on DVD are far from lavishly packaged, and the production values of the films are low, as the performers may have consisted of those on 'an unpaid trial session'. *Job Seekers Allowance: 'Extra Fuckin Benefits'*, for example, promises 'a whole host of new gob[b]y British geezers', who may then fall into that category. One wonders why the DVDs and downloads should be so expensive. To therefore guess that their market is a wealthy one would be a move typical of considerations of pornography; Lauret (1970: 92) notes the costliness of Danish 8-mm films imported to France – between £35 and £55, or equivalent currency, in 1970. Unlike 8-mm loops however, Triga's running times are typically in the region of 'epic' films: two and a half to three hours.

10. Johnson initially looks to a psychoanalytical reading of this, noting the relationship between sexual desire and sexual disgust (Johnson 2008: 73), but finds this approach unable to fully accommodate the inter-class nature of the imaginings (ibid.: 74). And so he turns to a consideration of the relationship between sexual desire, access to an inaccessible class and

assumed danger, before concluding that '[i]t is beyond the scope of this article to hypothesize the actual relationship between the class identifications of those who access these products and services [more generally chav porn culture] and their motivations for doing so' (ibid.: 75). Brewis and Jack are also cautious: faux-chavs '*apparently* become commodities for *others'* consumption; in this case, gay men who *supposedly* hail from the middle classes' (Brewis and Jack 2010: 252; first and last emphasis are mine, the middle emphasis is that of the authors). They conclude, as befitting a journal such as *Sociology*, that they are reluctant 'to go any further' and probe the nature of the consumption in what might be termed phenomenological terms, as that would 'risk putting the conceptual cart before the empirical horse' (ibid.: 265).

Conclusion

'That's What the Average Man Wants'

This study has worked with the fanciful notion of a spiritual warfare that the anti-permissives understood to be underway in their fight against the Permissive Society – and with pornography, for a while, as the major front in this battle. It is difficult now to imagine any kind of traction against pornography being achieved without this hysterical elevation. What kind of polluting, albeit tempting, spiritual quality was being offered by their opponents, in the desirable sexual displays on offer? And desirable here has been read in terms of opportunity that is class-inflected, and class-based, across a period of social upheaval (the late 1960s) and the dealignment of traditional political allegiances and class.

Pornography's intervention in this period, I have argued, has occurred in a number of areas, some of which have mingled: in terms of the sexual revolution across a long 1960s (expanding sexual cultures beyond monogamy, and tastes); in terms of the straight access to sex that Larkin envied (as suddenly readily obtainable; that 'brilliant breaking of the bank, / A quite unlosable gain'; Larkin 1974: 34); in terms of European integration (with the Continent mythologised as sexy exemplar); in educational terms (aspirational lifestyles on offer, as guilt-free hedonism for a secular age); and in respect to a revival of, even an attempted restoration of, the more far-flung frontiers of sexual subcultures (paedophilia). Much of this activity, from the perspective of half a century on, now seems so outré that this itself must be a measure of some quarter of victory for the anti-permissives on a longer timeline, in shifting a sense of the norm back to the middle ground. That fully and openly Swinging Society, envisaged by Harrison Marks, Russell Gay, John Lindsay and Derek Ford, did not occur. Glamour was stifled by austerity, by the AIDs pandemic, by a new moralism (and homophobic legislation), by that turned-on generation of the counterculture growing older, and by, with permissions dispensed locally, a depletion of a sense of transgression or naughtiness from activities that once seemed worth the effort. Chitty, writing around 2015 on 'the vanishing sensorium of titillation, shock, and intolerance towards differences of sexual taste', and the now non-contentious presence of homosexual characters in mainstream culture, observes that such a contemporary

> *waning of sexual affect is a distinctive feature of postmodernity, whatever causes one wishes to attribute to it: the ubiquity of hardcore pornography, the end of high bourgeois culture, digital cultures of over-sharing, the decline of the nuclear family, the dedifferentiation of public and private, and so on. The disappearance of shock and titillation at previously subversive or deviant sex acts and perversions has less to do with cultural representations of 'queeny' behaviour on television and a lot more to do with the historically unprecedented availability of pornography, the intensity of youth sexual hook-up cultures, the increasing feminization of culture, the prolongation of sexuality into old age with hormone therapies and erectile dysfunction pharmaceuticals, and the ways in which cybernetic technology is replacing the family in transmitting sexual norms and information to younger generations. (Chitty 2020: 175)*

Sexuality, as an idea, does not seem to have advanced in the way that the libertine proponents signalled – the potential to destabilise the norm peters out when the norm has no issue with silos of post-norm cultures. Belated Bacchanalia of swinging, as per the Triga coda to this study and my attempt to check-in on any advance, seem to hark back to the aspirational elements of 1970s British pornography in their contemporary freedoms – albeit in reverse, in looking to the wilder freedoms to be found in the downwardly mobile milieu. The class-based imagination of greater, sharper sexual freedom of D.H. Lawrence, then, holds good on the council estates of Triga's multiple marathons of mass sexual exertions. (Although, in terms of Triga's heterosexually coded queerness, a substantial advance on the idea of sexuality per se is at play in terms of the enactment of desire as decoupled from sexual identification.) My planned trip into the post-permissive future revealed some more of the same – as indeed bits of the future did to H.G. Wells's Time Traveller too.

It is difficult to summarise pornography's intervention in a way that finds consistent sense. Contradictory sentiments – or sentiments that seem to remain in a state of irresolution – cut across the field under review. At times, sex, as the lure of pornography itself, is presented as thrillingly subversive: a cinéma-vérité exposé of actuality – as putting paid to hypocrisies of Victorian moralism (old, and then revived; the immorality of Morality, as it were), in cracking open a secret, baroque society beneath a Protestant work ethic, or modern office cultures, or housewives and suburban cul-de-sacs. Some of this seems to resonate with the joie de vivre of revolutionary sentiment – but it also gains more anti-bourgeois traction from its condemnations and prosecutions than much that is intrinsic to, or particularly pointed in, sex films themselves (confirming Chitty's thesis), while at other times some of this seems of a piece with systems of exploitation, and to a far degree, of the performers involved. Female autonomy and empowerment in respect to this, as a facet of that revolutionary sentiment, has prompted a debate within feminisms that remains current – and indeed has fractured feminism along generational lines.[1] And the idea of class itself seems protean: class continues, across this study, to be equated to (and to excite) the notion of a heightened access – whether upwardly mobile, into sophisticated living, loving and swinging (with furs and Rolls Royces and aftershave), or downwardly mobile, into the rutting Rabelaisian hordes (with tracksuits, white vans and builders' piss – as per the performed clichés, noted as objectionable). So while class has remained the major structuring element of British pornography, in keeping with John Hefin's thesis about British cinema per se, and could be said to have been the very set dressing of pornography, articulating and rearticulating what aspiration could mean, pornography's critique of class has remained, at best, opaque. And pornography, in the scope of this study, seems to have been defenceless in terms of defending the ideals of the Summer of Love as they were remoulded into vistas of weekend amusements in the stockbroker belt. My initial intention to situate British pornography in the context of post-war socialist conceptions of the role of art, by way of conclusion, was defeated – and with the supplementary jab that it has mostly been the Anglican clerics of the anti-permissive front, discussed above, who espoused socialism. But Fisher's thesis of acid communism (reproduced in Ambrose 2018: 753–70), discussed above in respect to Lindsay's countering of the counterculture, offered just such a situating: pornography as the neoliberal mechanism for the depoliticisation of the radical project of sexual freedom. And Lindsay's tendency can also then apply to the great majority of films considered in this book. Fisher does not share Chitty's pessimism, further to the mundanity of the finally attained condition of sexual freedom, post-millennium. Fisher's intuition was akin to that of the Time Traveller of *The Time Machine*, discovering that the rural paradise is built on, and violently and nightly destabilised by, an underground of servitude in revolt. The lessons of the Summer of Love have yet to be fully utilised, or weaponised, from this perspective. In this respect, this book came to be aligned with Fisher's methodological scope in terms of acid communism, for which 're-thinking the 1970s is more important than revisiting the 1960s ... [t]he Seventies was a period of struggle and transition, in which the meaning and legacy of the previous decade was one of the crucial battlegrounds' (in Ambrose 2018: 757).

However, this irresolution on my part (and as put in this context by Fisher) is in respect to – as per my approach to the pornographic text – thinking about collective guesswork: images of desire that speak of the imagining of the imaginations of others, of pre-empting or engendering the kinds of desires to which pornography offers to speak, or about which pornography will educate, or to which pornography will enable. These pornographic texts, in this way, deliver a regime of fantasies, in the space in which we find answers to the fundamental question, voiced (and answered) by John Lindsay, regarding 'what the average man wants' (quoted in Duncan 1978: 71). Who is he? Who does he think he is? What is his pleasure? What does he think should be his pleasure? This is the space of imagination over or even in which spiritual warfare has been waged, by pro-sex and anti-permissive fronts, with each fearing for the well-being or wholeness of this average man's soul. But this is also a space that has been quite clearly identified, as it is about paying a price – either literally (i.e. the money to buy and have the porn, or gaining money to achieve an enviably 1970s lifestyle, and the sex that comes with that) or spiritually (the cost of the sinfulness to be exacted on the individual, and on the nation and its economy). Because the average man's pleasure seems to be understood, in pornographic terms, to be quite straightforward – images of that which Wilhelm Reich termed the 'genital embrace', and its surrounding rituals – this has resulted in an at times indistinguishable consistency to much hardcore pornography. That cinéma-vérité exposé of actuality seems to limit the experience and even, recalling further dialogue from E.M. Forster's *Maurice*, to reduce it to basic biological functioning, and as inappropriately considered if much beyond this:

> '*As I said before, I'm not here to get advice, nor to talk about thoughts and ideas either. I'm flesh and blood, if you'll condescend to such low things –*'
> '*Yes, quite right: I'm a frightful theorist, I know*'. (Forster 1971: 228)

The analysis, however, has also considered the soul of pornography – the essence that shapes the imagination. In considering the auteurs as they presented themselves and their work, for which I revised Stalin's conception of the engineering of the soul, clear indications of an erotic 1970s soul emerged: for Marks and Russell, an expanded wholeness to existence that can arise from sexual practices beyond or after moralistic restrictions – the bounty of a secular society. For Marks this seemed fun; and indeed Marks's comedy-inflected porn seems to have initiated a tradition, or channelled a Victorian music hall tradition that is, at first comparative glance, unique to British pornography. For Russell this seemed fully glamorous, whereas for Lindsay, this seemed soulless: his endpoint was the sexual entry point – with anything beyond simply erased, and loops wrapping up promptly post-money shot. With Ford, and then presences like Millington and Joan Collins, soul seemed luxurious – a plentiful life that was entirely different from the wartime deprivations suffered by the previous generation. For David Hamilton, the soul yearns for a sense of lost innocence and beauty that is particular, and presented as a matter of beyond-reach fantasy. For Mike Freeman, the soul is given free rein, even if this is then exercised in circumstances that seem less than joyful. And for Triga, the soul is de-alienated, through reconnection with a lost stratum of freedom. From these attributes, it is possible to delineate the imaginings of that which is desired by this abstract idea of an audience. Marks, Gay and Ford all speak to a notion of a will to break free from moral strictures – that their viewers imagine themselves as sexually mobile, and willing for more. This then belatedly makes up for the sexually thwarted society of *Brief Encounter*. Those 1940s Letchworth suburbs are reimagined as 1970s Essex suburbs: not the tedium of black-and-white married life, but the colourful adventures of sexual opportunism – fired by appropriated feminist ideas of female nymphomania and bisexuality, and difficult-to-categorise Ford fantasies. Ford fights against the sexual stagnation of *Brief Encounter* – as per the poster tagline of *Suburban Wives*, there will be no more 'nine-to-five widows in a sexual desert'.

These adventures were also fired by technology. There is a strain of this in many of the films discussed: opportunistic photographers, illicit filming, pornography as part of a cultural discourse of the 1970s, even rethinking the 'average housewife' as a potential porn star. And in this respect, mythical Soho could be considered to be a media operation as much as a location: the availability, for purchase or viewing, of images on celluloid and in magazines. But the technology is potentially sinning as well, imperilling the soul. Threading an 8-mm loop through a projector begins to automate the process of sinfulness, or sin-infused occurrence: the projector motor running until the sprockets catch, feeding the celluloid through; the lamp turning on, and projection beginning onto a wall or sheet or screen, the Danish maid arriving, and so on. The projector clatter itself, if at one of the parties that Marks talked about, seems a siren call: something happening in a side room, calling the curious over. And, as with *The Danish Maid*, the certainty that continuing to watch will result in watching disrobing, and sex: the machinery itself unspools the inevitable narrative. This is not a matter of needing to be proactive in seeking out pornography, but of simply being inactive in terms of failing to walk away: a lesser sin, surely? And yet this kind of small equivocation or hesitancy, then blown up to a national level, was the ground on which two competing conceptions of civilisation were understood to be in conflict for the soul of man, under a permissive, or remoralised, society.

Note

1. And this matter of free will and autonomy has also prompted me to redact information, to use anonymous sources at times, to sidestep naming the majority of the performers, and to obscure most of the images of performers, across this study. I extend my sincere apologies to anyone who has been encountered here but who would rather have been forgotten.

References

Acton, H. 1948. *Memoirs of an Aesthete*. London: Methuen & Co. Ltd.

———. (1970) 1986. *More Memoirs of an Aesthete*. London: Hamish Hamilton.

Acton, H., and N. Douglas (eds). 1930. *The Last of the Medici Done Into English*. Florence: G. Orioli.

Acton, H., and A. Zielcke. 1973. *The Villas of Tuscany*. London: Thames and Hudson.

Adams, R. 2013. 'The V&A, The Destruction of the Country House and the Creation of "English Heritage"'. *Museum and Society* (11)1: 1–18.

Aitken, J. 1967. *The Young Meteors*. London: Secker & Warburg.

Alison, M., and D.L. Edwards (eds). 1990. *Christianity and Conservatism*. London: Hodder & Stoughton.

Allsop, K. 1958. *The Angry Decade: A Survey of the Cultural Revolt of the Nineteen-Fifties*. London: Peter Owen Ltd.

Ambrose, D. (ed.). 2018. *K-Punk: The Collected and Unpublished Writings of Mark Fisher (2004–2016)*. London: Repeater Books.

Andersen, T. 2012. 'Bodil', in J. Nordstrom (ed.), *Dansk Porno / Danish Porn*. Hamburg: Ginkgo Press, pp. 272–79.

Angry Women, Leeds. (1981) 1984. 'Press Release from the Sex-Shop Arsonists', in H. Kanter, S. Lefanu, S. Shah and C. Spedding (eds), *Sweeping Statements: Writings from the Women's Liberation Movement, 1981–83*. London: The Women's Press, p. 49.

Anon. 1972. 'Union Council Elections', *The Courier* Issue 5, February, 3.

———. 1973a. 'The British X File / 2: Stanley Long', *Cinema X* (5)1, Issue 49: 34–41.

———. 1973b. 'The British X File / 3: Derek Ford', *Cinema X* (5)1, Issue 49: 45–49.

———. 1975. 'How Adult Movies Helped Our Sex Lives', *How To Give a Blue Film Party* (1)8: 32–38.

———. 1977. *Come Play With Me*. London: Kelerfern Ltd.

———. 1978. 'Jimmy's Special Award', *The Viewer and Listener*, January: 1.

———. 1979/80 [?] *Pornography: A Matter of Taste?* Colchester: National Viewers' and Listeners' Association.

———. 2011. 'David Holbrook', *The Daily Telegraph*, 17 October. Retrieved 21 November 2017 from http://www.telegraph.co.uk/news/obituaries/8832550/David-Holbrook.html.

Ardill, S., and S. O'Sullivan. 1989. 'Sex in the Summer of '88', *Feminist Review* (31)1: 126–34.

Arendt, H. (ed.). 1969. *Walter Benjamin: Illuminations*, trans. H. Zohn. New York: Schocken Books.

Armes. R. 1979. *A Critical History of British Cinema*. London: Secker & Warburg.

Arts Council, The. 1969. 'A Report by the Working Party set up by a Conference convened by the Chairman of the Arts Council of Great Britain'. *The Obscenity Law*. London: Andre Deutsch.

Ashby, J., and A. Higson (eds). 2000. *British Cinema, Past and Present*. London: Routledge.

August, A. 2009. 'Gender and 1960s Youth Culture: The Rolling Stones and the New Woman', *Contemporary British History* 23(1): 79–100.

Bailey, D. 1981. *David Bailey's Trouble and Strife*. London: Thames & Hudson.

Bakewell, J., and N. Garnham. 1970. *The New Priesthood: British Television Today*. London: Allen Lane / The Penguin Press.

Barlow, C. 2017. 'Introduction', in C. Barlow (ed.), *Queer British Art, 1861–1967*. London: Tate Publishing, pp. 11–17.

Barr, C. (ed.). 1986. *All Our Yesterdays: 90 Years of British Cinema*. London: British Film Institute.

Basannavar, N.R.G. 2019. 'Speaking about Speaking about Child Sexual Abuse in Britain, 1965–1991', PhD dissertation. Birkbeck, University of London.

Bateman, J. 1957. *The Soho Jungle*. London: Hale.

Baxter, J. 1973. *An Appalling Talent: Ken Russell*. London: Michael Joseph.

Bayldon, B. 1991. 'The Pleasures of Paula', *The Late Show: The Magazine of Adult Entertainment* (1)1 [?]: 51–55.

Bazin, A. 1967. *What Is Cinema?* Compiled and trans. H. Gray. Los Angeles: University of California Press.

Bengry, J. 2011. 'The Queer History of Films and Filming', *Little Joe: A Magazine about Queers and Cinema, mostly*, April: 31–41.

Berg, H. 2017. 'Porn Work, Feminist Critique, and the Market for Authenticity', *Signs: Journal of Women in Culture and Society* (42)3: 669–92.

Berrigan SJ, D. 1989. *Sorrow Built a Bridge: Friendship and AIDS*. Baltimore, MD: Fortkamp Publishing Company.

Bethmont, R. 2006. 'Some Spiritually Significant Reasons for Gay Attraction to (Anglo) Catholicism', *Theology & Sexuality* 12(3): 233–50.

Birdwood, J. 1970. 'Communist Tactics', *The Sunday Times*, 9 August, 7.

Biressi, A., and H. Nunn. 2013. *Class and Contemporary British Culture*. Basingstoke: Palgrave Macmillan.

Blachford, G. 1978. 'Looking at Pornography: Erotica and the Socialist Morality', *Gay Left: A Gay Socialist Journal*. Summer, Number 6: 16–20. Retrieved 20 October 2020 from http://gayleft1970s.org/issues/issue06.asp.

Bleakley, P. 2019. 'Cleaning Up the Dirty Squad: Using the Obscene Publications Act as a Weapon of Control', *State Crime Journal* 8(1): 19–38.

Board for Social Responsibility of the General Synod of the Church of England. 1970. 'Obscene Publications: Law and Practice'. London: Church House.

Booker, C. 1980. *The Seventies: Portrait of a Decade*. London: Allen Lane / Penguin Books.

Booth, R. 2012. 'Jimmy Savile Caused Concern with Behaviour during Visits to Prince Charles', *The Guardian*, 29 October. Retrieved 13 August 2021 from https://www.theguardian.com/media/2012/oct/29/jimmy-savile-behaviour-prince-charles.

Bourg, J. 2006. 'Boy Trouble: French Pedophiliac Discourse of the 1970s', in A. Schildt and D. Siegfried (eds), *Between Marx and Coca-Cola: Youth Cultures in Changing European Societies, 1960–1980*. New York: Berghahn Books, pp. 287–312.

Boyle, K. 2019. *#MeToo, Weinstein and Feminism*. London: Palgrave Pivot.

Boyson, R. 1996. *Boyson on Education*. London: Peter Owen Publishers.

Brandon, J. 1953. *A Scream in Soho*. London: Mellifont Press.

Brennan, M.G. 2013. *Evelyn Waugh: Fictions, Faith and Family*. London: Bloomsbury.

Brewis, J., and G. Jack. 2010. 'Consuming Chavs: The Ambiguous Politics of Gay Chavism', *Sociology* (44)2: 251–68.

Bridgewater, L. 2016. *Confessions of a Cyclist*. Newton-le-Willows: KFS Press.

Brooke, S. 2014. 'Living in "New Times": Historicizing 1980s Britain', *History Compass* (12)1: 20–32.

Brooks, R. 2020. 'Beyond Brideshead: The Male Homoerotics of 1930s Oxford', *Journal of British Studies* (59)4: 821–56.

Bronstein, C., and W. Strub (eds). 2018. *Porn Chic and the Sex Wars: American Sexual Representation in the 1970s*. Boston: University of Massachusetts Press.

Brown, A., and D. Barrett. 2002. *Knowledge of Evil: Child Prostitution and Child Sexual Abuse in Twentieth-Century England*. Devon: Willan Publishing.

Burgess, A., G. Greer and A. Biswell. 2018. *Obscenity & The Arts*. Manchester: Pariah Press.

Byrne, R. 2006. 'Beyond Lover's Lane: The Rise of Illicit Sexual Leisure in Countryside Recreational Space', *Leisure/Loisir* 30: 73–85.

Campbell, B. 1998. *Diana, Prince of Wales: How Sexual Politics Shook the Monarchy*. London: The Women's Press Ltd.

Campbell, H. 2014. *The Art of Neil Gaiman*. Lewes, East Sussex: ILEX.

Capon, J. 1972. *And There Was Light: The Story of the Nationwide Festival of Light*. London: Lutterworth Press.

Carlin, G. 2007. 'Rupert Bear: Art, Obscenity and the Oz Trial', in M. Collins (ed.). *The Permissive Society and its Enemies: Sixties British Culture*. London: Rivers Oram Press, pp. 132–44.

Caron, S. (ed.). c.1970. *Wife Swapping*. Surrey: Gadoline Limited / Gold Star Publications Limited.

Carpenter, E. 1896. *Towards Democracy*. Manchester: Labour Press.

Carpenter, H. 1989. *The Brideshead Generation: Evelyn Waugh and his Friends*. London: Weidenfeld & Nicholson.

Carter, O. 2018. 'Original Climax Films: Historicizing the British Hardcore Pornography Film Business', *Porn Studies* (5)4: 411–25.

Caulfield, M. 1975. *Mary Whitehouse*. Oxford: Mowbrays.

Chibnall, S. 2003. *Get Carter*. London: I.B. Tauris.

Chitty, C. 2020. *Sexual Hegemony: Statecraft, Sodomy, and Capital in the Rise of the World System*. Durham, NC: Duke University Press.

Ciment, M. 1985. *Conversations with Losey*. New York: Methuen.

Clark, A. 1993. *Diaries*. London: Weidenfeld & Nicholson.

Clark, K. 1978. 'Little Heroes and Big Deeds: Literature Responds to the First Five-Year Plan', in S. Fitzpatrick (ed.), *Cultural Revolution in Russia: 1928–1931*. Bloomington: Indiana University Press, pp. 189–206.

Cleves, R.H. 2020. *Unspeakable: A Life Beyond Sexual Morality*. Chicago: University of Chicago Press.

CNN. 1996. 'London Newspaper Says Diana Tape a Hoax', *World News*, 8 October. Retrieved 20 January 2021 from http://edition.cnn.com/WORLD/9610/08/diana.hoax/.

Coleridge, N. (1986) 1989. 'The New Club of Rich Young Men', in P. Marsden-Smedley (ed.), *Britain in the Eighties: The Spectator's View of the Thatcher Decade*, foreword by C. Moore. London: Grafton Books / Collins Publishing Group, pp. 101–8.

Collins, M. 2003. *Modern Love: An Intimate History of Men and Women in Twentieth-Century Britain*. London: Atlantic Books.

———. 2019. 'Permissiveness on Trial: Sex, Drugs, Rock, the Rolling Stones, and the Sixties Counterculture', *Popular Music and Society* 42(2): 188–209.

Comer, L. 1974. *Wedlocked Women*. London: Feminist Books Ltd.

Comfort, A. 1972. *The Joy of Sex: A Cordon Bleu Guide to Lovemaking*, illustrated by C. Raymond and C. Foss. New York: Crown Publishers, Inc.

Commission of Investigation into Mother and Baby Homes. 2021. 'Mother and Baby Homes Commission of Investigation Final Report'. Retrieved 16 April 2021 from https://assets.gov.ie/118565/107bab7e-45aa-4124-95fd-1460893dbb43.pdf.

Commission on Urban Priority Areas. 1989. *Faith in the City: A Call for Action by Church and Nation*. London: Church House Publishing.

Conkelton, S., and J. Newland (eds). 2014. *Free to Love: The Cinema of the Sexual Revolution*. Philadelphia: International House Philadelphia / The Sheridan Press.

Conrad, J., and P.L. Mallios (ed.). (1907) 2004. *The Secret Agent: A Simple Tale*, introduced by R.D. Kaplan. New York: The Modern Library.

Cook, H. 2004. *The Long Sexual Revolution: English Women, Sex, and Contraception 1800–1975*. Oxford: Oxford University Press.

Cook, M. 2011. '"Gay Times": Identity, Locality, Memory, and the Brixton Squats in 1970's London', *Twentieth Century British History* 24(1): 84–109.

Court, J.H. 1980. *Pornography: A Christian Critique*. Exeter, England: The Paternoster Press.

Cox, B., J. Shirley and M. Short. 1977. *The Fall of Scotland Yard*. Hammondsworth: Penguin.

Dallas, C. 1979. 'Religion, Morality and the Middle Classes', in R. King and N. Nugent (eds), *Respectable Rebels: Middle Class Campaigns in Britain in the 1970s*. London: Hodder & Stoughton, pp. 127–52.

Daly, A. 2018. *Playland: Secrets of a Forgotten Scandal*. London: Mirror Books.

D'Arch Smith, T. 1970. *Love in Earnest: Some Notes on the Lives and Writings of English 'Uranian' Poets from 1889 to 1930*. London: Routledge & Kegan Paul.
———. 1986. 'The Uranians', in W. Middleton (ed.), *The Betrayal of Youth: Radical Perspectives on Childhood Sexuality, Intergenerational Sex, and the Social Oppression of Children and Young People*. London: CL Publications, pp. 246–53.
Davenport-Hines, R. 2013. *An English Affair: Sex, Class and Power in the Age of Profumo*. London: HarperPress.
David, E. 1966. *Italian Food*. Middlesex: Penguin.
Davies, C. 1975. *Permissive Britain: Social Change in the Sixties and Seventies*. London: Pitman Publishing.
Davies, D. 2015. *In Plain Sight: The Life and Lies of Jimmy Savile*. London: Quercus Editions Ltd.
Deakin, M., and J. Willis. 1976. *Johnny Go Home*. London: Futura.
Delaney, S. (1959) 1989. *A Taste of Honey*. London: Heinemann-Methuen.
De-la-Noy, M. 1971. *A Day in the Life of God*. Derby: The Citadel Press.
Denham, A., and M. Garnett. 2001. *Keith Joseph*. Chesham, Bucks, UK: Acumen.
———. 2002. 'From the "Cycle of Enrichment" to the "Cycle of Deprivation": Sir Keith Joseph, "Problem Families" and the Transmission of Disadvantage', *Benefits* 10(3): 193–98.
De Rham, E. 1991. *Joseph Losey*. London: Andre Deutsch.
De Rome, P. 1984. *The Erotic World of Peter de Rome*. London: Gay Men's Press.
Derrick, R., and R. Muir (eds). 2005. *People in Vogue: A Century of Portraits*. London: Little, Brown.
Diamond, N. 1976. *Sexplay (Or The Book of the Film: Sexplay)*. London: Roydock Books.
Diver, B. 1983. 'Rock-Bottom Porn', *Razzle* (1)3: 6–7.
Dors, D. 1960. *Swingin' Dors*. London: WDL.
Duncan, A. 1978. 'John Lindsay: Sex is My Business', *Knave* 10(9): 24–27, 70–72.
Duplaix, S. 2009. 'Playing with Forms of "I"', in S. Duplaix et al. (eds), *Annette Messager: The Messengers*. London: Hayward Publishing, pp. 10–21.
Durham, M. 1991. *Sex and Politics: The Family and Morality in the Thatcher Years*. Basingstoke, Hampshire: Macmillan.
Dworkin, A. 1984. *Pornography: Men Possessing Women*. London: The Women's Press.
———. (1978) 1988. *Right-Wing Women: The Politics of Domesticated Females*. London: The Women's Press.
Dwyer, S. 2000. *Rapid Eye Movement*. London: Creation Books.
Eagleton, T. 1966. 'The Roots of the Christian Crisis', in A. Cunningham et al., *Slant Manifesto: Catholics and the Left*. London: Sheed & Ward, pp. 57–82.
———. 2010. 'Communism: Lear or Gonzalo?' in C. Douzinas and S. Žižek (eds), *The Idea of Communism*. Brooklyn: Verso, pp. 101–9.
Edwards, D.L. 1963. *The Honest to God Debate*. Philadelphia: The Westminster Press.
———. 1990. 'Towards an Understanding', in M. Alison and D.L. Edwards (eds), *Christianity and Conservatism*. London: Hodder & Stoughton, pp. 327–32.

Egan, K. 2020. '"The Film That's Banned in Harrogate": *Monty Python's Life of Brian* (1979), Local Censorship, Comedy and Local Resistance', *Historical Journal of Film, Radio and Television* 41(1): 152–71.

Eickhoff, L.F.W. 1967. 'Anxiety State after "Sex Education"', *British Medical Journal*, 30 September, 864–65.

———. 1975. 'Abortion and Promiscuity', *British Medical Journal*, 12 July, 99–100.

Ellis, J. 1992. 'On Pornography', in Screen Editorial Collective (ed.), *The Sexual Subject: A Screen Reader in Sexuality*. London: Routledge, pp. 146–70.

Elsom, J. 1973. *Erotic Theatre*. London: Secker & Warburg.

Escoffier, J. 2017. 'Sex in the Seventies: Gay Porn Cinema as an Archive for the History of American Sexuality', *Journal of the History of Sexuality* 26(1): 88–113.

Everywoman. 1988. *Pornography and Sexual Violence: Evidence of the Links*. London: Everywoman Ltd.

Faithfull, M., and D. Dalton. 1994. *Faithfull: An Autobiography*. Boston, MA: Little, Brown.

Farmer, R. 2018. '"An Almost Continuous Picture of Sordid Vice": The Keeler Affair, the Profumo Scandal and "Political" Film Censorship in the 1960s', *Journal of British Cinema and Television* 15(2): 228–51.

Feminist Anthology Collective (M. Barrett, S. Bruley, G. Chester, M. Millman, S. O'Sullivan, A. Sebestyen and L. Segal). 1981. *No Turning Back: Writing from the Women's Liberation Movement 1975–1980*. London: The Women's Press.

Filby, E. 2015. *God & Mrs Thatcher*. London: Biteback.

Fisher, M., and M. Colquhoun (eds). 2021. *Post-Capitalist Desire: The Final Lectures*. London: Repeater Books.

Fitzgerald, P. 1895. *Stonyhurst Memories; or, Six Years at School*. London: Richard Bentley & Son.

Flanagan. 1974. *Intimate Secrets of an Escort Girl*. London: Everest Books Limited.

Foot, Paul. 1969. *The Rise of Enoch Powell*. Middlesex: Penguin Books Ltd.

Ford, D. 1988. *Panic on Sunset*. London: Grafton Books.

Ford, D., and A. Sanders. 1972. *Secret Rites: Featuring Alex Sanders – King of the Witches*. Surrey: Gadoline Ltd / Gold Star Publications.

Ford, Simon. 1999. *Wreckers of Civilisation: The Story of COUM Transmissions & Throbbing Gristle*. London: Black Dog Publishing.

Forster, E.M. 1971. *Maurice*. London: Edward Arnold.

Foucault, M. 1978. *The History of Sexuality. Volume 1: The Will to Knowledge*, trans. R. Hurley. London: Allen Lane.

Fraser, F., and J. Morton. (1994) 2000. *Mad Frank: Memoirs of a Life of Crime*. London: Warner Books.

———. (2001) 2007. *Mad Frank's Underworld History of Britain*. London: Virgin Books Ltd.

Fraser, J. 1974. *Violence in the Arts*. London: Cambridge University Press.

Freeman, G. 1967. *The Undergrowth of Literature*. London: Thomas Nelson and Sons Ltd.

Frieze [J. Verwoert]. 2001. 'Sirens: David Hamilton', *Frieze* 60, 6 June. Retrieved 10 April 2017 from https://frieze.com/articles/sirens.

Fry, S. 1993. *Paperweight*. London: Mandarin.

Gibson, I. 1992. *The English Vice: Beating, Sex and Shame in Victorian England and After*. London: Gerald Duckworth & Co. Ltd.

Giles, J. 1995. *Women, Identity and Private Life in Britain, 1900–50*. New York: Palgrave Macmillan.

———. 2004. *The Parlour and the Suburb: Domestic Identities, Class, Femininity and Modernity*. Oxford: Berg.

———. 2018. *The Scala Cinema, 1978–1993*. Surrey: FAB Press.

Gleave, E. 2013. 'Fake Hero Stripped for Gay Porn Flick', *The Daily Star*, 16 June. Retrieved 5 October 2015 from http://www.dailystar.co.uk/news/latest-news/320646/Fake-hero-stripped-for-a-gay-porn-flick.

Glennie, J. 2018. *Performance: The 50th Anniversary of the Donald Cammell and Nicholas Roeg Cinematic Classic*. Chelmsford: Coattail Publishing.

Golding, P. 2001. *The Abomination*. London: Picador.

Gorfinkel, E. 2006. 'Wet Dreams: Erotic Film Festivals of the Early 1970s and the Utopian Sexual Public Sphere', *Framework* 47(2): 59–86.

Gorky, M., et al. 1977. *Soviet Writers' Congress, 1934: The Debate on Socialist Realism and Modernism*. London: Lawrence & Wishart.

Grant, C. 2012. *I & I: The Natural Mystics: Marley, Tosh and Wailer*. London: Vintage.

Graystone, A. 2021. *Bleeding for Jesus: John Smyth and the Cult of Iwerne Camps*. London: Darton, Longman and Todd.

Green, J. 1988. *Days in the Life: Voices from the English Underground, 1961–1971*. London: Heinemann.

Green, M. 1976. *Children of the Sun: A Narrative of 'Decadence' in England after 1918*. New York: Basic Books.

Greenidge, T. 1930. *Degenerate Oxford?* London: Chapman & Hall.

Greenwood, V., and J. Young. 1980. 'Ghettos of Freedom: An Examination of Permissiveness', in National Deviancy Conference (ed.), *Permissiveness and Control: The Fate of the Sixties Legislation*. London: Macmillan, pp. 149–74.

Grierson, J. 2017. 'Mass Grave of Babies and Children Found at Tuam Care Home in Ireland', *The Guardian*, 3 March. Retrieved 20 November 2020 from https://www.theguardian.com/world/2017/mar/03/mass-grave-of-babies-and-children-found-at-tuam-orphanage-in-ireland.

Grimley, M. 2012. 'Thatcherism, Morality and Religion', in B. Jackson and R. Saunders (eds), *Making Thatcher's Britain*. Cambridge: Cambridge University Press, pp. 78–94.

———. 2014. 'Anglican Evangelicals and Anti-Permissiveness: The Nationwide Festival of Light, 1971–1983', in A. Atherstone and J. Maiden (eds), *Evangelicalism and the Church of England in the Twentieth Century: Reform, Resistance and Renewal*. Suffolk: The Boydell Press, pp. 183–205.

Gummer, J. 1971. *The Permissive Society: Fact or Fantasy?* London: Cassell.

———. 1990. 'Conserving the Family', in M. Alison and D.L. Edwards (eds), *Christianity and Conservatism*. London: Hodder & Stoughton, pp. 306–16.

Habicht, F. 1969. *Young London: Permissive Paradise*. London: George G. Harrap & Co. Ltd.

Haigron, D. 2009 'Targeting "Essex Man" and "C2 Wives": The Representation of the Working Class Electorate in the Conservative Party Political Broadcasts (1970s–1980s)', in A. Capet (ed.), *The Representation of Working People in Britain and France: New Perspectives*. Newcastle upon Tyne: Cambridge Scholars Press, pp. 137–56.

Hall, S. 1980. 'Reformism and the Legislation of Consent', in National Deviancy Conference (eds), *Permissiveness and Control: The Fate of the Sixties Legislation*. London: Macmillan, pp. 1–43.

Halligan, B. 2003. *Michael Reeves*. Manchester: Manchester University Press.

———. 2014. 'From Countercultures to Suburban Cultures: Frank Zappa after 1968', in S. Whiteley and J. Sklower (eds), *Countercultures and Popular Music*. London: Routledge, pp. 187–202.

———. 2016. *Desires for Reality: Radicalism and Revolution in Western European Film*. Oxford: Berghahn Books.

———. 2017. 'Modeling Affective Labor: On Terry Richardson', *Cultural Politics* 13(1): 58–80.

———. 2018 '"This Is Father Berrigan Speaking from the Underground": Daniel Berrigan SJ and the Conception of a Radical Theatre', *TDR/The Drama Review* 62(2): 97–114.

Halligan, B., and L. Wilson. 2015. 'Use/Abuse/Everyone/Everything: A Dialogue on *LA Plays Itself*', *Framework: The Journal of Cinema and Media* 52(2): 299–322.

Hamilton, D. 1993. *David Hamilton: Twenty Five Years of an Artist*. London: Aurum Press.

Hamilton, N. 1971. 'Hard Rain', *The Courier*, Issue 8, 24 April: unnumbered [3–4].

———. 1972. 'God Save the Queen', *Feudal Reactionary*. Unnumbered [3].

Hanratty, J. 2016. *The Making of an Immigration Judge*. London: Quartet.

Hansen, S., and J. Jensen. 2014. *The Little Red Book*, trans. B. Thornberry. London: Pinter & Martin.

Hanson, E. 1997. *Decadence and Catholicism*. Cambridge, MA: Harvard University Press.

Harper, S., and J. Smith (eds and contributing authors). 2013. *British Film Culture in the 1970s: The Boundaries of Pleasure*. Edinburgh: Edinburgh University Press.

Harris, M. 1973. *The Dilly Boys: The Game of Male Prostitution in Piccadilly*. Rockville, MD: New Perspectives.

Hawkins, G. and F.E. Zimring. 1991. *Pornography in a Free Society*. Cambridge: Cambridge University Press.

HC Deb [House of Commons debate]. 1966. 'Sexual Offences (No. 2) Bill', 19 December, Vol. 738, cc. 1068–1129. Retrieved 10 April 2020 from https://api.parliament.uk/historic-hansard/commons/1966/dec/19/sexual-offences-no-2-bill.

———. 1975. 'Homeless Children', 31 July, Vol. 317, cc. 2359–2390. Retrieved 25 June 2019 from https://api.parliament.uk/historic-hansard/commons/1975/jul/31/homeless-children.

Healy, M. 2014. *Gay Skins: Class, Masculinity and Queer Appropriation*. London: Bread and Circuses.

Heawood, S. 2014. 'Princess Diana Was As Mad As Any Other Woman', *Vice*, 14 March. Retrieved 5 November 2020 from https://www.vice.com/da/article/ex9g3a/princess-diana-madness-the-firm-royal-family-phonebook.

Hebditch, D., and N. Anning. 1988. *Porn Gold: Inside the Pornography Business*. London: Faber and Faber.

Hefin, J. 2007. 'John Hefin: Director', in J. Hefin (ed.), *Grand Slam: Behind the Scenes of the Classic Film*. Ceredigion: Y Lolfa, pp. 14–34.

Hekma, G. 2013. 'Amsterdam's Sexual Underground in the 1960s', in C. Linder and A. Hussey (eds), *Paris–Amsterdam Underground: Essays on Culture Resistance, Subversion, and Diversion*. Amsterdam: Amsterdam University Press, pp. 49–61.

Hewison, R. 1981. *Monty Python: The Case Against*. London: Methuen Publishing Ltd.

Hickson, A. 1995. *The Poisoned Bowl: Sex, Repression and the Public School System*. London: Constable.

Hilderbrand, L. 2009. *Inherent Vice: Bootleg Histories of Videotape and Copyright*. Durham, NC: Duke University Press.

Hilliard, D. 1982. 'UnEnglish and Unmanly: Anglo-Catholicism and Homosexuality', *Victorian Studies* (Winter): 181–210.

Hilton, M., C. Moores and F. Sutcliffe-Braithwaite. 2017. '*New Times* Revisited: Britain in the 1980s', *Contemporary British History* 31(2): 145–65.

Hinton, P.R. 2016. 'Remembrance of Things Past: The Cultural Context and the Rise and Fall in the Popularity of Photographer David Hamilton', *Cogent Arts & Humanities* 3(1). Retrieved 11 July 2019 from https://www.tandfonline.com/doi/full/10.1080/23311 983.2016.1164930.

HL Deb [House of Lords debate]. 1971. 'Pornography in Britain', 21 April, Vol. 317, cc. 639–754. Retrieved 11 November 2019 from https://api.parliament.uk/historic-hansard/lords/1971/apr/21/pornography-in-britain.

Hobsbawm, E. 1978. 'The Forward March of Labour Halted?' *Marxism Today* 22(9): 279–86.

Hoggart, R. (1957) 1971. *The Uses of Literacy: Aspects of Working Class Life*. London: Chatto & Windus.

Holbrook, D. (ed.). 1972a. *The Case Against Pornography*. London: Tom Stacey Ltd.

Holbrook, D. 1972b. *The Masks of Hate: The Problem of False Solutions in the Culture of an Acquisitive Society*. Oxford: Pergamon Press.

———. 1972c. *The Pseudo-Revolution: A Critical Study of Extremist 'Liberation' in Sex*. London: Tom Stacey.

———. 1972d. *Sex and Dehumanization: In Art, Thought and Life in Our Times*. London: Pitman Publishers.

Holden, A. 2004. *Makers and Manners: Politics and Morality in Postwar Britain*. London: Politico's Publishing.

Hollis, C. 1976. *Oxford in the Twenties: Recollections of Five Friends*. London: Heinemann.

———. (1935) 2017. *The Church & the Modern Age*. London: The Incorporated Catholic Truth Society.

Holroyd, M. 1995. *Lytton Strachey: The New Biography*. New York: Farrar, Straus and Giroux.

Hooper, A. (ed.). (1973) 1980. *More Sex Life Letters*. London: Mayflower Publishing.

Houlbrook, M. 2006. *Queer London: Perils and Pleasures in the Sexual Metropolis, 1918–1957*. Chicago: University of Chicago Press.

Hunt, L. 1998. *British Low Culture: From Safari Suits to Sexploitation*. London: Routledge.

Hunter, H. 1973. 'The Over-Ambitious First Soviet Five-Year Plan', *Slavic Review* 32(2): 237–57.

Hunter, I.Q. 2008. 'Take an Easy Ride: Sexploitation in the 1970s', in R. Shail (ed.), *Seventies British Cinema*. London: Palgrave Macmillan, British Film Institute, pp. 3–13.

———. 2013. *British Trash Cinema*. London: Palgrave Macmillan, British Film Institute.

Hyam, R. 1991. *Empire and Sexuality: The British Experience*. Manchester: Manchester University Press.

IICAS (Independent Inquiry: Child Sexual Abuse). 2018a. 'Ampleforth and Downside Investigation Report. August 2018'. Retrieved 10 February 2020 from https://www.iicsa.org.uk/key-documents/6583/download/ampleforth-downside-investigation-report-august-2018.pdf.

———. 2018b. *Cambridge House, Knowl View and Rochdale: Investigation Report*. Retrieved 20 May 2020 from https://www.iicsa.org.uk/document/cambridge-house-knowl-view-and-rochdale-investigation-report-april-2018.

———. 2020. *Allegations of Child Sexual Abuse Linked to Westminster*. Retrieved 22 July 2020 from https://www.iicsa.org.uk/key-documents/17579/download/allegations-child-sexual-abuse-westminster-investigation-report-25-february-2020-amends-may-2020.pdf.

———. 2021. *Children in the Care of Lambeth Council*. Retrieved 1 July 2021 from https://www.iicsa.org.uk/key-documents/26649/download/children-care-lambeth-council_investigation-report_july-2021.pdf.

Jackson, K. 2004. *Withnail & I*. London: British Film Institute.

Janes, D. 2015. *Visions of Queer Martyrdom from John Henry Newman to Derek Jarman*. Chicago: University of Chicago Press.

Jeffreys, S. (1990) 1993. *Anticlimax: A Feminist Perspective on the Sexual Revolution*. London: The Women's Press Ltd.

Jenkins, P. 1988. *Mrs. Thatcher's Revolution: The Ending of the Socialist Era*. Cambridge, MA: Harvard University Press.

Joensen, B. 1973. 'My Men, My Pigs, My Orgasms', in W. Levy (ed.), *Wet Dreams: Films & Adventures*. Amsterdam: Joy Publications, pp. 156–65.

Joensen, B. [most probably another author]. 1974. 'Ask Bodil', *Screw*, 11 March: 8.

Johnson, P. 1977. *Enemies of Society*. London: Weidenfeld & Nicholson.

———. 2008. '"Rude Boys": The Homosexual Eroticisation of Class', *Sociology* 41(1): 65–82.

Jones, M. 2007. 'Down the Rabbit Hole: Permissiveness and Paedophilia in the 1960s', in M. Collins (ed.), *The Permissive Society and its Enemies: Sixties British Culture*. Sydney: Rivers Oram Press, pp. 112–31.

Jones, O. 2012. *Chavs: The Demonization of the Working Class*. New York: Verso.

Joseph, K. 1974. Speech at Edgbaston ('Our human stock is threatened'). Retrieved 10 August 2020 from https://www.margaretthatcher.org/document/101830.

Kaylor, M.M. 2006. *Secreted Desires: The Major Uranians: Hopkins, Pater and Wilde*. Brno: Masaryk University.

Keller, I. 1985. *Benjamin Rabbit and the Stranger Danger*. London: Ideals Children's Books.

Kerekes, D. 2000. 'Jolly Hockey Sticks! The Career of John Lindsay, Britain's "Taboo" Film-Maker of the Seventies', in J. Stevenson (ed.), *Fleshpot: Cinema's Sexual Myth Makers & Taboo Breakers*. Manchester: Critical Vision / Headpress, pp. 191–96.

Kerry, M. 2012. *The Holiday and British Film*. London: Palgrave Macmillan.

Killick, M. 1994. *The Sultan of Sleaze: The Inside Story of David Sullivan's Sex and Media Empire*. London: Penguin Books.

King, R. 1979. 'The Middle Class Revolt and the Established Parties', in R. King and N. Nugent, *Respectable Rebels: Middle Class Campaigns in Britain in the 1970s*. London: Hodder & Stoughton, pp. 153–82.

Kleinman, P. 1987. *The Saatchi & Saatchi Story*. London: Pan Books.

Kline, T.J. 1987. *Bertolucci's Dream Loom: A Psychoanalytic Study of Cinema*. Amherst: University of Massachusetts Press.

Krämer, P. 2011. *A Clockwork Orange*. Basingstoke: Palgrave Macmillan.

Kronhausen, P., and E. Kronhausen. 1976. *The Sex People*. Chicago: Playboy Press.

Kulze, L. 2013. 'That Time Margaret Thatcher Spanked Christopher Hitchens', *The Atlantic*, 8 April. Retrieved 5 August 2020 from https://www.theatlantic.com/sexes/archive/2013/04/that-time-margaret-thatcher-spanked-christopher-hitchens/274779/.

Lahr, John (ed.). 2001. *The Diaries of Kenneth Tynan*. London: Bloomsbury.

Lancaster, S. 1986. 'Boys in Wimpy Bar "Sold for Gay Sex"', *The Sun*, 3 May, p. 25.

Larkin, P. 1974. *High Windows*. London: Faber and Faber Ltd.

———. 2005. *Jill*. London: Faber and Faber Ltd.

Larsson, M. 2017a. 'Lasse Braun, Rape Scenarios, and Swedish Censorship: A Case Study of Two 8-mm Porn Films Featuring Rape', *Porn Studies* 4(1): 23–34.

———. 2017b. *The Swedish Porn Scene: Exhibition Contexts, 8-mm Pornography and the Sex Film*. Bristol: Intellect Books.

Lauret, J.-C. 1970. *The Danish Sex Fairs*, trans. A. Ryvers. London: Jasmine Press.

Laville, S. 2017. 'British Barrister Accused of Child Abuse Had Been Charged in Killing of Teen', *The Guardian*, 3 February. Retrieved 23 October 2019 from https://www.theguardian.com/society/2017/feb/03/british-barrister-john-smyth-child-abuse-allegations-church-england-charged-zimbabwe-killing.

Lawrence, D.H. (1928) 1960. *Lady Chatterley's Lover*. Complete unexpurgated edition. London: Heinemann.

Lee, L. 1959. *Cider with Rosie*, with drawings by J. Ward. London: The Hogarth Press.

Leech, K. 1973. *Keep the Faith Baby: A Close-up of London's Drop-outs*. London: SPCK.

Leeds Revolutionary Feminists. 1981. *Love Your Enemy? The Debate between Heterosexual Feminism and Political Lesbianism*. London: Onlywomen Press, Ltd.

Levy, G. 2015. 'The BBC "saint" who pounced on any woman in reach', *Daily Mail*, 27 February. Retrieved 23 October 2019 from https://www.dailymail.co.uk/news/article-2972833/The-BBC-saint-pounced-woman-reach-New-book-exposes-unholy-truth-moralist-Malcolm-Muggeridge.html.

Levy, W. (ed.). 1973. *Wet Dreams: Films & Adventures*. Amsterdam: Joy Publications.

Lieberstein, S. 1975. 'Technology, Work, and Sociology in the USSR: The NOT Movement', *Technology and Culture* 16(1): 48–66.

Light, B. 2014. *Disconnecting with Social Networking Sites*. Basingstoke: Palgrave Macmillan.

Limond, D. 2008. '"I Never Imagined That the Time Would Come": Martin Cole, the *Growing Up* Controversy and the Limits of School Sex Education in 1970s England', *History of Education* 37(3): 409–29.

———. 2009 '"I Hope Someone Castrates You, You Perverted Bastard": Martin Cole's Sex Education Film *Growing Up*', *Sex Education* 9(4): 409–19.

———. 2012. 'The UK edition of *The Little Red Schoolbook*: A Paper Tiger Reflects', *Sex Education* 12(5): 523–34.

Lodge, D. 1980. *How Far Can You Go?* London: Secker & Warburg.

Long, S., with S. Sheridan. 2008. *X-Rated: Adventures of an Exploitation Filmmaker*. London: Reynolds & Hearn Ltd.

Longford Committee, The. 1972. *Pornography: The Longford Report*. London: Coronet Books.

Lowles. 2000. 'A Very English Extremist', *Searchlight* (August), 17–21.

Malone, M. 1970. '"Some People Think I Am Entirely Responsible for the Permissive Society": John Trevelyan, Britain's Film Censor, Talks to Mary Malone', *Daily Mirror*, 17 September, pp. 12–13.

Manley, T. 1971. 'Europe's Mr Sex', *Fiesta* 1 Jan [?] 5(10): 24–28, 51, 62, 64.

Manners, E. 1971. *The Vulnerable Generation*. London: Cassell.

Marcus, S. 2007. *Between Women: Friendship, Desire, and Marriage in Victorian England*. Princeton, NJ: Princeton University Press.

Marle, H., B.A. Hardingham and D. Sullivan. 1972. *We Made £200,000: The Story of B.H. and D.S.* London: Silver Pub Co.

Matthews, T.D. 1994. *Censored*. London: Chatto & Windus.

McDermott, N. 2011. 'I Was That Cheeky Tennis Girl Says 52-Year-Old Mother of Three', *Daily Mail*, 23 March. Retrieved 13 April 2017 from http://www.dailymail.co.uk/femail/article-1368795/Athenas-iconic-Tennis-Girl-Fiona-Walker-revealed-35-years-on.html.

McFarlane, B. 1997. *An Autobiography of British Cinema*. London: Methuen.

———. 2015. *Twenty British Films: A Guided Tour*. Manchester: Manchester University Press.

McGillivray, D. 1992. *Doing Rude Things: The History of the British Sex Film, 1957–1981*. London: Sun Tavern Fields.

McLeod, H. 2010. *The Religious Crisis of the 1960s*. New York: Oxford University Press.

McManus, M. 2011. *Tory Pride and Prejudice: The Conservative Party and Homosexual Law Reform*. London: Biteback.

Meadows, P. 1992. 'How I Discovered CP', in Anon (ed.), *Janus: The Punishment Series of Authentic Model Interviews, Volume 1*. London: Gatisle Ltd, pp. 25–31.

Medhurst, A. 1991. 'That Special Thrill: *Brief Encounter*, Homosexuality and Authorship', *Screen* 32(2): 197–208.

Mercer, G. 2016. *Convert, Scholar, Bishop: William Brownlow, 1830–1901*. Bath: Downside Abbey Press.

Mercer, J. 2017. *Gay Pornography: Representations of Sexuality and Masculinity*. London: I.B. Tauris.

Middleton, W. 1986. 'Childhood Sexuality and Paedophilia: Some Questions Answered', in W. Middleton (ed.), *The Betrayal of Youth: Radical Perspectives on Childhood Sexuality, Intergenerational Sex, and the Social Oppression of Children and Young People*. London: Londonlications, pp. 141–88.

Mieli, M. (1977) 2018. *Towards a Gay Communism: Elements of a Homosexual Critique*, trans. D. Fernbach and E.C. Calder. London: Pluto Press.

Mishan, E.J. 1972. 'Making the World Safe for Pornography', *Encounter* XXXVIII(3): 9–30.

Mitchell, D. 2012. *Back Story*. London: HarperCollins.

Monahan, M. 2019. '"Tory-normativity" and Gay Rights Advocacy in the British Conservative Party since the 1950s', *British Journal of Politics and International Relations* 21(1): 132–47.

Monkhouse, B. 1994. *Crying With Laughter: My Life Story*. London: Random House.

Moody, R. 1986. 'Ends and Means: How to Make Paedophilia Acceptable...?', in W. Middleton (ed.), *The Betrayal of Youth: Radical Perspectives on Childhood Sexuality, Intergenerational Sex, and the Social Oppression of Children and Young People*. London: Londonlications, pp. 120–33.

Moore, C. 2013. *Margaret Thatcher: The Authorized Biography. Volume One: Not for Turning*. London: Allen Lane.

Moore, C., A.N. Wilson and G. Stamp. 1986. *The Church in Crisis*. London: Hodder & Stoughton.

Moore, L.J. 2007. *Sperm Counts: Overcome by Man's Most Precious Fluid*. New York: New York University Press.

Moorhead, J. 2014. 'The Little Red Schoolbook: Honest about Sex and the Need to Challenge Authority', *The Guardian*, 8 July. Retrieved 10 March 2021 from https://www.theguardian.com/education/2014/jul/08/the-little-red-schoolbook-republished-soren-hansen.

Mulvey, L. 1975. 'Visual Pleasure and Narrative Cinema', *Screen* 16(3): 6–18.

Mundy, J. 2007. *The British Musical Film*. Manchester: Manchester University Press.

Murphy, R. 1992. *Sixties British Cinema*. London: British Film Institute.

—— (ed.). 2014. *British Cinema: Critical Concepts in Media and Cultural Studies*. 4 volumes. Abingdon: Routledge.

——, C., P. Alcock, et al. 1994. *Underclass: The Crisis Deepens*. London: The IEA Health and Welfare Unit.

Murray, C., F. Field, et al. 1990. *The Emerging British Underclass*. London: The IEA Health and Welfare Unit.

Nash, D. 2017. 'Blasphemy on Trial', *History Today*, 15 November. Retrieved 1 July 2021 from https://www.historytoday.com/miscellanies/blasphemy-trial.

Niven, D. 1975. 'Introduction', in Anon (ed.), *The Complete Pirelli Calendar Book*. London: Pan Books Ltd, pp. 5–14 [unnumbered].

Nordstrom, J. (ed.). 2012. *Dansk Porno / Danish Porn*. Hamburg: Ginkgo Press.

Novotny, M. 1971. *King's Road*. London: Leslie Frewin Publishers.

O'Brien, J. 2020. *How Not to Be Wrong: The Art of Changing Your Mind*. London: WH Allen.

O'Carroll, T. 1980. *Paedophilia: The Radical Case*. Contemporary Social Issues Series, Number 12. London: Peter Owens.

O'Donnell, K., S. Pembroke and C. McGettrick. 2013. 'Oral History of Angelina Mayfield', *Magdalene Institutions: Recording an Oral and Archival History* project: 1–212. Retrieved 10 March 2020 from http://jfmresearch.com/wp-content/uploads/2017/04/MAGOHP49_Angelina-Mayfield_ANON.pdf.

Olympia Press, the. 1971. *The Obscenity Report*. London: The Olympia Press.

O'Mahony, J. 2012. 'Jimmy Savile: BBC Did Nothing When Director Caught Him in the Act', *The Telegraph*, 12 October. Retrieved 4 August 2020 from https://www.telegraph.co.uk/news/uknews/crime/jimmy-savile/9603743/Jimmy-Savile-BBC-did-nothing-when-director-caught-him-in-the-act.html.

One of the Boys. 1867. *School Days at Saxonhurst*. Edinburgh: A. & C. Black.

O'Toole, L. 1999. *Pornocopia: Porn, Sex, Technology and Desire*. London: Serpent's Tail.

Pagé, S., and B. Parent. 2009. 'Interview with Annette Messager', in S. Duplaix et al., *Annette Messager: The Messengers*. London: Hayward Publishing, pp. 152–55.

Pajaczkowska, C. 1992. 'The Heterosexual Presumption', in Screen (eds), *The Sexual Subject: A Screen Reader in Sexuality*. London: Routledge, pp. 184–96.

Palmer, J., and M. Riley. 1993. *The Films of Joseph Losey*. Cambridge: Cambridge University Press.

Palmer, T., and P. Medlicott (ed.). 1977. *All You Need Is Love: The Story of Popular Music*. London: Futura Publications Ltd.

Pasternak, A. 1996. *Princess in Love: The True Story of a Royal Love Affair*. London: Simon & Schuster Ltd.

Peraldi, F. (ed.). (1981) 1995. *Polysexuality [Semiotext(e) #10]*. New York: Semiotext(e).

Petley, J. 2001. 'There's Something about Mary…', in B. Babington (ed.), *British Stars and Stardom: From Alma Taylor to Sean Connery*. Manchester: Manchester University Press, pp. 205–17.

Petrie, D., M. Williams and L. Mayne (eds). 2020. *Sixties British Cinema Reconsidered*. Edinburgh: Edinburgh University Press.

Petronius. 1969. *London Unexpurgated*. London: New English Library.

Plante, D. 1995. 'A Last Fantasy in Florence', *New Yorker*, 10 July, pp. 40–55.

Preciado, B. 2014. *Pornotopia: An Essay on Playboy's Architecture and Biopolitics.* New York: Zone Books.

Pym, B. 1974. *Pressure Groups and the Permissive Society.* Newton Abbot: David & Charles.

Quinn, T. 2015. *Backstairs Billy: The Life of William Tallon, the Queen Mother's Most Devoted Servant.* London: The Robson Press.

Raile, A.L. 1928–1930. *The Defence of Uranian Love.* Three volumes. London: Cayme Press.

Reed, J. 2014. *The Dilly: A Secret History of Piccadilly Rent Boys.* London: Peter Owen Publishers.

Reich, W., and L. Baxandall (eds). 1972. *Sex-Pol: Essays 1929–1934,* trans. A. Bostock, T. DuBose and L. Baxandall. New York: Random House.

Renton, A. 2018. *Stiff Upper Lip: Secrets, Crimes and the Schooling of a Ruling Class.* London: Weidenfeld & Nicolson.

Rhymes, D. 1964. *No New Morality: Christian Personal Values and Sexual Morality.* London: Constable and Company Ltd.

Rialto Report. 2015. 'Lasse Braun Interview – Part 2: The American Years', 12 April. Retrieved 19 July 2021 from https://www.therialtoreport.com/2015/04/12/lasse-braun-interview-part-2/.

Richards, J. 1997. *Films and British National Identity: From Dickens to Dad's Army.* Manchester: Manchester University Press.

Roberts, J. 2020. *Red Days: Popular Music & the English Counterculture, 1965–1975.* Colchester: Minor Compositions / Autonomedia.

Robertson, G. 1979. *Obscenity: An Account of Censorship Laws and their Enforcement in England and Wales.* London: Weidenfeld & Nicholson.

Robinson, E., et al. 2017. 'Telling Stories about Post-War Britain: Popular Individualism and the "Crisis" of the 1970s', *Twentieth Century British History* 28(2): 268–304.

Robinson, J.A.T. 1963. *Honest to God.* London: SCM Press Ltd.

———. 1970. *Christian Freedom in a Permissive Society.* London: SCM Press Ltd.

Robinson-Brown, J. 2021. *Black, Gay, British, Christian, Queer: The Church and the Famine of Grace.* London: SCM Press.

Robson, C. 2001. *Men in Wonderland: The Lost Girlhood of the Victorian Gentleman.* Princeton, NJ: Princeton University Press.

Roddick, N. 1982/83. 'Soho: Two Weeks in Another Town', *Sight & Sound* 52(1): 18–22.

Roden, F.S. 2002. *Same-Sex Desire in Victorian Religious Culture.* New York: Palgrave Macmillan.

Rolph, C.H. (ed.). 1961. *Does Pornography Matter?* London: Routledge & Kegan Paul.

Rowe, M.W. 2001. 'On Being Brunette: Larkin's Schoolgirl Fiction', *Critical Quarterly* 43(4): 42–58.

Samuel, R. 1992. 'Mrs Thatcher's Return to Victorian Values', *Proceedings of the British Academy* 78: 9–29.

———. 2006. *The Lost World of British Communism.* London: Verso.

Särlvik, B., and I. Crewe. 1983. *Decade of Dealignment: The Conservative Victory of 1979 and Electoral Trends in the 1970s.* Cambridge: Cambridge University Press.

Saunders, F.S. 1999. *Who Paid the Piper? The CIA and the Cultural Cold War.* London: Granta.

Saunders, G. 2017. 'A Last Hurrah? Joe Orton's "Until She Screams", *Oh! Calcutta!* and the Permissive 1960s', *Studies in Theatre and Performance* 37(2): 221–36.

Saunders, K., and P. Stanford. 1992. *Catholics and Sex: From Purity to Purgatory.* London: Heinemann.

Savile, J. 1974. *As It Happens.* London: Barrie & Jenkins.

Schaefer, E. (ed.). 2014. *Sex Scene: Media and the Sexual Revolution.* London: Duke University Press.

Screen (eds). 1992. *The Sexual Subject: A Screen Reader in Sexuality.* New York: Routledge.

Seaton, J. 2015. *Pinkoes and Traitors: The BBC and the Nation, 1974–1987.* London: Profile Books.

Selwyn Ford. 1990. *The Casting Couch: Making It in Hollywood.* London: Grafton Books.

Sewell, B. 2011. *Outsider: Always Almost, Never Quite.* London: Quartet.

Shail, R. (ed.). 2008. *Seventies British Cinema.* London: BFI, Palgrave Macmillan.

Sheldon, K. 2011. 'What We Know About Men Who Download Child Abuse Images', *The British Journal of Forensic Practice* 13(4): 221–34.

Sheridan, S. 1999. *Come Play With Me: The Life and Films of Mary Millington.* Surrey: FAB Press.

———. 2011. *Keeping the British End Up: Four Decades of Saucy Cinema.* Fourth ['completely revised'] edition. London: Titan Books.

Sherman, A., and M. Garnett (eds). 2007. *Paradoxes of Power: Reflections on the Thatcher Interlude.* Exeter: Imprint Academic.

Shortt, R. 2008. *Rowan's Rule: The Biography of the Archbishop.* London: Hodder & Stoughton.

Simpson, A.W.B. 1983. *Pornography and Politics: A Look Back on the Williams Committee.* London: Waterlow.

Skeggs, B. 2004. *Class, Self, Culture.* London: Routledge.

Skousen, W.C. 1958. *The Naked Communist.* Salt Lake City: Ensign.

Smart, C., and B. Smart (eds). 1979. *Women, Sexuality and Social Control.* London: Routledge & Kegan Paul.

Smith, A. 2018. '*The Language of Love*: Swedish Sex Education in 1970s London'. *Film Studies* 18(1): 34–51.

Smith, Jonathan. 1971. 'Neil Hamilton – Informer. Aber Student Leads Tory Plot', *The Courier,* Issue 9, 14 May, p. 3.

Smith, Janet. 2016. *The Dame Janet Smith Review.* Volumes 1-3. Retrieved 28 December 2016 from http://www.bbc.co.uk/bbctrust/dame_janet_smith.

Snowden, Lord (A. Armstrong-Jones). 1983. *Snowden Sittings 1979–1983.* Introduced by J. Mortimer. London: Weidenfeld & Nicholson.

Soho Sixteen Support Sisterhood. 1981. 'The Soho Sixteen & Reclaim the Night', in Feminist Anthology Collective, *No Turning Back: Writing from the Women's Liberation Movement 1975-1980.* London: The Women's Press, pp. 221–23.

Soper, D. 1961. 'Rev Dr Donald Soper', in C.H. Rolph (ed.), *Does Pornography Matter?* London: Routledge & Kegan Paul, pp. 41–54.

Spender, D. 1988. *Women of Ideas and What Men Have Done to Them.* London: Pandora Press.

Spillman, R. 1957. 'Britain's No. 1 Glamour Photographer', *Art and Photography* VII(11–95): 4–9.

Stalin, J. 1953. *Problems of Leninism.* Moscow: Foreign Languages Publishing House.

Stanford, P. 2003. *The Outcasts' Outcast: A Biography of Lord Longford.* Stroud, Gloucestershire: Sutton Publishing Ltd.

Statham, J. 1986. *Daughters and Sons: Experiences of Non-Sexist Childraising.* Oxford: Basil Blackwell Ltd.

Stephenson, B. 2002. 'The Roots of the New Urbanism: John Nolen's Garden City Ethic', *Journal of Planning History* 1(2): 99–123.

Stevenson, J. 1994. 'Bodil of Denmark', in S. Jaworzyn (ed.), *Shock Xpress: The Essential Guide to Exploitation Cinema.* London: Titan Books Ltd, pp. 17–20.

———. 2000. 'Dead Famous: The Life and Movies of Erotic Cinema's Most Exploited Figure', in J. Stevenson (ed.), *Fleshpot: Cinema's Sexual Myth Makers & Taboo Breakers.* Manchester: Critical Vision / Headpress, pp. 176–89.

———. 2009. 'Porno to the People: The Danish Revolution that Liberated America', *Bright Lights Film Journal,* 31 October. Retrieved 10 December 2020 from https://brightlightsfilm.com/porno-to-the-people-the-danish-revolution-that-liberated-america/#.XzxpM16Wypo.

———. 2010. *Scandinavian Blue: The Erotic Cinema of Sweden and Denmark in the 1960s and 1970s.* Jefferson, NC: McFarlene and Co.

Saunders, F.S. 1999. 'How the CIA Plotted Against Us', *New Statesman,* 12 July. Retrieved 28 November 2021 from https://www.newstatesman.com/uncategorized/1999/07/how-the-cia-plotted-against-us.

Strachey, L. 1918. *Eminent Victorians: Cardinal Manning, Dr. Arnold, Florence Nightingale, General Gordon.* New York: Modern Library.

Strong, R. 1997. *The Roy Strong Diaries: 1967–1987.* London: Weidenfeld & Nicholson.

Strong, R., M. Binney and J. Harris (eds). 1974. *The Destruction of the Country House: 1875–1975.* London: Thames & Hudson.

Strub, W. 2019. 'Sanitizing the Seventies: Pornography, Home Video, and the Editing of Sexual Memory', *Feminist Media Histories* 5(2): 19–48.

Sturgeon, R. 1967. 'Jeremy Sandford Come Come', in T.A.B. Sinclair (ed.), *TABS 123.* Harrogate: The Watershed Press, pp. 19–24.

Sutcliffe-Braithwaite, F. 2012. 'Neo-Liberalism and Morality in the Making of Thatcherite Social Policy', *The Historical Journal* 55(2): 497–520.

———. 2018. *Class, Politics, and the Decline of Deference in England, 1968–2000.* Oxford: Oxford University Press.

Sutherland, J. 1982. *Offensive Literature: Decensorship in Britain, 1960–1982.* London: Junction Books.

Sweet, M. 2005. *Shepperton Babylon: The Lost Worlds of British Cinema*. London: Faber and Faber.

———. 2006. 'X Appeal: Britain's Oldest Living Sexploitation Star Tells All', *The Independent*, 29 January. Retrieved 10 April 2021 from https://www.independent.co.uk/arts-entertainment/films/features/x-appeal-britain-s-oldest-living-sexploitation-star-tells-all-6110509.html.

Szreter, S., and K. Fisher. 2011. *Sex before the Sexual Revolution: Intimate Life in England 1918–1963*. Cambridge: Cambridge University Press.

Tajiri, S. 1973. 'On Filming Bodil Joensen', in W. Levy (ed.), *Wet Dreams: Films & Adventures*. Amsterdam: Joy Publications, p. 166.

Tatchell, P. [partly disputed authorship] 1986. 'Questioning Ages of Majority and Ages of Consent', in W. Middleton, *The Betrayal of Youth: Radical Perspectives on Childhood Sexuality, Intergenerational Sex, and the Social Oppression of Children and Young People*. London: Londonlications, pp. 117–19.

Tatchell, P. 2017 'Under-age Sex: Statement of Clarification', 28 February. Retrieved 1 December 2021 from https://www.petertatchell.net/lgbt_rights/age_of_consent/under-age-sex-statement-of-clarification/.

Taylor, B. 1976. 'Motives of Guilt-Free Pederasty: Some Literary Considerations', *The Sociological Review* 24(1): 97–114.

Taylor, M., and E. Quayle. 2003. *Child Pornography: An Internet Crime*. London: Routledge.

Thatcher, M. 1982. 'Speech to Conservative Central Council'. Retrieved 21 January 2017 from http://www.margaretthatcher.org/document/104905.

———. 1983. 'TV Interview for London Weekend Television *Weekend World* ("Victorian Values")'. Retrieved 28 January 2017 from https://www.margaretthatcher.org/document/105087.

Thompson, B. 2013. *Ban This Filth! Mary Whitehouse and the Battle to Keep Britain Innocent*. London: Faber and Faber.

Thompson, B. 1994. *Soft Core: Moral Crusades against Pornography in Britain and America*. London: Cassell.

Thompson, W., and M. Collins. 2007. 'The Revolutionary Left and the Permissive Society', in M. Collins (ed.), *The Permissive Society and its Enemies: Sixties British Culture*. London: Rivers Oram Press, pp. 155–68.

Thrower, S., with J. Grainger. 2015. *Murderous Passions: The Delirious Cinema of Jesús Franco. Volume 1: 1959–1974*. London: Strange Attractor Press.

Todd, B. 2016. 'Marianne Faithfull talks Heroin, The Rolling Stones and '60s London', *Time Out*, 1 February. Retrieved 1 July 2021 from https://www.timeout.com/london/music/marianne-faithfull-interview.

Tolstoy, N. 1981. *Politics and Pornography*. Colchester: National Viewers' and Listeners' Association.

Tracey, M., and D. Morrison. 1979. *Whitehouse*. London: The Macmillan Press.

Travis, A. 1999. 'Oz trial lifted lid on porn squad bribery', *The Guardian*, 13 November. Retrieved 1 February 2019 from https://www.theguardian.com/uk/1999/nov/13/alantravis.

Travis, A. 2001. *Bound and Gagged: A Secret History of Obscenity in Britain*. London: Profile.

Trevelyan, J. 1977. *What the Censor Saw*. Preface by A. Walker. London: Michael Joseph.

Turner, V. 1975 'Many a Poem that Both Breeds and Wakes', in M. Bottrall (ed.), *Gerard Manley Hopkins: Poems*. London: Macmillan Press, pp. 126–39.

Tutti, C.F. 2017. *Art Sex Music*. London: Faber and Faber.

Tyler, I. 2013. *Revolting Subjects: Social Abjection and Resistance in Neoliberal Britain*. New York: Zed Books.

Tyler, P. 1993. *Screening the Sexes: Homosexuality in the Movies*. New York: Da Capo Press.

Tynan, K. (devisor). 1969. *Oh! Calcutta! An Entertainment with Music*. New York: Grove Press Inc.

Vane, R. 1951. *Sinful Sisters*. Cleveland, OH: Kaywin Publishers.

———. 1953. *Vice Rackets of Soho*. London: Archer Press.

Vassi, M. (ed.). 1976. *The Wonderful World of Penthouse Sex*. New York: Warner Books Inc.

Vermaat, A. 1994. 'Ex-pornokoning Joop Wilhelmus raakte steeds meer geisoleerd tot het doek viel' ['Former porn king Joop Wilhelmus became increasingly isolated until the curtain fell'], *Trouw*, 14 September. Retrieved 28 July 2017 from https://www.trouw.nl/home/ex-pornokoning-joop-wilhelmus-raakte-steeds-meer-geisoleerd-tot-het-doek-viel-twaalf-uur-na-vrijlating-uit-de-gevangenis-verdronken-in-dordtse-haven~acc342f0/.

Vyner, H. 1999. *Groovy Bob: The Life and Times of Robert Fraser*. London: Faber and Faber.

Walker, P. 2014. 'Rolf Harris jailed for five years nine months for indecently assaulting girls', *The Guardian*, 4 July. Retrieved 10 June 2018 from https://www.theguardian.com/uk-news/2014/jul/04/rolf-harris-jailed-indecent-assault-young-girls.

Wallsgrove, R. 1977. 'Pornography: Between the Devil and the True Blue Whitehouse', *Spare Rib* 65 (December): 44–46.

Ward, J. 2015. *Not Gay: Sex between Straight White Men*. New York: New York University.

Waugh, A. 1917. *The Loom of Youth*. London: G. Richards.

Waugh, E. 1945. *Brideshead Revisited: The Sacred & Profane Memories of Captain Charles Ryder*. London: Chapman & Hall, Ltd.

Weedman, C. 2019. 'A Dark Exilic Vision of 1960s Britain: Gothic Horror and Film Noir Pervading Losey and Pinter's *The Servant*', *Journal of Cinema and Media Studies* 58(3): 93–117.

Weeks, J. (1981) 1992. *Sex, Politics and Society: The Regulation of Sexuality since 1800*. Second edition. New York: Longman Group Ltd.

Wells, H.G. (1895) 1969. *The Wheels of Chance; The Time Machine*. London: Dent, Everyman's Library.

Wells, M., J. Wilson and D. Pallister. 1999. 'A Greedy, Corrupt Liar', *The Guardian*, 22 December. Retrieved August 2020 https://www.theguardian.com/uk/1999/dec/22/hamiltonvalfayed.conservatives.

Whipple, A.C. 2010. 'Speaking for Whom? The 1971 Festival of Light and the Search for the "Silent Majority"', *Contemporary British History* 24(3): 319–39.

White, C. 2006. 'The Spanner Trials and the Changing Law on Sadomasochism in the UK', *Journal of Homosexuality* 50(2–3): 167–87.

Whitehouse, M. 1972. *Who Does She Think She Is?* London: New English Library.

———. 1978. *Whatever Happened to Sex?* London: Hodder & Stoughton.

———. 1986. *Mightier than the Sword.* East Sussex: Knightsway Publications Ltd.

———. 1994. *Quite Contrary: An Autobiography.* Auckland: Pan Books.

Whiteley, S. 2003. *Too Much Too Young: Popular Music, Age and Gender.* London: Routledge.

Willetts, P. 2010. *Members Only: The Life and Times of Paul Raymond.* London: Serpent's Tail.

Williams, B. (chairman). 1979. 'Report of the Committee on Obscenity and Film Censorship'. London: Her Majesty's Stationary Office.

Williams, D.G. (ed.). 2021. *Raymond Williams: Who Speaks for Wales? Nation, Culture, Identity.* Cardiff: University of Wales Press.

Williams, H. 2018. 'John Smyth QC, 77, accused of shed beatings, dies in Cape Town', *Church Times*, 13 August. Retrieved 14 October 2019 from https://www.churchtimes .co.uk/articles/2018/17-august/news/uk/john-smyth-qc-77-accused-of-shed-beatings-dies-in-cape-town.

Williams, L. 1991. *Hard Core: Power, Pleasure, and the 'Frenzy of the Visible'.* London: Pandora Press.

Williams, M. 2021a. 'The Auteur Limits', *Sight and Sound* 31(6): 5.

———. 2021b. 'John Hefin', *Sight and Sound* 31(6): 53.

Williams, R.D. (1989) 2002. 'The Body's Grace', in E.F. Rogers Jr. (ed.), *Theology and Sexuality: Classic and Contemporary Readings.* Oxford, MA: Blackwell Publishers Ltd, pp. 309–21.

Willsher, K. 2016. 'David Hamilton Found Dead Amid Allegations of Historical Rape', *The Guardian*, 26 November. Retrieved 2 May 2017 from https://www.theguardian .com/uk-news/2016/nov/26/david-hamilton-found-dead-amid-allegations-of-historical.

Wingrove, N., and M. Morris. 2009. *The Art of the Nasty.* Surrey: FAB Press.

Wistrich, E. 1978. *'I Don't Mind the Sex, It's the Violence': Film Censorship Explored.* London: Marion Boyars.

Women's Report Collective. (1977) 1981. 'Pornography', in Feminist Anthology Collective, *No Turning Back: Writing from the Women's Liberation Movement 1975–1980.* London: The Women's Press, pp. 224–26.

Wood, F. (1967) 2017. *The Naked Truth: About Harrison Marks.* London: Wolfbait.

Wortley, R. 1969. *Skin Deep in Soho.* Photographs by J. Haynes. London: Jarrolds Publishers Ltd.

Wright, P., with P. Greengrass. 1988. *Spy Catcher: The Candid Autobiography of a Senior Intelligence Officer.* Port Melbourne, VIC: William Heinemann.

Young, H. 2013. 'Margaret Thatcher left a dark legacy that has still not disappeared', *The Guardian*, 8 April. Retrieved 10 November 2019 from https://www.theguardian.com/politics/2013/apr/08/margaret-thatcher-hugo-young.

Young, W. 1963. *The Profumo Affair: Aspects of Conservatism*. Harmondsworth, Middlesex: Penguin Books.

———. 1965. *Eros Denied*. London: Weidenfeld & Nicolson.

Zhdanov, A.A. (1934) 1950. *On Literature, Music and Philosophy*, trans. E. Fox, S. Jackson and H.G. Feldt. London: Lawrence & Wishart Ltd.

———. (1947) 1975. 'From *Report on the Journals Zvezda and Leningrad*, 1947', in D. Craig (ed.), *Marxists on Literature: An Anthology*. London: Penguin Books, pp. 514–26.

Index

Lightning Source UK Ltd.
Milton Keynes UK
UKHW021305190422
401728UK00003B/102